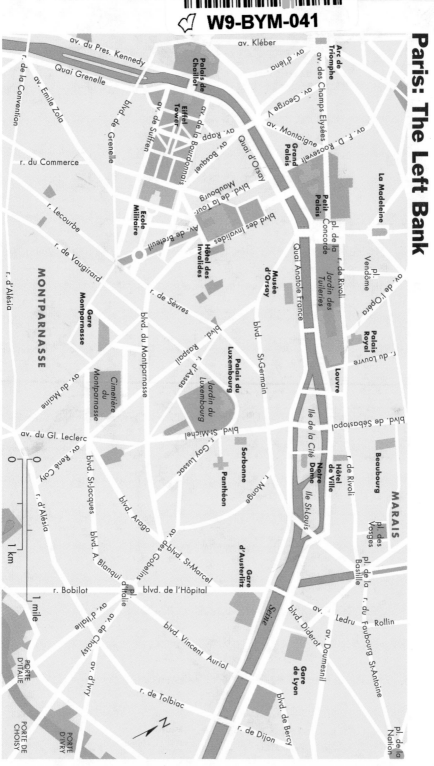

Paris: The Left Bank

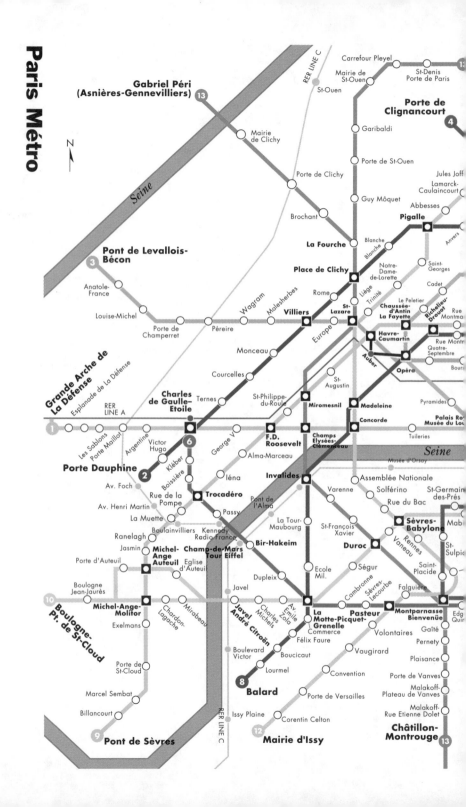

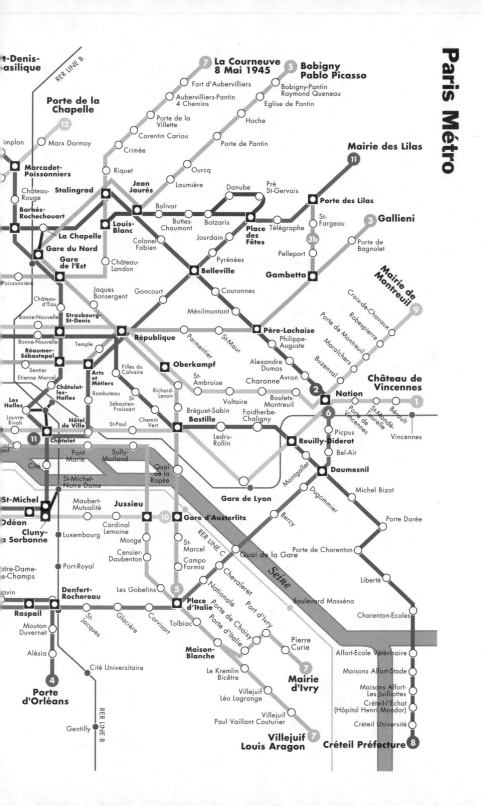

Paris Métro

Paris: The Right Bank

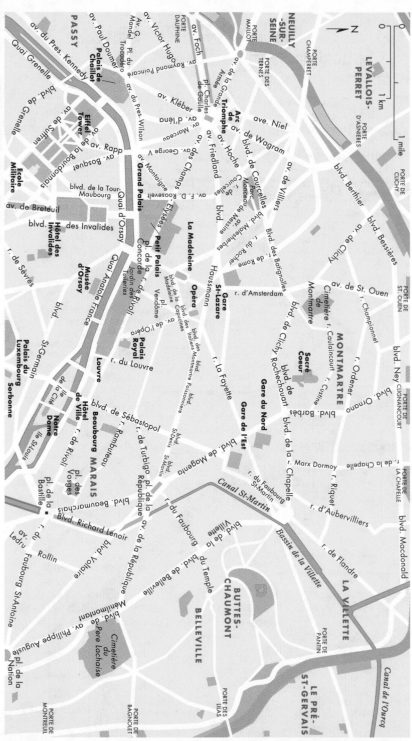

Critical acclaim for the Berkeley Guides

"[The Berkeley Guides are] brimming with useful information for the low-budget traveler—material delivered in a fresh, funny, and often irreverent way." —*The Philadelphia Inquirer*

"The [Berkeley Guides] are deservedly popular because of their extensive coverage, entertaining style of writing, and heavy emphasis on budget travel...If you are looking for tips on hostels, vegetarian food, and hitchhiking, there are no books finer." —*San Diego Union-Tribune*

"Straight dirt on everything from hostels to look for and beaches to avoid to museums least likely to attract your parents... they're fresher than Harvard's Let's Go series." —*Seventeen*

"The [Berkeley Guides] give a rare glimpse into the real cultures of Europe, Canada, Mexico, and the United States...with in-depth historical backgrounds on each place and a creative, often poetical style of prose." —*Eugene Weekly*

"More comprehensive, informative and witty than Let's Go." —*Glamour*

"The Berkeley Guides have more and better maps, and on average, the nuts and bolts descriptions of such things as hotels and restaurants tend to be more illuminating than the often terse and sometimes vague entries in the Let's Go guides." —*San Jose Mercury News*

"These well-organized guides list can't-miss sights, offbeat attractions and cheap thrills, such as festivals and walks. And they're fun to read." —*New York Newsday*

"Written for the young and young at heart...you'll find this thick, fact-filled guide makes entertaining reading." —*St. Louis Dispatch*

"Bright articulate guidebooks. The irreverent yet straight-forward prose is easy to read and offers a sense of the adventures awaiting travelers off the beaten path." —*Portland Oregonian*

On the Loose

On the Cheap

Off the Beaten Path

THE BERKELEY GUIDES

California '97
Central America (2nd Edition)
Eastern Europe (3rd Edition)
Europe '97
France (4th Edition)
Germany & Austria (4th Edition)
Great Britain & Ireland '97
Italy '97
London '97
Mexico '97
New York City '97
Pacific Northwest & Alaska (3rd Edition)
Paris (3rd Edition)
San Francisco '97

Fodor's **BERKELEY** budget guides

paris
third
edition

On the Loose
On the Cheap
Off the Beaten Path

WRITTEN BY BERKELEY STUDENTS IN COOPERATION WITH
THE ASSOCIATED STUDENTS OF THE UNIVERSITY OF CALIFORNIA

Third Edition

ISBN 0-679-03184-7

THE BERKELEY GUIDE TO PARIS

Editors: Sarah Fallon and Mielikki Org
Managing Editors: Tara Duggan, Kristina Malsberger, Sora Song
Executive Editor: Sharron Wood
Creative Director: Fabrizio La Rocca
Cartographers: David Lindroth, Inc.; Eureka Cartography
Text Design: Tigist Getachew
Cover Design: Fabrizio La Rocca
Cover Art: Poul Lange (3-D art), Nicholas DeVore/TSW (photo in frame), Paul D'Innocenzo (still life and digital imaging)

SPECIAL SALES

The Berkeley Guides and all Fodor's Travel Publications are available at special discounts for bulk purchases for sales promotions or premiums. Special editions, including personalized covers, excerpts of existing guides, and corporate imprints, can be created in large quantities for special needs. For more information, contact your local bookseller or write to Special Markets, Fodor's Travel Publications, 201 East 50th Street, New York, NY 10022. Inquiries from Canada should be directed to your local Canadian bookseller or sent to Random House of Canada, Ltd., Marketing Department, 1265 Aerowood Drive, Mississauga, Ontario L4W 1B9. Inquiries from the United Kingdom should be sent to Fodor's Travel Publications, 20 Vauxhall Bridge Road, London SW1V 2SA, England.

Contents

What the Berkeley Guides Are All About

Four years ago, a motley bunch of U.C. Berkeley students launched a new series of guidebooks—*The Berkeley Guides*. Since then, we've been busy writing and editing 14 books to destinations across the globe, from California, Mexico, and Central America to Europe and Eastern Europe. Along the way our writers have weathered bus plunges, rabies, and guerrilla attacks, landed bush planes above the Arctic Circle, gotten lost in the woods (proverbially and literally), and broken bread with all sorts of peculiar characters—from Mafia dons and Hell's Angel bikers to all those lunatics on the Métro. And don't forget about the train station sleep-ins, voodoo bus schedules, and hotel owners that just don't get it ("you only want *to see* a room? Non, c'est impossible.").

Coordinating the efforts of 65 U.C. Berkeley writers back at the office is an equally daunting task (have you ever tried to track manuscript from Morocco?). But that's the whole point of *The Berkeley Guides*: to bring you the most up-to-date info on prices, the latest budget-travel trends, the newest restaurants and hostels, where to catch your next train—all written and edited by people who know what cheap travel is all about.

You see, it's one of life's weird truisms that the more cheaply you travel, the more you inevitably experience. If you're looking for five-star meals, air-conditioned tour buses, and reviews of the same old tourist traps, you're holding the wrong guidebook. Instead, *The Berkeley Guides* give you an in-depth look at local culture, detailed coverage of small towns and offbeat sights, bars and cafés where tourists rarely tread, plus no-nonsense practical info that deals with the real problems of real people (where to get aspirin at 3 AM, where to launder those dirty socks).

Coming from a community as diverse as Berkeley, we also wanted our guides to be useful to everyone, so we tell you if a place is wheelchair accessible, if it provides resources for gay and lesbian travelers, and if it's safe for women traveling solo. Many of us are Californians, which means most of us like trees and mountain trails. It also means we emphasize the outdoors in every *Berkeley Guide* and include lots of info about hiking and tips on protecting the environment.

Most important, these guides are for travelers who want to see more than just the main sights. We find out what local people do for fun, where they go to eat, drink, or just hang out. Most guidebooks lead you down the tourist trail, ignoring important local issues, events, and culture. In *The Berkeley Guides* we give you the information you need to understand what's going on around you, whether it's the latest on Métro bombings or yet another protest for student rights in the Left Bank.

We've done our best to make sure the information in *The Berkeley Guides* is accurate, but time doesn't stand still: prices change, places go out of business, currencies get devalued. Call ahead when it's really important, and try not to get too stressed out.

Thanks to You

Putting together a guidebook that covers all of Paris is no easy task. From figuring out the Louvre to getting the lowdown on the bar scene in the Marais, our writers and editors relied on helpful souls along the way. We'd like to thank the following people—as well as the hundreds of others our writers encountered on the streets, in hotels, in bars—for the advice, encouragement, and free drinks.

We want to thank in particular: François Bel (Paris); Jean-Yves Boisson (Paris); Emily Buttinger (Seattle); Marlene Colburn (New York); Alison Desposito (San Francisco); Mme Devigne (Paris); Adam Diamant (Berkeley); The Fallons (Washington, D.C.); Nils Gilman (Paris); Joanna Honikman (Berkeley); Olivier Joly (Paris, Lyon); Noemi Kubiak (Paris); Andrew Lakoff (Paris); Sophie Macé (Paris); Gérard Mulot (Paris); Hugo Olliphant (Los Angeles); Pavel & Joy Švihra (California); Kathryn Tuma (Paris); San Vu Ngoc (Paris); The Vu Ngoc Family (Paris); Marjilein Westerbeek (Paris); Amy Zsigo (Berkeley).

In the Berkeley office, Kathleen Dodge, Maureen Klier, and Suzanne Stein provided invaluable help. We'd also like to thank the Random House folks who helped us with cartography, page design, production, and other pesky problems: Steven Amsterdam, Bob Blake, Denise DeGennaro, Tigist Getachew, Fabrizio La Rocca, Natasha Lesser, and Linda Schmidt.

Berkeley Bios

Behind every restaurant blurb, write-up, lodging review, and introduction in this book lurks a U.C. Berkeley writer. Maybe you know the type—perpetually short on time, money, and clean clothes. Two Berkeley students spent the summer in Paris researching and writing this book; every two weeks they sent their manuscript back to Berkeley, where Millie and Sarah whipped, squashed, and pummeled it into shape.

The Writers

After attending to the Mexican side of her genes by writing for the *Berkeley Guide to Mexico 1996,* **Viviana Mahieux** decided to ignore her French heritage no longer (her unpronounceable last name makes it hard to forget anyways). Her stay in Paris left her hopelessly addicted to coffee and taught her ways to avoid the question "What can you do with a degree in comparative literature and history?" She is now deciding between a lifelong career in denial or going to grad school to get a highly useful Ph.D. in literature.

Although she still thinks Prague is the best place on earth, **Julia Švihra** found Paris not a bad little city. She was sustained through bike rides in torrential rains and mysterious allergies by her unrelenting quest for the culinary delights of France; she taste tested *chocolat à l'ancienne* at innumerable salons throughout the city—all in the name of research, of course. Her quest also took her to dim nooks and crannies of villages in the Ile-de-France and Champagne. Special thanks must go to Andrew Lakoff, extraordinary traveling companion, and Gérard Mulot, extraordinary baker.

The Editors

At age nine, **Sarah Fallon** was dragged kicking and screaming to Paris. Three years later, she kicked and screamed just as much as she was dragged back to Los Angeles. Sick of the noise, her parents let her make her own travel plans; most recently these included a stint as the only French-speaking wrangler in Wyoming. After dabbling in organic chemistry and Russian, she decided to get her degree in English; after editing this book, she will specialize in organic chemistry books in Russian for French-speaking horses.

After fending off pyromanic strikers and uttering enough expletives to make even a French person take notice, **Mielikki Org** managed to make a hasty exit from Orly airport in November and hustle herself back to Berkeley in time to edit the books she just wrote for: *The Berkeley Guide to Paris 1996* and *The Berkeley Guide to France 1996.* Thinking that editing would be a peaceful respite from off-the-beaten-track travel, she would find yet more uses for foreign expletives, thanks to a thousand pages of Microsoft Word manuscript, temperamental computers, and the toxic UVB glow of an unchangeable, lime-green screensaver. Millie looks forward to someday blackmailing some of her French friends with the wealth of knowledge that she has acquired from plunging into the deepest bowels of Paris.

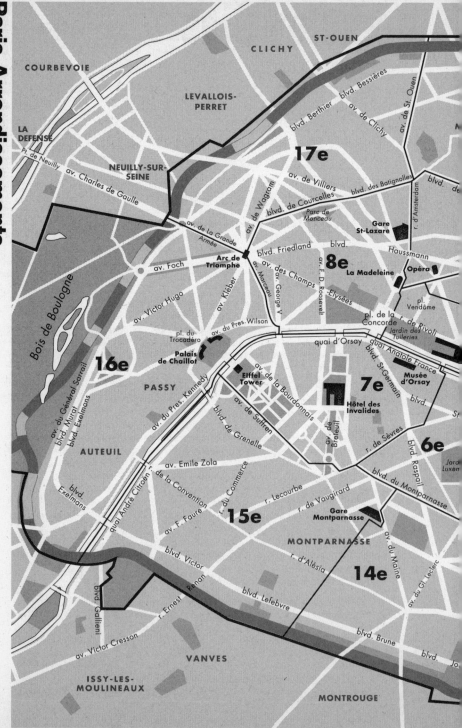

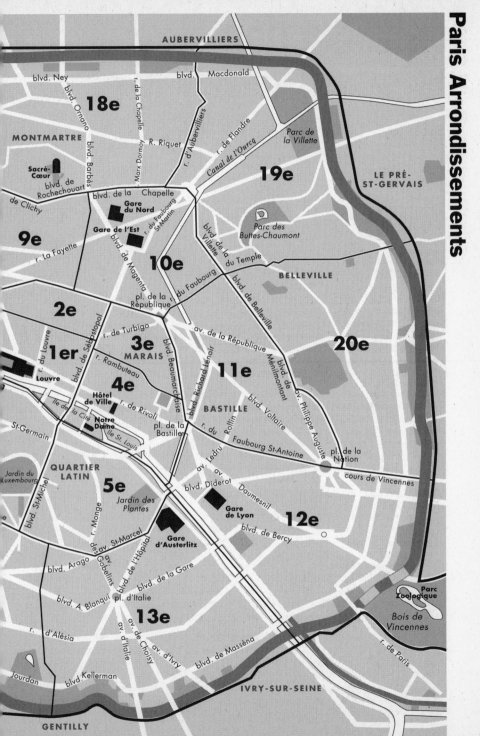

Introduction

To understand what Paris is all about, you need to understand the city's brooms.
Over a decade ago, Paris decided to remake itself as the cleanest metropolis in the world. The
city didn't want American-style urban renewal (this was tried unsuccessfully in the '60s and
'70s), nor did it want to turn deteriorated neighborhoods into cutesy historical districts (that's
Disney's domain). The idea was to keep Paris looking the same—only cleaner. Some bureau-
crat decided to institute the regular sweeping of every Paris street by hand. Of course, to do
this they needed the perfect broom. After a painstaking search for the most efficient street-
cleaning broom, a committee of urban undersecretaries settled on a traditional peasant model,
like the ones made out of a bunch of twigs bound to a big stick. Of course, rather than use
actual sticks and twigs, they came up with a durable plastic that could be cast in stick and twig
molds. The plastic brooms look like their ancestors in almost every way—except for their fluo-
rescent green color. Like the lime-green brooms used to sweep its streets, Paris is a strange
concoction of tradition and high technology, of highly developed aesthetics and slightly screwy
social conditions (observe the migrant workers pushing said peasant brooms).

Former president François Mitterrand was the man responsible for this project and other major
changes in the Parisian landscape. His *Grands Travaux* (literally Big Projects, like the Pyramides du Louvre and La Défense) established him as one of the great builders of Paris, along
with Philippe August, Louis XIV, and Napoléon III. New president Jacques Chirac, however, is
more intent on trimming the national budget than initiating new projects. The *fonctionnaire*
(government worker) strikes that ripped through Paris in 1995 were a reaction to drastic cut-
backs in social programs once taken for granted. If Chirac's program continues, the neon green
brooms and other urban renewal projects may someday elicit the same nostalgia as the original stick and twig ones they were based on.

Paradoxically, Paris is simultaneously the forum for self-appointed guardians of French tradition and a magnet drawing free-spirited poets, philosophers, and social butterflies. When the
government outlawed the commercial use of non-French (i.e., English) words in 1993, an odd
coalition of merchants, academics, and journalists came together to protest—and the law was
soon ruled unconstitutional. And, while keepers of the cultural flame try to preserve all that
they hold dear, they can't keep modernity from encroaching on this city, one of the great urban
centers of Europe. These contradictory forces might explain how the frumpiest, run-down
neighborhood bistro will swipe your credit card through a hand-held computer, instantly debit-
ing your account thousands of miles away for 1,000F of wine.

Paris's tension between tradition and modernity, though, is not always apparent as you walk
down the street. The city usually seems as carefully orchestrated as ever: Students spiff up to
see and be seen, and 85-year-old matrons do the shopping in smart little day suits. Even
Paris's parks, last bastions of nature, are carefully planned down to the last blade of grass. But
when you see a suited-up businessman chatting with an Algerian street sweeper leaning on his
broom in front of an Internet café, you'll suddenly realize that Paris is a city of sometimes
startling contradictions.

What to do when your *money* is done traveling before you are.

Don't worry. With **MoneyGram**,^{SM} your parents can send you money in usually 10 minutes or less to more than 18,000 locations in 86 countries. So if the money you need to see history becomes history, call us and we'll direct you to a **MoneyGram**^{SM} agent closest to you.

USA: **1-800-MONEYGRAM**   Canada: **1-800-933-3278**   France: **05-905311**
Germany: **0130-8-16629**   England: **0800-89-7198**   Spain: **900-96-1218**
                              or call collect **303-980-3340**

MoneyGram
MONEY IN MINUTES WORLDWIDE
SM

BASICS 1

By Viviana Mahieux and Julia Švihra

If you've ever traveled with anyone before, you know the two types of people in the world—the planners and the nonplanners. You also know that travel brings out the very worst in both groups: Left to their own devices, the planners will have you goose-stepping from attraction to attraction on a cultural blitzkrieg, while the nonplanners will invariably miss the flight, the bus, and the point. This Basics chapter offers you a middle ground; we hope it provides enough information to help plan your trip to Paris without saddling you with an itinerary or invasion plan. Keep in mind that companies go out of business and prices inevitably go up. Remain flexible; if you want predictability, stay home and watch reruns of *The Brady Bunch*.

Planning Your Trip

WHEN TO GO

Paris gets the bulk of its visitors between Easter and early September, and hotel owners know it, often jacking up prices 10F–20F in the high season. April–June is fine if you can bear the occasionally soppy weather. July brings an unsavory mix of crowds and heat, while in August many Parisians skip town for vacation, leaving a trail of closed stores and restaurants behind them. Cultural life comes out of hibernation in September, when the weather is usually glorious and music festivals abound. November through January—if you can stand the cold weather—offers a complete schedule of ballet, theater, and opera performances.

CLIMATE Telling your friends that you are going to Paris in the springtime may sound romantic, but it can be distressingly damp if you show up before Easter. The weather tends to be pleasantly warm (70°F, 20°C) by June but can be sultry and dusty in July and August (80°F, 30°C). September and early October are almost ideal, with lots of sun and moderate temperatures. Come November, expect a mixed bag of wet-and-cold and warmish-and-sunny days, while the temperatures frequently fall below freezing from December to March. Whenever you go, remember that you can usually expect rain—check the weather pages of your newspaper for the current situation.

NATIONAL HOLIDAYS France is a Catholic country and observes many holidays derived from the Church calendar. Also note that if a holiday falls on a Tuesday or Thursday, many businesses *font le pont* (make the bridge) and close on that Monday or Friday, too. Here's a quick list of major holidays:

January 1; March 31 (Easter Monday); **May 1** (Labor Day); **May 8** (World War II Armistice Day— a new holiday not observed as extensively as others—and Ascension Day in 1997, which will

be observed); **May 19** (Whit Monday); **July 14** (Bastille Day); **August 15** (Assumption); **November 1** (All Saints' Day); **November 11** (World War I Armistice); and **December 25** (Christmas).

FESTIVALS Paris loves to fête, and while most of the following festivals are Paris-specific, some are celebrated nationwide. Check the tourist offices (*see* Staying in Paris, Visitor Information, *below*) for details on dates and tickets.

➤ **SUMMER** • The **Fête de la Musique** is not to be missed. Held annually on June 21, the festival celebrates the summer solstice with an explosion of live music performed throughout the streets, cafés, and public spaces of Paris (and all of France). The Palais Royal, Bastille, and other areas host music until the sun comes up. **Fête du Pont Neuf** in mid-June is a festival of street performers, booths, and other funfare that takes place on the Pont Neuf and place Dauphine. The **Festival du Marais,** celebrated between mid-June and mid-July, stages music, dance, and theater in the churches and historic hotels of the Marais. Also in the classical music mode, the **Musique en l'Ile** series of concerts is held in the 17th-century Eglise St-Louis on the Ile St-Louis every July and August.

Fête du Cinema is a silver screen dream. One regular-price ticket is your passport to as many movies as your eyeballs can bear on this one special day in June. Ask a tourist office for this year's schedule.

Course des Garçons de Café is a notorious race in which more than 500 professional waiters dash through the streets of Paris carrying trays of bottles and glasses. The fastest racer who spills the least wins. The race happens at the end of June and starts and finishes at the Hôtel de Ville.

Foire International d'Art au Grand Palais happens in early July, when artists from around the world come to show their stuff in the modest confines of the Grand Palais.

Bastille Day (July 14), which celebrates the storming of the state prison during the early days of the Revolution, is a mix of parades, fireworks, alcohol, street music, and debauchery. Depending on your perspective, it's either one of the worst or best days to be in Paris.

The **Tour de France,** held annually at the end of July, is the world's most famous bicycle race. Anyone who is not along the route itself is glued to the TV set, and when the race winds up on the Champs-Elysées in Paris, the whole city pours into the streets to cheer.

➤ **AUTUMN AND WINTER** • Mid-September through mid-October is the time for **Musique Baroque au Château de Versailles,** a festival that takes place at Versailles and is well worth the trip. Hot on its heels is October's **Festival de Jazz de Paris,** the culmination of a summer full of jazz all over France. Subscription tickets are good for events in clubs and concert halls; for more info call 01–40–56–07–17. The **Festival d'Automne,** from mid-September to the end of December, features music, theater, and dance throughout Paris. Cafés and restaurants all over France celebrate the official release of new wine during **Beaujolais Nouveau** on the third Thursday of November. **Chinese New Year** is celebrated in the 13th arrondissement, between avenue d'Ivry and avenue de Choisy, in late January or early February, depending on when the New Year falls.

➤ **SPRING** • May 1 is **May Day,** honoring workers worldwide. Trade unions organize marches through the streets of Paris, museums and shops close, and newspapers stop their presses. Street vendors sell lilies of the valley, symbolic of the labor movement.

The **French Open** brings tennis greats and their fans to beautiful Roland-Garros Stadium every year at the end of May. If you plan a year in advance and can afford a ticket, you'll be able to watch the best battle it out on the red-clay courts. For info call the **French Tennis Federation** (tel. 01–47–43–48–00). Or write them (2 av. Gordon-Bennett, 75016 Paris) in January and ask for a reservation form. Tickets run anywhere from 45F to 295F.

GOVERNMENT TOURIST OFFICES

The **French Government Tourist Office,** also known as the **Maison de la France,** can answer general questions about staying in Paris or refer you to other organizations for more info. If you write to them, be specific about your interests—film, biking, food, whatever—or you'll get a stack of glossy brochures on cruises and shopping expeditions. *8 av. de l'Opéra, 1er, tel. 01–42–96–10–23.*

IN THE UNITED STATES The **French Government Tourist Offices** can mail you a stack of shiny brochures that advertise travel packages like "Paris Aristocrat" and "Monte Carlo Magnifique." If you want to ask specific questions, you'll have to call their Information Center (tel. 900/990–0040) and pay 50¢ per minute (9 AM–7 PM EST). *444 Madison Ave., 16th Floor, New York, NY 10022. 676 N. Michigan Ave., Suite 3360, Chicago, IL 60611. 9454 Wilshire Blvd., Suite 715, Los Angeles, CA 90212.*

IN CANADA Maison de la France. *1981 av. McGill Collège, Suite 490, Montréal, Qué. H3A 2W9, tel. 514/288–4264. 30 St. Patrick St., Suite 700, Toronto, Ont. M5T 3A3, tel. 416/593–4723.*

IN THE UNITED KINGDOM French Government Tourist Office. *178 Piccadilly, London W1V OAL, tel. 0171/629–1272.*

DOWN UNDER French Tourist Office. *BNP Building, 12th Floor, 12 Castlereagh St., Sydney, N.S.W. 2000, tel. 02/231–5244.*

BUDGET TRAVEL ORGANIZATIONS

The **Council on International Educational Exchange** ("Council" for short) is a private, nonprofit organization that administers work, volunteer, academic, and professional programs worldwide. Its travel division, **Council Travel,** is a full-service travel agency specializing in student, youth, and

---

Council Travel Offices in the United States

ARIZONA: Tempe (tel. 602/966–3544). **CALIFORNIA:** Berkeley (tel. 510/848–8604), Davis (tel. 916/752–2285), La Jolla (tel. 619/452–0630), Long Beach (tel. 310/598–3338), Los Angeles (tel. 310/208–3551), Palo Alto (tel. 415/325–3888), San Diego (tel. 619/270–6401), San Francisco (tel. 415/421–3473 or 415/566–6222), Santa Barbara (tel. 805/562–8080). **COLORADO:** Boulder (tel. 303/447–8101), Denver (tel. 303/571–0630). **CONNECTICUT:** New Haven (tel. 203/562–5335). **FLORIDA:** Miami (tel. 305/670–9261). **GEORGIA:** Atlanta (tel. 404/377–9997). **ILLINOIS:** Chicago (tel. 312/951-0585), Evanston (tel. 847/475–5070). **INDIANA:** Bloomington (tel. 812/330–1600). **IOWA:** Ames (tel. 515/296–2326). **KANSAS:** Lawrence (tel. 913/749–3900). **LOUISIANA:** New Orleans (tel. 504/866–1767). **MARYLAND:** College Park (301/779–1172). **MASSACHUSETTS:** Amherst (tel. 413/256–1261), Boston (tel. 617/266–1926), Cambridge (tel. 617/497–1497 or 617/225–2555). **MICHIGAN:** Ann Arbor (tel. 313/998–0200). **MINNESOTA:** Minneapolis (tel. 612/379–2323). **NEW YORK:** New York (tel. 212/822–2700, 212/666–4177, or 212/254–2525). **NORTH CAROLINA:** Chapel Hill (tel. 919/942–2334). **OHIO:** Columbus (tel. 614/294–8696). **OREGON:** Portland (tel. 503/228–1900). **PENNSYLVANIA:** Philadelphia (tel. 215/382–0343), Pittsburgh (tel. 412/683–1881). **RHODE ISLAND:** Providence (tel. 401/331–5810). **TENNESSEE:** Knoxville (tel. 423/523–9900). **TEXAS:** Austin (tel. 512/472-4931), Dallas (tel. 214/363–9941). **UTAH:** Salt Lake City (tel. 801/582–5840). **WASHINGTON:** Seattle (tel. 206/632–2448 or 206/329–4567). **WASHINGTON, D.C.** (tel. 202/337–6464). For U.S. cities not listed, call 800/2–COUNCIL.

budget travel. They offer discounted airfares, rail passes, accommodations, guidebooks, budget tours, and travel gear. They also issue the ISIC, GO25, and ITIC identity cards (*see* Student ID Cards, *below*), as well as Hostelling International cards. Forty-six Council Travel offices serve the budget traveler in the United States, and there are about a dozen overseas, including **Paris** (22 rue des Pyramides, 1er, tel. 01–44–55–55–65) and **Nice** (37 bis rue d'Angleterre, tel. 04–93–82–23–33). Council also puts out a variety of publications, including the free *Student Travels* magazine, a gold mine of travel tips (including info on work- and study-abroad opportunities). *205 E. 42nd St., New York, NY 10017, tel. toll-free 888/COUNCIL, http://www.ciee.org.*

Educational Travel Center (ETC) books low-cost flights to destinations within the continental United States and around the world. Their best deals are on flights leaving the Midwest, especially Chicago. ETC also issues Hostelling International cards. For more details request their free brochure, *Taking Off. 438 N. Frances St., Madison, WI 53703, tel. 608/256–5551.*

STA Travel, the world's largest travel organization catering to students and young people, has over 100 offices worldwide and offers low-price airfares to destinations around the globe, as well as rail passes, car rentals, tours, you name it. STA issues the ISIC and the GO25 youth cards (*see* Student ID Cards, *below*), both of which prove eligibility for student airfares and other travel discounts. Their useful web site is at http://www.sta-travel.com. Call 800/777–0112 or the nearest STA office (*see box, below*) for more info.

STA Offices

- **UNITED STATES. CALIFORNIA: Berkeley (tel. 510/642–3000), Los Angeles (tel. 213/934–8722), San Francisco (tel. 415/391–8407), Santa Monica (tel. 310/394–5126), Westwood (tel. 310/824–1574). FLORIDA: Miami (305/461–3444), University of Florida (tel. 352/338–0068). ILLINOIS: Chicago (tel. 312/786–9050). MASSACHUSETTS: Boston (tel. 617/266–6014), Cambridge (tel. 617/576–4623). NEW YORK: Columbia University (tel. 212/865–2700), West Village (tel. 212/627–3111). PENNSYLVANIA: Philadelphia (tel. 215/382–2928). WASHINGTON: Seattle (tel. 206/633–5000). WASHINGTON, D.C. (tel. 202/887–0912).**

- **INTERNATIONAL. AUSTRALIA: Adelaide (tel. 08/223–2426), Brisbane (tel. 07/221–9388), Cairns (tel. 070/314199), Darwin (tel. 089/412955), Melbourne (tel. 03/349–2411), Perth (tel. 09/227–7569), Sydney (tel. 02/212–1255). AUSTRIA: Graz (tel. 0316/32482), Innsbruck (tel. 0512/588997), Linz (tel. 0732/775893), Salzburg (tel. 0662/883252), Vienna (tel. 0222/401480 or 0222/5050–1280). DENMARK: Copenhagen (tel. 031/35–88–44). FRANCE: Paris (tel. 01–43–25–00–76). GERMANY: Berlin (tel. 030/281–6741), Frankfurt (tel. 069/430191 or 069/703035), Hamburg (tel. 040/442363). GREECE: Athens (tel. 01/32–21–267). ITALY: Bologna (tel. 051/261802), Florence (tel. 055/289721), Genoa (tel. 010/564366), Milan (tel. 02/5830–4121), Naples (tel. 081/552–7960), Rome (tel. 06/467–9291), Venice (tel. 041/520–5660). NETHERLANDS: Amsterdam (tel. 020/626–2557). NEW ZEALAND: Auckland (tel. 09/309–9995), Christchurch (tel. 03/379–9098), Wellington (tel. 04/385–0561). SPAIN: Barcelona (tel. 03/487–9546), Madrid (tel. 01/541–7372). SWEDEN: Göteborg (tel. 031/774–0025). SWITZERLAND: Lausanne (tel. 0121/617–58–11), Zurich (tel. 01/297–11–11). TURKEY: Istanbul (tel. 01/252–59–21). UNITED KINGDOM: London (tel. 0171/937–9962).**

Student Flights, Inc. specializes in student and faculty airfares and sells rail passes, ISE cards (*see* Student ID Cards, *below*), and travel guidebooks. *5010 E. Shea Blvd. Suite A104, Scottsdale, AZ 85254, tel. 602/951–1177 or 800/255–8000.*

Travel CUTS is a full-service travel agency that sells discounted airline tickets to Canadian students and issues the ISIC, GO25, ITIC, and HI cards. Their 25 offices are on or near college campuses. Call weekdays 9–5 for info and reservations. *187 College St., Toronto, Ont. M5T 1P7, tel. 416/979–2406.*

HOSTELLING ORGANIZATIONS

Hostelling International (HI), also known as IYHF, is the umbrella group for a number of national youth hostel associations. HI offers single-sex dorm-style beds ("couples" rooms and family accommodations are available at many hostels) and self-service kitchen facilities at nearly 5,000 locations in more than 70 countries around the world (three in Paris, over 100 in France). Membership in any HI national hostel association (*see below*), open to travelers of all ages, allows you to stay in HI-affiliated hostels at member rates (about $10–$25 per night). Members also have priority if the hostel is full; they're eligible for discounts around the world, including rail and bus travel in some countries. The French division of Hostelling International is **Fédération Unie des Auberges de Jeunesse (FUAJ)**; your HI card is good at all FUAJ hostels.

A one-year membership runs about $25 for adults (renewal $20) and $10 for those under 18. A one-night guest membership is about $3. Family memberships are available for $35, and a lifetime membership will set you back $250. If you forgot to get your card before you left home, you can pick one up for 100F at one of the FUAJ offices (*see* HI Hostels, in Chapter 3). Handbooks listing special discount opportunities (like budget cycling and hiking tours) are available from FUAJ and HI. There are also two international hostel directories: One covers Europe and the Mediterranean, while the other covers Africa, the Americas, Asia, and the Pacific ($13.95 each). *733 15th St. NW, Suite 840, Washington, D.C. 20005, tel. 202/783–6161.*

National branches of Hostelling International include **Hostelling International–American Youth Hostels (HI–AYH)** (733 15th St., Suite 840, Washington, D.C. 20005, tel. 202/783–6161); **Hostelling International–Canada (HI–C)** (400-205 Catherine St., Ottawa, Ont. K2P 1C3, tel. 613/237–7884 or 800/663-5777); **Youth Hostel Association of England and Wales (YHA)** (Trevelyan House, 8 St. Stephen's Hill, St. Albans, Herts. AL1 2DY, England, tel. 01727/855–215); **Australian Youth Hostels Association (YHA)** (Level 3, 10 Mallett St., Camperdown, New South Wales 2050, tel. 02/565–1699); and **Youth Hostels Association of New Zealand (YHA)** (Box 436, Christchurch 1, tel. 3/379–9970).

STUDENT ID CARDS

The **International Student Identity Card (ISIC)** entitles students to special fares on local transportation and discounts at museums, theaters, sports events, and many other attractions. If the popular ISIC card is purchased in the United States, the $19 cost also buys you $3,000 in emergency medical coverage; limited hospital coverage; and access to a 24-hour international, toll-free hotline for assistance in medical, legal, and financial emergencies. In the United States, apply to Council Travel or STA; in Canada, the ISIC is available for C$15 from Travel CUTS (*see* Budget Travel Organizations, *above*). In the United Kingdom, students with valid university IDs can purchase the ISIC at any student union or student-travel company. Applicants must submit a photo as well as proof of current full-time student status, age, and nationality. Upon request, purchase of the ISIC card includes the *International Student Identity Card Handbook,* which details the discounts and benefits available to cardholders. If you're only buying the card to get student discounts, you should know that most Parisian ticket agents will accept your school ID (after contorting their faces and turning the card over and over several times).

The **Go 25: International Youth Travel Card (GO25)** is issued to travelers (students and non-students) between the ages of 12 and 25 and provides services and benefits similar to those given by the ISIC card. The $19 card is available from the same organizations that sell the ISIC. When applying, bring a passport-size photo and your passport as proof of your age.

The World At a Discount

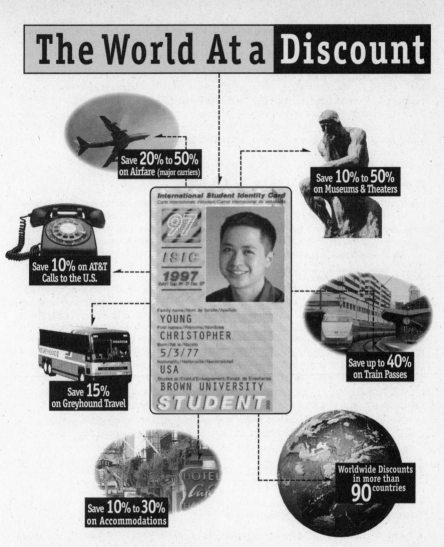

Save **20%** to **50%** on Airfare (major carriers)

Save **10%** to **50%** on Museums & Theaters

Save **10%** on AT&T Calls to the U.S.

Save up to **40%** on Train Passes

Save **15%** on Greyhound Travel

Save **10%** to **30%** on Accommodations

Worldwide Discounts in more than **90** countries

International Student Identity Card
Carte internationale d'étudiant/Carnet international de estudiante

97
ISIC
1997
Valid Sep. 96 - 31 Dec. 97

Family name/Nom de famille/Apellido
YOUNG
First names/Prénoms/Nombres
CHRISTOPHER
Born/Né le/Nacido
5/3/77
Nationality/Nationalité/Nacionalidad
USA
Student at/Etabli d'Enseignement/Establ. de Enseñanza
BROWN UNIVERSITY
STUDENT

The International Student Identity Card
Your Passport to Discounts & Benefits

With the ISIC, you'll receive discounts on airfare, hotels, transportation, computer services, foreign currency exchange, phone calls, major attractions, and more. You'll also receive basic accident and sickness insurance coverage when traveling outside the U.S. and access to a 24-hour, toll-free Help Line. Call now to locate the issuing office nearest you (over 555 across the U.S.) at:

Free 40-page handbook with each card!

1-888-COUNCIL (toll-free)

For an application and complete discount list, you can also visit us at **http://www.ciee.org/**

Council

CIEE: Council on International Educational Exchange

The **International Student Exchange Card (ISE)** is available to students and faculty members. You pay $18 and receive a $10 discount on flights within the United States and a $50 discount on certain flights to Europe. Write or call for more information or to enroll over the phone. *5010 E. Shea Blvd., Suite A104, Scottsdale, AZ 85254, tel. 602/951–1177 or 800/255–8000, fax 602/951–1216.*

The $20 **International Teacher Identity Card (ITIC),** sponsored by the International Student Travel Confederation, is available to teachers of all grade levels, from kindergarten to graduate school. With the ITIC you get benefits and services similar to those you get with the student cards. *The International Teacher Identity Card Handbook,* available when you buy the card, has all the details.

PASSPORTS AND VISAS

Although Brits need only a Visitor's Passport (a more restricted version of a passport) to enter France, everyone else needs a standard passport and possibly a visa (*see below*). If you lose these pieces of information while you're traveling, it's going to be a pain to get new ones, so make a couple of copies, leave one at home, and carry the other with you separate from the original. Better yet, give copies to your traveling companion.

OBTAINING A PASSPORT

➢ **U.S. CITIZENS** • First-time applicants, travelers whose most recent passport was issued more than 12 years ago or before they were 18, travelers whose passports have been lost or stolen, and travelers between the ages of 13 and 17 (a parent must also accompany them) must apply for a passport in person. Other renewals can be taken care of by mail. Apply at one of the 13 U.S. Passport Agency offices a *minimum* of five weeks before your departure. For fastest processing, apply between August and December. If you blow it, you can have a passport issued within five days of departure if you have your plane ticket in hand and pay the additional $30 fee to expedite processing. This method will probably work, but if there's one little glitch in the system, you're out of luck. Local county courthouses, many state and probate courts, and some post offices also accept passport applications. Have the following items ready when you go to get your passport:

- A completed passport application (form DSP-11), available at courthouses, some post offices, and passport agencies.

- Proof of citizenship (certified copy of birth certificate, naturalization papers, or previous passport issued in the past 12 years).

- Proof of identity with your photograph and signature (for example, a valid driver's license, employee ID card, military ID, student ID).

- Two recent, identical, 2"-square photographs (black-and-white or color head shots).

- A $55 application fee for a 10-year passport, $30 for those under 18 for a five-year passport. First-time applicants are also hit with a $10 surcharge. If you're paying cash, exact change is necessary; checks or money orders should be made out to Passport Services.

Those lucky enough to be able to renew their passports by mail must send a completed Form DSP-82 (available from a Passport Agency); two recent, identical passport photos; their current passport (less than 12 years old); and a check or money order for $55 ($30 if under 18). Send everything to the nearest Passport Agency. Renewals take from three to four weeks.

For more information or an application, contact the **Department of State Office of Passport Services** (tel. 202/647–0518) and dial your way through their message maze. Passport applications can be picked up at U.S. post offices, at federal or state courts, and at U.S. Passport Agencies in Boston, Chicago, Honolulu, Houston, Los Angeles, Miami, New Orleans, New York, Philadelphia, San Francisco, Seattle, Stamford, and Washington, D.C.

➢ **CANADIAN CITIZENS** • Canadians should send a completed passport application (available at any post office, passport office, and many travel agencies) to the **Bureau of Pass-**

ports (Suite 215, West Tower, Guy Favreau Complex, 200 Rene Levesque Boulevard West, Montréal, Qué. H2Z 1X4). Include C$60; two recent, identical passport photographs; the signature of a guarantor (a Canadian citizen who has known you for at least two years and is a mayor, practicing lawyer, notary public, judge, magistrate, police officer, signing officer at a bank, medical doctor, or dentist); and proof of Canadian citizenship (original birth certificate or other official document as specified). You can also apply in person at regional passport offices in many locations, including Edmonton, Halifax, Montreal, Toronto, Vancouver, and Winnipeg. Passports have a shelf life of five years and are not renewable. Processing takes about two weeks by mail and five working days for in-person applications. For more info call 514/283–2152.

➤ **U.K. CITIZENS** • Passport applications are available through travel agencies, a main post office, or one of six regional passport offices (in London, Liverpool, Peterborough, Belfast, Glasgow, and Newport). The application must be countersigned by your bank manager or by a solicitor, barrister, doctor, clergyman, or justice of the peace who knows you personally. Send or drop off the completed form; two recent, identical passport photos; and an £18 fee to a regional passport office (address is on the form). Passports are valid for 10 years (five years for those under 16) and take about four weeks to process. For more info, call the **Passport Office** (tel. 0171/279–4000; 0990/210–410 for recorded info).

➤ **AUSTRALIAN CITIZENS** • Australians must visit a post office or passport office to complete the passport application process. A 10-year passport for those over 18 costs AUS$81. The under-18 crowd can get a five-year passport for AUS$41. For more information, call toll-free in Australia 008/131–232 weekdays during regular business hours.

➤ **NEW ZEALAND CITIZENS** • Passport applications can be found at any post office or consulate. Completed applications must be accompanied by proof of citizenship and two passport-size photos. The fee is NZ$80 for a 10-year passport. Processing takes about 10 days.

OBTAINING A VISA If you are an American, Canadian, or New Zealander, you need a visa only if you plan to stay in France longer than 90 days in a row or if you're enrolling in classes or working in France. Brits need a visa only if enrolling in classes. Australians need a visa for a visit of any length. Student visas are pretty easy to get; just apply a few weeks in advance. Long-stay and work visas, on the other hand, take several months to go through the system, so plan ahead. Contact the French consulate nearest you for more info. If you didn't *plan* to stay but just can't bear to leave your hostel in the mountains or your new French lover, contact the French immigration officials well before your three months are up.

LOST PASSPORTS If your passport is lost or stolen, you should immediately notify the local police and nearest embassy or consulate (*see* Staying in Paris, Embassies, *below*). A consular officer should be able to wade through some red tape and issue you a new one, or at least get you back into your country of origin without one. The process will be slowed up considerably if you don't have some other forms of identification on you, so you're well advised to carry other forms of ID—a driver's license, a copy of your birth certificate, a student ID—separate from your passport.

A United States embassy or consulate will only issue a new passport in emergencies. In nonemergency situations, the staff will affirm your affidavit swearing to U.S. citizenship, and this paper will get you back into the United States. The British embassy or consulate requires a police report, any form of identification, and three passport-size photos. They will replace the passport in four working days. Canadian citizens face the same requirements as the Brits, but you must have a guarantor with you. Since most travelers do not know a local guarantor (for requirements *see* Obtaining a Passport, Canadian Citizens, *above*), there is also the option of paying an officer of the consulate/embassy to act in that capacity—proving that throwing money at a problem usually makes it go away. A replacement passport usually takes five working days. New Zealand officials ask for two passport-size photos, while the Australians require three, but both can usually replace a passport in 24 hours.

RAIL PASSES

Obviously, if you're flying into Paris and staying put for the length of your stay, you can skip right over this section. If, however, Paris is only one destination on your grand itinerary, read on. Rail passes are a great deal if you're planning to cover a lot of ground in a short period, and they certainly spare you the time waiting in lines to buy tickets. However, before plunking down hundreds of dollars on a pass, there are several issues to consider. First, add up the prices of the rail trips you plan. Some travel agents have a manual that lists ticket prices, or you can call **Rail Europe** (tel. 800/438–7245), **Railpass Express** (tel. 800/722–7151), or **DER Tours** (tel. 800/782–2424), three agencies that sell rail passes over the phone. If you're under 26, subtract about 30% from the prices quoted by Rail Europe or your travel agent; that's how much you can save by purchasing a BIJ ticket (*see below*) in Europe.

If you decide that you'll save money with a rail pass, you have three options: some sort of **EurailPass, France Railpass,** or **InterRail Pass** (InterRail is available only to those who have lived in a EU country for longer than six months). If you're under 26 years of age on your first day of travel, it's always a better deal to get a youth pass of some sort (Europass Youth, Eurail Youth Flexipass, or Eurail Youthpass). Youth passes are valid for second-class travel only. If you're 26 or over on your first day of travel, you're not eligible for a youth pass and have to buy one of the (much more expensive) passes valid for first-class travel. For this reason, rail passes are often not such a good deal for people 26 and older; you might do better buying individual tickets, since that way you can travel more cheaply in second class.

Be sure to buy your rail pass before leaving the United States; though Eurail passes are available in some European discount travel shops and major train stations (including Paris's Gare du Nord and Gare de Lyon), they're more expensive there. Also, if you have firm plans to visit Europe next year, consider buying your pass *this* year. Prices for Eurail passes generally rise on December 31, and your pass is valid as long as you start traveling within six months of the purchase date. The upshot is that a pass bought on December 30, 1996, can be activated as late as June 30, 1997. All the prices listed below are valid through December 30, 1996, after which you can expect a jump in rates.

Last warnings: Don't assume that your rail pass guarantees you a seat on every train. Seat reservations (tel. 08–36–35–35–35) are required on some trains, including all TGVs (*see* Coming and Going, By Train, *below*). *Couchettes* (sleeping compartments) on overnight trains cost about 90F extra. Also note that many rail passes entitle you to free or reduced fares on some ferries (though you should still make seat reservations in advance).

FRENCH RAIL PASSES A **France Railpass** is valid within France only for three days of travel within a one-month period. First-class passes go for $185, second-class for $145; added days (up to six allowed) cost $30 each for either class. The France Railpass isn't available once you arrive (in fact, it can't even be used by residents or citizens of France), so be sure to pick one up before leaving home. Another good deal is the **France Rail 'n Drive Pass**; for only a bit more than the plain ol' train pass, you get three days of train travel and two days of Avis car rental within one month. A second-class pass goes for $219, and you can add car days for $39 each and rail days for $30 each (per person). You get unlimited mileage and can pick up and drop off the car anywhere in France at no extra charge (Avis has 520 agencies in France), so this might not be a bad deal for seeing out-of-the-way châteaux. Car-rental reservations must be made directly with Avis at least seven days in advance (tel. 800/331–1084 in U.S.), and drivers must be age 24 or older. Neither the France Rail nor the France Rail 'n Drive pass is valid for travel in Corsica.

➤ **DISCOUNT CARDS •** You can buy a **Carte Carrissimo** discount card only in France and only if you're between the ages of 12 and 25. Passes are good for a year and cost 189F for four one-way trips, 295F for eight trips. Calendars given out with train tickets are color-coded to indicate different fare periods; with the Carrissimo, you get 50% off on blue days (*période bleue*) and 20% off on white days (*période blanche*). This discount card is good for small groups, since the discount applies to up to three other people traveling with you—just be sure to stamp the card, along with your tickets, one time for each person using it. If you're over 21 with a valid driver's license, Avis will give you a 20% discount with the card for cars rented from the train station.

Similar to the Carte Carrissimo, the **Carte Vermeil** gives people over age 60 two discount options. The first costs 143F and follows the same rules as the four-trip Carrissimo listed above; the second is 270F and allows an unlimited number of reduced-price trips within France and a 30% discount on trips outside of France for one year. With the **Carte Kiwi** (285F for four trips; 444F for an unlimited number of trips), up to four children under 16 accompanying an adult can get a 50% discount for a full year. Married couples (you have to have not only a copy of your marriage certificate but also one passport photo per person) can get the **Carte Couple** for free(!), which gives a 25% discount when traveling together in either class, although you can only travel in blue periods. If you know how to plan in advance, lower prices are also available by purchasing **Joker** (no joke) tickets up to two months before the date of departure (Joker 30, at least one month before, gives the best discount, while Joker 8, at least 8 days before, allows you to indulge your slacker side). Joker deals are available on some international destinations as well.

If you don't actually want a rail pass, you might want to consider a **Billet International de Jeunesse** (International Youth Ticket), usually known as a **BIJ** or **BIGE** ticket. Here's how it works: Travelers under the age of 26 can purchase a second-class ticket between two far-flung European cities at a 20%–30% savings and then make unlimited stops along the way for up to two months. BIJ tickets are available throughout Europe at budget travel agencies; try the European offices of STA and Council Travel (*see* Budget Travel Organizations, *above*).

EURAIL The **EurailPass** is valid for unlimited first-class train travel through 17 countries—Austria, Belgium, Denmark, Finland, France, Germany, Greece, Hungary, Italy, Luxembourg, Netherlands, Norway, Portugal, Republic of Ireland, Spain, Sweden, and Switzerland. It's available for periods of 15 days ($522), 21 days ($678), one month ($838), two months ($1,148), and three months ($1,468). If you're under 26, the **Eurail Youthpass** is a much better deal. One or two months of unlimited second-class train travel costs $598 and $768, respectively. For 15 consecutive days of travel you pay $418.

A **Eurail Saverpass,** which costs a little less than a comparable EurailPass, is intended for couples and small groups. A pass good for 15 days of first-class travel is $452, for 21 days $578, for one month $712. The pass requires that a minimum of two people each buy a Saverpass and travel together at all times. Between April 1 and September 30 there is a three-person minimum.

Unlike the EurailPass and Eurail Youthpass, which are good for unlimited travel for a certain period of time, the **Eurail Flexipass** allows you to travel for 10 or 15 days within a two-month period. The Flexipass is valid in the same 17 countries as the EurailPass and costs $616 for 10 days, $812 for 15 days. If you're under 26, the second-class **Eurail Youth Flexipass** is a better deal. Within a two-month period it entitles you to 10 ($438) or 15 ($588) days of travel.

For travel in France, Germany, Italy, Spain, and Switzerland, consider the **Europass** (first-class) or **Europass Youth** (second-class). The basic Europass is good for five, six, or seven days of travel in any three of the above-named countries, as long as they border one another. The five-day pass costs $316 (first-class) or $210 (second-class). The eight-, nine-, and 10-day passes are good in four of the five countries. The eight-day pass costs $442 (first-class) or $297 (second-class). The passes, good for any number of days from 11 to 15, are valid in all five countries. The 11-day pass costs $568 (first-class) or $384 (second-class). In all cases the days of travel can be spread out over two calendar months. Call Rail Europe or ask a travel agent for the brochures "1997 Europe On Track" or "EurailPass and Europass" for details on adding extra travel days, buying a discounted pass for your companion, or expanding the reach of your pass to Austria, Belgium, Greece, Luxembourg, and Portugal. FR, IT, SP, SW

➤ **PASS VALIDATION AND INSURANCE** • The very first time you use any Eurail pass you must have it validated. Before getting on the train, go to a ticket window and have the agent fill out the necessary forms—a painless but important procedure that could save you being asked to get off the train or being fined. Also, you might want to consider Eurail's "Pass

If you have any rail pass valid on French trains, show it to the station agent in the RER (the Métro that goes through Paris and out to the burbs), and he or she will hand you a free ticket.

Protection Plan," which costs $10 and must be arranged at the time of purchase. If you bought the protection plan and your pass mysteriously disappears, file a police report within 24 hours and keep the receipts for any train tickets you purchase. Then, upon your return home, send a copy of the report and receipts to Eurail. For your trouble you get a 100% refund on the *unused* portion of your stolen or lost pass.

INTERRAIL European citizens and anyone who has lived in the EU for at least six months can purchase an **InterRail Pass,** valid for 15 days' travel in one zone (1428F) or one month's travel in two or more zones (1,700F and up). The zones are organized more or less by geographic proximity: Great Britain, the Republic of Ireland (Zone A), Sweden, Norway, Finland (Zone B), Denmark, Germany, Switzerland, Austria (Zone C), Poland, the Czech Republic, Hungary, Croatia, Slovakia, Bulgaria, Romania (Zone D), France, Belgium, the Netherlands, Luxembourg (Zone E), Spain, Portugal, Morocco (Zone F), Italy, Slovenia, ferries between Italy and Greece, Greece, Turkey (Zone G). One month's travel in all of the zones will set you back 2,142F. The passes work much like Eurail, except that you only get a 50% reduction on train travel in the country where it was purchased. Be prepared to prove EU citizenship or six months of continuous residency. In most cases you'll have to show your passport for proof of age and residency, but sometimes they'll accept a European university ID. To prove residency, old passport entry stamps may do the trick, but be forewarned that each time passes are presented, the ticket controller has the option of looking at passports and confiscating "illegitimate" passes. InterRail can only be purchased in Europe at rail stations and some budget travel agencies; try the European branches of STA or Council Travel (*see* Budget Travel Organizations, *above*).

MONEY

The units of currency in France are the franc and the centime (1 franc = 100 centimes). Bills come in denominations of 20, 50, 100, 200, and 500 francs. Keep an eye out for the cool new 50F bills with images from St-Exupéry's *Little Prince* on them. Coins are worth ½, 1, 2, 5, 10, and 20 francs and 5, 10, and 20 centimes. Try to familiarize yourself with the look of the 10F coin; some bozo counterfeited it, and French salespeople are all too eager to dump the fake version on tourists. When you plan your budget, allow for fluctuating exchange rates; at press time, the exchange rate for the French franc was:

U.S.	Canada	Britain	Australia	New Zealand
$1 = 4F96	C$1 = 3F62	£1 = 7F68	AUS$1 = 3F93	NZ$1 = 3F41
1 F= 20¢	1F = 27¢	1F = 13p	1F = 25¢	1F = 29¢

The French use two methods of listing prices that include centimes. While 5 francs is always 5F, a price of 4 francs and 70 centimes may be rendered either 4F70 or 4,70F. In all our price listings we use the first method.

HOW MUCH IT WILL COST

➤ **LODGING** • While hostels are marginally the best deal for solo travelers, those traveling in twos or threes are better off splitting a hotel room. Parisian hostels average about 105F per night and charge 20F–50F for a meal. Singles in one- or no-star hotels run at least 100F, doubles 120F or more. Camping isn't an option in Paris. Single women new to Paris would be wise to pay more for a safer location—at least while they get their bearings. *See* Chapter 3 for more details.

➤ **FOOD** • If you don't plan to sit down for a Parisian multicourse meal at least once during your trip, stay home. A three-course dinner will run you at *least* 70F, though the same meal will cost a lot less (maybe 50F) at lunchtime. Unless you're from New York, expect to pay twice what you would at home for the same quality food. Throw yourself at the mercy of the markets, where you can survive quite well (and inexpensively) on fresh produce, cheese, and bread. Snacks like *tarte aux pommes* (apple tart) and chocolate croissants run anywhere from 5F to 15F, and drinkable wine starts at about 15F a bottle.

> **TRANSPORTATION** • Expect to pay 40F–50F for a short taxi ride, though often at night there'll be 20F or more on the meter when you get in. Métro and bus tickets run 5F–7F per trek, but Paris is a great city for strolling. For details on the intricacies of the Parisian transport system, *see* Getting Around Paris, *below*.

> **ENTERTAINMENT** • This is where you can go broke fast. Cover charges for nightclubs range 70F–140F and usually include one drink. Drinks in clubs are outrageously expensive—about 80F each, and the price is no guarantee of quality. A beer in a bar costs 15F–50F. Movies are pretty expensive (about 50F), but every theater has discount nights or matinées with tickets as low as 25F. Classical music and theater tickets are reasonable, and discounted student and rush tickets are often available. Museums can run 35F–45F a pop, with reductions of about 10F for students.

TRAVELING WITH MONEY A major U.S. credit card (especially Visa, known in France as Carte Bleue) with accompanying personal identification number (PIN) is often the safest and most convenient way to pay for goods and services in Paris; many hotels, restaurants, and shops accept credit cards, and you'll find numerous ATMs that will give you cash advances at favorable rates (*see* Getting Money from Home, *below*). Traveler's checks also come in handy. While few merchants accept them in foreign currencies, you can exchange them for cash at many banks and almost all bureaux de change. Whichever method you use, protect yourself by carrying cash in a money belt or "necklace" pouch, and by keeping records of your credit card numbers and traveler's check serial numbers in a few safe places.

You lose money every time you exchange currency, so try to avoid changing so much of your money to francs that you end up having to exchange it back when you leave the country.

You'll get a better deal buying French francs in France than at your bank in Australia or the States. Nevertheless, it's a good idea to exchange a bit of money into francs before you arrive in France in case the exchange booth at the train station or airport at which you arrive is closed. The Orly and Charles de Gaulle airports both have cash machines that will accept credit cards with PIN numbers but you need 50F to get to the city center by public transport, so better safe than stranded.

CHANGING MONEY The best place to exchange your cash or traveler's checks for francs varies, though, generally speaking, the Banque de France has good rates. Private exchange offices will occasionally have better rates—just watch out for commissions, which can run up to 5%. For info on specific locations to change your money in Paris, *see* Staying in Paris, Bureaux de Change, *below*.

TRAVELER'S CHECKS An increasingly outmoded form of currency in the face of ATMs, traveler's checks can be exchanged for cash at banks, some hotels, tourist offices, AmEx offices, or currency-exchange offices. AmEx checks are the most widely accepted; other brands are sometimes refused. Some banks and credit unions will issue checks free to established customers, but most charge a 1%–2% commission fee. The reward for paying this commission is being able to get your money back if some nimble-fingered thief takes off with your checks (*see* Lost and Stolen Checks, *below*). If you want to gamble on your country's currency weakening during your vacation, buy traveler's checks in French francs, which all banks in France must cash at face value (no commission)—they're also generally accepted for larger purchases and at small hotels that don't have bureaux de change. Just don't forget that any checks left over will have to be re-exchanged on your return home.

American Express card members can order traveler's checks in U.S. dollars and six foreign currencies by phone, free of charge (with a gold card) or for a 1% commission (with your basic green card). In three to five business days you'll receive your checks: Up to $1,000 can be ordered in a seven-day period. Checks can also be purchased through many banks, in which case both gold and green cardholders pay a 1% commission. AmEx also issues **Traveler's Cheques for Two**, checks that can be signed and used by either you or your traveling companion. If you lose your checks or are ripped off, true to Karl Malden's repeated pledges, AmEx has the resources to provide you with a speedy refund—often within 24 hours. At their Travel Services offices (about 1,500 around the world) you can usually buy and cash traveler's checks, write a personal check in exchange for traveler's checks, report lost or stolen checks, exchange foreign currency, and pick up mail. For locations of AmEx offices in Paris, *see* Staying in Paris, American Express, *below. Tel. 800/221–7282 in U.S. and Canada.*

Citicorp traveler's checks are available from Citibank and other banks worldwide in U.S. dollars and some foreign currencies. For 45 days from date of check purchase, purchasers have access to the 24-hour International S.O.S. Assistance Hotline, which can provide English-speaking doctor, lawyer, and interpreter referrals; assistance with loss or theft of travel documents; traveler's check refund assistance; and an emergency message center. The most useful Citibank office in Paris is at 30 avenue des Champs Elysées (tel. 01–40–76–33–00). *Tel. 800/645–6556 in U.S. or 813/623–1709 collect outside U.S.*

If you don't have an AmEx gold card, you can still get American Express traveler's checks free with an AAA membership. Talk to the cashier at your local AAA office.

Thomas Cook issues **MasterCard International** traveler's checks, available in U.S. dollars and several foreign currencies. If purchased through a Thomas Cook Foreign Exchange office (formerly Deak International), no extra charge is levied to get traveler's checks in French francs. There are nine Thomas Cook exchange offices/travel agencies in Paris, including one at 125 avenue des Champs-Elysées (tel. 01–42–89–80–32), another at 8 place de l'Opéra (tel. 01–47–42–46–52), yet another at 4 blvd. St-Michel (tel. 01–43–26–85–93). *Tel. 800/223–7373 in U.S. or 609/987–7300 collect from outside U.S.; in Europe, tel. 447/335–02–995 toll-free or 07/335–02–995 collect.*

Visa traveler's checks are available in U.S. dollars, British pounds, and various other currencies. Visa does not, however, issue traveler's checks in francs within the United States or Canada. *Tel. 800/227–6811 in U.S. and Canada.*

➤ **LOST AND STOLEN CHECKS** • Unlike cash, lost or stolen traveler's checks can be replaced or refunded *if* you can produce the purchase agreement and a record of the checks' serial numbers. Common sense dictates that you keep the purchase agreement separate from your checks. Caution-happy travelers will even give a copy of the purchase agreement and checks' serial numbers to someone back home. Most issuers of traveler's checks promise to refund or replace lost or stolen checks in 24 hours, but you can practically see them crossing their fingers behind their backs. If you are traveling in a remote area, expect this process to take longer. In a safe place—or several safe places—record the toll-free or collect telephone number to call in case of emergencies (*see above*).

CREDIT CARDS Many restaurants, cafés, bars, shops, and hotels will accept credit cards with a 100F minimum—look for the card logo on windows. Also keep in mind that any place that accepts the French card Carte Bleu also accepts Visa. MasterCard and Visa, but not always American Express, can be used at many banks and ATMs to get a cash advance (*see* Cash Machines, *below*).

Even if you have no job, no credit, no cards, and no respect, you can still tap into services offered by the **Visa Assistance Center** if one of your parents has a Visa Gold or Business card and you are a dependent of 22 years or less and at least 100 miles from home. Write down the card number in a safe place and call the center for emergency cash service, emergency ticket replacement, lost-luggage assistance, medical and legal assistance, and an emergency message service. Helpful, multilingual personnel await your call 24 hours a day, seven days a week. *Tel. 800/847–2911 in U.S. or 410/581–3836 collect from Europe.*

GETTING MONEY FROM HOME

Provided there is money at home to be had, there are at least six ingenious ways to get it:

- Have it sent through a large **commercial bank** that has a branch or sister bank in Paris. Unless you have an account with that large bank, though, you'll have to initiate the transfer at your own bank, and the process will be even slower and more expensive.

Stuck for cash? Don't panic. With Western Union, money is transferred to you in minutes. It's easy. All you've got to do is ask someone at home to give Western Union a call on US 1 800 3256000. Minutes later you can collect the cash.

- If you're an **American Express** cardholder, cash a personal check at an AmEx office for up to $1,000 ($2,500 for gold cardholders) every 21 days; you'll be paid in U.S. traveler's checks or, in some instances, in foreign currency. **Express Cash** further allows AmEx cardholders to withdraw up to $1,000 every 21 days from their personal checking accounts via ATMs (*see* Cash Machines, *below*).

- The **MoneyGram**[SM] service is a dream come true *if* you can convince someone back home to go to a MoneyGram agent and fill out the necessary forms. Simply pay up to $1,000 with a credit card or cash (and anything over that in cash) and, as quickly as 10 minutes later, it's ready to be picked up. Fees vary according to the amount of money sent, but average about 8% to send money from the United States to Paris. You have to show ID when picking up the money. For locations of MoneyGram agents call 800/926–9400; from overseas call 303/980–3340 collect.

- **MasterCard** and **Visa** cardholders can get cash advances from many banks in Paris and even in small towns. The commission for this handy-dandy service varies from none to almost 10%, so contact your credit card company for information before you leave. If you get a PIN for your card before you leave home, you may even be able to make the transaction with an ATM. For more info on this handy trick, *see* Cash Machines, *below*.

- Have funds sent through **Western Union** (tel. 800/325–6000). If you have a MasterCard or Visa, you can have money sent up to your card's credit limit. If not, have someone take cash, a certified cashier's check, or a healthy MasterCard or Visa to a Western Union office. The money will reach the requested destination in minutes, but it may not be available for several more hours or days, depending on the whim of local authorities. Fees range from about 5% to 15%, depending on the amount sent. In Paris there's a Western Union in the fourth arrondissement at 4 rue Cloître Notre Dame (tel. 01–43–54–46–12; Métro: St-Michel–Notre-Dame).

- In extreme emergencies (arrest, hospitalization, or worse) there is one more way American citizens can receive money overseas: by setting up a **Department of State Trust Fund.** A friend or family member sends money to the Department of State, which then transfers the money to the U.S. embassy or consulate in the city in which you're stranded. Once this account is established, you can send and receive money through Western Union, bank wire, or mail, all payable to the Department of State. For information, talk to the Department of State's Citizens' Emergency Center (tel. 202/647–5225).

CASH MACHINES Virtually all U.S. banks belong to a network of card-slurping, cash-expectorating ATMs. In Paris they are affiliated with the **Cirrus** and **Plus** systems only. In theory, the ubiquitous **BNP** (Banque National de Paris) machines will accept cards on both systems, but your card may only work sporadically, so when it does, withdraw as much as you think safe to carry. The most reliable Cirrus ATMs are housed at **Crédit Mutuel** banks; try 8 rue Saint Antoine, 4e (Métro: Saint-Paul); 2 rue de l'Arrivée, 15e (Métro: Montparnasse-Bienvenue); or 13 rue des Abbesses, 18e (Métro: Abbesses). Plus-system cardholders should try **Bred** banks with Right Bank–only locations, including 33 rue de Rivoli (Métro: Hôtel de Ville) and 14 boulevard des Capucines (Métro: Opéra). If you happen to be staying near a bank that accepts your card, this is the best way to get francs at the excellent commercial exchange rate, and the transaction fees may be lower than the interest charged by your credit card for cash withdrawals. In any case, make sure you have a back-up method of getting money.

To increase your chances of happy encounters with cash machines, take a few precautions *before* you go. ATMs in France accept PINs of four or fewer digits only; if your PIN is longer, ask your bank at home about changing it. If you know your PIN as a word, learn the numerical equivalent before you leave, since most French ATM keypads show numbers only, no letters. Foreign ATMs still abide by the withdrawal limits set for you by your bank at home, so make a rough estimate of that amount in French francs and round down to the nearest 100F. Many American banks will waive transaction fees for other-bank ATM use for the duration of lengthy trips; show them your plane ticket and ask nicely *before* you go.

Holders of **Citibank Citicards** can also use their own bank at 30 avenue des Champs–Elysées, 8e (tel. 01–40–76–33–00). The ATM works(!) around the clock, and the English-speaking staff can help you transfer funds from U.S. Citibank accounts. Note that most Citibank offices listed in the phone book are for business use and do not have ATMs or staffs particularly sympathetic to the woes of the cashless backpacker.

A **Visa** or **MasterCard** can also be used to access cash through certain ATMs (provided you have a PIN for it), but the fees for this service are usually higher than bank card fees. Also, a daily interest charge usually begins to accrue immediately on these credit card "loans," even if monthly bills are paid up. Check with your bank for information on fees and on the daily limit for cash withdrawals.

Express Cash allows AmEx cardholders to withdraw up to $1,000 in a seven-day period (21 days overseas) from their personal checking accounts via a worldwide network of ATMs. Gold cardholders can receive up to $2,500 in a seven-day period (21 days overseas). Each transaction carries a 2% fee, with a minimum charge of $2.50 and a maximum of $20. Apply for a PIN and set up the linking of your accounts at least two to three weeks before departure. Call 800/528–4800 for an application.

WHAT TO PACK

As little as possible. Besides the usual suspects—clothes, toiletries, camera, a Walkman, and a good book—bring along a day pack; it'll come in handy not only for day excursions but also for those places where you plan to stay for only one or two days. You can check heavy, cumbersome bags at the train or bus station (or leave it at your hotel) and just carry the essentials while you are out and about.

BEDDING Hostels require that you use a sleep sheet. Some include them in the price (including the three HI hostels in Paris) and some don't. If you have a backpack, consider bringing a sleeping mat too; it can be rolled tightly and strapped onto the bottom of your pack.

THE SLEEP SHEET:
Take a big sheet (flannel sheets are great for this). Fold it down the middle the long way. Sew one short side and the long, open side. Turn inside out. Get inside. Sleep.

CLOTHING Paris is a fashionable city; locals don't throw on sweats to run to the store. Though it's important to pack pragmatically (comfortable, easy-to-clean clothes), you may feel uncomfortable if you're always dressing down. It's better to have one decent shirt you can wear every other day (as the Parisians do) than a whole slew of tacky T-shirts. Athletic clothes are rarely worn outside the gym, and berets on foreign (that's you) men will provoke derision. Shorts or ski jackets will immediately mark you as a tourist; try to scrounge up some lightweight skirts or pants for the summer and a wool coat for winter. If you plan an extended stay, pack for all possible climates, and, whatever you do, don't forget your comfortable walking shoes.

ELECTRONIC STUFF Before tossing a blow-dryer into your bag, consider that European electrical outlets pump out 220 volts, enough to explode or implode American appliances. If you absolutely must have that electric toothbrush, you need a converter that matches your appliance's wattage and the outlet's current. In addition to taking up precious packing space, a converter costs about $20 and is not necessarily reliable in older hotels with bad sockets. Consider buying rechargeable battery sets in Paris if you're staying for a while.

LAUNDRY SUPPLIES Hotel rooms are the best place (certainly the cheapest) to do laundry. A bring-your-own laundry service includes a plastic bottle of liquid detergent (powder doesn't break down as well), about six feet of clothesline, and some plastic clips (bobby pins or paper clips can substitute). When faced with a plugless sink, stuff a sock or plastic bag in the drain. Be sure to bring a few extra plastic bags for damp laundry and dirty clothes. Note that it is against the law—and the police love to nab offending tourists—to display drying laundry from the windows of historic buildings. Use the bathtub.

TOILETRIES Use containers that seal tightly and pack them in a separate, waterproof bag; the pressure on airplanes can cause lids to pop off and create instant moisturizer slicks inside your luggage. Bring all the paraphernalia you need to conduct chemical warfare on your contact lenses if you wear them. Tampons (overpriced), deodorant, soap, shampoo, and toothpaste can all be bought in Paris, but you should bring any prescription drugs you might need. Condoms are expensive (at least 5F each), and French birth control pills can be more inconvenient than helpful/while your body adjusts. It's best to bring all the sexual paraphernalia you might need, especially if you don't know the French word for "dental dam" (*see* Staying Healthy, *below*).

MISCELLANEOUS Stuff you might not think to take but will be damn glad to have: (1) a flashlight, good for reading in the dark and exploring wine cellars; (2) a pocket knife for cutting fruit, spreading cheese, removing splinters, and opening bottles; (3) a water bottle; (4) sunglasses; (5) several large zip-type plastic bags, useful for wet swimsuits, towels, leaky bottles, and rancid socks; (6) a travel alarm clock; (7) a needle and small spool of thread; (8) extra batteries; (9) a few good books.

STAYING HEALTHY

There are few serious health risks associated with travel in France. Many travelers do suffer from mild diarrhea and nausea during their travels, but it's more often caused by stress and changes in diet than any nasty bacteria. In general, get plenty of rest, watch out for sun exposure, eat balanced meals—do we sound like your mother yet?

HEALTH AND ACCIDENT INSURANCE Some general health insurance plans cover health expenses incurred while traveling, so review your existing health policies (or a parent's policy, if you're a dependent) before leaving home. Most university health insurance plans begin and end with the school year, so don't count on school spirit to pull you through. Canadian travelers should check with their provincial ministry of health to see if their resident health insurance plan covers them on the road.

Organizations such as STA and Council (*see* Budget Travel Organizations, *above*), as well as some credit card conglomerates, include health-and-accident coverage with the purchase of an ID or credit card. If you purchase an ISIC card you're automatically insured for $100 a day for in-hospital sickness expenses, up to $3,000 for accident-related medical expenses, and $25,000 for emergency medical evacuation. For details, request a summary of coverage from Council (205 East 42nd St., New York, NY 10017, tel. 888/COUNCIL, http://www.ciee.org). Council Travel and STA also offer short-term insurance coverage designed specifically for the budget traveler. Otherwise, several private companies offer coverage designed to supplement existing health insurance for travelers; for more details contact your favorite student travel organization or one of the agencies listed below.

Carefree Travel Insurance covers emergency medical evacuation and accidental death or dismemberment. It also offers 24-hour medical phone advice. Basic coverage for an individual ranges from $86 for a 30-day trip to $180 for a 90-day trip. Deluxe coverage is about twice that. *100 Garden City Plaza, Box 9366, Garden City, NY 11530, tel. 516/294–0220 or 800/323–3149.*

International SOS Assistance offers insurance through Insure America, providing emergency evacuation services, medical reports on your destination, worldwide medical referrals, and medical and trip cancellation insurance. If all else fails, they also cover the return of "mortal remains." *Box 11568, Philadelphia, PA 19116, tel. 215/244–1500 or 800/523–8930.*

Travel Guard offers a variety of insurance plans, many of which are endorsed by the American Society of Travel Agents. A basic plan, including medical coverage and emergency assistance, starts at $53 for a five-day trip. Trip cancellation policies are available for as little as $19. *1145 Clark St., Stevens Point, WI 54481, tel. 715/345–0505 or 800/782–5151.*

Wallach & Company offers two comprehensive medical insurance plans, both covering hospitalization, surgery, office visits, prescriptions, and medical evacuation for as little as $3 per day. Both also buy you access to a network of worldwide assistance centers that are staffed 24 hours a day by English speakers. *107 W. Federal St., Box 480, Middleburg, VA 20118, tel. 800/237–6615, fax 540/687–3172.*

Your vacation.

Your vacation after losing your hard-earned vacation money.

All the best trips start with Fodor's.

MEDICAL ASSISTANCE International Association for Medical Assistance to Travellers **(IAMAT)** offers free membership (donations are much appreciated) and entitles you to a world-wide directory of qualified English-speaking physicians who are on 24-hour call and who have agreed to a fixed fee schedule. *United States: 417 Center St., Lewiston, NY 14092, tel. 716/754–4883. Canada: 40 Regal Rd., Guelph, Ont. N1K 1B5, tel. 519/836–0102. Switzerland: 57 Voirets, 1212 Grand-Lancy-Geneva. New Zealand: Box 5049, Christchurch 5.*

British travelers can join **Europe Assistance Worldwide Services** (252 High St., Croyden, Surrey CRO 1NF, tel. 0181/680–1234) to gain access to a 24-hour, 365-day, year-round telephone hotline that can help in a medical emergency. The American branch of this organization is **Worldwide Assistance Incorporated** (1133 15th St. NW, Suite 400, Washington, D.C. 20005, tel. 800/821–2828), which offers emergency evacuation services and 24-hour medical referrals. An individual membership costs $62 for up to 15 days, $164 for 60 days. Families may purchase coverage for $92 for 15 days, $234 for 60 days.

Diabetic travelers should contact the **American Diabetes Association** (1660 Duke St., Alexandria, VA 22314, tel. 703/549–1500 or 800/232–3472) or the **Canadian Diabetes Association** (15 Toronto St., Suite 1001, Toronto, Ont. M5C 2E3, tel. 416/363–3373) for resources and medical referrals. *The Diabetic Traveler* (Box 8223, Stamford, CT 06905, tel. 203/327–5832), published four times a year, lists vacations geared toward diabetics and offers travel and medical advice. Subscriptions are $18.95. An informative article entitled "Management of Diabetes During Intercontinental Travel" and an insulin adjustment card are available for free.

PRESCRIPTIONS Bring as much as you need of any prescription drugs (*ordonnance* in French), as well as your written prescription (packed separately). Ask your doctor to *type* the prescription and include the dosage, the generic name, and the manufacturer's name. To avoid problems clearing customs, diabetic travelers carrying syringes should have handy a letter from their physician confirming their need for insulin injections.

Most pharmacies close at 7 or 8 PM, but the *commissariat de police* in every city has a list of the *pharmacies de garde,* the pharmacists on call (literally, on guard) for the evening. This is an emergency-only service, and you may have to go to (as opposed to just call) the commissariat in order to get the name. Pharmacies de garde are also sometimes listed in newspapers or posted on the doors of closed pharmacies.

FIRST-AID KITS For about 97% of your trip, a first-aid kit may mean nothing to you but extra bulk. However, in an emergency you'll be glad to have even the most basic medical supplies. Prepackaged kits are available, but you can pack your own from the following list: bandages, waterproof surgical tape and gauze pads, antiseptic, cortisone cream, tweezers, a thermometer in a sturdy case, an antacid such as Alka-Seltzer, something for diarrhea (Pepto Bismol or Imodium), and, of course, aspirin. If you're prone to motion sickness, take along some Dramamine. Women: If prone to vaginal infections, you can now buy over-the-counter medication (Monistat or Gynelotrimin) in American pharmacies that will save you prolonged grief on the road. However, self-medicating should only be relied on for short-term illnesses; seek professional help if any medical symptoms persist or worsen. French pharmacies all have well-trained staffs ready to dispense medicine, but they don't necessarily speak English, and they won't let you just grab something off a shelf. Learn the generic names of your favorite drugs if you insist on something familiar to stop your headache or unstuff your nose.

For AIDS-related info and counseling in English, go to the Free Anglo-American Counseling Treatment Support (FAACTS) at the American Church (65 quai d'Orsay, 7e, tel. 01–45–50–26–49).

CONTRACEPTIVES AND SAFE SEX AIDS (in French, SIDA) and other *maladies sexuellement transmissibles* (MST, or sexually transmitted diseases) do not respect national boundaries; protect yourself when you travel as you would at home. If you're planning a rendezvous and have neglected to bring *un préservatif* (condom) from home, pick up some at a French pharmacy. You won't find nonoxynol-9 versions here, though; sales were discontinued a few years ago. However, women can add to condoms' effectiveness with *ovules* (spermicidal vaginal suppositories).

Condoms are available in dispensers outside many pharmacies and Métro stations for your late-night needs. In general, though, you'll have a hard time finding contraceptives in stores other than pharmacies. Condoms cost about 10F for two, 49F for a box of 12. Women should bring any birth control from home, because it may be difficult to find the exact equivalent in France. If you forget your prescription for *la pillule* (the Pill), a sympathetic pharmacist may forgo the formality, but the side effects of the switch to a French version may be such that you wish he or she hadn't. IUDs and diaphragms are available, but you have to see a doctor to get fitted, and it's hardly the sort of thing you'd want to do on a vacation. Pack condoms or diaphragms in a pouch or case where they will not become squashed or damaged. If all of the above fails and the *test de grossesse* (pregnancy test) from the pharmacy is positive, your options in France are limited: Given the more conservative political climate of late, abortion services are now legally available only to women who can prove they've been living in France for at least six months.

CRIME AND PUNISHMENT

DRINKING AND DRIVING The legal blood alcohol level for drivers has recently been reduced from 0.7% to 0.5%. To the frustration of the wine-loving French, this is the equivalent of about two glasses of wine for most drinkers.

DRUGS Many young Parisians are tolerant (even enthusiastic) about drug use. Heroin, LSD, amphetamines, cocaine, and marijuana are all bought and sold here. Drug possession and consumption, however, are punishable by hefty fines. Drug *selling* is also a big no-no—if you're caught, you'll go to jail for sure. If you get busted for drugs (or breaking any other law), your embassy might say a few sympathetic words but cannot give you one iota of legal help. You're on your own. But just in case you were wondering: *la came/la dope* (hard drugs), *la poudre/le drepou* (heroin), *l'extasie/des x* (ecstasy), *l'acide* (LSD), *le teuch/le chit* (hashish), *l'herbe/la beuh* (marijuana), *un pétard* (a joint).

PROTECTING YOUR VALUABLES Money belts may be dorky and bulky, but it's better to be embarrassed than broke. You'd be wise to carry all cash, traveler's checks, credit cards, and your passport in an inaccessible place: front or inner pocket, a bag that fits underneath your clothes, or even in your shoes. Keep a copy of your passport somewhere else, as it will be the biggest pain to replace. Neck pouches and money belts are sold in luggage and camping-supply stores. Waist packs are safe if you keep the pack part in front of your body, safer still if your shirt or sweater hangs over the pack. And it may go without saying, but *never* leave your pack unguarded, not even if you're only planning to be gone for a minute.

RESOURCES FOR WOMEN

Although times are changing, the idea still exists that women traveling alone are fair game for lewd comments, leering looks, and the like. The Left Bank tends to be less troublesome, as most male students are too worried about their academic reputation to risk looking like cads. The Right Bank, on the other hand, thanks to the sex trade that goes on around Les Halles near St-Denis, and on boulevard Clichy in Pigalle, deserves extra precaution, as do working-class areas. Harassment is usually verbal—always annoying, but not often violent. *Dragueurs* (men who persistently profess their undying love to hapless female passersby) tend to be very vocal, but the threat they pose is no greater than in any big city back home.

There are precautions you can take to avoid some harassment. Dressing conservatively helps; think about the area you're in before putting on that short skirt or tight body suit. Walk with a deliberate step and don't be afraid to show your irritation. Avoiding eye contact and conversation with potential sleazeballs also helps. Finally, be aware of your surroundings and use your head; don't do things abroad that you wouldn't do at home. Hitchhiking alone, for example, is not the brightest idea, nor is walking back to your hotel at night along deserted streets. If you get into an uncomfortable situation, move into a public area and make your fear widely known. That said, Paris is one of the safest big cities for the lone female, especially in areas that stay up late. Stick to the boulevards, memorize the time of the last Métro train to your station, and ride in the first car by the conductor.

PUBLICATIONS Along with the lesbian-oriented *Women's Traveller* and *Are You Two... Together?,* major travel publications for women include *Women Travel: Adventures, Advice, and Experience* ($12.95), published by Prentice Hall. More than 70 countries receive some sort of coverage in the form of journal entries and short articles. As far as practical travel information goes, it offers few details on prices, phone numbers, and addresses. The *Handbook for Women Travelers* ($14.95) by Maggie and Gemma Moss has some very good info on women's health and personal safety while traveling. For a nice companion book, look for *Maiden Voyages* ($14), edited by Mary Morris and published by Vintage Books. This collection of travel writings by women includes everyone from Mary Wollstonecraft to Joan Didion. All of these books should be readily available at any bookstore, or have your local shop order them for you.

ORGANIZATIONS Headquartered in Paris is **Mouvement Français Pour le Planning Familial** (4 sq. St-Irénée, 11e, tel. 01–48–07–29–10), part of the International Planned Parenthood Federation. You'll need a working knowledge of French to make much use of their services. **SOS Viol** (tel. 0–800–05–95–95) is a rape crisis hotline; they'll answer calls weekdays 10–6.

Pacific Harbor Travel specializes in independent adventure travel with an emphasis on women's travel. They're one of the better known agencies for women's travel. *519 Seabright Ave., Suite 201, Santa Cruz, CA 95062, tel. 408/427–5000.*

Women Welcome Women (WWW) is a nonprofit organization aimed at bringing together women of all nationalities, ages, and interests. Membership can put you in touch with women around the globe. *Betty Sobel, U.S.A. Trustee, 10 Greenwood Lane, Westport, CT 06880, tel. 203/ 259–7832.*

RESOURCES FOR GAY
AND LESBIAN TRAVELERS

The gay scene is alive and well in Paris, especially in the bars and clubs of the Marais, but lesbian spots are harder to find. Fewer hate crimes are committed against gays in France than in the United States and the United Kingdom, but once you leave Paris, a less-than-warm welcome may await you in the more conservative provinces.

PUBLICATIONS *Are You Two . . . Together?* is the best known guide to traveling in Europe. It's fairly anecdotal and skimps on practical details like phone numbers and addresses, but it still makes an excellent read. It costs $18 and is published by Random House; ask for it at your local bookstore.

Spartacus bills itself as *the* guide for the gay traveler, with practical tips and reviews of hotels and agencies in more than 160 countries. It's a bit expensive at $32.95, though you do get snappy color photos and listings in four languages. *Box 422458, San Francisco, CA 94142, tel. 800/462–6654.*

One of the better gay and lesbian travel newsletters is *Out and About,* with listings of gay-friendly hotels and travel agencies, plus health cautions for travelers with HIV. A 10-issue subscription costs $49; single issues cost about $5. *Tel. 800/929–2268 for subscriptions.*

The most comprehensive lesbian publication is *Women's Traveller* ($11.95), a dense guide to bars, hotels, and agencies throughout the United States, Canada, and the Caribbean. Rumor has it that a European edition will debut soon; keep your eyes open. *Box 422458, San Francisco, CA 94142, tel. 415/255–0404 or 800/462–6654.*

For the most detailed information about gay life in Paris, you should obviously look for gay publications in the city itself. The ultimate source of information and places to go for gay men in Paris is **Guide Illico** (64 rue Rambuteau, 3e, tel. 01–48–04–58–00), sold monthly for 9F at newsstands throughout Paris and available free at many gay restaurants and bars. Unfortunately, it's all in French. Publications Illico also put out *Double Face,* a free monthly supplement to gay life, and *Trixx* (35F), a collection of enticing photos. The *Guide Gai,* available for

21

50F from Les Mots à la Bouche (*see* Bookstores, in Chapter 6), lists restaurants, bars, cafés, and other popular gay hangouts in the city. The English-language version of *Paris Scene* costs 60F. For a large selection of gay magazines and other publications, check out Paris's **Le Kiosque des Amis** (29 blvd. des Italiens, 2e, tel. 01–42–65–00–94; Métro: Opéra).

ORGANIZATIONS For complete info on upcoming events, support groups, speakers, lists of gay-friendly establishments in Paris, literature (and even condoms!), head for the **Centre Gai et Lesbien** (3 rue Keller, 11e, tel. 01–43–57–21–47). Lesbian-specific info and support can be found at **Maison des Femmes** (8 cité Proust, 11e, tel. 01–43–48–24–91). You might also try **Act Up–Paris** (45 rue Sedaine, 11e, tel. 01–48–06–13–89).

International Gay Travel Association (IGTA) is a nonprofit organization with worldwide listings of travel agencies, gay-friendly hotels, gay bars, and travel services aimed at gay travelers. *Box 4974, Key West, FL 33041, tel. 800/448–8550, fax 305/286–6633.*

International Lesbian and Gay Association (ILGA) is an excellent source for info about conditions, specific resources, and trouble spots in dozens of countries, including France. *81 Rue Marche au Charbon, 1000 Brussels 1, Belgium, tel. 02/502–24–71.*

TRAVELERS WITH DISABILITIES

Accessibility may soon have an international symbol if an initiative begun by the Society for the Advancement of Travel for the Handicapped (SATH) catches on. A bold, underlined, capital *H* is the symbol that SATH is publicizing for hotels, restaurants, and tourist attractions to indicate that the property has some accessible facilities. While awareness of the needs of travelers with disabilities increases every year, budget opportunities are harder to find. Always ask if discounts are available, either for you or for a companion. In addition, plan your trip and make reservations far in advance, since companies that provide services for people with disabilities go in and out of business regularly.

Though Paris has spent a lot of money rebuilding itself during the past decade, only recently was a law passed requiring that new buildings be wheelchair accessible; you'll find very few buildings are barrier free. At least the government has published an excellent, free booklet (in French), "Touristes Quand Même." It details, region by region, which transportation systems and tourist attractions are accessible to the disabled. The booklet is available from tourist offices and from the **Comité National Français de Liaison pour la Réadaptation des Handicapés** (236 bis rue de Tolbiac, 13e, tel. 01–53–80–66–66). The tourist office will also charge you 60F for *Paris, Ile-de-France pour tous,* a reasonably complete guide book for travelers with disabilities.

ACCOMMODATIONS Whenever possible, reviews in this book will indicate if rooms are wheelchair accessible. However, most hotels in Paris are in buildings that are hundreds of years old and unsuited to guests with impaired mobility. In general, more expensive or chain hotels are better equipped. Talk to the **Association des Paralysés de France** (17 blvd. Auguste-Blanqui, 13e, tel. 01–40–78–69–00) for a list of wheelchair-accessible hotels.

GETTING AROUND

➤ **BY PLANE** • Most major airlines are happy to help travelers with disabilities make flight arrangements, provided they receive notification 48 hours in advance. Ask about possible discounts and check-in protocol when making reservations.

➤ **BY TRAIN** • The SNCF, France's rail service, has cars on some trains that are equipped for disabled travelers, and passengers in wheelchairs can be escorted on and off trains. All places for those in wheelchairs are now in nonsmoking cars. Contact SNCF in Paris (tel. 08–36–35–35–35) to request this service in advance and for tickets; for more wheelchair access information, try the **SNCF Accessibilité Service** (toll-free in France only, tel. 0–800–15–47–53). Most trains and train stations in Western Europe are wheelchair accessible, though many in more remote locations are not. The *Guide du voyageur à mobilité réduite* offers a comprehensive list of the services offered by every rail station in France and is available for free at all stations in Paris.

➢ **BY METRO** • Most of Paris's Métro lines (like the bus system) are unfortunately inaccessible to travelers with disabilities, but the RER is slightly more accessible. The following Paris RER stations have elevators: **Auber** (direction Etoile only), **Châtelet, Cité Universitaire** (direction south only), **La Défense, Denfert-Rochereau, Gare de Lyon, Gare du Nord, St-Michel** (elevator on side street rue Xavier-Privas), and **Vincennes.** Some of these may require escalator use as well, and you may have to push a call button for assistance. **Etoile** has escalators only, but they'll take you all the way to the street if you use one of the Champs-Elysées exits. **Nation** has an escalator for direction Marne-la-Vallée (toward Disneyland Paris, where the station is accessible). **Port Royal** has escalator access for direction Gentilly and access for exits only from direction Châtelet. For more details, ask the **Régie Autonome des Transports Parisiens (RATP)** (pl. de la Madeleine, 8e, tel. 01–40–46–42–17) for its brochure on accessibility.

PUBLICATIONS Twin Peaks Press publishes *Travel for the Disabled,* which offers helpful hints as well as a comprehensive list of guidebooks and facilities geared to disabled travelers. Their *Directory of Travel Agencies for the Disabled* lists more than 350 agencies throughout the world. Each is $19.95 plus $3 shipping and handling ($4.50 for both). Twin Peaks also offers a "Traveling Nurse's Network," which connects travelers with registered nurses to aid and accompany them on their trip. Fees range from $30 to $125. *Box 129, Vancouver, WA 98666, tel. 360/694–2462 or 800/637–2256 for orders only.*

ORGANIZATIONS **Directions Unlimited** organizes individual and group tours for disabled travelers. *720 N. Bedford Rd., Bedford Hills, NY 10507, tel. 800/533–5343 or 914/241–1700 in NY.*

Flying Wheels Travel arranges cruises, tours, and vacation travel itineraries. *143 W. Bridge St., Box 382, Owatonna, MN 55060, tel. 800/535–6790 or 507/451–5005 in MN.*

Mobility International USA (MIUSA) is a nonprofit organization that coordinates exchange programs for disabled people around the world. MIUSA also offers information on accommodations and organized study programs for members ($25 annually). The French affiliate is **Comité National Français de Liaison pour la Réadaptation des Handicapés** (*see above*). Nonmembers may subscribe to the newsletter for $15. *Box 10767, Eugene, OR 97440, tel. and TDD 541/343–1284, fax 541/343–6812, miusa@igc.apc.org.*

Moss Rehabilitation Hospital's Travel Information Service provides information on tourist sights, transportation, accommodations, and accessibility in destinations around the world. You can request information by phone only. The service is free. *Tel. 215/456–9900, TDD 215/456–9602.*

WORKING IN PARIS

If you're not currently a student (or recent grad), France won't grant you a work permit unless you already have a French employer who can convince immigration officials that he or she absolutely, positively needs *you,* and not a native French person, to fill the position. That said, plenty of native English speakers find work teaching their mother tongue to Francophones; hundreds of private language schools exist throughout the city, many in the 16th arrondissement. Each school has its own guidelines and restrictions: Many require a Teaching of English as a Foreign Language (TEFL) certificate, obtainable after an expensive, intensive four-week training course, and some hire only older, experienced teachers. The best place to get addresses and phone numbers is the Parisian *Pages jaunes* (Yellow Pages), and the best time to look is in late summer, since school generally starts around the beginning of October.

PUBLICATIONS Council (*see* Budget Travel Organizations, *above*) publishes two excellent resource books with complete details on work/travel opportunities. The most valuable is *Work, Study, Travel Abroad: The Whole World Handbook* ($13.95), which gives the lowdown on scholarships, grants, fellowships, study-abroad programs, and work exchanges. Also worthwhile is Council's *The High-School Student's Guide to Study, Travel, and Adventure Abroad* ($13.95). Both books can be shipped to you book rate ($1.50) or first-class ($3).

The U.K.-based Vacation Work Press publishes two first-rate guides to working abroad: **Directory of Overseas Summer Jobs** ($14.95) and Susan Griffith's **Work Your Way Around the World** ($17.95). The first lists more than 45,000 jobs worldwide; the latter has fewer listings but makes a more interesting read. Look for them at bookstores, or you can contact the American distributor directly. *Peterson's: 202 Carnegie Center, Princeton, NJ 05843.*

ORGANIZATIONS Au Pair Abroad arranges board and lodging for people between the ages of 18 and 26 who want to work as nannies for three to 18 months in France. Basic language skills are required, and all applicants must go through a somewhat lengthy interview process. *1015 15th St. NW, Suite 750, Washington, D.C. 20005, tel. 202/408–5380, fax 202/480– 5397, 708439@mcimail.com.*

The easiest way to arrange work in Britain, France, Ireland, and Germany is through Council's **Work Abroad Department** (205 E. 42nd St., New York, NY 10017, tel. 888/COUNCIL, http://www.ciee.org). The program enables you to work in Europe for three to six months. Participants must be U.S. citizens or permanent residents, 18 years or older, and a full-time student for the semester preceding their stay overseas. Past participants have worked at all types of jobs, including hotel and restaurant work, office and sales help, and occasionally career-related internships. A good working knowledge of French is required. The cost of the program is $200, which includes legal work permission documents, orientation and program materials, access to job and housing listings, and ongoing support services overseas. Contact Council for their free "Work Abroad" brochure.

Canadians are not eligible for the Council Work Abroad program and should contact **Travel CUTS,** which has similar programs for Canadian students who want to work abroad for up to six months. *187 College St., Toronto, Ont. M5T 1P7, tel. 416/979–2406.*

IAESTE sends full-time students abroad to practice their engineering, mathematics, and computer skills in more than 50 countries. You don't get paid much, though the program is designed to cover day-to-day expenses. Applications are due between September and December for travel the following summer, so get going. *10 Corporate Center, Suite 250, 10400 Little Patuxent Pkwy., Columbia, MD 21044, tel. 410/997–2200, fax 410/997–5186.*

The **YMCA** oversees a variety of international work exchanges in over 25 countries; the most popular is the **International Camp Counselor Program (ICCP),** which entails teaching English, building houses, hanging out with local kids, you name it. The program rarely lasts longer than a summer, and participants stay at local YMCAs or with families. Don't expect to make much money. Write for a detailed brochure. *71 W. 23rd St., Suite 1904, New York, NY 10010, tel. 212/727–8800.*

Once you're in Paris, the **CIDJ** (Centre d'information et de documentation de la jeunesse) will provide you with all the billboards and binders you need to research both short- and long-term job openings. *101 quai Branly, 15e, tel. 01–44–49–12–00. Métro: Bir-Hakeim. Open Mon.– Sat. 10–6.*

VOLUNTEER PROGRAMS

ORGANIZATIONS Council's **Voluntary Services Department** (205 E. 42nd St., New York, NY 10017, tel. 888/COUNCIL, http://www.ciee.org) offers two- to four-week environmental or community service projects in 25 countries around the globe. Participants must be 18 or older and pay a $195 placement fee. Also, Council publishes **Volunteer! The Comprehensive Guide to Voluntary Service in the U.S. and Abroad** ($12.95, plus $1.50 postage), which describes nearly 200 organizations around the world that offer volunteer positions.

Service Civil International (SCI) and **International Voluntary Service (IVS)** work for peace and international understanding through two- to three-week workcamps in Europe (fee $100– $150) and the United States (fee $50). You must be 16 or older to participate in U.S. camps, 18 and older for the European camps. *5474 Walnut Level Rd., Crozet, VA 22932, tel. 804/ 823–1826.*

Volunteers for Peace (VFP) sponsors two- to three-week international workcamps in the United States, Europe, Africa, Asia, and Central America. Registration is $175. Send for their *International Workcamp Directory* ($12); it lists more than 800 volunteer opportunities in 60 countries around the world. *43 Tiffany Rd., Belmont, VT, 05730, tel. 802/259–2759, fax 802/259–2922, http://www.vermontel.com/~vfp/home.htm.*

WorldTeach, a program run by Harvard University, offers excellent volunteer opportunities for those who want to teach in Europe, Africa, Central America, and parts of Asia. Subjects range from English and science to carpentry, forestry, and sports. You'll need a college degree and must be willing to commit for at least one year. *WorldTeach, c/o Harvard Institute for International Development, 1 Eliot St., Cambridge, MA 02138, tel. 617/495–5527 or 800/483–2240, fax 617/495–1599.*

STUDYING IN PARIS

Studying in another country is the perfect way to scope out a foreign culture, meet locals, and improve your language skills. You may choose to study through a U.S.-sponsored program, usually through an American university, or to enroll in a program sponsored by a European organization. Do your homework; programs vary greatly in expense, academic quality, exposure to language, amount of contact with locals, and living conditions. Working through your local university is the easiest way to find out about study-abroad programs in France. Most universities have staff members that distribute information on programs at European universities, and they might be able to put you in touch with program participants.

The **American Institute for Foreign Study** and the **American Council of International Studies** arrange semester- and year-long study-abroad programs in universities throughout France. Applicants must be enrolled as full- or part-time students. Fees vary according to the length of stay. *102 Greenwich Ave., Greenwich, CT 06830, tel. 800/727–2437.*

Council's **College and University Programs Division** administers summer, semester, and year-long study-abroad programs at various universities worldwide. To navigate the maze of programs, contact Council (205 E. 42nd St., New York, NY 10017, tel. 888/COUNCIL, http://www.ciee.org), or purchase their excellent *Work, Study, Travel Abroad: The Whole World Handbook* ($13.95).

The Information Center at the **Institute of International Education (IIE)** has reference books, foreign-university catalogues, study-abroad brochures, and other materials that may be consulted free of charge if you're in the neighborhood, or you can call for a recorded list of services. *809 U.N. Plaza, New York, NY 10017, tel. 212/984–5413. Information Center open Tues.–Thurs. 11–3:45.*

IIE also publishes the helpful *Academic Year Abroad* ($42.95), which lists more than 1,900 study-abroad programs for undergraduates and graduates. If you're more interested in summer-abroad and living-abroad programs, check out IIE's *Vacation Study Abroad* ($36.95). Order either from IIE Books (tel. 212/984–5412).

World Learning offers more than 100 different semester-abroad programs, many structured around home stays. *Kipling Rd., Box 676, Brattleboro, VT 05302, tel. 800/451–4465, fax 802/258–3248.*

Coming and Going

CUSTOMS AND DUTIES

`ARRIVING IN PARIS` Going through customs in Paris is usually pretty painless. The officials will check your passport but probably won't touch your luggage unless you look shady or their dogs have caught a whiff of something interesting in your bags. If you bring any foreign-made equipment with you from home, such as cameras or video gear, carry the original receipt or register it with customs before leaving the United States (ask for U.S. Customs Form 4457).

Otherwise, you may end up paying duty on your return. Don't even *think* about drugs. Being cited for drug possession is no joke, and embassies and consulates often can't or won't do much to persuade officials to release you if you get tossed into prison. On top of that, immigration officials have been getting tougher, conducting random searches of any traveler they think looks remotely suspicious.

RETURNING HOME It's best to have all the souvenirs and gifts you're bringing home in an easily accessible place, just in case the officials would like to have a peek. Don't wrap your gifts—it makes customs officers very inquisitive.

➢ **U.S. CUSTOMS** • Like most government organizations, the U.S. Customs Service enforces a number of mysterious rules. When you return to the United States you have to declare all items you bought abroad, but you won't have to pay duty unless you come home with more than $400 worth of foreign goods, including items bought in duty-free stores. For purchases between $400 and $1,000 you have to pay a 10% duty. You also have to pay tax if you exceed your duty-free allowances: one liter of alcohol or wine (for those 21 and over), 100 non-Cuban cigars (sorry, Fidel) or 200 cigarettes, and one bottle of perfume. A free leaflet about customs regulations and illegal souvenirs, "Know Before You Go," is available from the **U.S. Customs Service** (Box 7407, Washington, D.C. 20044, tel. 202/927–6724).

➢ **CANADIAN CUSTOMS** • Exemptions for returning Canadians range from $20 to $500, depending on how long you've been out of the country: for two days out, you're allowed to return with C$200 worth of goods; for one week out, you're allowed C$500 worth. Above these limits, you'll be taxed about 15%. Duty-free limits are: up to 50 cigars, 200 cigarettes, 400 grams of tobacco, and 1.14 liters of liquor—all must be declared in writing upon arrival at customs and must be with you or in your checked baggage. To mail back gifts, label the package: "Unsolicited Gift—Value under C$60." For more scintillating details, call the automated information line of the **Revenue Canada Customs, Excise and Taxation Department** (2265 St. Laurent Blvd. S., Ottawa, Ont., K1G 4K3, tel. 613/993–0534 or 613/991–3881), where you may request a copy of the Canadian Customs brochure "I Declare/Je Déclare."

➢ **U.K. CUSTOMS** • Travelers age 17 or over who return to the United Kingdom may bring back the following duty-free goods: 200 cigarettes or 100 cigarillos or 50 cigars or 250 grams of tobacco; 1 liter of alcohol over 22% volume or 2 liters of alcohol under 22% volume, plus 2 liters of still table wine; 60 ml of perfume and 250 ml of toilet water; and other goods worth up to £136. If returning from another EU country, you can choose, instead, to bring in the following, provided they were *not* bought in a duty-free shop: 300 cigarettes or 150 cigarillos or 75 cigars or 400 grams of tobacco; 1.5 liters of alcohol over 22% volume or three liters of alcohol under 22% volume, plus five liters of still table wine; 75 grams of perfume and ⅜ liter of toilet water; and other goods worth up to £250. For further information or a copy of "A Guide for Travellers," which details standard customs procedures as well as what you may bring into the United Kingdom from abroad, contact **HM Customs and Excise** (Dorset House, Stamford St., London SE1 9PY, tel. 0171/928–3344).

➢ **AUSTRALIAN CUSTOMS** • Australian travelers 18 and over may bring back, duty free: one liter of alcohol; 250 grams of tobacco products (equivalent to 250 cigarettes or cigars); and other articles worth up to AUS$400. If you're under 18, your duty-free allowance is AUS$200. To avoid paying duty on goods you mail back to Australia, mark the package: "Australian goods returned." For more rules and regulations, request the pamphlet "Customs Information for Travellers" from a local **Collector of Customs** (GPO Box 8, Sydney NSW 2001, tel. 02/226–5997).

➢ **NEW ZEALAND CUSTOMS** • Although greeted with a "*Haere Mai*" ("Welcome to New Zealand"), homeward-bound travelers face a number of restrictions. Travelers over age 17 are allowed, duty-free: 200 cigarettes or 250 grams of tobacco or 50 cigars or a combo of all three up to 250 grams; 4.5 liters of wine or beer and one 1,125-ml. bottle of spirits; and goods with a combined value up to NZ$700. If you want more details, ask for the pamphlet "Customs Guide for Travellers" from a New Zealand consulate.

GETTING THE BEST DEALS

While your travel plans are still in the fantasy stage, start studying the travel sections of major Sunday newspapers: Courier services, charter companies, and fare brokers often list incredibly cheap flights. Travel agents are another obvious resource, as they have access to computer networks that show the lowest fares before they're even advertised. However, budget travelers are the bane of travel agents, whose commission is based on the ticket prices. That said, agencies on or near college campuses—try STA or Council Travel (*see* Budget Travel Organizations, *above*)—actually cater to this pariah class and can help you find cheap deals.

While a last-minute, round-trip ticket to Paris on Air France can cost $1,200 from New York, bargain-basement prices can go as low as $450. Flexibility is the key to getting a serious bargain on airfare. If you can play around with your departure date, destination, amount of luggage carried, and return date, you will probably save money. When setting travel dates, remember that off-season fares can be as much as 50% lower. Ask which days of the week are the cheapest to fly on—weekends are often the most expensive. If you end up biting the bullet and paying more than you'd like for a ticket, keep scanning the ads in newspaper travel sections for last-minute ticket deals or a lower fare offered by desperate airlines. Some airlines will refund the difference in ticket price when they lower fares and you call them on it.

An extremely useful resource is Michael McColl's *The Worldwide Guide to Cheap Airfares,* an in-depth account of how to find cheap tickets and generally beat the system. The *Worldwide Guide* also includes a comprehensive listing of consolidators, charter companies, and courier services in budget travel hub cities all over the world. If you don't find it at your local bookstore, you can mail a check for $14.95 plus $2.50 for shipping and handling to Insider Publications (2124 Kittredge St., 3rd Floor, Berkeley, CA 94704), or call 800/782–6657 and order with a credit card.

STUDENT DISCOUNTS Student discounts on airline tickets are offered through **Council,** the **Educational Travel Center, STA Travel,** and **Travel CUTS** (*see* Budget Travel Organizations, *above*). Keep in mind that often you will *not* receive frequent-flyer mileage for discounted student, youth, or teacher tickets. For discount tickets based on your status as a student, youth, or teacher, have an ID when you check in that proves it: an International Student Identity Card (ISIC), Youth Identity Card, or International Teacher Identity Card.

Campus Connection, exclusively for students under 25, searches airline computer networks for the cheapest student fares to worldwide destinations. They don't always have the best price, but because they deal with the airlines directly you won't get stuck with a heavily restricted or fraudulent ticket. *1100 E. Marlton Pike, Cherry Hill, NJ 08032, tel. 800/428–3235.*

CONSOLIDATORS AND BUCKET SHOPS Consolidator companies, also known as bucket shops, buy blocks of tickets at wholesale prices from airlines trying to fill flights. Their tickets are generally lower than the published APEX fare, and you can often fly on a major airline with major airline comfort and convenience. Check out any consolidator's reputation with the Better

Paris Tonight . . . or in 21 Days, Dahhhling

There are two kinds of regular-fare tickets in this world: Full-fare and APEX (advance purchase excursion). The APEX price is the lowest published fare for any ticket purchased at least 21 days in advance. APEX tickets are what pleasure travelers buy if they aren't to be bothered with calling around to discount travel agencies and courier companies. Regular full-fare tickets are for business travelers on corporate accounts and supermodels who have to jet to Paris tonight. APEX fares are worth looking into, but real bargain hunters should focus on the three C's: consolidators, charters, and couriers.

Business Bureau before starting; most are perfectly reliable, but better safe than sorry. Travel agents can also get you good consolidator fares and usually deal with respectable companies.

There are some drawbacks to the consolidator ticket: You can't always be too choosy about which city you fly into. Consolidator tickets are not always refundable, and the flights available will sometimes involve indirect routes, long layovers in connecting cities, and undesirable seating assignments. If your flight is delayed or canceled, you'll also have a tough time switching airlines. However, you can often find consolidator tickets that are changeable, with no minimum or maximum stays required, and these tickets are often a very good deal at the last minute, when the deadline for the APEX fare has long since passed. Bucket shops generally advertise in newspapers—be sure to check restrictions, refund possibilities, and payment conditions. If possible, pay with a credit card, so that if your ticket never arrives you don't have to pay. One last suggestion: Confirm your reservation with the airline both before and after you buy a consolidated ticket. This decreases the chance of fraud and ensures that you won't be the first to get bumped if the airline overbooks. For more details, contact one of the following consolidators.

Airfare Busters. *5100 Westheimer Ave., Suite 550, Houston, TX 77056, tel. 713/961–5109 or 800/232–8783, fax 713/961–3385.*

Globe Travel. *507 5th Ave., Suite 606, New York, NY 10017, tel. 800/969–4562, fax 212/682–3722.*

UniTravel. *1177 N. Warson Rd., Box 12485, St. Louis, MO 63132, tel. 314/569–2501 or 800/325–2222, fax 314/569–2503.*

Up & Away Travel. *347 Fifth Ave., Suite 202, New York, NY 10016, tel. 212/889–2345, fax 212/889–2350.*

CHARTER FLIGHTS Charter flights have vastly different characteristics, depending on the company you're dealing with. Generally speaking, a charter company either buys a block of tickets on a regularly scheduled commercial flight and sells them at a discount (the prevalent form in the United States) or leases the whole plane and then offers relatively cheap fares to the public (most common in the United Kingdom). Despite a few potential drawbacks—among them infrequent flights, restrictive return-date requirements, lickety-split payment demands, frequent bankruptcies—charter companies often offer the cheapest tickets around, especially during high season when APEX fares are most expensive. Make sure you find out a company's policy on refunds should a flight be canceled by either yourself or the airline. Summer charter flights fill up fast and should be booked a couple of months in advance.

You're in much better shape when the company is offering tickets on a regular commercial flight. After you've bought the ticket from the charter folks, you generally deal with the airline directly. When a charter company has chartered the whole plane, things get a little sketchier: Bankrupt operators, long delays at check-in, overcrowding, and flight cancellations are fairly common. Other charter troubles: Weird departure times, packed planes, and a dearth of one-way tickets. Nevertheless, in peak season, charters are very often the cheapest way to go. You can minimize risks by checking the company's reputation with the Better Business Bureau.

Charter companies to try include **DER Tours** (Box 1606, Des Plains, IL 60017, tel. 800/782–2424), **MartinAir** (tel. 800/627–8462), **Tower Air** (tel. 800/34–TOWER), and **Travel CUTS** (187 College St., Toronto, Ont. M5T 1P7, tel. 416/979–2406). Council Travel and STA (*see* Budget Travel Organizations, *above*) also offer exclusively negotiated discount airfares on scheduled airlines.

COURIER FLIGHTS Courier flights are simple: You sign a contract with a courier service to babysit their packages (often without ever laying eyes on them, let alone hands), and the courier company pays half or more of your airfare. On the day of departure, you arrive at the airport a few hours early, meet someone who hands you a ticket and customs forms, and off you go. After you land, you simply clear customs with the courier luggage, and deliver it to a waiting agent.

Courier flights are cheap and easy, yes, but there are restrictions: (1) Flights can be booked only a week or two in advance and often only a few days in advance, (2) you are allowed carry-on luggage only, because the courier uses your checked-luggage allowance to transport the time-sensitive shipment, (3) you must return within one to four weeks, (4) times and destinations are limited, (5) you may be asked to pay a deposit, to be refunded after you have completed your assignment.

Find courier companies in the travel section of the newpaper, the yellow pages of your phone directory, or mail away for a telephone directory that lists companies by the cities to which they fly. One of the better publications is *Air Courier Bulletin* (IAATC, 8 South J St., Box 1349, Lake Worth, FL 33460, tel. 407/582–8320), sent to IAATC members every two months once you pay the $45 annual fee. Publications you can find in the bookstores include *Air Courier Bargains* ($14.95), published by The Intrepid Traveler, and *The Courier Air Travel Handbook* ($9.95), published by Thunderbird Press.

Discount Travel International has courier flights to destinations in Europe, Central America, and Asia from Chicago, Los Angeles, Miami, and New York. The prices are admirably cheap, but some restrictions apply, so call at least two weeks in advance. Couriers must be over 18. *169 W. 81st St., New York, NY 10024, tel. 212/362–3636.*

Now Voyager (tel. 212/431–1616) connects travelers scrounging for cheap airfares with companies looking for warm bodies to escort their packages overseas. Departures are from New York and Newark, and occasionally Los Angeles or Detroit; destinations may be in Europe, Asia, or Mexico (City, that is). Round-trip fares start at $150. A nonrefundable $50 registration fee, good for one year, is required. Call for current offerings.

LAST-MINUTE DEALS Flying standby is almost a thing of the past. The idea is to purchase an open ticket and wait for the next available seat on the next available flight to your chosen destination. Airlines themselves no longer offer standby tickets but some travel agencies do. Three-day-advance-purchase youth fares are open only to people under 25 and can only be purchased within three days of departure. Return flights must also be booked no more than three days prior to departure. If you meet the above criteria, expect 10%–50% savings on published APEX fares. Some courier companies keep a last-minute list of travelers who are willing to fly at a moment's notice. Call around to see which do and how you can be listed.

There are also a number of brokers that specialize in discount and last-minute sales, offering savings on unsold seats on commercial carriers and charter flights, as well as tour packages. If you're desperate to get to Paris by Wednesday, try **Last Minute Travel Club** (tel. 617/267–9800).

BY AIR

On your fateful departure day, remember that check-in time for international flights is a long two hours before departure. One more thing: International flights lasting more than six hours allow smoking—so if fumes make you queasy, book short hops or ask for seats as far away from the smoking section as possible; if you love to light up, book long and straight.

Paris's main airports lie a fair distance outside town—**Charles de Gaulle** (also called **Roissy**) is 26 kilometers (16 miles) to the northeast, **Orly** 16 kilometers (10 miles) to the south—but transportation to both is extensive (*see* Getting Around Paris, To and from the Airports, *below*). If you plan to fly out of Paris, arrive at the airport a full two hours before departure time; you'll probably encounter long lines at the ticket counters and baggage check and complete indifference from airline employees if you're about to miss your flight. Both airports have currency exchange desks and 24-hour cash exchange machines. *Airport info: Charles de Gaulle, tel. 01–48–62–22–80, 24 hours a day; Orly, tel. 01–49–75–15–15, 6 AM–11:30 PM.*

MAJOR AIRLINES WITH OFFICES IN PARIS

Air Canada, tel. 01–44–50–20–20; Air France, tel. 01–44–08–24–24; American Airlines, tel. 01–42–89–05–22; British Airways, tel. 01–47–78–14–14; Continental, tel. 01–42–99–09–09; Delta, tel. 01–47–68–92–92; Northwest, tel. 01–42–66–90–00; United, tel. 01–48–97–82–82.

If you can't get a cheap flight into Paris, look into other destinations. Flying into Brussels is convenient; the train trip to Paris costs about 250F second class and takes about three hours, and the train station connects to the airport in Brussels. Amsterdam and Frankfurt are also good bets. One-way second-class train tickets cost 390F and 550F respectively.

FROM NORTH AMERICA The flight from the East Coast to Paris takes about eight hours. Plenty of U.S. airlines, including **American** (tel. 800/433–7300), **Continental** (tel. 800/231–0856), **Delta** (tel. 800/221–1212), **TWA** (tel. 800/892–4141), and **United** (tel. 800/241–6522), fly from all over the United States to Paris. **Air France** (tel. 800/237–2747) has frequent flights to Paris and other French cities. Call around to see who is offering the best fare at the moment. If you're extremely lucky, you might find a special fare for as little as $450, but prices go all the way up to $1,200 or so. With a little advance planning and flexibility, you should be able to get a ticket for about $600 almost any time of year.

Air Canada (tel. 800/361–8620 in Québec or 800/268–7240 in Ontario) flies to Paris direct from Montréal, Toronto, and sometimes Vancouver. **Canadian Airlines** (tel. 800/426–7000) has lots of flights from Toronto.

FROM THE U.K. **Air France** (tel. 0181/759–2311) and **British Airways** (tel. 0181/897–4000) make the hour flight from London's Gatwick and Heathrow airports to Paris several times a day. The cost of a round-trip ticket is almost halved if you purchase it 14 days in advance and stay over a Saturday night. Both airlines also fly to Paris a few times every day from London's most central airport, London City. **Nouvelles Frontières** (tel. 0171/629–7772) in London has info on discounted airfares between the two countries.

FROM DOWN UNDER **Qantas** (tel. 02/957–0111) flies to Paris from Sydney by way of Bangkok and Frankfurt. **Continental** (tel. 02/693–5266 in Sydney or 09/379–5682 in Auckland) flies to Paris from Melbourne, Sydney, and Auckland, New Zealand, by way of Los Angeles and New York. Round-trip fares go as low as AUS$2,000 but are often as high as AUS$6,000. Talk to the STA offices in Victoria or Auckland (*see* Budget Travel Organizations, *above*) for info on discount fares.

TAKING LUGGAGE ABROAD You've heard it a million times. Now you'll hear it once again: Pack light. U.S. airlines allow passengers to check two pieces of luggage, neither of which can exceed 62 inches (length + width + height) or weigh more than 70 pounds. If your airline accepts excess baggage, it will probably charge you for it. Foreign airline policies vary, so call or check with a travel agent before you show up at the airport with one bag too many.

If you're traveling with a pack, tie all loose straps to each other or onto the pack itself, as they tend to get caught in luggage conveyer belts. Put valuables like cameras and important documents in the middle of packs, wadded inside clothing, because outside pockets are extremely vulnerable to probing fingers.

Anything you'll need during the flight (and valuables to be kept under close surveillance) should be stowed in a carry-on bag. Foreign airlines have different policies but generally allow only one carry-on in tourist class, in addition to a handbag and a bag filled with duty-free goodies. The carry-on bag cannot exceed 45 inches (length + width + height) and must fit under the seat or in the overhead luggage compartment. Call for the airline's current policy. Passengers on U.S. airlines are limited to one carry-on bag, plus coat, camera, and handbag. Carry-on bags must fit under the seat in front of you; maximum dimensions are 9 x 45 x 22 inches. Hanging bags can have a maximum dimension of 4 x 23 x 45 inches; to fit in an overhead bin, bags can have a maximum dimension of 10 x 14 x 36 inches. If your bag is too porky for compartments, be prepared for the humiliation of rejection and last-minute baggage check.

BY TRAIN

The railway system in France is fast, extensive, and efficient. All French trains have a first and second class. First class is 30%–50% more expensive, though the difference in comfort between the two is minimal, except on the lightning-fast TGV trains on which first class is really deluxe. First-class sleeping cars are very expensive, but second-class *couchettes,* bunks that come six to a compartment, cost only 90F more (and are worth every centime). On some international trips, you may be forced to pay a hefty supplement for a nice bed, whether you want to or not; check in advance to make sure you can get a 90F couchette. For long distances, it's best to take the TGV trains, though a seat reservation (which runs 20F–80F) is required *without* exception on these trains. For info on the various passes available, *see* Rail Passes, *above*. To make reservations on any train, call 08–36–35–35–35; you can't make reservations at the actual train station phone number—it's pretty much only for station open hours, etc.

Purchase tickets at the booth before boarding the train. Don't forget to validate them (*composter le billet*) at the orange ticket punchers, usually located at the entrance to the *quais* (platforms). That said, if you board your train on the run and don't have time to punch it, look for a *contrôleur* as soon as possible and get him to sign it. Otherwise, you're in for a nasty *amende* (fine). Train schedules for individual lines are available at all stations through which the line runs. Complete SNCF timetables are available at info counters in large stations. It's a good idea to bring food and drink with you on long trips; the food sold on the train is usually very expensive and very bad.

BY EUROTUNNEL Since the early 1800s, visionaries have dreamed of building a tunnel between France and England, but endless obstacles have stood in the way. The Channel itself wasn't a problem; the chalk on the Channel floor is actually quite firm and amenable to tunneling. Still, bureaucratic fumbling and money problems delayed the opening of the tunnel considerably. Yet despite this nearly two-century delay, the Eurotunnel is now complete, and it offers Parisians and Londoners daily opportunities for cultural exchange. **Eurostar** (19 Worple Rd., Wimbledon, tel. 0181/784–1333) sells second-class tickets for the train trip from London to Paris for 645F one-way (395F if bought 15 days in advance). The trip takes three hours. If you're traveling by car, **Le Shuttle** (19 rue des Mathurins, 9e, tel. 01–47–42–50–00) sells round-trip tickets from Calais to Folkstone for 350F and up. However, Le Shuttle prices fluctuate depending on time of day, the week you travel in, and the length of your stay, so be sure to check prices before making any plans. The trip takes about 40 minutes.

PARIS TRAIN STATIONS Six major train stations serve Paris; all have cafés, newsstands, bureaux de change, and luggage storage. You can abandon your belongings in a locker, usually with a coded lock, for 15F–30F for 72 hours. Most train stations have tourist offices (*see* Staying in Paris, Visitor Information *below*), and each is connected to the rest of Paris by the Métro system. To make a reservation from anywhere in France, call tel. 08–36–35–35–35.

➢ **GARE D'AUSTERLITZ** • Trains from here serve **southwest France** and **Spain,** including Toulouse (7 hrs, 470F), Barcelona (10–14 hrs, 470F), and Madrid (11 hrs, 670F).

➢ **GARE DE L'EST** • This station serves **eastern France, Germany, Austria,** and **Eastern Europe,** with trains leaving daily for Frankfurt (6 hrs, 556F), Prague (16 hrs, 775F), and Vienna (13 hrs, 905F). The station is smaller than nearby Gare du Nord and its services are more limited, but there's still a tourist office and a Thomas Cook bureau de change (open daily 7 AM–6:45 PM). The neighborhood is a bit scary at night.

➢ **GARE DE LYON** • Trains from here serve the **south of France, the Alps, Switzerland,** and **Italy.** Plenty of trains run to Lyon (5 hrs, 290F), Lausanne (4 hrs, 360F), Milan (7½ hrs, 400F), and Rome (14 hrs, 640F). This is one of the bigger stations, with a full range of services, including combination luggage lockers and a bureau de change (open 7 AM–11 PM).

➢ **GARE MONTPARNASSE** • Trains travel from here to **Brittany** and **southwestern France.** Daily trains run to Bordeaux (3 hrs, 340F), Rennes (2 hrs, 260F), and Biarritz (5 hrs, 410F).

➢ **GARE DU NORD** • Trains travel from here to **northern France** (Calais and Lille), and to **Belgium,** the **Netherlands,** and points in **Scandinavia.** Regular trains run to Amsterdam (6 hrs, 390F), Copenhagen (16 hrs, 1010F), and London (*see* By Eurotunnel, *above*). Showers cost 20F; soap and towels are extra. The neighborhood gets sketchy at night.

➤ **GARE ST-LAZARE** • This station serves **Normandy** and some destinations in **northern France.** International destinations include Amsterdam (6 hrs, 390F). This is the only major station without a tourist office.

BY BUS

Eurolines, Paris's lone bus company, offers international service only. If you take a bus into Paris, it will most likely drop you off at the Eurolines office close to Métro Gallieni. Some of its most popular routes are to London (9 hrs, 340F), Barcelona (15 hrs, 480F), and Berlin (12 hrs, 410F). The company's international buses also arrive and depart from Avignon, Bordeaux, Lille, Lyon, Toulouse, and Tours. Unfortunately, Eurail passes don't get you any discount. *28 av. du Général-de-Gaulle, Bagnolet, tel. 01–49–72–51–51. Métro: Gallieni. Other location: 55 rue St-Jacques, 5e, tel. 01–43–54–11–99. Métro: Cluny–La Sorbonne. Both open daily 9–6.*

Ferry companies are working hard to undercut the Eurotunnel, and P&O Ferries occasionally offers round trips for 20F a passenger. The catch is that you have to complete your trip within 48 hours— but how they force you to use the return portion of your ticket is unclear.

BY FERRY

Lots of ferry and Hovercraft companies transport travelers and their cars across the Channel. With the arrival of the Eurotunnel, many ferry companies are slashing their prices. Calais is becoming the Channel-crossing hub; only **Hoverspeed** (tel. 03–21–46–14–14) still sends speedy Seacats between Boulogne and Folkestone (mid-April–September only). From Calais, **Sealink** (tel. 01–44–94–40–40) and **P&O Ferries** (tel. 01–44–51–00–51) make the 1½-hour ferry trip to Dover all year long for 200F round-trip if you stay fewer than five days, 400F round-trip if you stay more. **Hoverspeed** (tel. 03–21–46–14–14) sends Hovercraft over in half the time and charges 200F round-trip for stays of fewer than five days.

HITCHING

While hitchhiking out of Paris is virtually impossible from the city center, a couple of organized carpool systems do exist. **Allostop Provoya** hooks up willing drivers with paying passengers. You simply call Allostop and see what they have available. The price runs 20 centimes per kilometer plus a 30F charge for trips under 200 kilometers, 70F for over 500 kilometers. Some sample prices for trips from Paris are: Marseille (223F), Montpellier (221F), Grenoble (183F), and Geneva (179F). Anyone is welcome to use this service, but if your French is rusty, make sure you've made your destination clear—you might end up in Barcelona instead of Munich. *84 passage Brady, 10e, tel. 01–42–46–00–66. Métro: Château d'Eau. Open weekdays 9–7:30, Sat. 9–1 and 2–6.*

Auto-Partage offers basically the same deal, but with a lot more international destinations. The charge again is 20 centimes per kilometer plus a 30F–90F service charge. Sample prices: Marseille (229F), Amsterdam (160F), Prague (298F), and Berlin (300F). *189 av. de Choisy, 13e, tel. 01–45–85–52–53. Métro: Place d'Italie. Open Mon. 2–7, Tues.-Sat. 10–1 and 2–7.*

Getting Around Paris

If you don't get anything else straight, for God's sake learn the difference between the **Rive Gauche** (Left Bank) and the **Rive Droite** (Right Bank) before you step off that plane. The simplest directions will refer to these two sides of the Seine River, and if you have to ask which is which, you're likely to be looked at scoldingly. In the most stereotypical terms, the Rive Gauche is the artistic area; the Sorbonne and the Quartier Latin are here, along with many other bustling neighborhoods full of young people. The Rive Droite, on the other hand, is traditionally more elegant and commercial, though its less central areas are actually much cooler than the Left Bank. It's home to ritzy shopping districts and most of the big-name sights like the Louvre and the Arc de Triomphe. Between the two banks you have the Ile de la Cité, where you'll find the Cathédrale de Notre-Dame, and the smaller Ile St-Louis.

Once you have the Left and Right Banks figured out, move on to the **arrondissements,** or districts, numbered 1 through 20. (For all addresses in this book, the arrondissement number is given, since it's the most common way to describe a location.) Arrondissements one through eight are the most central and contain most of the big tourist attractions, while the ninth through 20th gradually spiral outward toward the outskirts of the city.

To figure out the zip code of any point in Paris, just tack the arrondissement number onto the digits 750. For example, for the fifth arrondissement, 5e (cinquième), the five-digit zip code would be 75005—turning 5 into 05.

More than two million people somehow manage to cram themselves into the apartments, cafés, restaurants, bars, and streets of Paris. The long-running joke is that the streets—narrow, winding, labyrinthine, and vertiginous—were paved according to the paths the cows wandered in more pastoral times. You *will* get lost—hell, most of the natives do, too. But that's part of the fun.

When you've had enough walking and you just want to *get there,* the city has an excellent public transportation system consisting of the Métro (the subway system) and the municipal bus system, both operated by **RATP.** If you plan to stay in Paris for only a short time, stick to the Métro; it's easier to use than the buses. To avoid getting lost on a regular basis, as soon as you arrive buy *L'Indispensable Plan de Paris par Arrondissement,* a booklet of detailed maps showing all Métro stops and sights. An index at the front alphabetically lists all streets and their arrondissement. It costs 35F–60F, and it is available at large bookstores such as the FNAC (*see* Bookstores, in Chapter 6) and smaller bookstores marked *Presse.* You can also get less useful but free maps from the tourist offices (*see* Staying in Paris, Visitor Information, *below*). For info on all public transport, call 08–36–68–77–14 between 6 AM and 9 PM, though you may find it difficult to get through.

TO AND FROM THE AIRPORTS

Both airports are served by **Air France buses** that depart for Paris every 12–15 minutes between 6 AM and 11 PM. The bus from Charles de Gaulle (55F) stops at the Air France office at Porte Maillot, not far from the Arc de Triomphe; the one from Orly (40F) runs to the Hôtel des Invalides. The trip takes about 40 minutes from Charles de Gaulle and 20 minutes from Orly, depending on traffic.

If you can afford a **taxi** from the airport, you've got more money than we do; it costs about 200F to get to the center of Paris from Charles de Gaulle and 160F from Orly. If you have a lot of stuff, you might want to take the Air France bus or public transportation into Paris and then catch a cab to wherever you're staying. For taxi info, *see* Other Options, *below.*

CHARLES DE GAULLE/ROISSY If you're trying to catch a plane out of Paris, your safest bet is to take **RER B** from any Métro or RER station to **Roissy Aéroport Charles de Gaulle,** since you won't have to worry about traffic, which can delay the buses for up to an hour. A free *navette* (shuttle bus) takes you between the airport gates and the RER station in both directions. Tickets to airports cost 45F; they leave about every 10 minutes and the ride itself takes around 45 minutes. Trains start running at 5:30 AM toward the airport and at 6:30 AM toward town; either way they keep going until nearly midnight.

The **ROISSYBUS,** run by the RATP, is also easy and convenient, though traffic can thwart the projected 45-minute ride time. It costs 40F, and it takes you straight from your terminal to Métro Opéra every 15 minutes from 5:45 AM to 11 PM.

ORLY Orly has two terminals—Orly-Ouest and Orly-Sud—make sure you know which one you want. **RER C** to Orly plus a free shuttle brings you to the airport for 27F in about 30 minutes between 5:50 AM and 10:25 PM; trains in the other direction run 5:30 AM–11:30 PM. Trains in either direction leave about every 10 minutes. For 50F, you can take the **RER B** to Antony and grab the Orlyval shuttle to the airport. For 30F, the RATP-run **ORLYBUS** links the terminals with

Métro Denfert-Rochereau, just south of the Quartier Latin. Look for the emblem on the side of the shuttle.

BY METRO AND RER

Except for the fact that it closes soon after midnight, the Métro is the epitome of convenient public transportation. Thirteen Métro lines and five main RER lines crisscross Paris and the suburbs, and you will almost never be more than a 10-minute walk from the nearest Métro stop. Any station or tourist office can give you a free map of the whole system, or you can use the handy color map at the front of this book. Métro lines are marked in the station both by line number and by the names of the stops at the end of each line. Find the number of the line you want to take and the name of the terminus toward which you will be traveling, and follow the signs.

To transfer to a different line, look for orange signs saying CORRRESPONDENCE and for the new line number and terminus you need. The blue-and-white signs that say SORTIE (exit) will lead you back above ground. You can identify Métro stations by the illuminated yellow M signs, by the round red-and-white METRO signs, or by the old, green, art nouveau arches bearing the full name, METROPOLITAIN. The Métro tends to be pretty safe at night, as nocturnal Parisians will often be accompanying you on whatever train you take. Of course, bringing a companion is always a good idea. Otherwise, just look mean and uncommunicative.

The first Métro of the day heads out at 5:30 AM, the last at 12:30 AM. Often the directional signs on the quays indicate the times at which the first and last trains pass that station. Individual tickets cost 7F, but it's much more economical to buy a *carnet* (book of 10) for 45F. You can use one ticket each time you go underground for as many transfers as you like. For extended stays consider getting a **Carte Orange,** for which you need a picture of yourself. (Large Métro stations usually have photo booths that cost 20F, and many film stores offer passport photos.) You can fill the card with a *coupon semaine* (weekly pass; 67F, valid Mon.–Sun.) or *coupon mensuel* (monthly pass; 230F, valid from the first day of the month). You can buy these at any tabac with the abbreviation "RATP" on the window. Whatever you use, hang on to your ticket until you exit the Métro in case some uniformed French dude wants to see it, a particular danger toward the end of the month. Young people who hop the barriers get a rough word from the attendant—or a fine of up to 250F.

Several Métro stations also act as **RER** stations. The RER is a high-speed rail system that extends into the Parisian suburbs and is a fast way to travel between major points in the city. The five principal RER lines are also marked on the Métro maps. You can use normal Métro tickets on them within Zones 1 and 2, which will get you pretty much anywhere in Paris. To venture farther into Zones 3–5, to Versailles, for example, or to the airports, you need to buy a separate, more expensive ticket.

BY BUS

The buses are safe, and they offer the distinct advantage of letting you see where you're going, how you're getting there, and anything interesting along the way. During rush hour they offer the distinct disadvantage of getting you there verrry, verrry slowly.

The Noctambus is a good way to meet drunk people of all nationalities and possibly learn some dirty songs in French.

Métro tickets are accepted on the buses. Theoretically you need one to three tickets, depending on how far you're going, but it is highly unlikely anyone's going to check up on how many you use. In fact, even a *used* Métro ticket will fly on most buses if you're subtle and don't mind a slight risk factor. If you're caught, though, you'll have to pay an 80F fine. Stamp your ticket in the machine at the front of the bus. If you have a Carte Orange, though, don't *ever* stamp it, or it will become invalid—just flash it to the driver.

There are maps of the bus system at most bus stops; all 63 bus lines run Monday through Saturday from 6:30 AM to 8:30 PM, with limited service until 12:30 AM and all day on Sunday. A handy little service, the **Noctambus,** runs 10 lines every hour on the half hour between 1:30

AM and 5:30 AM; all lines start at Métro Châtelet, leaving from just in front of the Hôtel de Ville. Stops served by the Noctambus have a yellow-and-black owl symbol on them. Technically, a single ride gobbles up four tickets, though rarely does anyone pay all four; a monthly or weekly Carte Orange works on Noctambuses, too. For a map of the night-bus routes, ask for a "Grand Plan de Paris" at any Métro station; the Noctambus lines are drawn in the corner. April 15 through September, on Sundays and holidays from noon until 9, the RATP runs a bus line called the **Balabus,** which hits all major sights in the city and takes about an hour one-way. Buses start at the La Défense or Gare de Lyon Métro stations and stop at all bus stops with the sign BB-BALABUS. The full ride costs three normal tickets, though again you can probably get away with stamping just one.

BY CAR

You can save as much as 30% if you reserve a car before leaving home, rather than renting one on the spot abroad.

Getting around Paris by car is a very bad idea, but if you're planning to cruise the countryside, having a car gives you the ultimate travel freedom. Gas, however, is expensive in France (about 5F30 per liter for regular unleaded, 5F70 for super unleaded). Remember that, in France, the driver on your right has the right of way—and will take it. If you plan to rent a car abroad, you should probably get an **International Driver's Permit (IDP)** before leaving home. The IDP is available from the American Automobile Association (AAA) for $10 if you bring two of your own passport-size photos. Some offices can take photos for you ($6 for AAA members;

Rues with a View: Scenic Bus Rides in Paris

There are several bus lines that you can ride for a good, cheap tour of Paris, sans irritating commentary. Some of these lines are traveled by buses with small balconies at the rear, though the proximity to gusts of carbon monoxide is less than pleasant.

- *No. 29: The interesting section of the 29 stretches from Gare St-Lazare, past Opéra Garnier and the Pompidou, and through the heart of the Marais, crossing the place des Vosges before ending up at the Bastille. This is one of the few lines that run primarily through the small streets of a neighborhood, and it has an open back.*

- *No. 69: Get on at the Champ de Mars (the park right by the Eiffel Tower) and ride through parts of the Quartier Latin, across the bridge to the Right Bank near the Louvre, by the Hôtel de Ville (City Hall), and out to the Bastille area.*

- *No. 72: River lovers will appreciate this line. It follows the Seine from the Hôtel de Ville east past the city limits, hitting the Louvre, the Trocadéro, and most of the big-name Right Bank sights. You also get good views of the Left Bank, including the Eiffel Tower.*

- *No. 73: You can pick up this short line at the top of the Champs-Elysées or all the way out at La Défense. It travels all the way down the Champs-Elysées, through the place de la Concorde, crossing the river, and ending up at the Musée d'Orsay.*

- *Montmartrobus: If you want to see all of Montmartre without facing the hills "à pied" (by foot), pick up this bus at Pigalle for a winding tour of the area, including a pass under the Sacré Cœur. No special ticket is needed.*

$8 for nonmembers). Nonmembers must pay cash. Some offices can issue an IDP on the spot in about 15 minutes, but be sure to call ahead; during the busy season IDPs can take a week or more.

The French **Automobile Club National (ACN)** (5 rue Auber, 75009 Paris, tel. 01–44–51–53–99, fax 01–49–24–93–99) charges a small fee for roadside breakdown service and 24-hour towing (tel. 0-800–05–05–01). FYI, *remorquer* means "to tow," while the noun form is *la remorque*. If you're an AAA member, you can get reimbursed for ACN charges when you get home. For more info stop by your local AAA branch and ask for the pamphlet "Offices to Serve You Abroad," or send a S.A.S.E. to the AAA's head office (1000 AAA Dr., Heathrow, FL 32746).

RENTING A CAR Although renting a car is more expensive in France than in the U.S., several agencies offer pretty reasonable rates. However, they rarely offer cars with automatic transmission, so learn to drive a stick before you go. The cheapest cars are very small stick-shifts that go for around 300F per day or 1,000F–1,500F a week. Some agencies include mileage in the cost, while others may charge you extra once you reach a certain number of kilometers. Many agencies require that you be at least 23 years old and have a credit card.

Many small cars in France use diesel (gazole) instead of gas. The pumps are easy to confuse, and a mistake can wreck your engine.

Rental rates vary widely and usually include unlimited free mileage and standard liability coverage. Most major car-rental companies are represented in Europe, including **Avis** (tel. 800/331–1212, 800/879–2847 in Canada, 0181/848–8765 in the United Kingdom); **Budget** (tel. 800/527–0700, 800/268–8900 in Canada); **Hertz** (tel. 800/654–3131 in the U.S. and Canada, 0990/99–6699 in the United Kingdom); **National** (tel. 800/227–7368, 0113/242–2233 in the United Kingdom).

Other sources of savings are the several companies that operate as wholesalers—companies that do not own their own fleets but rent in bulk from those that do and offer good rates to their customers. Rentals through such companies must be arranged and paid for before you leave the United States. Among them are **Auto Europe** (39 Commercial St., Box 7006, Portland, ME 04112, tel. 207/828–2525 or 800/223–5555); **Europe by Car** (mailing address: 1 Rockefeller Plaza, New York, NY 10020; walk-in address: 49th St., New York, NY 10020, tel. 212/581–3040 or 800/637–9037); **Bon Voyage By Car** (5658 Sepulveda Blvd., Suite 201, Van Nuys, CA 91441, tel. 818/786–1960 or 800/272–3299); and **Kemwel** (106 Calvert St., Harrison, NY 10528, tel. 914/835–5555 or 800/678–0678). Always ask for all the fine-print details (required deposits, cancellation policy, etc.) in writing.

OTHER OPTIONS

BY MOTORBIKE AND MOPED Any two-wheeled vehicle that goes over 50 kilometers (31 miles) per hour needs to be registered and licensed at the nearest *préfecture* (local police department). This means most mopeds don't have to be registered and most motorbikes do. Renting a moped is expensive but may be worth doing to really get off the beaten track for a day or two. It's also a good way to zip through Parisian traffic—most Parisian drivers are used to mopeds and won't try too hard to run you over. A good place to pick up a scooter is **Mondial Scooter** (14 rue St-Maur, 11e, tel. 01–43–48–65–80), if you're willing to part with 150F–300F per day, or **Dynamic Sport** (149 rue Montmartre, 2e, tel. 01–42–33–61–82). To buy a used moped or motorcycle, check the listings in *Argus,* a weekly publication available at most newsstands.

BY BOAT During the summer, hordes of **bateaux mouches** (tel. 01–40–76–99–99) creep up and down the river, offering commentary in five languages and shining floodlights on the buildings at night. The lights show off the buildings (and the flies that give these "fly boats" their name) to their best advantage, but they make people living along the river mad as hell. Dress warmly enough to ride on the upper deck, and you might avoid the crush below. Board the boat for a 40F, 1¼-hour tour at the Pont de l'Alma. From April to September, a less touristy alternative is **Bateaux Parisiens** (tel. 01–44–11–33–55), a small boat-bus that runs between Pont de la Bourdonnais at the Eiffel Tower and the Hôtel de Ville. There are five stations along the way, and you'll pay 20F for the journey from Hôtel de Ville to the Eiffel Tower; 60F gets you a day pass to the whole line. The boats begin running daily at 10 AM and leave about every 30 minutes until 9 PM.

BY BIKE It's not uncommon to see hardy souls with baguettes in their backpacks pedaling their way through Paris's treacherous traffic—bicycling is one of the more efficient ways to get around the city, especially if you manage to emerge with your baguette intact. Your lungs, however, might not be so lucky: Many French bikers have started wearing masks to protect themselves from the pollution. **Paris-Vélo** rents bikes for 90F per day, 140F for 24 hours, 160F for two days and one night, and 500F per week. Again, you have to provide a hefty 2,000F deposit. They accept MasterCard and Visa. *2 rue du Fer-à-Moulin, 5e, tel. 01–43–37–59– 22. Métro: Censier-Daubenton. Open Mon.–Sat. 10–12:30 and 2–7.*

BY ROLLERBLADE Rollerblades are taking over the world, and Paris is no exception. Rollerbladers of all ages zip around unsuspecting pedestrians, especially along the Seine, the Arche de le Défense, and the Trocadéro. If you've arrived in Paris without wheels, you're gonna have to shell out some cash; you can't rent them (yet), and the cheapest pair at **Go Sport** (Forum des Halles, 1er, tel. 01–45–08–92-96) goes for 499F.

BY TAXI Getting a taxi in Paris can be frustrating, especially in summer. During peak times (7–10 AM and 4–7 PM), allow yourself a couple of hours to secure one—only taxis with lit signs are available, and these are few and far between. Your chances of picking one up are best at major hotels. In the better-traveled parts of the city, people line up at makeshift taxi stations; try to find one of these, or call individual taxi companies. Rates are approximately 8F per kilometer; they may go up a bit after dark, but not more than 50 centimes or so per kilometer. Two good companies are **Taxis Radio 7000** (tel. 01–42–70–00–42) and **Taxis Bleus** (tel. 01– 49–36–10–10). Your taxi driver may be able to sputter an English word or two, but don't expect him or her to understand complicated directions; a map, finger, and half-coherent verb phrase ought to do the trick.

Staying in Paris

VISITOR INFORMATION

OFFICE DE TOURISME DE PARIS Paris's main tourist office is an attraction in itself, with its gift shop, lodging desk, and multitude of glossy brochures—all a few seconds' walk from the Arc de Triomphe on the famed Champs-Elysées. The helpful multilingual staff can give you info on public transport and other practicalities, and they're happy to tell you about current cultural events. The office sells Télécartes (*see* Phones, *below*), museum passes (*see* Museums, in Chapter 2), and Paris Visite passes. Paris Visite passes are good for one, three, or five days of unlimited travel on Métro, bus, and RER lines; if you plan to hop on the Métro six or more times a day it's kinda worth it . . . kinda. If you're in a bind they can find lodging for you, but only if you come down to the office in person. They'll charge you 8F to find you a youth hostel, 20F to put you in a one-star hotel, and 25F to set you up in a two-star hotel—needless to say, this is not how you'll find the cheapest places to crash. They run out of brochures pretty regularly during peak tourist season, but try to secure "**Les Marchés de Paris,**" which lists all the markets in Paris, and "**Paris la nuit,**" which highlights nightclubs and late-night restaurants. Both are free and in French. For 24-hour info in English on upcoming art exhibits and festivals, dial the cultural hotline at 01–49–52–53–56. *127 av. des Champs-Elysées, 8e, tel. 01–49–52–53–54. Métro: Charles de Gaulle–Etoile. Open daily 9–8.*

Six branch offices also reserve rooms and dole out general info on the city. The one at the **Eiffel Tower** (7e, tel. 01–45–51–22–15) is open May through September only, 11–6. Other branch offices in the main train stations are open 8–8 most of the year and until 9 in summer (though Austerlitz closes at 3 PM): **Gare d'Austerlitz** (13e, tel. 01–45–84–91–70); **Gare de l'Est** (10e, tel. 01–46–07–17–73); **Gare de Lyon** (12e, tel. 01–43–43–33–24); **Gare Montparnasse** (15e, tel. 01–43–22–19–19); and **Gare du Nord** (10e, tel. 01–45–26–94– 82). All of them are closed on Sunday.

ACCUEIL DES JEUNES EN FRANCE (AJF) The Reception Center for Young People in France is more in tune with the backpack set. The friendly folks that staff AJF's four offices book rooms in hostels for a 10F fee and sell ISIC cards (*see* Planning Your Trip, Student ID Cards, *above*) for 60F. The AJF also acts as a travel agency for many budget-travel packages (most including breakfast and lodging)—a great way to have someone organize your trip for you and to meet some mellow people. To avoid the huge crowds during the summer tourist rush, arrive right after it opens at 9 AM. *119 rue St-Martin, 4e, tel. 01–42–77–87–80. Métro: Rambuteau. Open Mon.–Sat. 9–5:45. Other locations: Gare du Nord, 10e, tel. 01–42–85–86–19; Métro: Gare du Nord; open summer, daily 8 AM–10 PM. 139 blvd. St-Michel, 5e, tel. 01–43–54–95–86; RER: Port Royal; open Mar.–Oct., Mon.–Sat. 10–6.*

THE AMERICAN CHURCH This utterly helpful church hosts concerts and holiday meals; lists jobs, apartments, and contacts for expatriates; and is a great place to meet other Americans staying in the city. *65 quai d'Orsay, 7e, tel. 01–47–05–07–99. Métro: Invalides. Open Mon.–Sat. 9 AM–10:30 PM and Sun. 2 PM–7:30 PM.*

AMERICAN EXPRESS

At any of Paris's three AmEx travel offices, cardholders can pick up mail, buy traveler's checks in several currencies, and cash personal checks (*see* Planning Your Trip, Money, *above*). The rue Scribe location is the most central and has several Métro lines running by it. Have your mail addressed to: your name, c/o American Express Voyages France, 11 rue Scribe, 75009 Paris. The office holds mail for 30 days. Non-cardholders can also receive mail (though it costs 5F for each pickup) and buy traveler's checks with French francs. Everyone can use the travel agencies and currency exchange offices. *11 rue Scribe, 9e, tel. 01–47–77–79–50. Métro: Opéra. Open weekdays 9–6:30, Sat. 9–5:30. Other locations: 38 av. de Wagram, 8e, tel. 01–42–27–58–80; Métro: Ternes; open weekdays 9–5:30. 5 rue de Chaillot, 16e, tel. 01–47–23–72–15; Métro: Iéna; open weekdays 9–5.*

BUREAUX DE CHANGE

During business hours (9 or 10 AM–5 or 6 PM) you can get good currency-exchange rates around the Opéra Garnier, the Champs-Elysées, and the Palais Royal (rue de Rivoli); just be sure you stop in at an official bank and not one of the bureaux de change, which keep longer hours but get away with worse rates. The bureaux at the train stations stay open until at least 8 PM, sometimes as late as 10 PM, and have slightly worse rates than banks. There are other bureaux around the Champs Elysées and the Quartier Latin around the intersection of boulevards St-Germain and St-Michel. There are a few others scattered around the rue de Rivoli close to the Métro Hotel de Ville. Rates are generally worse on the Left Bank than on the Right.

For late-night currency exchange, use one of the automatic cash-exchange machines that are popping up all over. To use exchange machines you need cash—and relatively crisp cash at that—and the exchange rate is not that great but, at 3 AM, who cares? Locations of 24-hour exchange machines include **Crédit du Nord** (24 blvd. Sébastopol, 1er); **CCF** (115 av. des Champs-Elysées, 8e); and **BNP** (2 pl. de l'Opéra, 2e).

BUSINESS HOURS

Most museums are closed one day a week (usually Monday or Tuesday) and on national holidays (*see* Planning Your Trip, When to Go, *above*). Normal opening times are from 9:30 AM to 5 or 6 PM, occasionally with a long lunch break between noon and 2. Large stores stay open without a lunch break from 9 or 9:30 AM until 6 or 7 PM. Smaller shops often open an hour or so earlier and close a few hours later, with a lengthy lunch break in between. Banks are open weekdays (and sometimes Saturdays) roughly 9:30–4:30. Most banks, but not all, take a one-hour to 90-minute lunch break. Almost all stores (large and small), food shops, and government offices close on Sundays.

DISCOUNT TRAVEL SHOPS

Several places offer discount plane tickets and other travel services for the cash-strapped voyager. The following agencies can get you cheaper rates than most commercial travel agencies, as well as student identification cards (ISICs):

Access Voyages: *6 rue Pierre-Lescot, 1er, tel. 01–40–13–02–02. Métro: Rambuteau. Open weekdays 9–7, Sat. 10–6.* **Council Travel:** *6 rue de Vaugirard, 6e, tel. 01–46–34–02–90. Métro: Odéon. Open weekdays 9:30–6:30, Sat. 10–5. Other location: 22 rue des Pyramides, 1er, tel. 01–44–55–55–65. Métro: Pyramides.* **CPS Voyages (STA):** *20 rue des Carmes, 5e, tel. 01–43–25–00–76. Métro: Maubert-Mutualité.* **Forum Voyages:** *140 rue du Faubourg-St-Honoré, 8e, tel. 01–42–89–07–07. Métro: Champs Elysées Clémenceau. Open weekdays 9:30–7, Sat. 10–1 and 2–5.* **Usit Voyages:** *6 rue de Vaugirard, 6e, tel. 01–42–34–56–90. Métro: Odéon. Open weekdays 10–7, Sat. 1:30–5.*

Nouvelles Frontières. This is the place to go for discount airfares. *Central office: 63 blvd. des Batignolles, 8e, tel. 01–43–87–99–88. Métro: Villiers. Open Mon.–Sat. 9–7 (Thurs. until 8:30).*

Wasteels. This is the best-represented youth travel organization in town, with branches near most train stations. Here those under 26 can get 20% discounts on all train tickets beginning or terminating in France. *113 blvd. St-Michel, 5e, tel. 01–43–26–25–25. RER: Luxembourg. Other location: 5 rue de la Banque, 2e, tel. 01–42–61–53–21. Métro: Bourse. Open weekdays 9–7.*

EMBASSIES

Australia. *4 rue Jean-Rey, 15e, tel. 01–40–59–33–00, 01–40–59–33–01 in emergencies. Métro: Bir-Hakeim. Open weekdays 9–5:30.*

Canada. *35 av. Montaigne, 8e, tel. 01–44–43–29–16. Métro: Franklin D. Roosevelt. Open weekdays 8:30–11.*

Ireland. *4 rue Rude, 16e, tel. 01–45–00–20–87. Métro: Charles de Gaulle–Etoile. Open weekdays 9:30–noon.*

New Zealand. *7 ter rue Léonard-de-Vinci, 16e, tel. 01–45–00–24–11. Métro: Victor Hugo. Open weekdays 9–1 and 2–5:30.*

United Kingdom. *35 rue du Faubourg-St-Honoré, 8e, tel. 01–42–66–91–42. Métro: Madeleine. Open weekdays 9:30–1 and 2:30–6.*

United States. *2 rue St-Florentin, 1er, tel. 01–40–39–84–11 (in English) or 01–42–96–14–88 (in French). Métro: Concorde. Open weekdays 9–4.*

EMERGENCIES

As in any big city, if you encounter trouble in the streets of Paris, the best thing to do is yell for help (*au secours!*) and attract as much attention as possible. There are a number of hotlines you can call if you or one of your companions is ill, but not all of them speak English. In case you lose your French with your cool, here are a few phrases to keep you going: *urgence* (emergency), *samu* (ambulance), *pompiers* (firemen), *poste de police* (police station), *docteur* (doctor) and *hôpital* (hospital). For the **police** dial 17 from any phone. For an **ambulance** dial 15, for the **fire department** 18.

EMERGENCY HOTLINES Hotlines to **doctors** (tel. 01–47–07–77–77), **dentists** (SOS Dentaire, tel. 01–43–37–51–00), a **suicide hotline** (tel. 01–45–39–40–00), and a **poison center** (Centre Anti-Poison, tel. 01–40–37–04–04) are available for emergencies, but there's no guarantee the staff will speak English. **SOS Viol** (tel. 0–800–05–95–95) is a rape crisis hotline; they'll answer calls weekdays 10–6. There are no doctors on call at English-speaking **SOS Help** (tel. 01–47–23–80–80), but between 3 PM and 11 PM they'll help you with medical referrals. For drug-related issues, **Drogues Info Service** (tel. 0-800–23–13–13) is a free 24-hour hotline. The staff speaks some English.

ENGLISH-LANGUAGE BOOKS AND NEWSPAPERS

The Free Voice, a free monthly paper available at English-language bookstores, some restaurants, and the American Church (*see* Visitor Information, *above*), provides an outlet for English-language comment upon Parisian life and lists upcoming events for the Anglophone community. English-language bookstores also carry the free *France-USA Contacts,* which has classified listings in English and French for apartment rentals, goods for sale, work exchange, et cetera. Most newsstands carry the *International Herald-Tribune,* as well as international versions of *Time* and *Newsweek.*

Pariscope (3F) has an English-language section called "Time Out," with recommendations for concerts, theater, movies, museum expositions, and even restaurant and bar picks. Their info can be slow on the update, so cross-check with the French-language listings. For more information on English-language bookstores in Paris, *see* Chapter 6, Shopping.

LAUNDRY

Your socks have a life all their own and people move away from you as you board the Métro. You might have more leg room, but you also need a *laverie* (laundromat). You'll have to shell out 30F to clean 7 kilograms (15 lbs) of laundry. Dryers cost about 2F for 5 minutes. Most laundromats will also dispense soap for 2F. Make sure you come with handfuls of 10F and 2F coins because there are rarely change machines. You shouldn't have any problem finding a laundromat near you, but here are a few **Laverie Libre Service** to get you started: 9 rue de Jouy, 4e; 212 rue St-Jacques, 5e; 28 rue des Trois-Frères, 18e; 2 rue du Lappe, 11e; 28 rue Beaubourg, 3e; 113 rue Monge, 5e; 27 rue Vieille du Temple, 4e.

LOST AND FOUND

Service des Objets Trouvés. The entire city shares one lost-and-found office, and this is it. They won't give info over the telephone; you have to trek over to see if you can find your grubby backpack among the Louis Vuitton bags. *36 rue des Morillons, 15e, tel. 01–45–31–14–80. Métro: Convention. Open weekdays 8:30–5 (Tues. and Thurs. until 8).*

MAIL

You can identify post offices by the yellow signs with blue letters that say LA POSTE. Mailboxes are yellow, with one slot for letters to Paris and one for AUTRES destinations (everywhere else). Airmail letters and postcards to the United States and Canada cost 4F30 for 20 grams. Letters to the United Kingdom cost 2F80. Postcards sent to most European countries cost 2F80, 5F10 to Australia and New Zealand. Buy stamps in post offices if you really like standing in line. Otherwise, head to one of Paris's ubiquitous *tabacs* (tobacco shops) and say "*J'aimerais des timbres*" (I'd like some stamps). Make sure to mention whether you're sending *lettres* (letters) or *cartes postales* (postcards). Mail takes about seven days to make its way from France to the United States, about half that to reach Britain, and 10 days to two weeks to reach Australia.

Hôtel des Postes. Paris's central post office is open 24 hours. At any time, day or night, the office offers mail, telephone, telegram, Minitel (*see* Phones, *below*), photocopy, and poste restante services. During regular business hours (weekdays 8–7, Saturday 8–noon) you can also use the fax machines and exchange money. All post offices in Paris accept poste restante mail, but this is where your mail will end up if the sender fails to specify a branch. Have your mail addressed to: Last name (in capital letters), first name, Poste Restante, 75001 Paris. Bring your passport with you to pick it up. *52 rue du Louvre, at rue Etienne-Marcel, 1er, tel. 01–40–28–20–00. Métro: Sentier.*

The **post office** near the rond point des Champs-Elysées (a major intersection on the avenue) has extended hours for mail, telegram, and telephone service. *71 av. des Champs-Elysées, 8e, tel. 01–44–13–66–00. Métro: Franklin D. Roosevelt. Open Mon.–Sat. 8 AM–10 PM, Sun. 10–8.*

MEDICAL AID

`HOSPITALS AND CLINICS` **Hôpital Américain.** The American Hospital, about a 45-minute trip outside Paris, operates a 24-hour emergency service, and, just like American hospitals, is very expensive. A consultation with a doctor costs 500F. If you're American and lucky enough to have Blue Cross/Blue Shield (carry your card with you), they should cover the cost at the time of your visit. Otherwise, you have to pay up front and hope to be reimbursed by your insurance company when you return to the States. EU citizens also have to pay first but can be reimbursed while still in France if they have form E-111, available at some of the bigger post offices. *63 blvd. Victor-Hugo, Neuilly-sur-Seine, tel. 01–46–41–25–25. Take Métro to Pont de Neuilly, then follow blvd. du Château 15 min.*

On Wednesdays 1:30 PM–4:30 PM, anyone can walk into the Centre du Planning Familial (10 rue Vivienne, 2e, tel. 01–42–60–93–20; Métro: Bourse) for free info on contraception and STDs.

Hôpital Anglais. The English Hospital, also known as the *Hôpital Britannique,* in Levallois, again about 45 minutes outside Paris, has 24-hour emergency service and two British doctors on duty. Consultations vary between 150F–220F, depending on which doctor you get. Here again, Americans have to pay up front and get reimbursed at home; EU citizens pay up front and can be reimbursed through form E-111. Most of the staff speaks no English. *3 rue Barbès, Levallois, tel. 01–46–39–22–22. Métro: Anatole-France.*

Centre de Soins MST. The Center for Sexually Transmitted Diseases provides free consultations on a drop-in basis, weekdays 5–7 PM. You can sign in at 4:30. Although the staff speaks some English, flip through your dictionary before you come in to prevent hazardous misunderstandings. *At Institut A. Fournier, 25 blvd. St-Jacques, 14e, tel. 01–40–78–26–00. Métro: St-Jacques.*

In a pinch, the American embassy (01–40–39–84–11) has a list of **English-speaking doctors.** For **AIDS** info, call 0–800–36–66–36; for **sexual disease** info and diagnosis, call 01–40–78–26–00. Women who have been assaulted should call **SOS Femmes Battues** (14 rue Mendelssohn, 20e, tel. 01–43–48–20–40; Métro: Porte Montreuil).

`PHARMACIES` Besides basic over-the-counter medication, pharmacies (identifiable by green neon crosses) provide all sorts of useful health and beauty aids. If you're looking for herbal (homeopathic) medicines, try the *pharmacies homéopathiques.*

While regular pharmacy hours are about 9 AM to 7 or 8 PM, **Pharmacie Dhéry** (84 av. des Champs-Elysées, 8e, tel. 01–45–62–02–41; Métro: George V) is open 24 hours. **Drugstore Publicis** (149 blvd. St-Germain, at rue de Rennes, 6e, tel. 01–42–22–92–50; Métro: St-Germain-des-Prés) is open daily until 2 AM. Three more pharmacies open until midnight are **Cariglioli** (10 blvd. Sépastopol, 4e, tel. 01–42–72–03–23; Métro: Châtelet); **La Nation** (13 pl. de la Nation, 11e, tel. 01–43–73–24–03; Métro: Nation); and **Caillaud** (6 blvd. des Capucines, 9e, tel. 01–42–65–88–29; Métro: Opéra).

PHONES

Public phones are never far away in Paris; you will find them at post offices and often in cafés. On October 18, 1996, the French revamped their phone system and the old eight-digit phone number grew to ten digits: All Paris numbers now start with 01, all numbers in the northwest start with 02, in the northeast 03, in the southeast 04, and in the southwest 05. If you come across an eight-digit number (now terribly passé), you have to know what part of France the number is in so you can tack on the new prefix.

To make a call *to* France from another country, dial France's country code (33), drop the initial zero from the telephone number, and then dial the remaining nine digits.

LOCAL CALLS Local calls cost a minimum of 1F for six minutes. Most French phones only accept the **Télécarte**, a handy little card you can buy at tabacs, post offices, or Métro stations; it costs 41F for 50 units or 96F for 120 units. The digital display on the phone counts down your units while you're talking and tells you how many you have left when you hang up. The occasional old-fashioned phone will take 50-centime, 1F, 2F, and 5F coins, but it won't make change. Dial 12 with a card or coin to reach directory inquiries from any phone (though operators rarely speak English).

MINITEL In 1990, France Telecom proudly launched the distribution of an information device called the Minitel: a monitor/modem that can receive electronic mail, conduct data searches, dole out addresses and telephone numbers, and even tell you the weather. You can use them for free in any post office, where Minitel terminals have for the most part replaced telephone books. Here's how it works: Press the button with a phone-receiver symbol on it and dial "11." When you hear the high-pitched tone, press ANNIHILATION. Database fields will then appear on the screen. Type in the *nom* (name), *activité* (subject), *localité* (city), or address relating to the info you're seeking. To advance a line press SUITE, to go back a line press RETOUR, to backspace press CORRECTION, and to begin a new search press ANNIHILATION. Press ENVOI to send your query; responses will then appear on the screen. To end your session, press CONNEXION/FIN.

INTERNATIONAL CALLS To dial direct to another country, dial 00 + the country code (61 for Australia, 64 for New Zealand, 44 for the United Kingdom, and 1 for the United States and Canada) plus the area code and number. The cheapest time to call is between 10:30 PM and 6 AM (about 4F50 per minute to the States, 3F50 per minute to Britain). Middling rates apply 6–8 AM and 9:30–10:30 PM; rates are reduced all day Sunday and holidays.

To use an **AT&T** calling card or to speak with an AT&T international operator, dial 0–800–99–00–11. For **MCI**, dial 0–800–99–00–19; for **Sprint**, dial 0–800–99–00–87. Within France, you can call collect by dialing 12 for the operator and saying "*en PCV*" (pronounced "on pay say vay"). If you want international directory info, dial 00–33–12 and then the country code (listed in all phone booths).

TIPPING

At restaurants, cafés, and brasseries, service is undoubtedly included, and it's 100% normal not to leave a centime. If you love the service, though, or someone called you a cab, then leave anywhere from 2F to 5F. In the case of taxi drivers and hairdressers, tip 10%. Ushers who help opera- and theater-goers to their seats should be tipped about 5F.

Resident Resources

ACADEMIC AND CULTURAL RESOURCES

AMERICAN LIBRARY Here you'll find the largest collection of English-language books in Paris, with more than 80,000 volumes. Anyone can use it, as long as they're willing to pay 70F for a single day's admittance—so much for free public libraries. If you actually want to take books out, you have to sign up for the year (550F, 440F students). A summer subscription, good June through August, costs 240F. Membership also gets you into the smaller collection at the American University in Paris. *10 rue du Général-Camou, 7e, tel. 01–45–51–46–82. Métro: Ecole Militaire or Alma-Marceau. Open Tues.–Sat. 10–7; shorter hrs in Aug.*

BIBLIOTHEQUE FORNEY Housed in the beautiful Hôtel de Sens is the best collection of art and architecture materials in Paris. The extensive collection of books and periodicals, in both French and English, are accessible to all for free, but to check out materials you need a picture ID and proof that you've lived in Paris for at least three months. *1 rue du Figuier, 4e, tel. 01–42–78–14–60. Métro: Pont Marie or St-Paul. Open Tues.–Fri. 1:30–8:30, Sat. 10–8:30.*

BIBLIOTHEQUE NATIONALE DE FRANCE The Bibliothèque Nationale de France traces its origin to 1368, when Charles V first founded a library in the Louvre. François I expanded the collection in 1537 when he ordered publishers to send him a copy of every book they published—this brought in more books *and* allowed the king to keep a close eye on what was being written. A seat in this megalibrary's splendid 19th-century reading room is by far the most coveted study space in all of France. The intelligentsia of the world vie for access to what is considered to be the largest library collection ever: 10 million books, 1.5 million photographs, 1.5 million music manuscripts, 1.1 million discs and videos, 650,000 maps, 350,000 manuscripts, and 350,000 periodicals—and this doesn't even count the collections in the satellite libraries and what's in storage in Versailles. The collection won't be fully accessible until the big move to the new Grande Bibliothèque is completed sometime in 1997. Access is open to citizens of all nations, provided they present a letter of accreditation from their university stating that they are either a professor or a graduate student in their third year of a Ph.D. program. The unaccredited can merely peek in and look around. *58 rue Richelieu, 2e, tel. 01–47–03–81–26. Métro: Bourse. Main reading room open daily 10–6.*

BIBLIOTHEQUE STE-GENEVIEVE Founded when the library of the now-demolished Eglise Ste-Geneviève was nationalized during the Revolution, the Bibliothèque Ste-Geneviève sports a collection spanning all disciplines, with an emphasis on 19th- and 20th-century documents. The library is a popular study space for students from the neighboring universities and is free to students from any university (even non-French) and to anyone over 18 or with a high school degree; for a library card, bring a passport-size photo, a student ID, and a phone bill or other proof that you're a Paris resident of at least three months. If you lack these items, a day pass can provide you with limited access. Both cards get you into the study hall only—there is no borrowing. *10 pl. du Panthéon, 5e, tel. 01–44–41–97–97. Métro: Maubert-Mutualité. Open Mon.–Sat. 10–10; closed Aug. 1–15.*

BRITISH CULTURAL CENTER The British center has a large and sunny reference library and occasionally hosts art expos and lectures. Although the events are usually free, you have to pay 230F a year (or 30F for a day pass, homesick Brits allowed in free of charge) to access the library. Stop by or call for a list of upcoming events. *9–11 rue Constantine, 7e, tel. 01–49–55–73–00. Métro: Invalides. Open weekdays 11–6 (Wed. until 7).*

CENTRE DE DOCUMENTATION JUIVE CONTEMPORAINE Above the Mémorial du Martyr Juif Inconnu, this center is the best resource for Jewish studies in town. The small but rich library has Jewish history and philosophy in any language you could possibly want, with the bulk in French, English, and Hebrew. Technically, there's a 30F fee per day or 150F (80F students) annual membership, but if you just want to use it for a short time they're usually pretty lax about collecting. *17 rue Geoffroy-l'Asnier, 4e, tel. 01–42–77–44–72. Métro: Pont Marie or St-Paul. Open Mon.–Thurs. 2–5:30.*

CENTRE GEORGES POMPIDOU The Pompidou is like a kingdom of city-states sparring amicably: In addition to housing the **Musée National d'Art Moderne (MNAM)** (*see* Major Attractions, in Chapter 2), the Centre hosts services that fall under the control of the **Centre des Créations Industriel (CCI)**, a contemporary architecture, urban planning, and design institute; the **Bibliothèque Publique d'Informations (BPI)**, a very popular library; and the **Institut de Recherche et Coordination de l'Acoustique et la Musique (IRCAM)**, sponsoring musical programs. All of these organizations are devoted to former President Pompidou's stated goal of allowing people to experience tons of art and culture all within a single building.

The **BPI** (tel. 01–44–78–44–83), on the ground, first, second, and third floors, is about as exciting as a library can be: several huge open floors filled to capacity with books and quiet people doing mind-expanding stuff. Anyone can have free access to the 3,000 periodicals (including foreign presses), 14,000 records and CDs (with listening stations), 2,000 films on video (with monitors), and 400,000 books (many in English). The BPI has an extensive CD-ROM library, with over 150,000 images catalogued to date, all of which must be used on the premises. More than 13,000 people use the place daily (it was designed to handle 1,500), and there's often a line to get in. If you're willing to brave the lines, get a pass around the corner from the main entrance, on rue St-Merri. The library staff does no reshelving during the day, so if you come in the evening you'll have a hell of a time finding what you need.

The first floor of the BPI holds the **Salle Jorge Luis Borges,** a room named after the Argentine writer and designed especially for use by the visually impaired. The room is staffed by volunteers and open only by appointment; call Monday, Tuesday, Thursday, or Friday to set something up (tel. 01–44–78–44–83 or 01–44–78–60–98). *31 rue St-Merri, on pl. Igor-Stravinsky, 4e, tel. 01–42–17–12–33. Open Mon.–Thurs. 9:30–1 and 2–6, Fri. 9:30– 1 and 2–5; library open Mon. and Wed.–Fri. 2–6. Tickets for events at the ticket counter on the ground floor of the Centre. Wheelchair access.*

GRANDE BIBLIOTHEQUE DE FRANCE Scheduled to open sometime in 1997, this new 5.2-billion–franc home for the Bibliothèque Nationale's collection is the latest of Paris's *grands projets.* The massive library—its 395 kilometers (245 miles) of shelves make it one of the largest in the world—is a tribute to urban renewal. Four buildings designed to look like huge books standing open will enclose a vast rectangular park. The buildings were constructed almost entirely of clear glass until architect Dominique Perrault realized that the sun would damage the books—the windows have since been tinted. A giant tepee has been set up to provide info about the library and the incredible urban renewal going on all around it. A few reading rooms will be open to the public early in 1997, but at press time the move was still in progress. Call or stop by for more information. *Quai de la Gare, 13e, tel. 01–53–79–53–79. Métro: Quai de la Gare.*

INSTITUT DU MONDE ARABE This institute has become the center of Arabic studies in all of France. Its library has 50,000 volumes and 1,000 periodicals in Arabic, French, and English. The stacks and reading room are open to the public, but only a small number of volumes can be checked out. More than anything, the institute acts as a meeting place for those interested in Arabic studies; the café and terrace on the ninth floor are the main gathering spots. *1 rue Fossés-St-Bernard, 5e, tel. 01–40–51–38–38. Métro: Jussieu or Cardinal Lemoine. Open Tues.–Sat. 1–8. Wheelchair access.*

PAVILLON DE L'ARSENAL The library of the Centre d'Urbanisme et d'Architecture de la Ville de Paris (*see* Museums, French History and Culture, in Chapter 2) has a fine collection of French- and English-language books and periodicals, but its collection of 70,000 photographs and images of Paris is truly spectacular. The modern steel-and-exposed-conduit renovation of the old arsenal makes for a nice study space. *21 blvd. Morland, 4e, tel. 01–42–76–33–97. Métro: Sully-Morland. Open Tues.–Sat. 2–6.*

MEDIA

NEWSPAPERS AND MAGAZINES The French press has taken a beating in the last several years, with newspapers and magazines going out of business at an alarming rate. The following are a few of the more popular choices.

Le Monde is an eminently respectable centrist daily with good arts and books supplements. Famous philosophers often write difficult articles—sometimes stridently nationalist—for the front page. The Paris daily *Le Figaro* has been around since 1866. It leans to the right a little more than the others, and its business section is very reputable. Jean-Paul Sartre was the first editor of *Libération,* a witty, slangy weekly paper that is one of the best and most accessible. The slant is to the left but is becoming less so. Looking for something a little further to the left? Affiliated with the French Communist Party, *L'Humanité* is still running, though with a little ideological confusion. You have to be *very* up on your French slang to understand the satirical weekly *Le Canard Enchaîné,* which has funny cartoons and investigates the latest political scandals with biting humor.

Weekly magazines include the extremely popular *Le Nouvel Observateur,* with middle-of-the-road articles on politics à la *Time* or *Newsweek. L'Evenement de Jeudi* also tackles politics but specializes in random, amusing articles on topics like "The Ten Smallest Countries in the World." *L'Express* is less fun, more businesslike, and conservative, and *Le Point* tends to lean even a little more to the right than *L'Express.* For those dying for celebrity gossip and scandal, check out *Paris-Match,* where you can read stories about various royal families. *L'Equipe* is a comprehensive magazine for sports buffs.

RADIO France has an enormous array of stations. Some to check out are **Fréquence Gaie** (94.4), aimed at the gay community; **Fréquence Juive** (94.8), for Jewish listeners; and **France Maghreb** (94.2), which targets Paris's North African community.

Africa No. 1: 107.5. This station is generally upbeat, playing mostly West and Saharan African tunes with few interruptions. *Tel. 01–45–74–83–83.*

FIP: 105.1. Not for those who cling to stability, this station spins an arbitrary mix of classical, contemporary French favorites, and jazz. They're short on commentary but will usually tell you what you're listening to. *Tel. 01–42–20–12–34.*

France Infos: 105.5. This nonstop news station will give you the latest news (in French) again, and again, and again. *Tel. 01–42–30–10–55.*

France Musique: 91.7 and 92.1. This classical station usually vacillates between Rossini melodies and Schoenberg dissonance but also gives air time to non-Western classical music. Artists performing in Paris often come by for a chat and an occasional studio performance. *Tel. 01–42–30–18–18.*

M40: 105.9. In the wee hours of the morning (around 4:30), this mainstream station actually counts down *Billboard*'s weekly Top 40. *Tel. 01–40–39–09–09.*

Ouï Rock You: 102.3. The best of all the rock stations, Ouï FM is the most "alternative," featuring lots of new cuts from England and the Americas, as well as many interviews with bands. Music varies greatly from thrash to metal to reggae to English Pop, with an occasional classic rock tune.

Radio Classique: 101.1. As the name implies, it's classic, with operas thrown in now and then. *Tel. 01–40–08–50–00.*

Radio Libertaire: 89.4. On Friday nights from 10:30 to 1 an anarchist political program takes over this station. All in French. *Tel. 01–42–62–90–51.*

Radio Montmartre: 102.7. Mostly traditional French tunes. Sing along with Edith Piaf and Jacques Brel. *Tel. 01–42–54–37–06.*

Radio Nova: 101.5. A cool mix of traditional and contemporary jazz makes this the favorite of many a Parisian jazz buff. *Tel. 01–43–46–88–80.*

TELEVISION French television can be a shock, especially if you expected programs created, say, in France. French television offers only six *chaînes* (channels), and most feature dubbed versions of American originals. The French have a peculiar fetish for early '80s shows; watch out for old favorites like *Les drôles de dames* (roughly translated as "those crazy ladies," otherwise known as *Charlie's Angels*) and *Dallas*.

Most channels offer news in the mornings and evenings. Channels One through Three form the network core and tend to show series, talk shows, and films. Channel Four is the cable station, but sometimes it broadcasts films for free. If your Franch slang and political savvy is up to par, you'll enjoy **Guignols de l'Info** (7:50 PM–8:05 PM), a puppet show that lambasts politicians and newscasters. For something more comprehensible, catch Dan Rather (in English) on at 7:30 AM. Channel Five is the intellectual channel and is the only channel to subtitle its films instead of dubbing them. Channel Six is a rather pathetic MTV substitute with cheesy music videos in the mornings.

HOUSES OF WORSHIP

American Cathedral of the Holy Trinity. Episcopal-Anglican. Holy Eucharist Sundays at 9 AM and 11 AM, weekdays at noon. *23 av. George V, 8e, tel. 01–47–20–17–92. Métro: George V or Alma-Marceau.*

American Church in Paris. Interdenominational Protestant. Sunday adult church school at 10 AM, worship service at 11 AM. *65 quai d'Orsay, 7e, tel. 01–47–05–07–99. Métro: Invalides or Alma-Marceau.*

Christian Science Church. *36 blvd. St-Jacques, 14e, tel. 01–47–07–26–60. Métro: St-Jacques.*

Great Synagogue. Synagogue and offices of the Consistoire Israëlite de Paris, where you can get info on the Jewish community in Paris. Services in Hebrew. *44 rue de la Victoire, 9e, tel. 01–45–26–90–15. Métro: Le Peletier.*

La Mosquée de Paris. *Pl. du Puits de l'Ermite, 5e, tel. 01–45–35–97–33. Métro: Monge.*

Liberal Synagogue. Services in Hebrew. *24 rue Copernic, 16e, tel. 01–47–04–37–27. Métro: Victor Hugo.*

Quaker Society of Friends. *114 bis rue de Vaugirard, 6e, tel. 01–45–48–74–23. Métro: Montparnasse or St-Placide.*

St. Joseph's Church. Roman Catholic. *50 av. Hoche, 8e, tel. 01–42–27–28–56. Métro: Charles de Gaulle–Etoile.*

Temple Kagyu Dzong. Buddhist. Meditation held Saturday and Sunday at 5 PM. *40 route de Ceinture du Lac Daumesnil, 12e, tel. 01–40–04–98–06. Métro: Porte Dorée.*

Unitarian Universalist Fellowship of Paris. *1 rue de l'Oratoire, 1er, tel. 01–42–78–82–58. Métro: Louvre-Rivoli.*

EXPLORING PARIS   2

By Viviana Mahieux and Julia Švihra

Proudly bearing the scars of an illustrious 2,000-year history and home today to more than two million people, Paris could take you multiple lifetimes to explore from top to bottom—and that's not counting the Louvre. If you have only a few days or weeks in the city, strategy is key. The Métro system is extremely efficient and will aid those of you in the see-and-flee mode of sightseeing; however, moving around on the bus—or, better yet, your feet—is much better if you want to get a real feel for the city. The center of town is quite walkable, and Parisian street life—its action, its glamour, its little piles of doggie doo—is an important element of any visit. You might also consider a ride on a scenic *bateau mouche*. Paris's hideous "fly" boats, equipped with enough wattage to illuminate a small nation, churn their way down the Seine, riling pedestrians and riverside habitants with their incomprehensible loudspeakers. But they do take you past some awesome sights, especially at night. Try **Bateaux Mouches** (Pont de l'Alma, tel. 01–42–25–96–10, 8e; Métro: Alma-Marceau) on the Right Bank, which offers 30F boat tours every half hour, 10 AM–11 PM. Otherwise, consider one of the following walks through the center of Paris:

- Along the Seine between the Eiffel Tower and Cathédrale Notre-Dame. You'll see the Trocadéro, the Louvre, the Musée d'Orsay, the Ile de la Cité, and the Ile St-Louis.

- The Louvre to the Arc de Triomphe. Majestic with a capital "M," this walk hits many vestiges of aristocratic Paris, including the Jardin des Tuileries, the place de la Concorde, and the Champs-Elysées.

- The Louvre to the Panthéon. Cross the Pont Neuf, walk through place Dauphine toward Notre-Dame, cross the bridge at the west of place Parvis, and walk along rue St-Jacques to see the crowded little streets of the Latin Quarter.

- From place de la Bastille, head toward the Marais along rue Rambuteau. You'll pass through the active Les Halles area, and if you rejoin rue de Rivoli around the Louvre, you can rest your aching feet in the Jardin des Tuileries.

- From the Pigalle métro stop, head up to Montmartre along rue des Martyrs, hike up to the Sacré Cœur, and wander around the cobblestoned streets of upper Montmartre.

With luck you'll have time for a little aimless wandering as well; the **Bastille** (11e), **Belleville** (20e), the **Champs-Elysées** (8e), the **Marais** (4e), **Montmartre** (18e), the **Quartier Latin** (5e), and **St-Germain-des-Prés** (6e) (*see* Neighborhoods, *below*) will all treat you well if you get lost in their little streets. Visiting the obelisk at place de la Concorde is also a rich treat; nowhere else in Paris can you turn 360° and see so many monuments at once.

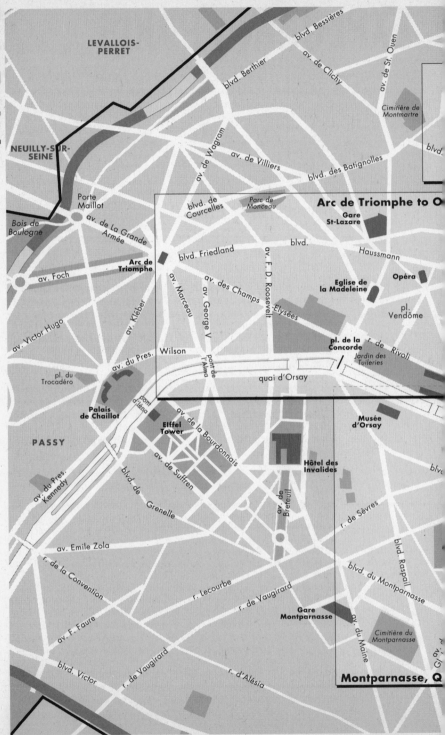

LEVALLOIS-PERRET

blvd. Bessières

blvd. Berthier

av. de Clichy

av. de St. Ouen

Cimitière de Montmartre

blvd.

av. de Wagram

av. de Villiers

blvd. des Batignolles

NEUILLY-SUR-SEINE

Porte Maillot

blvd. de Courcelles

Parc de Monceau

Arc de Triomphe to O

Gare St-Lazare

Bois de Boulogne

av. de La Grande Armée

blvd. Friedland

blvd.

Haussmann

Arc de Triomphe

av. Foch

av. Marceau

av. des Champs

av. George V

av. F. D. Roosevelt

Eglise de la Madeleine

Opéra

pl. Vendôme

av. Victor Hugo

av. Kléber

Elysées

pl. de la Concorde

r. de Rivoli

Jardin des Tuileries

pl. du Trocadéro

av. du Pres. Wilson

pont de l'Alma

quai d'Orsay

Palais de Chaillot

pont d'Iéna

av. de la Bourdonnais

Musée d'Orsay

Eiffel Tower

PASSY

av. de Suffren

av. de Breteuil

Hôtel des Invalides

blvd

av. du Pres. Kennedy

blvd. de Grenelle

r. de Sèvres

av. Emile Zola

blvd. Raspail

r. de la Convention

r. Lecourbe

r. de Vaugirard

blvd. du Montparnasse

r. F. Faure

r. de Vaugirard

Gare Montparnasse

av. du Maine

Cimitière du Montparnasse

blvd. Victor

r. de Vaugirard

r. d'Alésia

G. av.

Montparnasse, Q

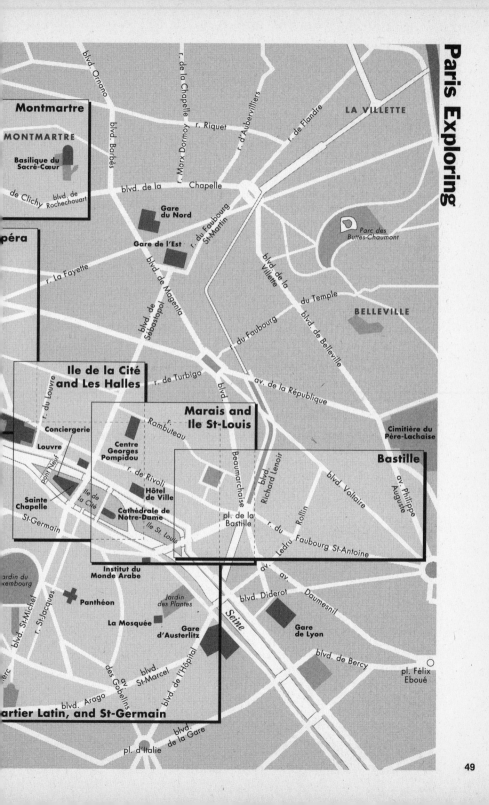

Montmartre

MONTMARTRE

Basilique du
Sacré-Cœur

LA VILLETTE

blvd. Ornano

blvd. Barbès

r. de la Chapelle

r. Marx Dormoy

r. Riquet

r. d'Aubervilliers

r. de Flandre

de Clichy

blvd. de
Rochechouart

péra

r. La Fayette

blvd. de la   Chapelle

Gare
du Nord

Gare de l'Est

r. du Faubourg
St-Martin

Parc des
Buttes-Chaumont

blvd. de la
Villette

du Temple

BELLEVILLE

blvd. de
Sébastopol

blvd. de Magenta

du Faubourg

blvd. de Belleville

**Ile de la Cité
and Les Halles**

r. du Louvre

r. de Turbigo

blvd.

av. de la République

**Marais and
Ile St-Louis**

Cimitière du
Père-Lachaise

Conciergerie

Louvre

r.
Rambuteau

Centre
Georges
Pompidou

r. de Rivoli

Bastille

Beaumarchaise

blvd. Richard Lenoir

blvd. Voltaire

av. Philippe
Auguste

Pont Neuf

Sainte
Chapelle

St-Germain

Ile de
la Cité

Hôtel
de Ville

Cathédrale de
Notre-Dame

Ile St. Louis

pl. de la
Bastille

r. du Faubourg St-Antoine

Rollin

Ledru

Institut du
Monde Arabe

ardin du
xembourg

blvd. St-Michel

r. St-Jacques

Panthéon

La Mosquée

Jardin
des Plantes

Gare
d'Austerlitz

Seine

av.

av.

av.
Daumesnil

blvd. Diderot

Gare
de Lyon

blvd. de Bercy

pl. Félix
Eboué

erc

des Gobelins

blvd.
St-Marcel

blvd. de l'Hôpital

blvd. Arago

artier Latin, and St-Germain

blvd.
de la Gare

pl. d'Italie

Paris' major sights are listed first in alphabetical order in the following pages. Other sights are arranged by category (Museums, Houses of Worship, Dead Folk, Parks and Gardens, and Neighborhoods). You'll find descriptions and maps of individual neighborhoods in the Neighborhoods section at the end of the chapter.

Major Attractions

ARC DE TRIOMPHE

Never one renowned for subtlety or modesty, Napoléon I, celebrating his successful battles of 1805–1806, commissioned the architect Jean-François Chalgrin to design a permanent monument to his military prowess. Definite plans weren't accepted until 1809, and when Marie-Louise of Austria arrived in 1810 to marry the little man, only the foundation had been completed. No problem—he simply had a full-size wooden mock arch set up, disguised by trompe-l'oeil canvas. In 1815, when Napoléon met his waterloo, the Arc de Triomphe was still only half finished, but Louis-Philippe completed it in 1836. Although the plaque on it now calls the arch simply a "tribute to the French military," the names of Napoléon's 128 victorious battles and 660 generals are inscribed on the inner faces.

Napoléon's coffin was rolled under the Arc de Triomphe in 1840, inaugurating the arch as a site for public ceremonies. Victor Hugo's remains rested underneath for a night before being moved to the Panthéon. In 1919, the triumphal parade marking the end of the war passed below, and in 1920 the Unknown Soldier was buried here; an eternal flame, relit each evening, has watched over him ever since. Hitler strode through the arch in 1940 to encounter a largely deserted Paris; four years later Charles de Gaulle victoriously followed the same route, this time met by thousands of jubilant Parisians.

The Arc de Triomphe remains the largest triumphal arch in the world. The sculpture surrounding it includes François Rude's famous *La Marseillaise,* depicting the uprising of 1792. Climb the 50-meter (164-foot) arch for one of the better views of Paris, highlighting the city's unmistakable design. The arch marks the intersection of the 8th, 16th, and 17th arrondissements, and radiating out from the arch are 12 avenues, hence the plaza's name *place de l'Etoile* (star plaza). Gaze along the precise lines to La Défense, down the Champs-Elysées to place de la Concorde, and on to the Louvre. *Pl. Charles de Gaulle–Etoile, tel. 01–43–80–31–31. Métro: Charles de Gaulle–Etoile. Admission: 31F, 20F students. Take the underground passage from the Champs Elysées, on the even numbers side. Open Apr.–Sept., daily 9:30–6 (Fri. until 10); Oct.–Mar., daily 10–5:30.*

BASILIQUE DU SACRE-CŒUR

This horrific white concoction was dreamt up by overzealous Catholics to "expiate the sins" of the citizens participating in the Paris Commune of 1871 (*see box,* The Paris Commune, *below*). Designed by architect Paul Abadie and built between 1875 and 1914, the Sacré-Cœur met with criticism even before construction, but today tourists have made it the most popular postcard subject in Paris. The Romanesque-Byzantine structure looks white because the stones (taken from Château-Landon, southeast of Paris) secrete calcite when wet; the more it rains, the more the Sacré-Cœur gleams. The interior is hardly awe-inspiring, though the red-toned stained glass can give off a fiery glow in the evening. The 15F admission fee to the 112-meter (367-foot) bell tower offers a magnificent view of the city, but you can get the same view for free from the front of the basilica. *35 rue du Chevalier-de-la-Barre, tel. 01–42–51–17–02. Métro: Anvers. Basilica open daily 6:45 AM–11 PM. Tower open summer, daily 9–7; winter, daily 9–6.*

CATHEDRALE DE NOTRE-DAME

For centuries Notre-Dame (built between 1163 and 1361) has watched Paris go through all sorts of phases, riding out periods of neglect and hostility like a patient parent. Such patience is not without its payoffs, and today Notre-Dame is one of the best-known houses of worship in the world. Unfortunately, its current condition barely gives us an idea of its previous states: During the Gothic era, the fashion was to cover everything in bright paint, so the statuary on the facade was colorful and highlighted by a gilded background. The now-colorless portals are still fantastic, depicting (from left to right) the Virgin (to whose glory the cathedral is dedicated), the Last Judgment, and Ste-Anne, Mary's mother. Above is a row of statues depicting 28 kings of Judah and Israel, all of which lost their heads during the Revolution, when the cathedral became the Temple of Reason. Once all the fuss had died down, the great architect Viollet-le-Duc rolled up his sleeves and took on serious restoration, including replacing the kings' heads. Turns out, some Royalist had stashed the originals away in his basement; they were discovered a couple of decades ago and are on display in the Musée de Cluny (*see* Museums, *below*).

The interior of Notre-Dame is vast and hollow; again, this hardly reflects its original state. Before the Revolution, rich tapestries and paintings adorned the interior, diminishing the tomblike aura of today. Even the stained-glass windows have changed: In the 18th century, the originals were removed to let in more light! The gray windows that replaced them were then replaced this century by abstract patterns created with medieval colors and techniques. Luckily, three spectacular rose windows were left intact.

Throughout the centuries, kings, lords, generals, and other churches have sent gifts of everything from statues to war banners; in the 13th century, the side chapels had to be added to hold all the gifts. Notice the statues flanking the altar: One is Louis XIII, who, after years of trying unsuccessfully for a child, promised to repay the Virgin if she would grant him a son; and the other Louis XIV, who carried out his father's vow with these gifts to the cathedral. Climb the cathedral's towers (around to the left as you face the building) for a gape at tons (literally) of bells and gargoyles, and a terrific view of Paris. *Pl. du Parvis Notre-Dame, 4e, tel. 01–42–34–56–10. Métro: Cité. Admission to towers: 28F, 18F students. Cathedral open daily 8–7. Towers (tel. 01–43–29–50–40) open daily 9:30–6:30.*

CENTRE GEORGES POMPIDOU AND MUSEE NATIONAL D'ART MODERNE

Along with the Louvre and the Musée d'Orsay (*see below*), the Musée National d'Art Moderne, housed within the Centre Georges Pompidou, completes the chronological triumvirate of national museums. Also known as the Beaubourg, the wacky and modern Centre brings a circuslike multitude of fire-eaters, tourists, and caricaturists to its plaza and fountains out front. Inside, a museum, a library, a theater, and a cinema act as the "laboratory" envisioned when the Centre was first conceived in the early 1970s. The Pompidou once declared itself the fulcrum of contemporary thought; looking at the digital clock in front of the building counting down the seconds left in the millennium, you almost believe that the year 2000 will start right here.

For those in desperate need of some Internet contact, the café on the mezzanine of the Pompidou will grant you Web access (50F for an hour, 30F for half an hour) and strong coffee.

BASICS The lobby is a huge tangle of signs, televised images, chairs, art, pipes, escalators, and people. In addition to the museum, public library, theater, and cinema, the center has countless conference rooms (for more on the Pompidou's other resources, *see* Resident Resources, in Chapter 1).

Two breeds of art exhibits exist here: Those that cost money and those that don't. The free ones are scattered throughout the temporary galleries on the ground floor and in the library halls; these are usually related to the blockbuster temporary exhibit housed in the fifth-floor Grande Galerie. For everything else you need to buy a ticket corresponding to the exhibits you want to see. The permanent collection is more than enough for one day, as is the Grande Galerie, though the ambitious will pace themselves and get an all-gallery pass. The cashier will issue you a ticket that you pop into a machine, Métro-style, at the entrance to the galleries. The info desks have a bimonthly program of events printed in English, as well as a full listing of gallery events, prices, and the wheres and whens of guided tours in your mother tongue.

The Centre is one of the best buildings adapted for disabled visitors. There are no steps that can't be avoided by a lift, and elevators are all over the place. *4e, tel. 01–44–78–12–33 or 01–42–77–11–12. Métro: Rambuteau. Admission: permanent collection 35F, 24F ages 18–25, under 18 free, Sun. 10–2 free for everyone; Grande Galerie 35F, 24F under age 24; Forum and Galeries Nord and Sud 27F, 20F under age 24; all galleries and permanent collection 70F, 45F ages 13–25, under 13 free. Open weekdays noon–10 PM, weekends 10–10. Closed Tues. and May 1st. Wheelchair access/barrier free.*

". . . you have been trapped by this glass serpent that brings alive, with its flow of humanity, the facade of this big body. The joke is on you! You are a spectator on view!"—a reference to the Pompidou's glass-encased escalators, from its melodramatic "Practical Guide."

HISTORY The decrepit Beaubourg district, in decline since the late 17th century, had an estimated five million rats when Georges Pompidou, the French president from 1969 to 1974, declared in December of 1969 that a new contemporary art museum and intellectual center would be placed in the decaying heart of Paris. The staid, conservative Pompidou seems like an unlikely cultural hero, but apparently the idea of creating a multimedia cultural center (with his name on it) seemed like a good urban renewal project. This new center, he promised, would be more than a building; it would be a statement.

In 1977, after six years of demolition and construction, the riot of steel crossbraces and snaky escalators designed by Italy's Renzo Piano and Gianfranco Franchini and Britain's Richard Rodger was inaugurated before an astonished city—the Pompidou looks like God turned the building inside out and then went to town on it with a box of crayons. The exposed pipes in bright primary colors (green for water, blue for air, yellow for electricity, red for communications) may be the most memorable part of the building, but it is with the interior structure that the architects were truly innovative. To eliminate the need for columns to hold the building up, steel beams were cross-strutted and hinged over its length and width, connecting to the exterior skeleton. Water fills the large steel tubes, stabilizing the outward push made on the structure from the pressure of the floors. This never-before-tried system was supposed to give the Centre an unheard-of flexibility—walls could be taken down or put up anywhere at will, allowing the building to change shape to accommodate different exhibitions and displays.

While the building itself became the topic of architecture classes everywhere, its two major tenants, the museum and the **Centre des Créations Industriel** (CCI), soon defined the Pompidou's role in Parisian life. The CCI, the interactive part of the center, is composed of two parts: the **Bibliothèque Publique d'Information** (BPI) (*see* Resident Resources, in Chapter 1) and the **Institut de Recherche et Coordination de l'Acoustique et de la Musique** (**IRCAM**) (*see* Opera, Classical Music, and Dance, in Chapter 5). The BPI, with its massive open stacks and technological resources (microfiche back then, CD-ROM today), was supposed to revolutionize the traditional library, while the IRCAM offered a venue for contemporary dance, music, and theater performances, not to mention provocative colloquia and films.

THE COLLECTION The Pompidou is justly proud of its permanent collection, which picks up around 1904, where the Orsay leaves off: Encompassing more than 40,000 works, it is the largest single gathering of modern art in the world. Only 850 works can be displayed at any one time, though, and even then the galleries on the third and fourth floors are crammed with major pieces. The fourth floor houses the historical part of the collection, while the third has later pieces. The historical part starts off with Matisse, then takes off through the cubists, futurists, suprematists, surrealists, Bauhaus, European abstractionists, abstract expressionists, pop artists, minimalists . . . don't worry, the museum has thoughtfully placed quartets of chairs throughout the galleries for you to flop down in.

Because the museum got into the collecting business rather late in comparison to New York's Museum of Modern Art or Guggenheim Museum, there aren't as many postcard-famous works here as you'd expect. Of course, there are some stunners: **Alexander Calder**'s (1898–1976) *Josephine Baker* was one of the sculptor's earliest and most graceful versions of the mobile—a form he invented. Also here is **Marcel Duchamp**'s (1887–1968) *Valise,* a collection of miniature reproductions of his most famous dada sculptures and drawings conveniently displayed in their own ironic carrying case. One of the last works by the piously abstract **Piet Mondrian**

(1872–1944), *New York,* marks one of the few breaks with the style of the *Compositions* he had been painting for the previous 25 years. The Russian **Kazimir Malevich** (1878–1935) declared that his *Black Square* was the point from which painting left behind the frivolity of illusionism in favor of abstraction. The museum displays his work where Malevich intended— hanging above eye level, as Eastern Orthodox Church icons were placed in pre-Revolution Russian homes. Also here is *Out of the Deep,* **Jackson Pollock**'s (1912–56) attempt a year before his death to return to the abstraction of his earlier drip paintings, though alcoholism and fame were suffocating his career.

Accessible only from an escalator within the fourth-floor galleries is the third floor, home to more recent works from the permanent collection. While the fourth floor has the unspoken need to spell out a history of early modern art, the third is far more playful. In general, though, the Musée National d'Art Moderne's best asset is the natural light, which shines through the building's large windows and gives the visitor the illusion of walking through an outdoor gallery.

SPECIAL EXHIBITIONS Temporary shows play an important role in the life of the Pompidou; nine or so galleries are set up to serve that purpose, not to mention the countless partitions that pop up in the lobbies and other public spaces. The Grande Galerie on the fifth floor holds the big exhibitions, for which the Pompidou plasters the city with advertisements. Exhibition admission is separate (*see* Basics, *above*). Next door to the Grande Galerie is Studio 5, a cinema that screens films and videos related to the exhibition. Smaller displays relating to the main exhibition are scattered around the building; some are free, and the ones that charge admission are available in a package deal with the Grande Galerie. The Galerie Nord and Galerie Sud on the mezzanine level offer shows not connected to the big ones upstairs, and they usually focus on the work of a single artist.

In October 1997 the Pompidou will start undergoing an 18-month-long gradual renovation. The Centre will never close down completely, but certain galleries and resource centers will be inaccessible to the public for months at a time.

CIMETIERE DU PERE-LACHAISE

The world's most celebrated necropolis, Père-Lachaise is the final stop for more illustrious people than you could ever meet in a lifetime. The former farm of Louis XIV's confessor, Father Lachaise, it has since been transformed into *the* mini-city of death and remembrance. Plots in the 118-acre cemetery are prime real estate, and now only the outrageously wealthy can afford to be laid to rest with the famous. The tattooed and leather-clad rage on at the eternal party in Division 6, but otherwise a serene gothic aura pervades the place. While the famous names deserve a visit, it's just as fun to wander aimlessly amid the disorderly array of decaying tombstones.

The oldest residents at Père-Lachaise are the celebrated lovers **Abelard** (1079–1142) and **Héloïse** (1101–64). But let's face it, most young travelers are tromping out here to see lizard

Jim Who?

If you're a fan of The Doors, check out the shrine dedicated to Jim Morrison at the Czech restaurant across the street from where Jimmy once lived (17 rue Beautreillis, 4e). To celebrate Jim's birthday on December 8, people start the festivities over his grave at Père-Lachaise and then bring the party back to Restaurant Le Beautreillis. You can sit in the same wicker chair where the Lizard King once slammed whiskey shots, and the restaurant owner will fill you in on all the "connections" he and Jim share. The catch is that Vieran had never even heard of The Doors until he bought the restaurant . . . years after Jim died.

king James Douglas Morrison (1943–71). A gendarme is now posted to keep crowds from mussing up nearby graves; Jim's grave site is periodically cleaned of spray-painted messages left by well-intentioned devotees. There was once a bust of Jim here, but it was stolen. (The artist has offered to replace it, but only the Morrison estate is allowed to make decisions regarding the plot, and it seems they are less than pleased with his lifestyle—both living and dead.) Die-hard Jim fans insist he must still be roaming the earth somewhere, because the grave is too small.

The precocious composer **Georges Bizet** (1838–75) finally found success with his opera *Carmen*, but only after a pitiful death in the bath (the water was too cold for his weak heart). Entombed with the negligent family he immortalized in over 3,000 pages of artful diatribes, **Marcel Proust** (1871–1922) now has the undivided attention of his mother. The dramatic death by strangulation (her long scarf got tangled up in a wheel of her sporty convertible) of dancer **Isadora Duncan** (1878–1927) wasn't the only freak accident in the family; 14 years earlier her children Deirdre and Patrick were swallowed by the Seine when their limousine fell into it. The body of **Oscar Wilde** (1854–1900) was moved here nine years after his death—the quicklime that was supposed to decompose him actually preserved the corpse, shocking the poor guys who had to dig him up. Wilde's tombstone, by Sir Jacob Epstein, is famous for its fantastic penis; it was originally covered up by the order of the cemetery, only to be later lopped off by an adoring fan. In a similar vein, the family jewels of **Victor Noir** (1848–70) are in dan-

The Paris Commune

While musicians and writers make a beeline for the graves of cultural icons like Jim Morrison and Oscar Wilde, others make a pilgrimage to the Mur des Fédérés at the southeast corner of Père-Lachaise. Since 1880, when socialists first staged a demonstration at "the Wall," socialists, anarchists, and other free thinkers have come to this place where the last 147 people to die during the Paris Commune of 1871 are buried.

The commune was begun by fiercely patriotic Parisians who intended to resist the Prussian invasion. Yet on January 28, 1871, Paris capitulated to a dishonorable peace: The Treaty of Frankfurt granted the Prussians Alsace, Lorraine, five billion francs, and the right to parade victoriously through Paris and install their government in the Château de Versailles, a symbol of the old absolute order. Outraged Parisians resisted this treaty by electing a radical municipal government, and Paris's National Guard soon joined the citizens, giving them the firepower they needed to form the independent Commune and resist the onslaught of troops faithful to the national government in Versailles. Statues were toppled, the Hôtel de Ville burned to the ground, and general chaos ensued.

The Communards used their newly seized power to pass social legislation intended to shorten the workday, improve education, and empower the working classes. Parisians held outdoor concerts and parties during what Lenin later described as a "festival of the oppressed" and what Marx considered to be a precursor of the greater socialist revolution to come. The Communards' main goal was to organize the country into a system of politically autonomous, democratic enclaves, but their vision was short lived. Government troops entered Paris only 72 days after the start of the Commune, brutally killing over 3,000 Parisians fighting from barricades and summarily massacring over 25,000 others.

ger of being completely rubbed off. The journalist/gigolo, killed in a duel, is depicted in bronze at the moment of death; ever since the statue's, um, erection, young lovers have been petting his pride and joy for fortune and fertility. Irreverent fans pick at the face of the sculpted angel watching over the timid virtuoso **Frédéric Chopin** (1810–49), and have even gone so far as to tear off her fingers.

Even in death, there are those who are greater among equals. Here they include city planner **Baron Haussmann** (1809–91); writers **Colette** (1873–1954), **Honoré de Balzac** (1799–1850), **Gertrude Stein** (1874–1946) and (in the same grave) **Alice B. Toklas** (1877–1967), and 1967 Nobel Prize winner **Miguel Angel Asturias** (1899–1974); poet and critic **Guillaume Apollinaire** (1880–1918); playwrights **Jean-Baptiste Molière** (1622–73) and **Pierre-Augustin Beaumarchais** (1732–99); fabulist **Jean de La Fontaine** (1621–95); painters **Théodore Géricault** (1791–1824), **Jean-Auguste Ingres** (1780–1867), **Eugène Delacroix** (1798–1863), **Jacques-Louis David** (1748–1825), **Amedeo Modigliani** (1884–1920), **Camille Pissarro** (1830–1903), **Georges Seurat** (1859–91), and **Max Ernst** (1891–1976); illustrator **Honoré Daumier** (1808–79); philosopher **Auguste Comte** (1798–1857); doctor and revolutionary **François Raspail** (1794–1878); actress **Sarah Bernhardt** (1845–1923); and singer **Edith Piaf** (1915–63). Near the **Mur des Fédérés** in the southeast corner are equally humbling memorials to World War II concentration camp victims and Resistance workers. All of these graves (and oh-so-many more) are located on free photocopied maps occasionally available at the cemetery office. Or you can buy a detailed map (10F) from nearby florists. *Blvd. de Ménilmontant, 20e, tel. 01–43–70–70–33. Métro: Père-Lachaise or Gambetta. Open daily 8 AM–6 PM.*

EIFFEL TOWER

It's funny to think that a construction so abhorred by the French public upon its conception could become the monument most closely associated with the country. A synthesis of national pride and egotism, of grandeur and artifice, of the beautiful and the grotesque soaring to an obscene height yet graciously straddling all of Paris, this old hulk o' steel is instantly recognizable the world over as *the* Parisian icon. And chances are that you'll be cursed with some vague sense of emotional unfulfillment until you've actually seen it during your strolls about Paris.

It all started in 1885, when the city held a contest to design a 300-meter (984-foot) tower for the 1889 World Exposition. Competing with proposals for a monster sprinkler and a giant commemorative guillotine, Gustave Eiffel, already well known for his iron works, won the contest with his seemingly functionless tower, which was slated for the junkyard even as it was being built. Somewhere along the way, however, people realized it might actually have a practical use or two, and it was saved; it has gone on, to help decipher German radio codes during World War I, capture Mata Hari, measure atmospheric pressure, and act as the ideal launch pad for 350 airborne suicides. To top it all off, artists and sensitive hearts galore have all gotten their willies off painting, singing about, writing to, and philosophizing from the tower that has come to symbolize Paris.

The Eiffel Tower, which receives about 15,000 visitors a day, lost $120,000 per day during the workers' strike that closed it in May 1996.

The close-up view of the tower—a 10,000-ton dark metal structure—is considerably more striking than that from across town. This was the world's tallest building until New York's Chrysler Building took over that title in 1930. Nowadays, it's simply a source of awe to legions of visitors, especially at night when it's entirely lit up. The hour-long lines to ascend the tower in summer are decidedly less wonderful; to avoid them, try visiting early in the morning or late at night. The best view, though, is on a clear day an hour before sunset, when visibility from the top extends 90 kilometers (56 miles). You can walk up to the second level to save money and work off some crêpes and take the elevator from there to the top. The post office with that famous postmark is open daily 10–7:30, so bring your postcards. *Champ de Mars, 7e, tel. 01–44–11–23–23. Métro: Bir-Hakeim. RER: Champ de Mars–Tour Eiffel. Admission (elevator): 20F for 1st level, 40F to 2nd level, 56F to top. Admission (stairs): 12F to 2nd level. Open daily 9 AM–11 PM.*

Just across the Pont d'Iéna bridge from the Eiffel Tower is the **Trocadéro** plaza, home to gardens, spectacular fountains, and the Palais de Chaillot museum complex. The view of the Eiffel Tower from here is unsurpassed, especially when the fountains are shooting up and framing it.

GRANDE ARCHE DE LA DEFENSE

Paris's major monuments follow the longest urban axis in the world: A straight line starts at the Louvre, passes through the Jardin des Tuileries, the place de la Concorde, and the Arc de Triomphe, and terminates at the Grande Arche de La Défense. Resembling a tremendous, mirrored Rubik's Cube floating in air with its center removed, the Grande Arche is a sort of monumental office building commisioned by the king of grands projets ("great projects"), François Mitterrand. Designed by Danish architect Otto von Spreckelsen and inaugurated on July 14, 1989, the futuristic structure is impressive, if not a bit weird: Uncomfortably perched on top of 12 narrow piers, the Grande Arche crosses the cold sleekness of its concrete beams and pure white marble with the optical brilliance of its 2,800 panes of clear glass. Over the years, the French government has come to realize that stark concrete is a bit drab and has gradually spruced up the area with a monumental fountain and a few dozen sculptures. A 40F (30F students) elevator ride will whisk you up through the belly of the building for a view of Paris. For tickets, head for the booth near the elevator; there's also a larger info booth just out front. *Tel. 01–49–07–27–57. Métro: Grande Arche de La Défense. Open daily 10–7 (ticket booth closes at 6).*

HOTEL DES INVALIDES

The Hôtel des Invalides was commissioned by Louis XIV to house soldiers wounded during his many military campaigns. The free digs must have come as a mixed blessing to the 4,000 veterans who lived here under Louis: Although they had what was essentially a small town within the elaborate and admittedly beautiful complex, their lives were still run by the military, and they were watched over by captains who supervised daily work in artisanal studios. Napoléon Bonaparte, too, came to rest on his sickbed—and final deathbed—here, and the **Musée de l'Armée,** located inside, has the death mask to prove it. Along with all sorts of war paraphernalia, the museum has mildly interesting costumes, armor, weapons, maps, and models of soldiers in war garb, as well as some imposing cannons in the central courtyard. Admission to the museum also buys a visit to Napoléon's tomb, housed in the **Eglise du Dôme.** Here the little megalomaniac lies ensconced in five coffins, one inside the next, keeping him nice and cozy. Wounded soldiers are still housed in the Hôtel des Invalides, and they attend mass in the **Soldier's Church** in the courtyard. *Esplanade des Invalides, 7e, tel. 01–44–42–37–67. Métro: Latour-Maubourg or Varenne. RER: Invalides. Admission (valid for 2 days): 35F, 25F students under 30 and Sun. Open Apr.–Sept., daily 10–6; Oct.–Mar., daily 10–5.*

HOTEL DE VILLE

The first Hôtel de Ville (Town Hall), built in 1532, was burned to the ground in the 1871 rebellion by the Communards (*see box,* The Paris Commune, *above*), who preferred to set it on fire than see it occupied by their foes. Rebuilt in 1874 by Haussmann, Napoléon III's prefect, the Hotel de Ville's construction spanned 14 years in an attempt to make the replica even better than the original (which, in 19th-century architectural terms meant bigger). In 1944, German troops set up camp in the building, but not for long—General de Gaulle celebrated the liberation of the city from the place de l'Hôtel de Ville on August 25, 1944. Today, the building is the seat of local government, as well as an international cultural center that continually sets up expos on the city of Paris. *Pl. de l'Hôtel de Ville, 4e, tel. 01–42–76–43–43. Métro: Hôtel de Ville. Admission free. Official tour Mon. 10:30 AM.*

INSTITUT DU MONDE ARABE

More than a museum, this is a monstrous multimedia cultural center. Built with funds from the French and most Arab governments, the institute is attempting to become a "cultural bridge" between Europe and the Arab world. In addition to its huge library and audiovisual center, the institute has two exhibition spaces, one for the permanent collection and the other for travel-ing exhibitions. The permanent collection (admission 25F, 20F age 25 and under) is a combi-nation of the institute's and some of the Louvre's Arab artifacts, with works dating from the pre-Islamic era to the present. The traveling exhibitions are usually blockbuster events, well-publicized by a large banner on the facade. Films are shown in the cinema on weekends, all in their original language with French subtitles (22F, 18F students and senior citizens). A café and a restaurant reside on the ninth floor, though the former makes you pay dearly for the view (one of the best in Paris), while the latter serves surprisingly bland food.

The building itself is a source of pride to Parisians, Arabs, and French-Arabs, all of whom con-sider the graceful glass institute one of Paris's finest modern structures. Designed by Jean Nou-vel (*see box,* Jean Nouvel, *below*), it is famous for the way it manipulates light. Behind the glass south wall are 240 mechanized metal plates that act like the aperture on a camera—a contem-porary interpretation of the moucharabieh (traditional Arab light-filtering latticework). Photo cells in the wall respond to the intensity of light outside, opening and closing the spiraling plates so that the interior of the institute is never too bright or too dim. This filtering system attracts hordes of visitors each day, though the complex mechanics have been known to break down. The interior courtyard plays with light in a less flashy manner: Small squares of thinly cut white mar-ble in the walls are carefully held in place by metal pins, allowing the sunlight to pass through the stone's patterns and illuminate the interior of the building with a soft glow. On top of this it's hard to get over the view—the spectacular panorama from the ninth-floor terrace encompasses Paris in all her glory. *1 rue des Fossés-St-Bernard, 5e, tel. 01–40–51–38–38. Métro: Jussieu or Cardinal Lemoine. Open Tues.–Sun. 10–6. Wheelchair access/barrier free.*

MUSEE DU LOUVRE

One of the grandest and most stunning museums in the world, and certainly one of the most visited, the Louvre houses an overwhelmingly comprehensive collection of art and artifacts from just about all cultures and regions, from ancient times up to the 19th century. Join the crowds of tourists flocking to the Mona Lisa for a photo and then leaving. Or, take some time to bask in the grandeur for awhile—at least so you can say you did. A 100F *carte jeune* for those under 26 will give you unlimited access to the museum for the whole year. *1er, tel. 01–40–20–53–17. Métro: Palais Royal–Musée du Louvre or Louvre–Rivoli. Admission: 45F, 26F daily after 3 PM and all day Sun., under 18 and art or architecture students free. Open Wed. 9 AM–10 PM, Thurs.–Mon. 9–6 (Richelieu open Mon. until 10 PM); galleries start empty-ing 30 min before closing time. Cafés and stores in Carrousel du Louvre open daily 9 AM–10 PM.*

The Grande Pyramide is not the quickest way into the Louvre. Try the staircases by the Arc du Carrousel (called the Porte Jaujard), or enter through the Métro stop Palais Royal–Musée du Louvre, both of which put you directly inside the underground mall, the Carrousel du Louvre.

François Mitterrand

The death of François Mitterrand, the Socialist president of France from 1981 to 1995, was met with mixed emotions by the French Republic in 1996. The driving force behind the construction of eleven "grands projets," including the pyramids of the Louvre, the Grande Arche de La Défense, and the Institut du Monde Arabe, Mitterrand helped to infuse France with a new pride (arrogance?) in its culture. His involvement with the Franco-German Vichy government in World War II, however, not to mention indiscreet interludes with the likes of Coco Chanel models, cast considerable suspicion upon his career during his final years, until prostate cancer ended his life on January 8, 1996.

BASICS To get into the Louvre, you may have to wait in two long lines: one outside the Pyramide and another downstairs at the ticket booths. Unless you come during the midday tourist rush, the first line shouldn't be a problem. If you're buying a full-price ticket, the second one isn't either, because you can buy a ticket from the vending machine to save time. Or, avoid both of these lines by entering through the Carrousel du Louvre. Your ticket will get you into any and all of the wings as many times as you like during one day.

Before you skip down that escalator and turn into the first wing you see, remember that the Louvre is *enormous*. We've outlined a simple guide in the following pages that is broken up by location (wing, floor, collection, and room number). If you want more comprehensive stuff, the museum bookstore kindly offers—in addition to the general maps at the information desk— books and leaflets outlining four different prepackaged strategies. The simplest is the **Guide for the Visitor in a Hurry** (20F), which directs you to the biggies with room numbers and illustrations. The *Visitor's Guide* (60F) ups the number of covered works but cuts the directions— it's an abridged catalogue. The weighty *Louvre: The Collections* (130F) covers even more of the museum's works, but it's too cumbersome to be a good visitor's guide and too incomplete to be a true catalogue. Finally, you've got the cool cellular-phone–style recorded tours (30F), which lead you through the galleries and explain the highlights. The Louvre is a great place to wander mapless in the hope of stumbling past fantastic bits of art, but don't get frustrated if you don't happen upon the Mona Lisa after hoofing it for five hours. Some pieces may also have been moved because of museum renovations.

Disabled visitors have about as easy a time as could be expected getting around a Renaissance palace; you can get to everything, and in some sections you can breeze through with almost no trouble at all. Ironically, the newest wing, Richelieu, is sometimes the most problematic: There are often a few steps leading from one room to another, forcing you to have to use a series of lifts and out-of-the-way elevators. Wheelchair-accessible rest rooms are in the lobby under the Pyramid.

HISTORY The Louvre spent its first 600 years alternately as a fortress and a palace. The original Louvre was a fortification built by Philippe Auguste in the late 12th century. A young, nervous Charles V expanded the building in the mid-14th century to distance himself from the potentially revolutionary masses on the Ile de la Cité, creating a Cinderella-like castle of moats and round towers. In the mid-16th century, François I demolished the old castle and started the Vieux Louvre, now encompassed within the Sully wing, and he initiated a cycle of major building projects that have continued more or less nonstop to this day. As construction lagged through the reign of Henri II, Catherine de Médicis started to build her Palais des Tuileries (named for the tileworks that stood close by) to the west of the Vieux Louvre. Catherine connected the two buildings with a hallway along the banks of the Seine; this hallway eventually became the Galerie Médicis of the Denon wing.

The wings were expanded and refined over the next 100 years, but it was the construction of the east facade, begun in 1668, that marked the beginning of the Louvre as we see it today. When a competition for architects to design the facade was held, a young draftsman named Claude Perrault worked with the seasoned illustrator and painter Charles Le Brun to come up with the winning proposal. Though his facade helped define French neoclassicism, Perrault didn't have the best timing—Louis XIV left the Louvre for Versailles in 1682, thus abandoning Perrault's elegant style for Versailles's frilly French baroque design.

The Louvre remained virtually untouched by royalty for the next century. The palace's apartments were rented out and very poorly kept; some even considered tearing it down in the mid-18th century. Then, in 1793, during the Revolution, the National Assembly voted to turn part of the Louvre into a public museum. The galleries were stocked with nationalized art taken from the churches, the king, and other members of the French nobility, but the greatest boon to the collection came when a tiny corporal from Corsica measured his power by how much Great Art he could take away from the rest of the world. Napoléon Bonaparte moved into the Louvre in 1800 as his armies were marching across Europe and the Mediterranean. They stole for him the world's most famous treasures, including entire fresco-covered walls and ancient temples, which were all brought to the Louvre, then called the Musée Napoléon. Although the Louvre had always been home to royalty, the emperor's residency in the complex marked the beginning of its role as France's premier palace. With Napoléon's removal (twice) from power, the museum was forced in 1815 to return many of its works to the original owners. However, not everything found its way back home—most notably, many Spanish and Italian paintings.

During the reign of Napoléon III (1852–71), the Louvre saw its most intensive period of construction ever: The Denon and Richelieu wings were finished, the Jardin du Carrousel was landscaped, and the facades of the Cour Napoléon and on rue de Rivoli were completed in the baroque/Renaissance/neoclassical mixture that came to be known as Second Empire. During the uprisings that followed the end of the Franco-Prussian War, the royal apartments were stormed and the Tuileries were burned to the ground during the Commune, leaving the Cour Napoléon without a west side. Napoléon III was forced out of power, and little was done to improve the collection for many years. During World War II, the invading Germans looted the Louvre and used parts of the museum as office space; a classical-art buff, Hitler had the *Victory of Samothrace* installed in his office. Most of the stolen pieces were recovered after the Liberation, but no large-scale changes or innovations were made until Mitterrand was elected. In his first year in office, 1981, the president announced a plan to commence a 20-year, three-phase, seven-billion-franc ($1.3 billion) renovation and expansion.

THE LOUVRE TODAY Mitterrand declared that the remaking of the Louvre was to be the central element of his *Grands Travaux* (Great Works), which makes it, according to the French, the most important building project in the world. Mitterrand, who always participated in choosing architects for Parisian projects, offered the commission to I. M. Pei, a New York–based Chinese American architect who made his reputation designing modernist mega-structures. The French were not pleased with the selection, the cost, or the proposal—namely, the relocation of all central services to an excavated Cour Napoléon, which would then be topped by a two-story glass pyramid. Pei explained that by moving the ticket windows and stores underground, the Louvre could have a single entrance that would be capable of handling the massive crowds of visitors (an estimated eight million people in 1995). At the same time, he argued that the stark style of his design for the Pyramide, lobby, and gallery space was intentionally modern so as to contrast with the older parts of the Louvre, rather than coming up with new designs that would mimic the frilly columns and statuary. In 1988 the Pyramide was inaugurated to a chorus of mixed reviews. The public and critics eventually warmed up to the new entrance, and when it came time to decide on an architect for the 2.7-billion-franc ($500 million) phase-two renovations, Pei was again chosen.

The most controversial part of recent renovations was the expansion of the underground Carrousel du Louvre mall, a series of upscale boutiques selling clothing, records, and other decidedly non-Louvre-related merchandise. There is even a massive fast-food court—now you can get a 30F Quick Burger and check out David's *Coronation of Napoleon and Josephine* all in the same building. The one saving grace to the Carrousel du Louvre is the inverted glass pyramid that plunges down into the middle of it, flooding the hallway with sunlight.

The most important part of the second phase has been the renovation of the old galleries, including 39 new rooms in the Sully wing dedicated to French paintings. By annexing the Richelieu wing, the Louvre also acquired three courtyards, which have been turned into stunning sculpture galleries. Just as the Pyramide became the symbol of the first phase of construction, these courtyards have become the postcard image of phase two (and not the inverted pyramid in the Carrousel du Louvre, as had been expected). The 76-year-old Pei was honored with a higher position in the Légion d'Honneur when the newest Louvre was inaugurated on November 18, 1993, exactly 200 years after the first Musée du Louvre was opened to the public.

The dream of every self-respecting art thief is to rip off the Mona Lisa (La Gioconda). This amazing feat was actually pulled off in 1911 when a burglar, disguised as a workman, snatched the then-405-year-old painting. It wasn't until two years later that Mona was found in Florence and safely returned to her glass-encased resting place in the Louvre.

Renovation is still marching on; painters, builders, and architects are furiously redoing, rearranging, and spiffing up the Louvre. Due to the work, the entire **Egyptian department** will be closed until March 1997; the **Grande Galerie** is being divided into two sections, and until renovations are complete some 15th- and 16th-century Italian and Spanish works will be unavailable to view. For more info on changes or for up-to-date info on renovations, inquire at the knowledgeable, English-speaking information desk, or call 01–40–20–53–17.

RICHELIEU WING

➣ **BELOW GROUND AND GROUND FLOOR** • As you enter the Richelieu wing from the Pyramide, on the left and up a flight of stairs is a gallery that displays temporary exhibits that comprise the Louvre's most recent aquisitions in **French sculpture.** Straight ahead is **Salle 20,** filled with more French sculpture, including frilly busts of members of the court of Louis XIV, but most people pass through this room to get to the dramatic Cour Marly to the west or Cour Puget to the east. The **Cour Marly** is filled with sculptures taken from a garden commissioned by Louis XIV in the early 18th century. The sculptures were intended to be lighthearted additions to ultrapompous Versailles; you can just imagine all these Greco-Roman gods set into the bushes of the Sun King's garden, their clothes falling away from their perfect bodies for all eternity. The **Cour Puget** is named for the artist who created the sculpture at the place des Victoires, now mostly reassembled in the lower court. Sculptures that once dotted the estates of nobility fill the rest of the courtyard, while the upper level has some busts of characters from the Revolution and the 1830 uprising.

Back to the southeast corner of Cour Marly: Here you will find **Salle 1** of French sculpture. The first truly French sculpture—that is, not Gallo-Roman—dates to the 11th century, when the carved column heads produced by regional artisans began to display figures or beasts instead of Corinthian capitals. In **Salle 2** are fragments of Romanesque chapels from Cluny, the powerful abbey in Burgundy that dominated French Catholicism in the 11th century. In **Salles 4–6** you can see the refinement of sculpture encouraged by the wealthy communities in the Ile de France. The **funerary art** of **Salles 7–10** ranges from spooky to risible. The late 15th-century tomb of Philippe Pot in **Salle 10** is especially eerie: You see Philippe stretched out in eternal prayer, held aloft by eight black-robed pallbearers.

Walking through **Salles 11–19,** you can see how the piety and stiffness of medieval French sculpture began to give way to the more natural style of the Italian Renaissance. Many local artists were traveling to Italy during the 16th and 17th centuries, while the French nobility were importing noted Italian sculptors. Bronze, out of favor since Roman times, was being cast again, and the subject matter, which had rarely strayed from Madonnas or saints, could now be mythological, allegorical, or classical.

To the north of the Cour Puget are **Salles 25–33,** filled with the products of the Académie Royale, *the* art school of 18th-century France. The smaller works in **Salle 25** are all qualification pieces for the Académie—once admitted into the school based on previous works, the student was asked to produce a sculpture as proof of continuing worth. Mythology was a popular subject, as in Jean Thierry's 1717 *Leda and the Swan,* which depicts the unorthodox seduction scene between the queen of Sparta and Zeus in the form of a large bird. While beautiful art did emerge during the 18th century, the individual artists are of questionable creative merit: The Académie became a sort of aesthetics factory, churning out thousands of decorative marble statues depicting yet another stock Apollo figure.

To the east of the Cour Puget is the start of the Louvre's **Oriental Antiquities** collection. Within the glass case of **Salle 1** are many ancient Mesopotamian carvings, including a 5.4-centimeter (2-inch) Neolithic figure dating to the 6th millennium BC. Facing the case are the pieced-together fragments of the 3rd millennium BC *Stela of the Vultures,* containing the oldest written history known to humankind: On one side, King Eannatum catches his enemies in a net and thanks the disembodied head of his patron goddess; on the other side, vultures eat the corpses of the enemy, while the king leads chariots and infantry over more bodies and a sacrifice is offered for the victory.

Farther along, **Salle 1b** has countless examples of the wide-eyed alabaster statues produced by the Sumerians during the 3rd millennium BC. **Salle 2** is filled with statues and fragments of Gudea, a prince who supported a neo-Sumerian artistic culture in his 23rd-century BC kingdom of Lagash. Gudea commemorated his achievements through countless portraits of himself he had carved from diorite, the hardest stone on earth; notice the one headless statue depicting Gudea presiding over the architectural plans for a temple.

The centerpiece of **Salle 3** is the "Codex of Hammurabi," an 18th-century BC diorite stela that contains the oldest written laws known to humanity. Near the top of the text you can see Hammurabi, king of the first Babylonian dynasty, meeting a seated Shamash, the god of justice. On the east side of Salle 3 is a lion glazed onto a piece of a terra-cotta-tile wall—just one of hundreds of similar beasts that decorated the multistory 6th-century BC Gates of Babylon. (The rest of the Gates have been re-erected in the Pergamon Museum in Berlin.)

Salle 4 is the Cour Khorsabad, a re-creation of the temple erected by the Assyrian king Sargon II in the 8th century BC at the palace of Dur-Sharrukin. Walking among the temple's five massive, **winged bulls** known as *lamassu,* or benign demigods, is one of the most spectacular experiences in the Louvre, even though only three of the bulls and almost none of the re-erected reliefs are authentic. The originals were lost on a sunken frigate.

➢ **FIRST FLOOR** • The newly restored rooms from the **royal apartments** of Napoléon III, opened to the public in March 1996, fill the southwestern portion of the first floor of the Richelieu wing. **Salle 79** is the most spectacular of the lot; the corner reception room, decorated for Napoléon III's secretary of state, gives you a good idea of the audacious luxury of the Second Empire. The **gallery** running between the Cour Marly and the Cour Puget is filled with **French medieval artifacts** saved from the Revolution's zeal to destroy all things Christian and Roman. It also contains **Byzantine objects** taken as booty from non–Roman Catholic churches in Constantinople during the Crusades.

➢ **SECOND FLOOR** • Just to the east of the escalators is **Salle 1,** which begins the section devoted to **French and Northern School paintings.** At the entrance to this room is a single 14th-century gold-backed painting of John the Good—the oldest known individual portrait from north of Italy. In **Salle 4** is the *Madonna and Chancellor Rolin,* by the 15th-century Dutch master Jan van Eyck. The first artist to extensively use oil paints, van Eyck defined what became known as the "northern style," characterized by a light source illuminating one area on an otherwise dark background. One of the first self-portraits ever painted—a bizarre and disheveled offering by Albrecht Dürer (1471–1528)—hangs in **Salle 8.** Walking through **Salles 9–17,** you can see how the Dutch developed a fluid and comfortable representation of the body while playing with the shiny, dark palette of oil paints. **Salle 12** houses the 1514 *Banker and His Wife,* where Quentin Metsys (1456–1530) deftly depicts the effect of light on glass, gold, and mirrors.

The most dramatic gallery in this section is **Salle 18,** where a cycle of epic Peter Paul Rubens (1577–1640) canvases recounts the journey Marie de Médicis made from Florence to Paris— an overbearing immortalization of a relatively cushy trip. The swirling baroque paintings were commissioned by Marie herself and originally hung in the Palais du Luxembourg. The riveting *Disembarkation of Marie de Médicis at the Port of Marseilles* depicts an artificially slimmed-down Marie about to step over the roly-poly daughters of Poseidon as a personified France beckons her to shore.

Though the still life genre may seem dull today, it was loaded with meaning for the Dutch. Ambriosius Bosschaert's (1573–1621) *Bouquet of Flowers in an Arch* (1620) in **Salle 27** is meant to represent the power of the colonially minded Dutch merchants: The flowers brought together in the vase in this painting couldn't have been gathered at any one moment in real life because of their diverse and exotic origins. In **Salle 31** are several paintings by Rembrandt van Rijn (1606–69), including a late self-portrait in which he goes nuts with the chiaroscuro. In his 1648 *Supper at Emmaüs,* he challenges many painting conventions, such as centering the subject and delineating objects with bold brush strokes. The masterpiece of the Dutch collection is the *Lacemaker,* by Jan Vermeer (1632–75), in **Salle 38.** Obsessed with optical accuracy, Vermeer

The French philosopher/writer Roland Barthes noted that only the Dutch painters allowed patricians and cows to look out and make eye contact with the viewer—glance around Salle 34 of the second floor of Richelieu and see if you agree.

painted the red thread in the foreground as a slightly blurred jumble, just as one would actually see it if focusing on the girl.

SULLY WING   The entrance into the Sully wing is more impressive than the entrances to the other wings—you get to walk around and through the foundations and moat of the castle built by Philippe Auguste in the 12th century and expanded by Charles V in the 14th.

➤ **BELOW GROUND** • The foundations of Philippe Auguste's castle were accidentally discovered during renovations of the building in 1988. Notice that many of the stones have squares, circles, or hearts cut roughly into them: These were used by the illiterate masons to identify the parts. Take a look at the model in the side room to get an idea of what the place used to look like.

➤ **GROUND FLOOR** • The northern galleries of the Sully are a continuation of the ancient **Iranian collection** started on the ground floor of the Richelieu wing. Conflicting styles emerged as the Greco-Roman art exported by the Roman and Byzantine empires influenced the work of indigenous artisans.

Adjacent to the Egyptian galleries—under renovation and temporarily closed through most of 1997—is **Salle 13**, housing the **Greek, Etruscan,** and **Roman collections** and the famous 2nd-century BC *Venus de Milo*. The armless statue, one of the most reproduced and recognizable works of art in the world, is actually as beautiful as they say—it is worth your trouble to push past the lecturing curators and tourist groups to get a close look at the incredible skill with which the Greeks turned cold marble into something vibrant and graceful. **Salles 13–17** are filled with all kinds of statuary: funerary stelae, body fragments, architectural detailings. One important form for Greek figurative statues was the *kouros,* which depicts an idealized youth standing staring straight ahead, an "archaic smile" (the lips are pulled back to resemble a grin, but the mouth isn't actually smiling) on his face, his shoulders squared with his hands at his sides, and one foot slightly in front of the other. You can see in these galleries how sculptors relaxed and naturalized the stance over the centuries. The statues in **Salle 17,** known as the Caryatid Room (named for the 16th-century female figures standing as columns at either end of the hall), are Roman copies of original Greek works.

➤ **FIRST FLOOR** • The northern galleries of the first floor continue with the **objets d'art collection** started in the Richelieu wing, picking up at the 17th century and continuing through the Revolution to the Restoration. Running alongside the Egyptian galleries to the south are works from the early period of the **Greek collection**—a smattering of coins, pottery, and other everyday objects from the 7th to 3rd centuries BC.

➤ **SECOND FLOOR** • Sully picks up French painting where the Richelieu wing leaves off, somewhere around the 16th century. At this point, a conscious battle was under way in French art between the northern style, centered on the work of the Dutch, and the southern one, coming from Florence, Venice, and Rome. The result was a blending of northern style and technology (darkly painted interiors and oil paints) with southern subjects and technique (ruins-filled landscapes and one-point perspective). Charles Le Brun (1619–90), Louis XIV's principal adviser on the arts, painted massive "History Paintings," jam-packed with excruciating details depicting biblical, historical, or mythological stories. Displayed in **Salle 32** are the four canvases of his late 17th-century *Story of Alexander,* with a powerful view of the trials of the emperor (and no small reference to Louis XIV).

An academic painter of a different genre was Jean-Antoine Watteau (1684–1721). In scenes such as his 1717 *Pilgrimage to the Island of Cythera* in **Salle 36,** he depicted in wispy pastel brush strokes the bucolic and often frivolous lifestyle of the baroque-age court set. In the same room is Watteau's enigmatic 1718 *Pierrot* (also called *Gilles*), a portrait of a boyish-looking actor whose costume and surroundings reflect the popularity of Italian commedia dell'arte at the time. Maurice Quentin de La Tour (1704–88) was another favorite court painter; his 1755 *Marquise de Pompadour* in **Salle 45** captures the frivolous pomp of Louis XV's court. Madame de Pompadour, mistress to the king, is shown with everything a good courtesan should have: books, music manuscripts, engravings, fine clothing, and, of course, pale skin.

One Revolution and two Republics after the court painters of the 17th and 18th centuries, the Académie continued to define what Good Taste was. In **Salle 55** you can see the paintings of Jean-Auguste-Dominique Ingres (1780–1867), which depict the exotic themes popular in the Age of Empires. His 1862 *Turkish Bath* portrays an orgy of steamy women who look anything but Turkish. You can see more of his work in **Salle 77** of the Denon wing and across the Seine at the Musée d'Orsay (*see below*).

DENON WING

➤ **BELOW GROUND** • To the south and east from the Pyramide entrance are newly renovated galleries displaying **Italian sculpture** from the early Renaissance, including a 15th-century *Madonna and Child* by the Florentine Donatello (1386–1466).

➤ **GROUND LEVEL** • In **Salle 9** you can see the 1513–15 *Slaves* of Michelangelo (1475–1564). Carefully selecting his slab of marble, Michelangelo would then spend days envisioning the form of the sculpture within the uncut stone. The sculptures that finally emerged openly eroticized the male body. The fact that many were left "unfinished" (i.e., parts of the marble were left rough, making it look as if the sculptures were trying to free themselves from the stone blocks) was controversial at first, but the style went on to inspire Rodin and other modern artists. In **Salle 10** is the 1793 *Eros and Psyche* by the great Italian neoclassicist Antonio Canova (1757–1822), whose delicate and precise touch made him the darling of European royalty.

To the east of the Italian sculpture collection are the galleries containing the sculptures of the **Greek, Etruscan,** and **Roman** periods. In **Salle 18** is the 6th-century BC Etruscan *Sarcophagus from Cerveteri,* pieced together from thousands of clay fragments.

➤ **FIRST FLOOR** • Stretching out from a tiny entry next to the Sully wing is the **Galerie d'Apollon,** a 17th-century hall decorated by the painter Charles Le Brun (who immortalized himself in one of the portraits on the wall) that now holds what remains of France's **Crown Jewels.** Around the corner from the jewels, the *Victory of Samothrace* stands regally, if headless, at the top landing of the staircase leading down to the ground floor. The spectacular 2nd-century BC statue, found on a tiny Greek island in the northern Aegean, was probably a monument to a victorious battle at sea.

The **Italian painting** collection begins at the western end of the Denon wing, but Salles 6 and 7 may be partially closed in 1997. The paintings in **Salle 6** are large-scale canvases from the 16th-century Venetian School. Dominating the room is the massive 1562 *Feast at Cana* by Veronese (1528–88), a sumptuous scene centered on Jesus turning water into wine. Spread across the canvas are hundreds of still lifes and portraits, all little masterpieces within this huge painting; it is said that the great painters of the Venetian School—Titian, Bassano, Tintoretto, and even Veronese—are depicted as the musicians. In the same room is the 1525 *Entombment* by the quintessential Venetian painter, Titian (1488–1576). Titian used the translucent shine of the oil paints characteristic of Venetian art while contrasting dark colors against extreme whites to create a sense of light. The last great artist from the Venetian School was Tintoretto (1518–94), whose latter works look almost impressionistic, since he rejected a brush in favor of smearing the paint onto the canvas with his fingers.

And now for **Salle 7,** home to the Most Famous Painting in the World, the **Mona Lisa** (officially known as *La Gioconda*). Somewhere behind the legion of videotaping tourists (think about it: videotaping *paintings!*) and layers of bulletproof glass is the painting that has inspired so much awe, emulation, and disbelief—you, too, may find yourself asking "Is this it?" when you are faced with this 70-by-50-centimeter (2½-by-1¾-foot) painting of an eyebrow-less woman with yellowing skin and an annoyingly smug smile. But if you can somehow move to the front of the crowd to squint through the glare of the protective coating, you'll have a close look at a truly beautiful painting.

The 1458 *Calvary* in **Salle 8,** painted by Andrea Mantegna (1431–1506), a follower of the Florentine architect Brunelleschi's treatises on perspective, is one of the first paintings ever with a vanishing point. While the angling of the roads and people may seem severe, he opened the door for exploration of the concepts of background and foreground. Though more accomplished during his lifetime as an anatomist and inventor, Leonardo Da Vinci (1452–1519) was originally trained as a painter. His 1483 *Virgin of the Rocks* has a pretty nifty sense of spatial relationships—the four figures create the four corners of a pyramid, while their glances and gestures keep all activity contained within this form. On the way from Salle 8 to the landing where the *Victory of Samothrace* is standing, you'll pass by Sandro Botticelli's (1445–1510) *Venus and the Graces,* a fresco chipped out of its villa in Tuscany. The painting is full of the sidelong glances and lengthy fingers associated with the mannerist movement.

Behind the *Feast at Cana* are two passages leading to **Salles 75–77,** home of the great epic-scale canvases produced in Paris during the 19th century. When official court painter Jacques-Louis David (1748–1825) produced the 1806 *Coronation of Emperor Napóléon I, 2 December 1804,* now hanging in **Salle 75,** he wisely decided *not* to capture the moment when Napóléon snatched the crown from the hands of Pope Pius VII to place it upon his own head—choosing instead to paint the new emperor turning to crown Josephine. In the same room is the 1805 painting *Empress Josephine* by Pierre-Paul Prud'hon (1758–1823), depicting the wife of Napóléon one year after her crowning.

In **Salle 75** hang the two most famous works in the history of **French painting**: the 1819 *Raft of the Medusa* by Théodore Géricault (1791–1824) and the 1830 *Liberty Leading the People* by Eugène Delacroix (1798–1863). The *Medusa,* painted when Géricault was only 27 years old, was inspired by the real-life story of the wreck of a French merchant ship: The captain lost control, the ship was without lifeboats or supplies, and ultimately the survivors resorted to cannibalism. The painting caused a stir with the government, which took offense at the stab made at the inefficiency of authority. The Académie was aghast for formal reasons: The painting had no central subject, no hero, no *resolution.* The survivors are a mess of living and dead bodies jumbled in and out of ominous shadows.

If you're lucky enough to have a 100F note in your posession, you'll notice Delacroix's famous "Liberty Leading the People" gracing its design. Might make you think twice about spending the cash on beer.

Even though Delacroix wasn't directly involved in the "Trois Glorieuses"—a three-day revolution in 1830 that ousted Charles X's autocracy and brought in a parliamentary monarchy with Louis-Philippe as king—he was compelled to paint *Liberty* to commemorate the Parisians who attempted to restore the Republic. Once again, it is an unorthodox subject for a painting: Poorly armed bourgeoisie and pugnacious street urchins step over the dead bodies of comrades and kill other French folk in the name of an ultimately short-lived government. The allegorical figure of Liberty is quite a character: She is shown walking barefoot over barricades, her peasant dress falling away from two nippleless breasts, the Tricolore (French flag) held aloft with one well-muscled limb while the other grips a rifle. The painting was immediately bought by an appreciative Louis-Philippe, who hid it to keep from inciting his enemies.

SPECIAL EXHIBITIONS AND EVENTS Temporary photography shows, exhibits of new acquisitions and donations, and events honoring individual painters or subjects usually take place in either the Napóléon Hall, the basement galleries of the Richelieu and Sully wing, the second-floor galleries of the Denon wing, or the showrooms of the Carrousel du Louvre. Your Louvre ticket may give you free access, or you may have to shell out another 28F, depending on the exhibit. Lectures and films take place in the Louvre Auditorium on topics such as archaeology, architecture, and art criticism (25F–50F); the films showcase everything from silent works to the history of art in Paris (25F–100F). Chamber music concerts happen infrequently in the auditorium as well (130F, 100F students). A smattering of films, lectures, concerts, and exhibits are included in what's called **Les Midis du Louvre**; these noontime events cost 25F–50F. For a recorded message announcing the week's agenda, call tel. 01–40–20–52–99; if you'd rather talk to a human being, call tel. 01–40–20–51–86 between 9 AM and 7 PM. You can also pick up the free three-month schedule of events called *Louvre* at the information desk under the Pyramide, or look at the TV monitors behind the desk.

MUSEE D'ORSAY

For those who have just visited the Louvre and are oozing antiquity from every orifice, the Musée d'Orsay presents a refreshingly more modern collection, encompassing art produced between 1848 (where the Louvre drops off) and about 1904 (where the Pompidou picks up). Since the most talented artists at this time, at least according to Parisians, were French, and coincidentally a French movement called impressionism was taking root, the Orsay seems to have a peculiar bias for French works. Far from being just an impressionist museum, however, the Orsay also does a fine job of representing other trends of the time, including the rise and fall of the literary salons and the creation of the concept of the avant-garde. For those of you itching to see a Van Gogh, Monet, Toulouse-Lautrec, or Renoir, this is the place to be. *62 rue de Lille, 7e, tel. 01–40–49–48–14. Métro: Solferino. RER: Musée d'Orsay. Admission: 36F, 24F ages 18–25, under 18 free; separate admission for temporary exhibits. Open Tues.–Sat. 10–6 (Thurs. until 9:45), Sun. 9–6; in summer (June 20–Sept. 20), from 9 AM. Wheelchair access.*

BASICS Although not as chaotic as the Louvre, the interior of this former train station may overwhelm you with its weighty postmodern architecture, sculptures, and hordes of people furiously milling around. The museum shop offers *Guide for Visitors in a Hurry* (20F), an abbreviated outline of the most important works of the collection, and *Guide to the Orsay* (110F), a more comprehensive look at the collection with better pictures.

General English-language tours are offered Tuesday through Saturday at 11 AM (also 7 PM Thursdays); tours at 11:30 are in French. Tours related to the special exhibitions vary—ask for the monthly calendar *Au jour le jour* when you buy your ticket to learn what's being offered that day.

Even though the Orsay is wheelchair accessible, it is far from barrier-free. Elevators take you to all three levels of the museum, but individual galleries may be five or more steps up or down from each other, forcing you to circumnavigate to get where you're going. Check with the information desk to find out how to operate the elevators.

HISTORY The Orsay was only christened a "musée" in 1986. Built in 1898, the original Gare d'Orsay was meant to handle the onslaught of trains expected for the 1900 World's Fair. Architect Victor Laloux, a professor at the nearby Ecole des Beaux-Arts, designed all kinds of ornamental frippery appropriate to the dawning of the modern age. The platforms of the station were soon too short for modern trains, and the building was mostly abandoned only a few years after it opened. There were a few tenants now and then—Orson Welles shot *The Trial* in the station, and at one point a circus set up shop—but it was slated for demolition as a part of the urban renewal schemes of the early 1970s. Parisians couldn't stand the thought of this beloved, unused, oversized neo-rococo dinosaur being torn down, so they successfully petitioned President Pompidou to designate it a national monument in 1973. Four years later, a competition was announced for a design to turn the old station into a museum, and the project was awarded to Italian architect Gae Aulenti.

When François Mitterrand assumed the presidency in 1981, the renovation of the Orsay had completely stalled. With a deft stroke of his pen, Mitterrand tripled the reconstruction budget; five years later the Musée d'Orsay was inaugurated, now displaying the combined collections of the Jeu de Paume (*see* Museums, *below*) and the 19th-century galleries of the Louvre. The crowds love Aulenti's renovation design: While preserving a single grand, statue-lined promenade along the length of the building, Aulenti broke up the spacious shell of the old train station by dividing and subdividing the galleries into smaller rooms. But while Aulenti successfully turned the old antiseptic, white-walled, picture-in-splendid-isolation cliché of museums on its head, she also created tight doors and stairways easily clogged by tourists.

THE COLLECTION Earlier paintings and sculptures are displayed on the ground level, later sculpture and architectural design on the middle level, and the heart of the impressionist collection on the upper level. If impressionism is this museum's draw for you, take an elevator directly to the third floor—otherwise all the walking will have you beat by the time you hit your favorites.

➢ **GROUND FLOOR** • As you walk up the Grande Promenade, the first gallery on the right contains the works of sensualist **Jean-Auguste-Dominique Ingres** (1780–1867), whose erotic style was called "classic" by the other sensualists at the Académie Francaise. The next gallery along the promenade has the works of **Eugène Delacroix** (1798–1863), who managed to remain in favor with the French government throughout his career; Delacroix did a fair bit of business repainting canvases and frescoes in churches desecrated during the Revolution. Like many painters, as he got older he became more liberal with color and technique, becoming an unintentional innovator.

Back across the promenade, the first gallery has figurines by the satirical illustrator **Honoré Daumier** (1808–79). Working at the beginning of the popular-press age, Daumier spent his energies mocking various members of the government and intelligentsia with biting little etchings. The caricatures included wicked likenesses of members of the National Assembly; you can see some of his paintings on the upper level. In the next gallery are works by **Jean-Baptiste-Camille Corot** (1796–1875). His uncentered landscapes are associated with the Barbizon school, an approach to painting inspired by the writings of Rousseau and the invention of the camera.

In the first room on the left in the next bank of galleries on the promenade is the notorious *Olympia* (1863) by **Edouard Manet** (1832–83). When it was unveiled at the Salon des Refusés, it drew scathing remarks: The image of a nude, youngish courtesan with unfinished hands (they were described as monkey paws) stretched out next to a black cat (a symbol of female sexuality) with a bouquet of flowers *sketched* in paint was far too much. Reviews of the painting (save two) were negative. Next door is **Claude Monet**'s (1840–1926) pre-1870 work.

Between the banks of galleries running along the Seine side of the Orsay is a large, open room containing the works of **Gustave Courbet** (1819–77), considered by current scholars to be the first modernist. Courbet's highly gestural brush strokes were abhorred by the Académie Française; no matter—the painter hated the Académie just as much. Courbet's subjects— muddy country roads, poor farmers, rural dogs—embodied everything the sophisticated Parisian art scene was not, making the artist a hero to future generations of realists. His controversial *Origine du Monde,* a portrait of a woman's vagina in the heat of passion, was a gift for a women-loving friend. For more Courbet, check out the **Petit Palais** (*see* Museums, *below*).

Standing under the twin battlements at the end of the promenade is the **Salle Garnier,** a spiffy cluster of rooms devoted to the architect **Charles Garnier** (1825–98) and his crowning achievement, the Opéra de Paris (*see* Opera, Classical Music, and Dance, in Chapter 5). Here you can look at models and sketches examining the Opéra's structure, but the best part is the scale model of the Opéra and its surrounding neighborhood that is set into the floor under see-through tiles. Trailing up along the staircase in the northeast corner of the museum is a montage of Parisian facades, starting from the Restoration and moving chronologically through the July Monarchy, Second Republic, Second Empire, and Third Republic.

➢ **MIDDLE FLOOR** • On the terrace overlooking the promenade are early 20th-century sculptures, including works by **Auguste Rodin** (1840–1917) and **Camille Claudel** (1864– 1903). Rodin, arguably the greatest sculptor of his era, spent the last 37 years of his career working on figures for his never-finished bronze *Gate of Hell,* a plaster version of which stands between the two battlements. The *Gate* was originally supposed to depict the *Divine Comedy* of Dante, but an obsessed Rodin overreached the concept of visual narration by packing the doors with scores of plunging figures twisted in agony and ecstasy. (For more on the *Gate* and on Rodin and Claudel, *see* Museums, Musée Rodin, *below.*)

The galleries on either sides of the battlements are filled with architecture and furniture design from the turn of the century. To the north are several rooms filled with art nouveau, including a completely reconstructed dining room by **Alexandre Charpentier** (1856–1909). Across the terrace are rooms dedicated to non-French designers of the same period, including the American "Prairie School" architect **Frank Lloyd Wright** (1867–1959) and the Scot **Charles Rennie Mackintosh** (1868–1928), an early modernist.

➢ **UPPER FLOOR** • Entering the first gallery from the northeastern stairs or elevator, you'll finally hit the impressionist stuff you've been waiting for. The impressionists challenged the status quo with their highly detailed theories about the effects of light, movement, and color, finding a slew of new subjects to paint with the advent of the Haussmann boulevards, cafés, and department stores just beginning to dominate Parisian culture in the late 19th century. A growing middle class was having a great time in the parks and dance halls while the Second Empire was out reaping the spoils of a colonized world. In the middle of this new era, Manet did his controversial *Déjeuner sur l'herbe.* The subject, naked ladies and clothed men in a bucolic setting, wasn't new to the French public in 1863; everybody was familiar with similar scenes from the Italian Renaissance and French baroque paintings hanging in the Louvre. But there was something about the modern dress of the men, the discarded clothes of the women, and the way two of the figures look out at the viewer with a slightly confrontational glance that upset the critics.

In the next gallery is the famous portrait of the mother of **James McNeill Whistler** (1834–1903), embodying all the spartan puritanism associated with the rural United States and the late 19th-century American aesthetic. In the next gallery, the work of **Claude Monet** shows how the painter replaced hard delineation with soft brush strokes and colors from a muted palette. His *Fête du 30 juin 1878* tries to capture the shimmering vitality of a Paris street celebration. In the same gallery is the work of **Pierre-Auguste Renoir** (1841–1919), who used to spend long hours in Parisian parks catching the newly idle petite bourgeoisie at play.

The last gallery in this series is devoted to **Paul Cézanne** (1839–95), who challenged the salons of Paris by entirely ignoring them. Though he had contact with other painters like Degas and Manet and a few young artists who came to study with him in his Aix-en-Provence studio, Cézanne painted almost entirely for himself. And he painted and painted, continually playing with color and spatial relationships while selling only a few works to a wealthy doctor.

Around the corner, past the Café des Hauteurs, is a room filled with the work of **Vincent van Gogh** (1835–90), the slightly insane Dutch painter who spent most of his years working in France. Van Gogh was doomed to a bizarre life from the outset—he was named for a dead brother who'd had the same birthday. Sure, there's the ear story, and the problems he had with prostitutes and his brother Theo, but the contribution he made to painting cannot be underestimated. Van Gogh painted a stone bridge yellow and a wheat field red because that's the way he painted them—a simple idea for later generations of artists to figure out.

Turning the corner, you have the work of **Henri Rousseau** (1844–1910), whose cool and flattened touch delineated fairy-tale-like jungle scenes complete with exotic animals hidden in the dense underbrush. This jungle motif was popular with the style-conscious French, who were eager to get images of what they imagined to be Edenic colonies in Africa, East Asia, and the Caribbean. The symbolist **Paul Gauguin** (1848–1903) titillated an audience back in Paris with the primitivist paintings he produced while living in Tahiti, but the lightheartedness of his earlier stuff is naïve compared with the fatalistic imagery that came later.

Farther along are works by **Georges Seurat** (1859–91), whose use of dots of color became known as pointillism (though he found the term "divisionism" much more appropriate). At the end of the hallway are early works by **Henri Matisse** (1869–1954), whose 1904 *Luxe, Calme, et Volupté* helped him earn the label *fauvist,* an uncomplimentary term coined by the critics, who thought his bright colors were *comme un fauve* (like a beast). Matisse was much more than just a colorist, but his early works mark the official end (at least according to French museums) of post-impressionism and the beginning of modern art—for more Matisse, go to the Pompidou (*see above*). For another big batch of impressionists and post-impressionists in a smaller setting, make time for the Musée de l'Orangerie; and Monet fans can't miss the Musée Marmottan (for both, *see* Museums, *below*).

PLACE DE LA CONCORDE

In no other spot in Paris can you turn 360° and see so many monuments. Place de la Concorde is a Kodak dream come true, provided you aren't flattened by the hundreds of cars that tear through it. Architect Jacques-Ange Gabriel designed the square for Louis XV and, as with so many of Paris's historical sites, a lot of blood has been spilled around it. In 1763, a statue of Louis XV was erected in the center of the square, which was then named after his egotistical majesty. However, in 1792 the statue was replaced by a big symbol of Liberty (and complemented, ironically enough, by a guillotine that same year). It was at this spot that Louis XVI lost his head (literally), as did Marie-Antoinette and hundreds of others. In 1795 it was finally dubbed place de la Concorde.

The place is flanked on the northern side by Gabriel's 1763 mansions, the **Hôtel de la Marine** and the **Hôtel Crillon,** with the **Madeleine** (*see* Houses of Worship, *below*) rising up between them. To the west you can stare right up the Champs-Elysées to the **Arc de Triomphe** and, on unusually clear days, to **La Défense:** The eastern side boasts the **Jardin des Tuileries,** which leads to the Louvre. Finally, to the south you have the fancy **Pont de la Concorde,** built in 1788. Smack-dab in the middle of the square, and looking decidedly un-French, is the **Obelisque de Luxor.** A gift to King Louis-Philippe in 1831 from Egyptian leader Mohammed Ali, the obelisk originally stood before the gates of Thebes. The hieroglyphics, which run 23 meters high, tell the tales of Ramses II; the more modern tale of how they got the 230-ton monument from Egypt to Paris is engraved on the bottom (a special ship equipped with cranes and pulleys was built to carry it). The eight statues encircling place de la Concorde, added in 1871, represent the biggest cities in France. *Métro: Concorde.*

SAINTE-CHAPELLE

Sainte-Chapelle is a Gothic chapel made sublime by its fantastic room of wall-to-wall stained glass, the only one in Paris. Ascending to the upper chapel, especially on sunny days, is like climbing into a jewel box: Brilliantly colored windows flood the interior with light—you get the exhilarating feeling that the building has walls of glass. The less-grand lower chapel, once reserved for the king's servants, is paved with the faceless, worn tombstones of clerics and forgotten knights. Listening to solo instrumental or vocal concerts here is a particularly glorious experience.

This chapel remains a fine example of the extremes to which people will go when they get hold of a holy relic or two. In the mid-13th century, Louis IX bought the alleged crown of thorns and a part of *the* Cross from Constantinople. In order to adequately house these treasures, as well as a portion of John the Baptist's skull and Mary's milk and blood, he ordered the building of Sainte-Chapelle. The elegant result was completely unlike massive contemporaries Chartres (*see* Chartres, in Chapter 7) and Notre-Dame (*see above*); rather than impressing with scale, Sainte-Chapelle turns its efforts toward piously luxuriant details. Louis's influence is everywhere in the cathedral; he even had his own private entryway to the chapel so he wouldn't have to mix and mingle with the rabble. As the first staunchly Catholic French king, he was understandably enthusiastic about the then-new royal symbol of purity, the fleur-de-lis: He had the icon painted all over the place, along with the symbol of his mother, a golden church. *Inside Palais de Justice, 4 blvd. du Palais, 1er, tel. 01–53–73–78–50. Métro: Cité. Admission: 26F, 21F students, 45F joint ticket with the Conciergerie (see museums, above). Open Apr.–Sept., daily 9:30–6:30; Oct.–Mar., daily 10–5.*

Museums

Paris's museums range from the ostentatiously grand to the delightfully obscure—the French seem hell-bent on documenting everything any of its citizens have ever done. In addition to the three biggies covered above in Major Attractions—the Louvre, the Musée d'Orsay, and the Pompidou—we've listed all sorts of smaller spaces that may fit your various moods, including science and history museums, photography galleries, and world culture centers. The city also has many galleries that have no permanent collections but host traveling shows; check *Pariscope* (*see* English-Language Books and Newspapers, in Chapter 1) and posted flyers to find out what's in town.

Paris museums are not cheap, and youth/student discounts are iffy—sometimes they're given only to those 25 and under, sometimes only to students, sometimes only to students 25 years and under. Other discounts are available to the elderly, children, and the unemployed (though you must be a citizen of a European Union nation to get this one); in national museums, visitors in wheelchairs and their attendants also receive reduced rates. All kinds of other special stipulations exist, but no matter what the rule is, a reduction may depend largely on the mood of the person in the ticket booth—bring all kinds of ID and hope for the best.

If you want to pop into a museum just before closing, keep in mind that ticket offices close 15–45 minutes before the posted closing time of the galleries.

The association InterMusée spends a large sum of money advertising its **Carte Musées et Monuments,** valid for entry to most of Paris's museums. The pass—valid for either one day (70F), three days (140F), or five days (200F) and sold at participating museums and most major Métro stations—is only a deal if you both (a) don't qualify for any discount admissions; and (b) have the stamina of a marathon runner. Remember that at the Louvre 40F gets you 6,000 years of art; if you also plan to go to the d'Orsay (36F) and then pay your respects to the Parisian dead at the Catacombs (27F) all in the same day, this pass might be for you.

ART MUSEUMS

ESPACE MONTMARTRE–DALÍ Boasting more than 300 works by the self-proclaimed master of surrealism, **Salvador Dalí** (1904–89), this museum isn't quite as exciting as the Dalí museum in Spain. Nonetheless the dark, sunken chambers of Espace Montmartre still contain an impressive display of the artist's dream landscapes, psychedelic sculptures, and illustrations of *Alice in Wonderland.* But be warned: Most of the works in the collection are lithographs and castings produced in the winter of the artist's life, when a sick and senile Dalí was signing his name to prints and sculptures that were mainly reproductions of his earlier works, and the museum uses somewhat tacky New Age music and light effects to display them. *11 rue Poulbot, 18e, tel. 01–42–64–40–10. Métro: Pigalle, Anvers, or Abbesses. Admission: 35F, 25F students. Open July–Aug., daily 10–7; Sept.–June, daily 10–6.*

FONDATION CARTIER The Fondation Cartier has a reputation as one of the corporate world's greatest patrons of contemporary art. Designed by Jean Nouvel (*see box, below*), the building is one of Paris's most stunning, a mélange of vast glass panes, complicated steel structures, and exposed mechanical work, all done so damn elegantly that you can't accuse the building of being some cheesy, high-tech cliché. While the watch-and-jewelry empire executives work upstairs in the Cartier headquarters, the basement and ground floor of this ultramodernist building hold galleries and museum staff who act like they genuinely want to help you enjoy yourself. Exhibitions are always changing and manage to be extremely sophisticated in such a relatively small space—it *is* Cartier, after all. The best way to experience both the art and Nouvel's building is to come on Thursday nights, when the series "**Les Soirées Nomades**" (Evenings of the Nomad) offers dance, performance art, or live music around and about the art, except for in July and August. *261 blvd. Raspail, 14e, tel. 01–42–18–56–50 or 01–42–18–56–51. Métro: Denfert-Rochereau. Admission: 30F, 20F under age 26; "Les Soirées*

Jean Nouvel

Jean Nouvel, an emerging visionary of Parisian architecture, has designed two of the city's most intensely scrutinized buildings: the Institut du Monde Arabe and the Fondation Cartier. His philosophical obsession with "transparency" inspired the light-manipulating wall at the institute and the mobile 8-by-3-meter (26-by-10-foot) glass panels at Cartier. Critics have termed his style "façadism," but Nouvel is quick to differentiate between his innovative use of glass—panes that fog, LCD-tinted panels, thermal plates—from run-of-the-mill corporate architecture. His latest project is the proposed Tour Sans Fin, a 400-meter (1,312-foot) cylindrical tower at La Défense, to be enclosed entirely by, of course, glass.

Nomades" included in admission. Open Tues.–Sun. noon–8 (Thurs. until 10). Wheelchair access/barrier free.

GRAND PALAIS AND PETIT PALAIS Intended as temporary additions to the Parisian landscape for the 1900 Exposition Universelle, these domed extravaganzas dodged the wrecking ball to become full-time tourist attractions. The Grand Palais became a salon space and the site of ballooning exhibitions, at which well-heeled ladies and gentlemen would gather under the glass-domed ceilings, heads tilted toward the puffed-up names of Michelin and Goodyear, and marvel at the future of travel. In more recent years, big-time art exhibitions have been filling the modest halls of the building's wings. *3 av. du Général Eisenhower, 8e, tel. 01–44–13–17–17. Métro: Champs-Elysées–Clemenceau. Admission 25F–40F, depending on exhibit. Open Thurs.–Mon. 10–8, Wed. 10–10. Wheelchair access (entrance to left of main entrance); rest rooms not accessible.*

The Petit Palais, across the street, displays works in rich, vaulted halls that ironically are grander than those of the Grand Palais. In addition to temporary exhibits, there's a permanent collection featuring 17th-century Flemish works and particularly strong coverage of 19th-century French painters, including large and plentiful works by Courbet—his risqué 1866 *Le Sommeil,* of two naked women napping together, is especially popular—and a healthy handful of impressionist-era pieces, such as Cézanne's *Les Baigneuses* (1880). There are also large cases of turn-of-the-century jewelry, including many art nouveau pieces. *Av. Winston-Churchill, 8e, tel. 01–42–65–12–73. Métro: Champs-Elysées–Clemenceau. Admission: 27F, 15F students; temporary exhibits 25F–45F extra. Open Tues.–Sun. 10–5:40.*

JEU DE PAUME Named for the indoor tennis court that once stood in the royal Jardin des Tuileries, the Jeu de Paume held much of the national impressionist collection until the Musée d'Orsay laid claim to all things 19th century. The building stood neglected until a recent renovation created one of Paris's most inviting spaces. Exhibitions feature modern and contemporary masters, while the cinema shows related documentaries (free with gallery admission). There's a small, loungeable café and a bookstore with a strong collection of French- and English-language art criticism and catalogues. Admission prices and hours may vary with exhibits. *Pl. de la Concorde, 1er, tel. 01–47–60–69–69. Métro: Concorde. Admission: 35F, 25F students. Open Tues. noon–9:30, Wed.–Fri. noon–7, weekends 10–7. Wheelchair access.*

MUSEE D'ART MODERNE DE LA VILLE DE PARIS Even though it was founded at the turn of the century, this museum has had a difficult time convincing the world that there is another major venue for modern art in Paris besides the Pompidou (*see* Major Attractions, *above*). Many of the 30,000 works forming the permanent collection were donated by artists such as Henri Matisse and Robert Motherwell, but there is still unfortunately a dearth of high-profile pieces. Wisely deciding not to compete with the Goliath across town, the Musée d'Art Moderne focuses on the contemporary works of more controversial artists, although not ignoring those of historical importance. The museum also hosts fantastic temporary exhibits (German expressionists seem to be frequent guests), as well as occasional concerts.

The museum has been housed in the east wing of the Palais de Tokyo since 1967. Originally constructed for the Exposition Universelle in 1937, this building stands where Louis XII's royal rug factory once operated. The columned modern terrace offers a great view of the Eiffel Tower and is popular with skate rats, whose racket echoes off the building's walls. On the way to the top floor it is impossible not to notice Raoul Dufy's (1877–1953) *Fée Electricité,* in which 600 square meters (720 square yards) of bright colors fervently depict the harnessing of electricity by humanity. At its creation, this was the largest displayed painting known in the world. Off the terrace on the ground floor are a café and a bookstore that stocks a diverse selection of academic books and journals in English and French. *11 av. du Président-Wilson, 16e, tel. 01–47–23–61–27. Métro: Iéna. Admission: permanent collection 27F, 19F age 25 and under; temporary exhibitions 30F–40F, 19F–30F age 25 and under. Open Tues.–Fri. 10–5:30, weekends 10–6:45.*

MUSEE DE CLUNY This museum began in 1832 as the private—most people thought quirky—medieval art collection of Alexandre du Sommerand in an *hôtel particulier* (mansion) built over and around the ruins of some Roman baths. The state purchased the hôtel and collection soon after and turned the place into a full-time museum. Today the collection features medieval stained glass, furniture, jewelry, carvings, music manuscripts, and some exquisite tapestries. One of the finest tapestry series—found half-eaten by rats before being brought here—is The Lady and the Unicorn, comprising six panels in which a refined lady demonstrates the five senses to a unicorn. The museum recently acquired a set of sculpted heads of the kings of Judea that once looked out from the facade of the Cathédrale de Notre-Dame (*see* Major Attractions, *above*); thought to have been lost during the Revolution, they were rediscovered in a bank vault in 1977. *6 pl. du Paul-Painlevé, 5e, tel. 01–43–25–62–00. Métro: Cluny–La Sorbonne. Admission: 27F, 18F students and Sun. Open Wed.–Mon. 9:15–5:45.*

MUSEE DE L'ORANGERIE This small but rewarding collection of impressionist and post-impressionist paintings sits peacefully near the Jardin des Tuileries. Like the Musée Marmottan (*see above*), this museum is especially nice if you're in the mood for turn-of-the-century art but can't deal with the enormity of the Musée d'Orsay. Below generous rooms of Renoirs and displays of Cézanne, Manet, and Modigliani lies the museum's most popular room: a magical, watery oval space lined with Monet's huge water-lily paintings. Inspired by Monet's home at Giverny (*see* Chapter 7), the *Nymphéas* are perhaps the best-known of his "series" works—repeated studies of the effects of different lighting upon the same subject. After the 1918 armistice, Monet donated the *Nymphéas* to the state, though he requested they not be displayed until after his death. *Pl. de la Concorde, 1er, tel. 01–42–97–48–16. Métro: Concorde. Admission: 27F, 18F age 25 and under and Sun. Open Wed.–Mon. 9:45–5:45.*

MUSEE DES ARTS DECORATIFS You may finally realize just how big the Louvre palace is when you consider that this major collection of decorative arts occupies only a portion of one of its wings. Spread confusingly over the museum's four floors are chairs, vases, sword cases, and other necessities of life from the Middle Ages to the present. There are also many rooms that have been meticulously redecorated with furniture and other appropriate items: The game room has a backgammon board, the bathroom a soap dish, the salon an ostentatious number of chairs. The art-nouveau era is best represented. *107 rue de Rivoli, 1er, tel. 01–44–55–57–50. Métro: Palais Royal–Musée du Louvre. Admission: 25F, 16F under age 26. Open Wed.–Sat. 12:30–6, Sun. noon–6.*

MUSEE GUSTAVE MOREAU Symbolist painter Gustave Moreau (1826–98), the mentor of an entire generation of young artists and teacher of subsequent celebrities Matisse and Rouault, spent the final years of his life forming a little collection in his apartment. At his death, the collection became a public museum. Other than a few small works by Rembrandt and Poussin, the museum is devoted to the works of Moreau himself and can be a bit drab unless you appreciate the effect Moreau had on others. *14 rue de La Rochefoucauld, 9e, tel. 01–48–74–38–50. Métro: Trinité. Admission: 17F, 11F students and Sun. Open Thurs.–Sun. 10–12:45 and 2–5:15, Mon. and Wed. 11–5:15.*

MUSEE JACQUEMART ANDRE A breathtaking, newly restored hôtel houses the fantastic 19th-century collection of Edouard André and Nélie Jacquemart, a bourgeois couple whose hankering for Italian and Flemish art spurred the creation of one of the most beautiful private art collections in Paris. Highlights among the impressive Botticellis, Donatellos, Tintorettos, and Canalettos include Uccello's *Saint George Killing the Dragon*. The entrance fee includes an audio guide (in English and French) that explains the entire exhibit in detail. *158 blvd. Haussmann, 8e, tel. 01–42–89–04–91. Métro: St-Philippe du Route or Mirosmesnil. Admission: 45F, 35F students 25 and under. Open daily 10–6.*

MUSEE MARMOTTAN CLAUDE MONET A couple of years ago this museum tacked "Claude Monet" onto its official name—and justly so, as this may be the best collection of the artist's works anywhere. A sampling of works by fellow impressionists and portraitists like Louis Léopold Boilly fill out the areas of this airy hôtel particulier not claimed by Claude. Small displays include letters exchanged by impressionist painters Berthe Morisot and Mary Cassatt. While Monet shares the wall space of the bright upstairs rooms, his most spectacular display is down in the basement, where large, oval rooms enclose his dizzying masterpiece, the luminous, circular wall-painting *Nymphéas*. Among such well-known works as the series *Cathédrale à Rouen* and *Parlement à Londres*, you'll find *Impressions: Soleil Levant* (1873), now recognized as the first impressionist painting. Some of the rooms make you feel as if you're at an actual salon, with comfortable couches and grand windows overlooking the Jardin de Ranelagh on one side, the hôtel's private yard on the other. *2 rue Louis-Boilly, 16e, tel. 01-42-24-07-02. Métro: La Muette. Admission: 35F, 15F students 24 and under. Open Tues.-Sun. 10-5:30.*

MUSEE NATIONAL EUGENE DELACROIX This modest museum is housed in the last apartment Delacroix occupied before his death in 1863. Bits of Delacroix paraphernalia and furniture—a paint box here, a divan there—decorate the tiny complex of rooms, and prints and paintings cover the walls. Knowing that he painted in this space is, however, more exciting than the artwork itself. Through the back is his high-ceilinged, generously windowed studio, over-looking a quiet courtyard. *6 pl. de Furstenberg, 6e, tel. 01-43-54-04-87. Métro: St-Germain-des-Prés. Admission: 15F, 10F age 25 and under. Open Wed.-Mon. 10-5.*

MUSEE PICASSO When Spaniard Pablo Picasso's family couldn't come up with enough cash to settle the taxes on his estate, they decided to donate a large number of his works to the French government. Now all nestled within a beautiful 17th-century Hôtel Salé in the heart of the Marais district, the Musée Picasso is one of the most popular museums in Paris. Rooms in the museum are arranged chronologically, and information in each (in English) tells about major events in the artist's life. Although he was known as the greatest artist of his generation, Picasso was also an arrogant, misogynistic cad who made a habit of seducing other artists' wives. When his contemporaries (including Georges Braque and Guillaume Apollinaire) were shipped off to World War I, Picasso used his Spanish passport to stay safely in Paris. His loutish behavior, however, could not detract from his artistic contributions. Taking their cues from the field of physics, Picasso, Braque, and Juan Gris reformulated the way three-dimen-

Museums Strange and Obscure . . .

- *Musée de Cire Grévin. Since 1882, this wax museum has been covering all the big names from French history and American pop culture. Your overpriced ticket also grants you a magic show and entrance into the 1900 Palace of Illusion. 10 blvd. Montmartre, 9e, tel. 01-42-46-13-26. Métro: Rue Montmartre. Admission: 50F. Open daily 1-7.*

- *Musée de la Contrefaçon. The Paris Manufacturers' Union, egged on by such power-ful companies as Cartier, opened this tiny museum to document the problem of prod-uct counterfeiting. Compare fake perfume bottles, liquor labels, and designer shirts to the real thing. 15 rue de la Faisanderie, 16e, tel. 01-45-01-51-11. Métro: Porte Dauphine. Admission free. Open Mon. and Wed. 2-4:30, Fri. 9:30-noon.*

- *Musée de la Curiosité. Built in the underground caves of the former residence of the Marquis de Sade, this museum has rotating exhibits and all the trademark funhouse mirrors, optical illusions, historical artifacts, and variations on the magic wand. A tal-ented magician performs card tricks between more formal shows, given every half hour or so. 11 rue St-Paul, 4e, tel. 01-42-72-13-26. Métro: St-Paul. Admission: 45F, 30F children. Open Wed. and weekends 2-7 PM.*

- *Musée du Vin: All you need to know about French winemaking, exposed in a musty 14th-century cellar. 5 rue des Eaux, 16e, tel. 01-45-25-63-26. Métro: Passy. Admission: 35F, glass of wine included. Open daily 10-6.*

sional space was represented on canvas. Though best known as a painter, Picasso was also an innovative sculptor, constructing cubist guitars and using a toy Renault for the snout of a bronze baboon. This collection represents a sampling of every stage of Picasso's work, but there are no blue-chip pieces to be found here—those are all in New York. The covered garden out back makes a pleasant setting for a summertime café and shades many of his sculptures. *5 rue Thorigny, 3e, tel. 01–42–71–25–21. Métro: Chemin Vert or St-Paul. Admission: 26F, 17F ages 17–25 and Wed. Open Wed.–Mon. 9:30–6.*

MUSEE RODIN The Musée Rodin is one of the most beautiful museums in Paris. The undisputed master of 19th-century French sculpture left his house, the early 18th-century Hôtel Biron, and all the works in it to the state when he died. The mansion, with the second-largest garden in the neighborhood (after the prime minister's), is as much a part of the museum as the art. In addition to the beautiful garden (5F), you can also see a pavilion exhibiting temporary shows. The main building houses Rodin's personal collection of impressionist and post-impressionist paintings. The life of Auguste Rodin (1840–1917) was one riddled with intrigue, deception, and controversy. When he died at the height of World War I, his wake drew the largest nonmilitary crowd of the time (26,000). While living, however, Rodin was simultaneously loathed and praised by the French, who both appreciated his genius and despised his vision. His career took off in 1876 with *L'Age d'Airain* (The Age of Bronze), a sculpture—in bronze, of course—inspired by a pilgrimage to Italy and the sculptures of Michelangelo. Because the work was so realistic, some critics accused Rodin of having stuck a live boy in plaster, while others blasted him for what was seen as a sloppy sculpting and casting technique. His seeming messiness, though, was intentional; Rodin sought to capture the sculpting process through the imprints of fingers, rags used to keep the clay moist, and tools he left on his works.

Four years later, Rodin was commissioned to create the doors for the newly proposed Musée des Arts Décoratifs. He set out to sculpt a pair of monumental bronze doors in the tradition of Italian Renaissance churches, calling his proposal *The Gate of Hell* (*La Porte de l'Enfer*). The *Gate,* a visual representation of stories from Dante's *Divine Comedy,* became his obsession: He spent the last 37 years of his life working on it. *The Gate* was never completed, and no metal casts of the masterpiece were made during Rodin's life—the museum's bronze out in the garden is posthumous.

Possibly Rodin's most celebrated work is his 1880 piece *The Thinker* (Le Penseur), the muscular manly man caught in a moment of deep thought and flex. The version here in the garden is the original—the city of Paris, its intended owner, refused to accept it. Before installing the permanent bronze statue on the steps of the Panthéon, Rodin set up a full-scale plaster cast. Its physicality horrified the public; crowds gathered around the statue, debates ensued, and Rodin was ridiculed in the press. A man who was later tried and found criminally insane hacked away at some of the plaster cast with a hatchet, giving the city a convenient excuse to refuse the statue.

Rodin may have hogged the limelight, but his museum allows some space to works by **Camille Claudel** (1864–1943). Rodin's mistress, Claudel was a remarkable sculptor in her own right. (Look at her *L'Age Mûr,* done in 1900, for the dynamics: The young girl is Claudel, the man Rodin, and the old woman his wife.) Shunning the monumental except for her *Perseus and the Medusa* (Medusa's face was a self-portrait), Claudel experimented with smaller figures in well-defined, almost architectural settings. Her torturous relationship with Rodin drove her out of his studio—as though life weren't difficult enough for female sculptors doing nonconventional work in the late 19th century. In 1913 her family committed her to an asylum on the Ile St-Louis (*see* Neighborhoods, *below*), where she remained, barred from any artistic activities, until her death in 1943. Had Claudel's talent not been straitjacketed, her work might have its own space today instead of being squished in among Rodin's. Her work is definitely a relief for anyone annoyed by the megalomaniacal masculinity of some of Rodin's pieces. *77 rue de Varenne, 7e, tel. 01–47–05–01–34. Métro: Varenne. Admission: 28F, 18F students 25 and under and Sun, 5F gardens only. Open Tues.–Sun. 9:30–5:45.*

MUSEE ZADKINE The former studio of Ukrainian-born Ossip Zadkine (1890–1967) has become, in the 14 years since his widow bequeathed it to Paris, one of the nicest museums to visit in the city—regardless of what you think of Zadkine's work. Dozens of sculptures from his

Parisian career (he moved to the city in 1909) pack the few small but bright rooms; feeling the sculptures is particularly tempting, since Zadkine worked with natural and treated woods, brass, and stone, giving the materials varying levels of shine. Only the sight-impaired can touch, though. No great innovator, Zadkine was instead a skilled imitator of the styles that passed through Paris during the early to mid-20th century—cubism, futurism, primitivism, you name it. Check out the free sculpture garden in front. *100 bis rue d'Assas, 6e, tel. 01–43–26–91–90. Métro: Vavin. Admission: 18F, 9F students 25 and under. Open Tues.–Sun. 10–5:30.*

PHOTOGRAPHY

CENTRE NATIONAL DE LA PHOTOGRAPHIE Photographs previously housed in the Palais de Tokyo have been relocated to the ground floor of the expansive Hôtel Salomon de Rothschild, home of the Centre National de la Photographie. Big-name shows focusing on a single genre or artist dominate the main gallery, though peripheral rooms may display works from the permanent collection. Institutes related to photography are on the upper floors. The sizable grounds are well tended but off-limits, affording a strictly visual appreciation of nature. Balzac died in 1850 in a house that once stood in the west garden. *11 rue Berryer, 8e, tel. 01–53–76–12–31. Métro: George V. Admission: 30F, 15F students 26 and under (may vary by exhibition). Open Wed.–Mon. noon–7. Closed Aug.*

ESPACE PHOTO DE PARIS Despite its location in a mall, this tiny gallery is able to stage consistently great photography exhibits, thanks to an association with the cultural muscle of the Mairie de Paris. *4–8 Grande Galerie des Halles, 1er, tel. 01–40–26–87–12. Métro: Les Halles. Admission: 10F. Open Tues.–Fri. 1–6, weekends 1–7.*

FNAC GALERIE PHOTO FNAC Forum Les Halles hosts some wonderful free photography shows, as do the lesser branches in Montparnasse and in the 17th arrondissement on avenue Wagram, close to the Arc de Triomphe. Monthly brochures provide details on the nature of the exhibitions. *1 rue Pierre-Lescot, 1er, tel. 01–40–41–40–00. Métro: Châtelet–Les Halles. Open Mon.–Sat. 10–7:30.*

MAISON EUROPEENNE DE LA PHOTOGRAPHIE This beautiful museum, unveiled in 1996, is a conversion of two old hôtels particuliers, complete with creaky floorboards, a cave to house experimental projects, and a café. Despite its name, the museum has an impressive

Free Art

To get a feel for Paris's current art scene, cruise through the multitude of galleries that display artwork. All galleries are open Tuesday–Saturday 2–7. Anyone can enter for free, although looking rich and artsy helps deter snobby looks from gallery owners.

In the Bastille area, check out the huge, funky sculptures at Durand Desert (28 rue du Lappe, tel. 01–48–06–92–93), or the fantastic photography at Galerie Carlihan (37 rue de Charonne, tel. 01–47–00–79–28). In the Marais, Farideh Cadot (77 rue des Archives, tel. 01–42–78–08–36) hosts avant-garde work, while rue Quincampoix is a good place to look for abstract art. On the Left Bank, rue de Seine, rue Daguerre, and rue du Bac all have lots of small galleries. Near the Montmartre cemetery, the Hôpital Ephémère (2 rue Carpeaux, tel. 01–46–27–82–82) is a collection of artist studios, a theater, and an auditorium. The place has a funky, offbeat image. Another collection of artist workspaces, the Quai de la Gare (91 quai de la Gare, tel. 01–45–85–91–91), hosts frequent "portes ouvertes" (open doors) where you can wander freely among the 250 studios.

selection of American works as well, with exhilarating examples of recent fashion photography and photojournalism. Check out the rare documentaries shown in the "videotheque," or find out about lectures on historical and contemporary issues in photography. Although entirely wheelchair-accessible, the museum is hardly barrier-free, requiring an unwieldy navigation of elevators to get to different parts of the same floor. *5 rue de Fourcy, 4e, tel. 01–44–78–75–00. Métro: St-Paul. Open Wed.–Sun. 11–8. Admission: 30F, 15F 25 and under, free Wed. after 5 PM.*

MISSION DU PATRIMOINE PHOTOGRAPHIQUE Set up by the Ministry of Culture, this small photography gallery, with continually changing exhibits, focuses frequently on avant-garde and contemporary work. Housed in a corner of the hôtel particulier Sully, the gallery overlooks a beautiful courtyard leading into place des Vosges. *62 rue St-Antoine, 4e, tel. 01–42–74–30–60. Métro: St-Paul. Admission: 25F, 10F students and age 24 and under. Open Wed.–Mon. 1–6.*

FRENCH HISTORY AND CULTURE

LA CONCIERGERIE This complex of towers and halls served as the royal palace until 1358, when a young Charles V sought to place a safe distance between himself and his potentially revolutionary masses by building the Louvre across the Seine. Since the 14th century, the Conciergerie (named after the official who administered the castle) has served as a tribunal hall and prison, but its most macabre period came in the 18th century when the Revolutionary court mercilessly issued death proclamations—2,780 to be exact—from its halls. While much of the nobility passed through these cells, the most famous resident was Marie Antoinette, who spent her final days here before being hauled off on a garbage cart to be guillotined. The court disbanded after the execution of Robespierre, who became the victim of the Terror he had himself initiated. Now the Conciergerie is merely the basement of the Palais de Justice, though a motley collection of empty halls and dusty approximations of cells brings in tourists. *1 quai de l'Horloge, 1er, tel. 01–43–54–30–06. Métro: Pont Neuf or Cité. Admission: 28F, 18F age 25 and under. Open Apr.–Sept., daily 9:30–6:30; Oct.–Mar., daily 10–5.*

MAISON DE VICTOR HUGO The former home of France's literary hero has become a two-story museum in his honor. What is interesting here is the re-created rooms on the second floor (where Hugo's apartment was) and the artwork on the first, including some rather bizarre watercolors by Hugo and illustrations for his writings by other painters; Bayard's rendition of Cosette from Les Misérables (now a famous T-shirt) can be found here. The rooms upstairs represent Hugo's living style in several of his many homes; the central room of the floor, for instance, is decorated with Chinese-theme panels and woodworks he created for his mistress's home outside town. *6 pl. des Vosges, 4e, tel. 01–42–72–10–16. Métro: Chemin Vert or St-Paul. Admission: 18F, 9F age 24 and under. Open Tues.–Sun. 10–5:40.*

The Ecole Vétérinaire d'Alfort, in Maisons-Alfort just south of the Bois de Vincennes, houses the gruesome yet fascinating works of anatomist Honoré Fragonard (1732–99). Among the human and animal bodies flayed to display veins and muscles are preserved peculiarities like a 10-legged sheep. Its sign advises: "If you enjoy the museum, why not send us your friends—if not your enemies."

MUSEE CARNAVALET It takes two hôtels particuliers in the Marais—the Carnavalet and Le Peletier de St-Fargeau—to house this worthwhile collection paying homage to Parisian history. Basically, the Carnavalet (through which you enter) covers ancient Paris through the reign of Louis XVI, the Peletier the Revolution through the 20th century—though you could go crazy trying to move through the poorly marked rooms chronologically. In the courtyard off rue de Sévigné stands the last remaining bronze statue of a Louis: Louis XIV, whose representation by Antoine Coysevox was saved from Revolutionary meltdown only by oversight—the people simply didn't notice it in the too-obvious Hôtel de Ville. Back inside, other treasures include Jean-Jacques Rousseau's inkwell and blackened blotting sponge, keys to the Bastille, and Napoléon I's death mask. Most entertaining, however, are the re-created rooms, particularly Marcel Proust's bedroom, the turn-of-the-century Fouquet jewelry shop, and a room from the art nouveau Café de

75

Paris. *23 rue de Sévigné, 3e, tel. 01-42-72-21-13. Métro: St-Paul. Admission: 27F, 15F students. Open Tues.-Sun. 10-5:40.*

MUSEE DE LA MODE ET DU COSTUME In the 1920s, Paris decided it needed a fashion museum, and after a couple of trial runs at World Expos, this is where it wound up. The strictly temporary exhibits, usually centering on fashionable aspects of Paris's past, feature hundreds of items of clothing and accessories. Admission is 35F-40F, with a reduction of about 10F for anyone 25 and under. *10 av. Pierre-1er-de-Serbie, 16e, tel. 01-47-20-85-23. Métro: Iéna. Open Tues.-Sun. 10-5:40.*

MUSEE DE LA POSTE This whole museum is dedicated to stamps and the history of written communication, including the balloon used to get mail out of Paris during the 1870 Prussian siege. *34 blvd. de Vaugirard, 15e, tel. 01-42-79-23-45. Métro: Montparnasse. Admission: 25F, 13F students. Open Mon.-Sat. 10-6.*

MUSEE DE LA VIE ROMANTIQUE See the memorabilia of woman writer, bohemian, and cross-dresser George Sand (1804-76) in the onetime studio of painter Ary Scheffer, where Chopin, Delacroix, Liszt, and other greats would gather in the evenings to swap artistic views and perform for one another. The museum occasionally hosts temporary exhibits, such as "The life and work of Ary Scheffer." On sunny days, don't miss the opportunity to picnic on the sunny patio. *16 rue Chaptal, 9e, tel. 01-48-74-95-38. Métro: Pigalle or Saint Georges. Admission: 27F, 19F students and age 24 and under. Open Tues.-Sun. 10-5:40.*

MUSEE DE MONTMARTRE This space houses a fascinating but small collection of photos and changing exhibits on life in Montmartre, including displays about famous former inhabitants, drawings by Toulouse-Lautrec, and minor works by Modigliani, Vlaminck, Utrillo, and others. *12 rue Cortot, 18e, tel. 01-46-06-61-11. Métro: Lamarck-Caulaincourt. Admission: 25F, 20F students. Open Tues.-Sun. 11-6.*

MUSEE DES MONUMENTS FRANCAIS Architects will appreciate this collection, which displays models of all of Paris's great monuments in one small space. Hundreds of reproductions of portals, statues, and other pieces—many of them full size—represent all the blockbuster structures in France from Chartres to Mont-St-Michel. *1 pl. du Trocadéro, 16e, tel. 01-44-05-39-10. Métro: Trocadéro. Admission: 21F, 14F age 25 and under. Open Wed.-Mon. 10-6. Wheelchair access.*

PAVILLON DE L'ARSENAL Home to the Centre d'Urbanisme et d'Architecture de la Ville de Paris, this spacious late 19th-century arsenal is devoted entirely to documenting and exploring the buildings of Paris. Dominating the ground floor is the Grande Modèle, a 40-square-meter (432-square-foot) model of Paris, complete with interactive video screens—you can direct a CD-ROM terminal to display any of 30,000 images of the city and its buildings. Temporary exhibits take up the ground floor and upper loft, and a library (*see* Resident Resources, in Chapter 1) provides art and architecture periodicals and books, plus 70,000 photographs of Paris. *21 blvd. Morland, 4e, tel. 01-42-76-33-97. Métro: Sully-Morland. Admission free. Open Tues.-Sat. 10:30-6:30, Sun. 11-7.*

WORLD HISTORY AND CULTURE

MUSEE DES ARTS AFRICAINS ET OCEANIENS This building, one of the first made with reinforced concrete, was designed for the 1931 Exposition Coloniale, held in the Bois de Vincennes. The museum's collection, first named Museum of the Colonies, was updated and renamed Museum of France Overseas after World War II—the "Virtues of French Colonization" display, however, still held a prominent position. In 1960 the museum settled upon its current name under the advice of France's Ministry of Cultural Affairs.

Today, the slightly rundown museum is ignored by most visitors to Paris, and its glorious Expo days are definitely over. The displays, however, are very complete. They're divided by region and well explained, if you read French. The ground floor houses displays on South Pacific cultures—including a generous selection from New Guinea—and temporary exhibits, usually featuring contemporary African artists. The first floor turns to central African cultures, looking at great kingdoms in the Congo and Benin. The importance of funerary rites in this region, particularly among the Ashanti, is evidenced in the death masks and other funerary objects on display. The top floor is dedicated to the heavily colonized countries of the Maghreb (Algeria, Tunisia, and Morocco); items from this area include some impressive Algerian jewelry, which will instill new respect in you for your mostly intact earlobes and neck. Finally, in the basement lurk crocodiles of the Nile, in a ditch that curators have tried their damnedest to transform into a natural habitat. The calm aquarium surrounding the crocs is home to a second ditch (filled with turtles) and some rather beautiful sea creatures. A small library, open weekdays 10–6, is on the east side of the building. *293 av. Daumesnil, 12e, tel. 01–44–74–84–80. Métro: Porte Dorée. Admission: 28F, 18F age 25 and under. Open Mon. and Wed.–Fri. 10–5:30, weekends 10–6.*

MUSEE NATIONAL DES ARTS ASIATIQUES–GUIMET This enormous collection of religious and secular artwork from China, Japan, India, Indochina, Indonesia, and central Asia spans more than 3,000 years of history. As specified in the late 19th century by founder Emile Guimet, the collection is divided by country; info centers in each area explain individual histories and religious developments but only in French. Highlights include seductive statues of Hindu gods and goddesses and stunning finds from the Chinese Silk Route, including painted silk banners. Don't miss the annex at 19 avenue d'Iéna (same ticket), which thoroughly explores the Buddha in images from China and Japan. A comfortable library upstairs in the main building houses more than 10,000 works on Asian arts and religions and is open to the public Monday and Wednesday–Friday from 10 to 5. *6 pl. d'Iéna, 16e, tel. 01–47–23–61–65. Métro: Iéna. Admission: 35F, 26F age 25 and under and Sun. Open Wed.–Sun. 9:45–5:45.*

NATURAL HISTORY

MUSEE DE L'HOMME Visiting this anthropology museum in the Palais de Chaillot is like taking a trip around the world and through about three million years of history. Permanent exhibits show clothing, musical instruments, and other artifacts of the major cultures of the world (African, Asian, Middle

The Musée de l'Homme's prize piece is Descartes's skull, the solution to the mind-body problem preserved forever in a little glass case.

Eastern, European, Native North and South American, indigenous Australian, South Pacific, Arctic) and fossil displays from prehistory to the present. Excellent temporary exhibits highlight topics like prehistoric funeral rites and traditions of Turkish households. *Pl. du Trocadéro, 16e, tel. 01–44–05–72–72. Métro: Trocadéro. Admission: 30F, 20F students. Open Wed.–Mon. 9:45–5:15.*

MUSEE NATIONAL D'HISTOIRE NATURELLE This natural history museum is popular with children and includes a grand interior hall filled with stuffed bears, tigers, elephants, and whales. TV screens in front of comfortable leather chairs document the fascinating art of taxidermy. Thursday nights the museum hosts a debate, lecture, or film on some aspect of natural history, included in the admission price. *Jardin des Plantes, 36 rue Geoffroy St-Hilaire, 5e, tel. 01–40–79–39–39. Métro: Gare d'Austerlitz or Censier-Daubenton. Admission: 40F, 30F age 25 and under. Open Wed.–Mon. 10–6 (Thurs. until 10). Wheelchair access/barrier free.*

SCIENCE AND TECHNOLOGY

CITE DES SCIENCES ET DE L'INDUSTRIE This museum is a mammoth orgy of everything industrial and scientific, inviting you to interact with its many exhibits. Give yourself at least half a day to see everything. The structure is indeed the size of a small city—it's three times the size of the Pompidou—and was built in 1986 on land that once housed Paris's slaughterhouses. Now the area is all glass and stainless steel, criss-crossed by bridges and suspended walkways. The permanent exhibit is dedicated to scientific exploration, with multilingual explanations. Hands-on experiments include futuristic musical instruments, environmental manipulation, a simulated space voyage, and cutting-edge photography. The

Sticking out of the ground near the Cité des Sciences et de l'Industrie are bits of a gargantuan bicycle by Claes Oldenberg. The sculpture is popular with children, who fortunately don't know the difference between a slide and "art."

second-floor planetarium is well worth a stop. The magnificent steel sphere in front of the exhibit building is the Géode cinema (tel. 01–40–05–80–00), which has the largest projection screen in existence that completely surrounds the spectators; tickets for films (usually nature flicks) are sold separately for 45F, 37F for those 25 and under. The Cité backs up to the equally playful Parc de la Villette (*see* Parks and Gardens, *below*). *Parc de la Villette, 30 av. Corentin-Cariou, 19e, tel. 01–40–05–70–00. Métro: Porte de la Villette. Admission: 45F, 35F age 25 and under. Open Tues.–Sun. 10–6. Wheelchair access.*

PALAIS DE LA DECOUVERTE The worst thing about this museum, in a back wing of the Grand Palais (*see above*), is the preponderance of grammar-school student groups. The best thing is its quality displays on all branches of science, from the solar system to the human brain. The exhibits are rarely hands-on, but they are informative and eye-catching. Planetarium shows cost an extra 40F (18F students). *Av. Franklin D. Roosevelt, 8e, tel. 01–40–74–80–00. Admission: 25F, 18F students. Open Tues.–Sat. 9:30–6, Sun. 10–7.*

Houses of Worship

Unfortunately, many of these important houses of worship in Paris tend to be dwarfed by the existence of big timers like the Cathédrale de Notre-Dame and the Basilique Sacré-Cœur (*see* Major Attractions, *above*). Their isolation from the Kodak crowd and their own historical importance, however, make them more pleasant places to reflect, admire the architecture, or even lounge around naked sipping tea (although only in the Mosquée, and only in their Turkish baths, at that). Many of them offer free concerts; check *Pariscope* for listings.

BASILIQUE DE ST-DENIS

The first major Gothic building built anywhere in the world, the Basilique de St-Denis sits in the square of a villagelike suburb to the north of Paris. The place achieved Christian sanctity somewhere between the 3rd and 6th centuries, when the just-decapitated St-Denis wandered head-in-hand from Montmartre with a choir of angels before keeling over on the hill. In the 12th century, Abbot Suger decided to build a church on the site according to his notion that God equaled light, and that daring expanses of glass allowing light into a cathedral would bring worshipers closer to the divine. The resulting cathedral—with loads of stained glass, high-pointed arches, and a rose window with the signs of the zodiac—would set the style for French cathedrals over the next four centuries.

Legend has it that at the foot of the Montmarte hill Paris's first bishop, St-Denis, had his head lopped off by angry Romans in AD 250. Not one to give up without a few dramatics, St-Denis picked up his head and made his way to the top of the hill before calling it quits at the site where the Basilique de St-Denis now looms.

The 27F admission (18F students) to the choir, ambulatory, and crypt allows access to 15 centuries of French royalty, including peeks at their mismatched bones and a delightful cabinet of embalmed hearts—including one encased in a glass bulb. All of your favorites are here, including Catherine de Médicis (depicted in one statue conspicuously young, dead, and naked), Marie Antoinette (gently grazing her right nipple for all eternity), and Louis XIV (buried under a modest black stone). While checking out the corpses, note the foundations of previous crypts; the site has been used as a necropolis since Roman times. *Tel. 01–48–20–02–47. Métro: St-Denis–Basilique, north of 18e. Crypt open Mon.–Sat. 10–5:30 in winter, 10–6:30 in summer, Sun. noon–5:30 in winter, noon-6:30 in summer. Sun. mass at 7:30, 8:30, and 10 AM.*

EGLISE DE LA MADELEINE

Under sporadic construction for 80 years, the Eglise de la Madeleine finally opened its huge bronze doors in 1842, becoming one of the largest French neoclassical buildings. The church stands alone in the center of a busy thoroughfare as a proudly inflated, though unfaithful, version of the classic Greek temple. The loose interpretation was intentional: The overproportioned porticoes, the interior barrel vaults-cum-domes, and the opulent versions of the Ionic and Corinthian orders were meant to be Parisian one-uppings of anything Athens had to offer. Changing political moods continued to alter the building's purpose—a Greek basilica one day, a temple to Napoléon's glory another, a National Assembly hall the next. The building suffered from all these vacillations, as designers razed foundations and eliminated details; much of the church's gloominess results from one architect filling in the stained-glass windows of another. Nowadays the opulent interior witnesses lots of expensive concerts, as well as daily masses. And if sitting in the cool interior of a Catholic church is not enough to make you reflect upon your sins, try viewing the huge fresco of the Last Judgment above you.

A world away from the scale and politics of the church proper is the **crypt** (admission free), in whose intimate chapel weekday masses (7:30 and 8 AM) are held. The crypt is accessible from either the nave of the church or the northwest side of place de la Madeleine. *Pl. de la Madeleine, 8e, tel. 01–42–65–52–17. Métro: Madeleine. Open daily 8–7. Sun. mass at 8, 9, 10 (choral mass), and 11 AM, 12:30 and 6 PM.*

EGLISE ST-ETIENNE-DU-MONT

Tucked away behind the grandiose Panthéon, the chapel of St-Etienne, begun in the 13th century, is home to the remains of Ste-Geneviève, the patron saint of Paris. Recent restorations have left the place clean, luminous, and one of Paris's best churches to visit. The interior features subtly creative interpretations of various forms of the Gothic style: Arches blend into the nave's columns without capitals, and a double-spiral staircase ascends the only remaining rood screen in Paris. A stroll behind the altar reveals plaques marking the remains of Ste-Geneviève, Pascal, Racine, and Marat. A faded red engraving at the portal end of the nave indicates where Monseigneur Sibour, a 19th-century archbishop of Paris, was stabbed to death by a mad priest. A perfect, cool place to rest after hiking around the Quartier Latin. *1 rue St-Etienne-du-Mont, 5e, tel. 01–43–54–11–79. Métro: Cardinal Lemoine. Sun. mass at 9 AM, 11 AM, and 6:45 PM.*

EGLISE ST-EUSTACHE

Right next door to the ultramodern shopping structure Les Halles, the Eglise St-Eustache presents a ponderous reminder that the Right Bank wasn't always all glitz and neon: The site was once the city's main marketplace and happenin' spot, which Emile Zola called "the belly of Paris." Over the years St-Eustache has seen lots of famous people: The composer Rameau was buried here; little Louis XIV took his first communion here; and both Richelieu and Molière were baptized here. Lesser notables have also left their mark: Much of the chapel and artwork were donated by the food guilds and merchants of the old Les Halles.

Few people realize that the huge head and hand in front of the Eglise St-Eustache are modeled after those of Henry Miller.

The structure was built over nearly a hundred years (1537–1632), at the tail end of the Gothic era, but it was during the 19th century, when Liszt directed his *Messe de Gran* here and Les Halles was still a real market, that the cathedral was at its height. These days, however, the bland reconstructed facade and gloomy interior are a letdown. The presence of a Rubens painting in one of the side chapels potentially salvages the church's appeal, except that no one is quite able to prove *which* Rubens did it. Do look for the painting *The Departure of the Fruits and Vegetables from the Heart of Paris* (1968), Raymond Mason's animated and very unchurchlike interpretation of the closing of Les Halles marketplace. *Pl. René-Cassin, 1er, tel. 01–42–36–31–05. Métro: Les Halles. Open daily 8:30–7 in winter, 8:30–8 in summer. Sun. mass at 8:30, 9:30, and 11 AM and 6 PM.*

EGLISE ST-GERMAIN-DES-PRES

The oldest church in Paris, St-Germain-des-Prés traces its roots to the 6th century, when then-archbishop Germanus (now known as St-Germain) built an altar to St-Symphorien on land left to the Benedictine monks by Childebert I. Though most of the present church dates from the 12th and 13th centuries, the purported remains of the original altar still stand near the south side of the entrance. The abbey became one of the great centers of learning in France, with its complex of buildings stretching from the Seine well into the present-day Quartier Latin. Here the Benedictines busied themselves completing the first French translation of the Bible in 1530 and amassing a library that would be appropriated during the Revolution to found the Bibliothèque Nationale (*see* Resident Resources, in Chapter 1). Almost all of the abbey buildings were torn down in the years after the Revolution, while a renovation in the 1950s removed the paint on the ceiling ribbing. Some of the remains of René Descartes (his heart, to be precise) have found peace in the seventh chapel. The church now holds a series of usually choral concerts, alas rarely free (80F–200F). *Pl. St-Germain-des-Prés, 6e, tel. 01–43–25–41–71; for concert info, tel. 01–44–62–70–90. Métro: St-Germain-des-Prés. Sun. mass at 9, 10, and 11:15 AM and 5 (in Spanish) and 7 PM.*

EGLISE ST-SEVERIN

This ivy-covered Gothic isle of calm dates from the 11th century, though most of what you see comes from 16th-century construction efforts and 18th- and 19th-century renovations. The double aisle of the ambulatory has a subterranean feel, with the ribbing of the vaults looking more as if it were holding up the earth than soaring toward the heavens, while the column behind the altar is twisted like a contorted tree trunk. The church is at its best at night, when the only lighting comes from the base of the columns and from behind the altar. Daylight, however, has the advantage of showing off the stained-glass windows (1966–1970) depicting the Seven Facets of the Sacrament. Occasional free concerts are performed on Sundays. *Cnr rues St-Jacques and St-Séverin, 5e, tel. 01–43–25–96–63. Métro: St-Michel. Sun. mass at 10 AM, noon, and 6 PM.*

EGLISE ST-SULPICE

Facing a tranquil place just off bustling boulevard St-Germain, St-Sulpice is an unusual departure from most Parisian churches: The double-story loggia with freestanding columns was the first example of French neoclassicism on a monumental scale. The facade was designed in 1736 (after most of the church had already been built) by painter Jean Nicolas Servandoni, who conceived the scheme with little regard for stodgy architectural tradition. Although not the most attractive church in Paris, there are faded Delacroix murals inside, as well as a regular stream of free concerts on the recently restored 18th-century organ. The fountain in the place matches the church in hulking scale, but both are softened by nighttime lighting. Star-watcher alert: Catherine Deneuve lives on the square. *Pl. St-Sulpice, 6e, tel. 01–46–33–21–78. Métro: St-Sulpice. Sun. mass at 7, 9, 10:15 AM, noon, and 6:45 PM. Half-hour organ concerts Sun. 11:30–noon; call for other scheduled concerts.*

Turkish Delights

For a decadent experience, spend an afternoon at the hammam (39 rue Geoffroy-St-Hilaire, 5e, tel. 01–43–31–38–20), the Turkish baths in la Mosquée. Lie around naked in one of the steam rooms or in the bathing area, listening to Arabic music and drinking mint tea (10F). All-out hedonists can get a rubdown for 50F. To maximize your sensual pleasure, bring some clay or something else to slather all over your body, a loofah or sponge, and some water and fruit so you don't get dehydrated. Women are admitted Monday and Wednesday through Saturday; men on Tuesday and Sunday. Admission is 85F and towel rental is 12F. The baths are open Wednesday through Monday 10–9 and Tuesday 2–9.

LA MOSQUEE

Behind the Jardin des Plantes, the city's main mosque is the religious and the intellectual center of the Parisian Muslim community. Built in the 1920s as a memorial to North African Muslims who died fighting for France in World War I, its modest white walls enclose colorful, intricately tiled courtyards, which surround the prayer room, *hammam* (baths), and an equally opulent tearoom (*see* Salons de Thé, in Chapter 4), all designed in the tradition of North African secular architecture. Upstairs from the peaceful public gardens are institutes devoted to the study of Islam and Arab cultures. Admission to the whole complex is 15F, students 10F, but you can wander around the garden for free.

Since the prayer room is used continually throughout the day (daily prayer times are posted inside), you should be aware of some basic customs before entering. Cover all skin above the elbow and above the calf and remove your shoes; the more traditional insist that you also cleanse your face, neck, ears, arms, and hands with water. The carved wooden altar indicates the direction of Mecca; if you sit, point your feet away. Non-Muslims are never allowed in during daily calls to prayer, and at other times, depending on the orthodoxy of the person nearest the door, women, non-Muslims, or both may be asked to view the prayer room only from the courtyard. *Pl. du Puits-de-l'Ermite, 5e, tel. 01–36–68–70–05. Métro: Monge. Open for tours Sat.–Thurs. 10–noon and 2–6:30; in winter, until 5:30.*

Dead Folk

From carefully tended plots of crumbling tombstones to eerie, skull-filled channels leading deep into the bowels of the city, Paris has been perfecting its postmortem practices since the Revolution. More than just eternal hangouts for famous dead folk, Paris's cemeteries also offer tree-lined cobblestone paths, well-tended flowers, and ample benches where we mortals can sit and contemplate the erosive quality of time. Visitors seeking the ultimate mortal experience should venture through the Catacombes—miles and miles of bones and grinning skulls ensconced in dark, dank passages.

That Which Lurks Below

Since the Middle Ages, Paris has been abused, prostituted, and exploited for her earthy treasures—mostly limestone, clay, and sand quarried with the use of a 300-kilometer (186-mile) labyrinth of passageways and immense caverns beneath the streets of Paris. Mining didn't stop until the early 1800s, despite ominous warnings that the weight of the city was too great for the caverns to support. And it wasn't until whole streets began collapsing (taking with them buildings, trees, and poodles) that Parisians wised up, mining was stopped, and most passages were closed off. Today, the greatest danger is not a cave-in but getting lost: All the tunnels look virtually the same.

The subterranean "égouts" (sewers) of Paris were immortalized in "Les Misérables," in which Jean Valjean used them to escape, and in "The Phantom of the Opera," which places the phantom's lair in the depths below the Paris Opéra. The Communards used the quarries in 1871 to flee from approaching government troops; and in 1944 occupying Germans set up offices here with lights, pumped-in air, and communication lines. The setting is ideal for Gothic parties, late-night carousing, and drunken graffiti stints. Legally, the passageways are off-limits, but that doesn't mean they aren't used.

While Père-Lachaise, Montmartre, and Montparnasse hog the limelight, there are plenty of enchantingly haunting burial grounds where the famed can remain a little more incognito. The intimate, high-walled **Cimetière de Passy** (2 rue du Commandant-Schlœsing, 16e; Métro: Trocadéro) is particularly inviting; it's also the everlasting home of French impressionist **Edouard Manet** (1832–83), and modern music pioneers **Gabriel Fauré** (1845–1924) and **Claude Debussy** (1862–1918).

For a more offbeat funerary excursion, head to the **Cimetière des Chiens** (Dog Cemetery) (along the Seine, Asnières-sur-Seine; Métro: Gabriel Péri), where lots of Fifis have been put out to pasture. The privately owned pet cemetery has hundreds of lapdogs, cats, and even a wolf and bear. On the second-highest point in all of Paris you'll find the **Cimetière de Belleville** (40 rue du Télégraphe, 20e; Métro: Télégraphe), with no famous folks, but a fabulous view. *All city cemeteries open Mar. 16–Nov. 5, weekdays 8–6, Sat. 8:30–6, Sun. 9–6; Nov. 6–Mar. 15, weekdays 8–5:30, Sat. 8:30–5:30, Sun. 9–5:30.*

LES CATACOMBES

"Arrête! C'est ici l'Empire de la Mort." This message scrawled at the entrance to the "Empire of Death" was enough to convince German troops in World War II to leave promptly. They never guessed that Resistance fighters used the tunnels in the catacombs as a base. This dire warning now welcomes tourists after a winding descent through dark, clammy passages to Paris's principal ossuary and most disturbing collection of human remains. Bones from the notorious **Cimetière des Innocents,** a stinky, overcrowded plot of common graves under what is now place des Innocents, were the first to be transplanted here in 1786, when decomposing bodies started seeping into neighboring cellars, bringing swarms of ravenous rats with them. Other churchyard cemeteries, also facing unhealthy conditions, were happy to dispose of the decomposed in the catacombs. The legions of bones dumped here are arranged not by owner but by type—witness the rows of skulls, stacks of tibias, and piles of spinal disks. There are also some bizarre attempts at bone art, like skulls arranged in the shape of hearts. It's all very macabre and makes you feel quite . . . mortal. Among the bones in here are those of **Mirabeau** (1749–91), the Revolution leader who found an early resting place in the Panthéon (*see below*) but was transferred when his ideas became unfashionable; keeping him company are the remains of fellow rebels, many of them brought fresh from the guillotine. Sixteenth-century satirist and writer **Rabelais** (1490–1553) was transplanted from the former cemetery at the Eglise St-Paul-St-Louis, and famous courtesan **Madame de Pompadour** (1721–64) is mixed in with the rabble after a lifetime spent as the mistress to Louis XV. Be prepared to walk long distances when you come here—the tunnels stretch for kilometers, and the only light comes from your flashlight. *1 pl. Denfert-Rochereau, 14e, tel. 01–43–22–47–63. Métro: Denfert-Rochereau. Admission: 27F, 19F students. Open Tues.–Fri. 2–4, weekends 9–11 and 2–4.*

CIMETIERE DE MONTMARTRE

Though it's crammed underneath a busy traffic bridge, the Montmartre cemetery still manages to be a beautiful resting place, where trees hang over crumbling stones and the occasional prowling cat. A smaller and more peaceful version of the Cimetière du Père-Lachaise (*see above*), it has the advantage of not being mobbed by Jim Morrison fans. Though the neighborhood was once home to a lively art scene, today the dead artists draw more attention than the breathing ones. Among the former is **François Truffaut** (1932–84), who turned from critic to filmmaker with *Les 400 Coups* (1959), the flick that kicked off the French New Wave. (Ironically, Truffaut was once booted out of the cemetery, while still living, for trying to film here without permission.) You can also seek out composer **Jacques Offenbach** (1819–80)—the Montmartre soirée scene is forever indebted to him for his legendary cancan music.

Other colorful residents include painters **Edgar Degas** (1834–1917) and **Jean-Honoré Fragonard** (1732–1806), writers **Stendhal** (1783–1842) and **Alexandre Dumas** *fils* (1824–95), composer **Hector Berlioz** (1803–69), Russian ballet dancer **Vaslav Nijinski** (1890–1950), physicist **Jean Bernard Foucault** (1819–68), and German poet **Heinrich Heine** (1797–1856). **Emile Zola** (1840-1902) had a brief stint here—until he moved up to fancier digs in the Panthéon (*see below*), where he has remained. If you don't want to get lost among the tombstones, pay close attention to the map next to the front gate. *20 av. Rachel, 18e. Métro: Blanche or Place de Clichy.*

CIMETIERE DU MONTPARNASSE

A leafy canopy hides the modern buildings looming above this peaceful cemetery of flat, orderly rows of tombstones. Residents include angst-ridden existentialist **Jean-Paul Sartre** (1905–80), who is buried with longtime companion and early feminist **Simone de Beauvoir** (1908–86). **Charles Baudelaire** (1821–67) is memorialized here with a striking sculpture; the poet reclines nearby in a tomb with other members of his family. American actress **Jean Seberg** (1938–79) became France's sweetheart when she relocated to Paris and started adding her girlish accent to French films like Jean-Luc Godard's *Breathless.* Admirers of sculptor **Constantin Brancusi** (1876–1957) can pay their respects twice: once at his grave, and again at his famous sculpture *The Kiss*, which portrays the close bodies of two lovers. You'll find the couple hovering over **Tanosa Gassevskaia** (1888–1910), who killed herself over unrequited love.

The eternal party also includes author **Guy de Maupassant** (1850–93), theater-of-the-absurd guru **Eugène Ionesco** (1912–94), composer **Camille Saint-Saëns** (1835–1921), American artist **Man Ray** (1890–1976), Russian sculptor **Ossip Zadkine** (1890–1967), anarchist **Pierre-Joseph Proudhon** (1809–65), carmaker **André Citroën** (1879–1935), and **Alfred Dreyfus** (1859–1935), the Jewish army captain falsely convicted of spying for the Germans. *3 blvd. Edgar-Quinet, 14e. Métro: Raspail or Edgar Quinet.*

PANTHEON

The final resting place for the officially great citizens of France, the Panthéon wasn't originally intended to serve this purpose. Louis XV ordered the building of a church to replace nearby St-Etienne-du-Mont (*see* Houses of Worship, *above*) as home to the relics of Ste-Geneviève, who became the patron saint of Paris when her constant praying in 451 supposedly made Attila the Hun change his plans to invade the city. Construction began in 1755, with architect Jacques-Germain Soufflot's design for a Greek cross plan supporting a dome on a scale never before seen—a soaring masterpiece of technical achievement and visual harmony. Though his vision wasn't that bad, his engineering sucked, and the perfect building has been trying desperately to fall apart ever since. The original windows had to be filled in, interior columns braced, the dome restructured; in 1985, falling stones prompted its temporary closure. The structure was finished in 1790, 10 years after the death of the architect, and just in time for . . . the Revolution. Thereafter, the building alternated as a church and a nondenominational burial ground—until the funeral procession of Victor Hugo came rolling up from the Arc de Triomphe into the crypt, cementing its status as the tomb for French VIPs.

Victor Hugo (1802–85), the prolific author and chronicler of his generation, wasn't the first resident of the Panthéon; he was joining philosopher **Jean-Jacques Rousseau** (1712–78) and Rousseau's philosophical opposite, **Voltaire** (1694–1778). The heart—yep, we mean heart—of **Léon Gambetta** (1838–82), a leader of the Paris Commune (*see box, above*) and eponym for countless French streets, sits quietly in its little vase. Writer **Emile Zola** (1840–1902) was a populist intellectual and a supporter of labor movements. His condemnation of anti-Semitism during the Dreyfus Affair brought out as many supporters as protesters to his funeral. **Louis Braille** (1809–52) was considered worthy of a spot in the Panthéon, too—100 years after his death—except for his all-important hands, which remain in his parish churchyard. Blind, Braille taught himself to read by feeling embossed Roman letters, eventually devising the system of raised dots we know today. Resistance leader and Nazi vic-

The remains of Nobel Prize–winning scientist Marie Curie and her daughter were moved into the Panthéon on April 19, 1995, thereby making her the first woman to rest among France's great dead citizens based solely on her own merit (Marcelin Berthelot's wife is here with her husband).

tim **Jean Moulin** (1899–1943) has found an eternal place in the basement of the Panthéon. Climb to the top of the dome for an ethereal view of Paris, or just rest a moment on the main floor to watch Foucault's pendulum swing back and forth across the nave. *Pl. du Panthéon, 5e, tel. 01–43–54–34–51. RER: Luxembourg. Admission: 32F, 21F ages 18–25, 17F ages 12–17. Open daily 9:30–6:30.*

Parks and Gardens

If you feel trapped by Paris's bustling streets and you just want a place to sit down without having to order a cup of coffee, over 350 green spots come to the rescue. Watch for kids floating boats in fountains, gossiping old ladies, poodle-walkers, and randy French men preying on tourists. Two large *bois* (woods) on the western and eastern edges of the city make you feel like you've escaped Paris altogether. Parks are either *à l'anglaise,* which means they're naturally overgrown in the style of English gardens, or *style français,* which means everything's planted in maddeningly neat, symmetrical rows. In most parks, you can stroll along paths and read on benches, but stay the hell off the grass—the *gendarmes* will not hesitate to lecture (and pursue) trespassers. Exceptions to the rule include the user-friendly grass in Bois de Boulogne, Bois de Vincennes, Parc des Buttes-Chaumont, and Parc de la Villette. Most parks open at dawn and are locked at dusk.

BOIS DE BOULOGNE

Stretched along the western side of the 16th arrondissement, the Bois de Boulogne—"Le Bois"—is the largest park in Paris and has played an important role in Parisian life for the past

Pick a Park

- **Bassin de l'Arsenal.** *This small canal-side park south of place de la Bastille, complete with a café/restaurant, is a sunny, peaceful spot to eat lunch and watch the boats. Napoléon created the canal to increase water movement through the city, and Jacques Chirac commissioned the park in the '80s. 12e. Métro: Bastille.*

- **Parc André-Citroën.** *Named for the automobile magnate, this park has all the French basics and more. Greenhouses and shallow waterways share the park with carpetlike lawns you can play on and trees arranged like an army regiment. 15e. Métro: Balard.*

- **Parc Georges Brassens.** *Once an abattoir (slaughterhouse), this park has secluded paths, rocks to climb, Ping-Pong, and a theater. There's also a huge used-book market on weekends in the old horse stalls. 15e. Métro: Porte de Vanves.*

- **Parc de Monceau.** *In the posh eighth arrondissement, this garden was the setting for the steamy love scenes in Zola's "La Curée." Besides au pairs pushing expensive strollers, you'll find fake grottos, made-to-look-ancient Greek sculptures, a waterfall, and the Musée Cernuschi—a small museum featuring ancient Chinese art. 8e. Métro: Monceau.*

- **Square du Vert-Galant.** *Created in 1884 and occupying a prime location at the tip of the Ile de la Cité, this is the place to go to smooch, catch a sunset, and watch the Seine flow by. 1er. Métro: Pont Neuf.*

100 years. It owes its existence to Louis XI, who protected the park's game with his personal guards; Napoléon III shaped it into its present form, modeling the previously unlandscaped grounds after London's Hyde Park. The late 19th-century Bois became one of Paris's great social hot spots, a place to ride disdainfully on horseback or in carriages watching everybody watching everybody else. It was the playground of the wealthy, with polo fields, a racetrack, tennis lawns, and the court that eventually became the Stade Roland-Garros of French Open fame (*see* Planning Your Trip, Festivals, in Chapter 1).

The Bois is such a convenient and pleasant place to get away from the crowds of Paris that only the Eiffel Tower has more annual visitors. You are allowed to sit on (most of) the lawns, climb the trees, and do all those other park-type things you never thought you'd miss until you visited the Jardin du Luxembourg (*see below*). Boating on **Lac Inférieur** is an integral part of many a Parisian Sunday; you can rent a boat here for 45F per hour (200F deposit). Or take the ferry to the lake's islands, well worth the 7F round-trip ticket. The café out there serves expensive snacks and 17F cafés; you may want to bring a picnic and sit under the cherry trees with the strutting peacocks. Other attractions include the **Jardin d'Acclimatation,** a hands-on kiddie park/zoo/playground at the north end of the park, and the incredible flower collection of the **Parc de Bagatelle.**

Families and nice folks frequent the Bois during the day, but at night sleaze creeps down the access roads and into the Bois. The Bois has always been the city's prostitution center; it is estimated that over five million francs—about $1 million—change hands here every night. Unless you yearn for the attentions of a transvestite, her/his pimp, and a police officer dogging you all, avoid the park at night.

The park is huge and can be difficult to navigate, so look at the Métro station map carefully to orient yourself. The Métro stops at the perimeter, and buses (like the 52 and 241 from Porte d'Auteuil or 244 from Porte Maillot) cross the Bois. You can also rent bikes (25F per half hour, 40F per hour) from the stand at the entrance to the Jardin d'Acclimatation and close to the Pavillion Royal, on the northwest of Lac Inférieur. *16e. Métro: Porte Maillot, Porte Dauphine, or Porte d'Auteuil. RER: Avenue Foch.*

BOIS DE VINCENNES

Southeast of the city is another huge, relatively unmanicured, wooded area. You can rent a row-boat on either of two major lakes (30F per half hour, 55F per hour), **Lac des Minimes** or **Lac Daumesnil,** at which you can also rent bikes (25F per half hour, 40F per hour). Also near Lac Daumesnil are the **Musée des Arts Africains et Océaniens** (*see* Museums, *above*), a zoo, and a Buddhist center, including a Tibetan Buddhist temple where you can meditate on Saturday and Sunday at 5 PM (Métro: Porte Dorée). **The Château de Vincennes** (Métro: Château de Vincennes) was a long time coming: Started by Philippe VI in 1337, it wasn't completed until his grandson, Charles V, rolled around. The château served as, among other things, a country home for François I, and it later became a fortified bastion under Emperor Napoléon I—his failing empire's last stronghold against the invading western European powers. The proud general on guard, Daumesnil, refused to capitulate to the Russians, British, Austrians, and Prussians, waiting until he could surrender to a Frenchman. The château now houses a museum. The **Parc Floral,** near the château, features diverse floral displays of aquatic and land-bound varieties. The **Zoo de Vincennes** (Métro: Porte Dorée), open daily 9–5 and charging 35F admission, attracts hordes of schoolchildren who want to gape at wild animals. A look at the exotic birds in "virtual" freedom is well worth the trip. *12e. Métro: Château de Vincennes, Porte Dorée, Porte de Charenton, or Liberté. RER: Vincennes.*

JARDIN DU LUXEMBOURG

The Jardin du Luxembourg possesses all that is unique and befuddling about Parisian parks: swarms of pigeons, cookie-cutter trees, ironed-and-pressed dirt walkways, and immaculate lawns meant for admiring, not touching. The tree- and bench-lined paths offer a necessary reprieve from the incessant bustle of the Quartier Latin, as well an opportunity to discover the dotty old women and smooching university students who once found their way into Doisneau

photographs. Somewhat austere during the colder months, the garden becomes intoxicating as spring fills the flowerbeds with daffodils, tulips, and hyacinths; the pools teeming with boats nudged along by children (17F per hour to rent), and the paths with Parisians thrusting their noses toward the sun. The park's northern boundary is dominated by the **Palais du Luxembourg,** which is surrounded by a handful of well-armed guards; they are protecting the senators who have been deliberating in the palace since 1958. Feel free to move the green chairs around to create your own picnic area or people-watching site.

While the garden may seem purely French in its curious treatment of greenery and promenades, the original 17th-century planting took its inspiration from Italy. When Marie de Médicis acquired the estate of the recently deceased Duke of Luxembourg in 1612, she decided to turn its hôtel into a version of the Florentine Médicis home, the Palazzo Pitti. She ended up with something more Franco-Italian than strictly Florentine. The land behind the palace was loosely modeled on the Boboli Gardens. The landscapers, like the architects, didn't design a true version of the Florentine garden, opting for the emerging style of heavy-handed human manipulation of nature—linear vistas, box-trimmed trees, and color-coordinated flowerbeds—thereby further defining the "French" garden. A tiny corner of the park still possesses that nature-on-the-brink-of-overwhelming-civilization look that was the trademark of the Renaissance Italian garden—namely, the intentionally overgrown cluster of trees and bushes lining the 1624 **Fontaine de Médicis.** The park captured the hearts of Parisians when it became public after the Revolution; thousands turned out in the mid-1800s to prevent a Haussmann-directed boulevard from being built through its middle.

Paris has not one but TWO tiny models of the Statue of Liberty (a likeness of sculptor Frédéric Bartholdi's mom): one in the west gardens of the Jardin du Luxembourg, the other on the Allée des Cygnes (15e; Métro: Bir-Hakeim).

One of the great attractions of the park is the **Théâtre des Marionnettes,** where on Wednesday, Saturday, and Sunday at 3 and 4 PM you can catch one of the classic *guignols* (marionette shows) for 20F. The wide-mouthed kiddies, though, are the real attraction; their expressions of utter surprise, despair, or glee have fascinated the likes of Henri Cartier-Bresson and François Truffaut.

And finally, for those eager to burn off those pastry breakfasts: The Jardin de Luxembourg has a well-maintained trail around the perimeter, and it is one of the few public places the French will be seen in athletic clothes (this is a riot). It takes an average jogger 20 minutes to get all the way around, and water fountains are strategically placed along the way. Men of all ages are also strategically placed; their comments to female runners are irritating, but otherwise this is a great escape. *Bordered by rues de Vaugirard, de Medicis, Guynemer, and Auguste Comte and blvd. St-Michel, 6e. RER: Luxembourg.*

JARDIN DU PALAIS ROYAL

It's odd that the "Royal Palace" is the only place in the city that never sheltered a monarch. Cardinal Richelieu laid claim to the land, buying up property until he found himself with a palace. When he died in 1642 he left the digs to the crown. Anne of Austria promptly took advantage of the gift, moving here in 1643 to escape the stuffy Louvre. Five years later, La Fronde, a period of unrest between nobility and royalty, broke out; Anne fled Paris, and the Orléans family took her place, sticking around until the Revolution. The last Orléans, Philippe Egalité, expanded the complex in a clever attempt to make some francs by selling lots and building town houses. It quickly became a fashionable place to live, and the ground level filled with cafés and bordellos. The garden became a public forum for voicing complaints against the government, ultimately witnessing many of the key meetings leading up to the Revolution. People gathered here on July 14, 1789, before stomping off to the Bastille.

The Jardin du Palais Royal as we know it today is devoid of bordellos, and little old men who talk to sparrows have replaced the dissenters. You can still order a cup of coffee from one of the cafés overlooking the grounds, and it's a good place to take a break from all the hectic sightseeing activity nearby. The park itself is the picture of Parisian romance, with lines of trees, a dramatic central fountain, and benches for snuggling couples. The southern end of the park, however, receives the most attention—and controversy. In truly Parisian style, in 1986 artist Daniel Buren decided to juxtapose the traditional with the ultramodern. His black and white columns rise up from water flowing beneath the courtyard, accompanied by fountains of rotating silver balls. At night, airport runway lights glow green and red, while blue lights illuminate the columns. Although conservative Parisians shudder at the sight of all this modernity in royal surroundings, skateboarders and roller skaters give the smooth concrete the thumbs-up. *1er. Métro: Palais Royal–Musée du Louvre. Open Apr.–May, daily 7 AM–10 PM; June–Aug., daily 7 AM–11 PM; Sept., daily 7 AM–9:30 PM; Oct.–Mar., daily 7 AM–8:30 PM.*

JARDIN DES PLANTES

In 1626, Louis XIII intended for this park to become "The King's Garden of Medicinal Herbs." Today, the Jardin des Plantes is the city's official botanical garden and houses over 10,000 varieties of plants (all tidily arranged in little rows and labeled, of course), a zoo (the animals also tidily arranged—in 19th-century cages), an aquarium, huge collections of rocks and insects, the **Musée National d'Histoire Naturelle** (*see* Museums, *above*), and lots of traffic from students attending the nearby Ecole Normale Supérieure. With the Gare d'Austerlitz along its southeastern edge, the park is a great discovery if you have a long wait for your train. The **Open-Air Sculpture Garden** is between the Jardin des Plantes and the Seine—yet another great place to wait for your train. *57 rue Cuvier, 5e. Métro: Jussieu, Monge, or Gare d'Austerlitz. Admission to museums: 12F–40F.*

JARDIN DES TUILERIES

A stroll around this stately (albeit dusty) onetime royal garden is like an abbreviated monument tour: You'll see the Louvre, place de la Concorde, the Musée d'Orsay, the Eiffel Tower, and the Seine. A palace by the same name had been around for centuries when Catherine de Médicis arrived in the mid-16th century, bringing Renaissance influences from Tuscany and coercing architect Philibert de l'Orme to design a private park; the result was the first classical French garden in the structured, manicured style we know today. A century later, André "Versailles" Le Nôtre gave the place a face-lift before it was opened to the public; it instantly became the fashionable center for strolling and showing off. The palace burned down during the Commune of 1871, but the gardens stuck it out and went on to form a nice piece of Haussmann's Paris: In one direction you can see straight down the Champs-Elysées all the way to the Arc de Triomphe; in the other, you see a long, orderly expanse of garden between you and the Louvre.

Besides small lawns you can't sit on and a huge pick-up scene for gay men along the Seine, the Tuileries offer a series of women sculpted by Aristide Maillol (1861–1944) as well as a place to rest your weary feet after the trek down the Champs-Elysées. The park is still undergoing renovations until the end of 1997, but the garden remains completely accessible. Hanging by the big fountain near place de la Concorde is about as relaxing as it gets in the heart of Paris. If the summer heat makes you delirious, take refuge in one of the two art museums at the west end, the **Orangerie** and the **Jeu de Paume** (for both, *see* Museums, *above*). *1er. Métro: Tuileries or Concorde. Open summer, daily 8–9; winter, 8–7.*

PARC DES BUTTES-CHAUMONT

The Parc des Buttes-Chaumont wins the prize for most dramatic transformation: It's been a quarry for plaster of paris, a garbage dump, a slaughterhouse, and refuse pile for dead horses. A treatise on the merits of simulated nature, this park near Belleville now hosts steep lawns, a mountain made of cement and rock, and a waterway and grotto. One of the most comfortable places in the city to collapse, the hill and the small lake are a welcome relief after you've seen one too many stodgy French gardens where the trees

Running across the waterway at Buttes-Chaumont you'll find the Pont des Suicidés (Suicide Bridge). So many distraught young lovers leapt from here to a watery death that a barricade has been put up.

all grow in a row. The park has gorgeous views of the city below, ducks to feed, and a small neo-classical temple at the top of the hill. This little oasis is brought to you by Napoléon III and Baron Haussmann, who wanted to give the working folk a green spot where they could take their families. Kids (big and small) will enjoy a stop at the **Théatre de Guignols** (puppet theater) on the northern side of the parc. Shows start daily (weather permitting) at 3 PM and cost 10F. *Bordered by rues de Crimée, Manin, and Botzaris, 19e. Métro: Buttes-Chaumont.*

PARC MONTSOURIS AND CITE UNIVERSITAIRE

Another Haussmann project, Parc Montsouris almost succeeds in convincing you that you have found an arcadian paradise. The hilly park (its name means mouse mountain) is filled with sloping fields, clusters of stately trees, and a pond. Unfortunately, abandoned railway tracks and active RER lines cross the park, and traffic speeds around its perimeter. Across boulevard Jourdan from the park is the Cité Universitaire, a collection of residences built by foreign countries to house their nationals while they study at Parisian universities. Funded by John D. Rockefeller in the 1920s, each of the 35 buildings was designed with a world's fair–like attitude toward national identity and architectural design. Le Corbusier designed two houses, the **Fondation Suisse** and **Fondation Franco-Brasil,** and both continue to attract architectural pilgrims. The cité is a nice complement to the Parc Montsouris across the street, and you can run around, throw a Frisbee, or climb a tree without being pestered by park police. *14e. RER: Cité Universitaire.*

PARC DE LA VILLETTE

What was Paris's largest complex of slaughterhouses and stockyards is now a nice big green park with tons of high-tech buildings and toys to run around in and play with. The sheep that were once driven through this neighborhood on their way to becoming mutton left in the mid-1970s; you can check out photos documenting these days at the **Maison de la Villette** (tel. 01–40–03–75–10; closed Mon.). Most people come here to enjoy the gigantic lawns, nifty mega-playgrounds, and bike paths. The largest park this side of the Bois de Boulogne, it's also the city's most fun. There's things like Claes Oldenberg's oversize *Buried Bicycle* to ogle, a monstrous dragon slide, catwalks, and no less than 11 special theme gardens, including the meditative **Jardin des Bambous** (Bamboo Garden), the steamy **Jardin des Brouillards** (Fog Garden), the **Jardin des Miroirs** (Mirror Garden), the **Jardin des Vents** (Wind Garden), and the **Jardin des Frayeurs Enfantines** (Garden of Childhood Frights). Park architect Bernard Tschumi divided the area into a 5- by 9-unit grid and put a big red steel contraption called a *folie* at each grid point, each with some sort of artistic or other purpose—like the *folie vidéo,* the *folie arts plastique,* or the Quick folly, which sells nasty fast food.

The park is bordered by the canal St-Denis to the west and is split by the canal de l'Ourcq through the middle; the **information folly** (211 av. Jean Jaurès, tel. 01–40–03–75–03; Métro: Porte de Pantin), near the confluence of the canals, dispenses maps and general park info. To the north of the canal de l'Ourcq is the **Cité des Sciences et de l'Industrie** museum and the attached **Géode** (*see* Museums, *above*), as well as the semiburied *Argonaute,* a 1950s nuclear submarine. To the south of the canal de l'Ourcq is the slaughterhouse-turned-concert-venue **Grande Halle,** which hosts jazz festivals and other big events, and the **Théâtre Paris-Villette** (tel. 01–42–02–02–68). Nearby is the **Cité de la Musique,** an assortment of theaters and recital rooms, including the campus of the **Conservatoire National Supérieur de Musique et de Danse** (*see* Opera, Classical Music, and Dance, in Chapter 5). On the western corner is the **Zénith,** a major concert hall hosting big-name international acts. *19e. Métro: Porte de la Villette or Porte de Pantin.*

Neighborhoods

One of the many names for Paris is *la cité aux cent villages*—the city of a hundred villages. The modernization and centralization of the 19th century meant grand boulevards and imposing government buildings cut wide swaths into these villages, sometimes linking them to other towns, sometimes obliterating them entirely. With the waves of immigration from former colonial territories in this century, new "villages" have formed within Paris. To really experience the hidden Paris, explore the winding side streets; they frequently squirm through tiny communities that huddle in the shelter of modern high-rises.

The following neighborhoods are ordered alphabetically. If you'd rather tackle things geographically, the neighborhoods on the Right Bank are the Bastille, Belleville, the Champs-Elysées, La Défense, the Gares de l'Est and du Nord, Les Halles and Beaubourg, Louvre to Opéra, the Marais, and Montmartre. On the Left Bank you'll find Montparnasse, the Quartier Latin, and St-Germain-des-Prés. And right in the heart of the city are the Seine's two islands, the Ile de la Cité and the smaller Ile St-Louis.

BASTILLE

You probably won't feel compelled to visit the place de la Bastille, at the intersection of the 4th, 11th and 12th arrondissements, just to see the monument erected here—it's just a column, after all. But as you'll almost certainly end up in the neighborhood surrounding it, either hopping from one bar to another or shopping at the megastores and boutiques, you should at least have a vague idea of what once happened here.

The Revolution

In the late 18th century, the French aristocracy was frantically trying to hold on to its privileges; the middle class was frustrated by its lack of power; and the peasants were furious about being taxed into oblivion. It all exploded with the French Revolution. The bourgeois members of the government kicked things off on June 17, 1789, by proclaiming themselves a new legislative body called the National Assembly and vowing to write a new constitution. On July 14, Parisians of every political stripe joined the fray, storming the Bastille in search of arms for the citizen militia. During the next two years, aristocrats fled the country in droves—their property was being forcibly taken away, and they figured their heads would be next. (Some of them were right.) The Parisians forced Louis XVI to leave his royal pleasure palace in Versailles and slum it at the Tuileries palace, where they could keep an eye on him. He and his wife, Marie "Let them eat cake" Antoinette, later tried to flee France but were recognized in Varennes and dragged back to the capital.

In September 1791, the National Assembly adopted a constitution, all but shutting Louis out of the political proceedings. Unfortunately for him, that wasn't enough for the radical antimonarchists, called the Jacobins, who eventually gained control. They tried and executed the king in January 1793 at place de la Révolution (place de la Concorde). Throughout the year, the newly appointed Committee of Public Safety manned the guillotines, beheading thousands of "enemies of the Revolution" during a period known as the "Reign of Terror." Revolutionary ideals seemed to fall by the wayside as more and more heroes of the Revolution were tried on unlikely treason charges. In 1794 the frenzy had reached such a pitch that Jacobin leader Maximilien Robespierre lost his own head. With Robespierre out of the way, the quasi-tyrannical Directory of Five took control of the country until Napoléon Bonaparte worked his way up from General of the Interior to "Emperor of the French."

Bastille

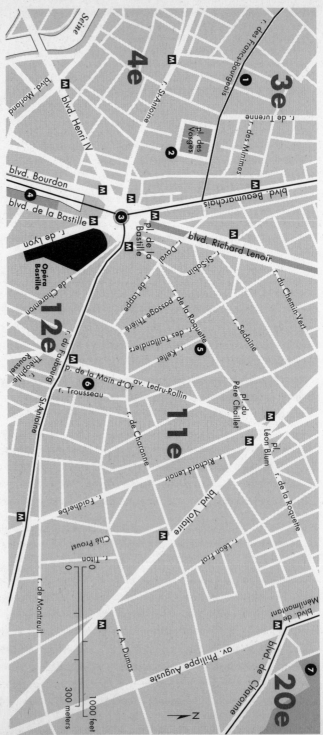

The original Bastille was a fortress developed under the reign of Charles V and had the works: a moat, drawbridges, and towers. It was designed to defend the eastern entrance to Paris, but gradually it was transformed into a prison used for political offenders. On July 14, 1789, thousands of French citizens, frustrated by Louis XVI's hapless rule, tore apart the Bastille prison to liberate the contents of the meager arsenal (and not the prisioners, as you might expect). Nowadays, all you see around the place de la Bastille are swarms of Parisian drivers circling a pole with an angel on top of it—the **July Column,** erected in memory of the 504 victims who died during the "Trois Glorieuses" revolution of 1830. These victims are supposedly buried in a vault underneath the column. The victims of the 1848 revolution were also buried here and added to the inscription on the column.

The only folks likely to storm the Bastille these days are Opéra-goers lining up for seats and predatory Parisians cruising the nightlife. The place de la Bastille is a traffic nightmare and today the area around the former prison is undergoing a revolution of a different sort: gentrification. Galleries, shops, theaters, cafés, restaurants, and bars have taken over formerly decrepit buildings and alleys, bringing an artsy crowd to mingle with blue-collar locals—and jacking up prices considerably; brave artists and penniless students are already defecting to cheaper places like Belleville. Don't expect too much activity and excitement during daylight hours—what's left of the hip Bastille spirit wakes up (and keeps going) after dark.

To get away from the crowds, try exploring **rue de la Roquette** and **rue de Charonne,** which lead you into areas largely inhabited by African and Arab Parisians. A myriad of small streets between the two, such as **rue Keller** and **rue des Taillandiers,** hide cool art galleries and nifty clothing and music boutiques. Nocturnal activities are the Bastille's specialty. Parisians from the farthest corners of the city make the trip to hit their favorites among the amazing variety of bars here. **Rue de Lappe, rue de la Roquette,** and **rue de Charonne** are packed with bars, restaurants, and the self-consciously hip.

BELLEVILLE

Belleville is one of Paris's most unique and, unhappily, quickly changing neighborhoods. Victim to the city's urban renewal frenzy, the area's gentle old buildings are being replaced with harsh modern structures. When the powers that be suggested virtually demolishing Belleville's oldest, most characteristic corner (the western corner, crossed by rue de Belleville and boulevard de Belleville), neighbors united to fight the plan, forming a group known as the "Bellevilleuse"; they've had mixed success in gaining promises to restore rather than raze some areas. But the stretch between the original Belleville and Père-Lachaise cemetery still warrants some rambling. Take **rue de Ménilmontant,** which goes up, up, up, from boulevard de Belleville and still has many of the old buildings. Other good places to really experience the area's (slightly run-down) charm are the **Parc de Belleville, rue Dénoyez,** or **rue de Belleville** up to **rue des Pyrénées.**

A more refreshing change taking place in Belleville is the recent influx of grunge—artists, musicians, and slackers who can still afford this part of town. Part of the area's appeal stems from the fact that it never charmed the bourgeoisie. Originally a country village with farmland and vineyards, it had less than 1,000 inhabitants right up to the Revolution. The late 18th century saw the beginning of a long, slow migration into Belleville, and in the mid-19th century the village was incorporated into Paris. Pushed out of central Paris by Haussmann's huge boulevards, the laboring class came here to live. The arrival of waves of immigrants in the 20th century, most fleeing persecution in their homelands, has contributed to Belleville's international esprit: Polish, Russian, German, and Sephardic Jews; Armenians; Greeks; Africans; Eastern Europeans; Chinese . . . all have brought their specialties to shops, markets, and restaurants throughout the district. Groups of men chat amicably on corners and doorsteps in this approachable, friendly quartier—although women traveling alone might find it a little *too* friendly. But, if you need a respite from the picture-book Paris of grand boulevards and Chanel boutiques, this is the neighborhood for you.

CHAMPS-ELYSEES

What was once an aristocratic pleasure park is now a commercialized tourist trap living off its former glory. While there's a certain thrill about strutting down the world's most famous street in the shadow of the Arc de Triomphe, the abundance of bland shops and restaurant chains (and the lack of actual Parisians) makes the experience feel suspiciously like a trip to Disneyland. The city's attempt at bringing back splendor has included widening the white-granite sidewalks and planting lots of trees, but it still feels like the world's grandest outdoor shopping mall: lots of French kids and tourists cruising around, scoping each other out, and taking breaks at Burger King. The only exclusive things left in the area are the power-lunch bistros and the private nightclubs.

Originally an expanse of green frequented by cattle, the Champs was built for Louis XIV by the landscape designer Le Nôtre to extend the line of the Tuileries. Though place de la Concorde, at the eastern end, saw plenty of activity—including a few hundred heads rolling around during the Revolution—the extending stretch stayed rural, except for a few wealthy folks' homes. In the mid-1800s, the Champs became a popular Sunday strolling ground, encouraging more ice-cream stands, pavilions, and parties as the century went on. The decline of World Expos in the mid-20th century saw a parallel decline in the Champs-Elysées, which had been the stomping grounds of many a fair-goer. A few designer names still hang around, but the avenue has lost its novelty. For a map of the Champs, *see* map Arc de Triomphe to Opéra, *below.*

LA DEFENSE

With sleek modern buildings and funky urban art, La Défense is Paris's version of Disney's Futureland. About 2 kilometers (1¼ miles) outside Paris proper, La Défense does not exactly fit the traditional idea of a "neighborhood." The 35,000 residents who live in the high-rise housing projects are easily eclipsed by the 110,000-plus people who work in the complex of business towers and shops. Development of this huge commercial conglomeration of hypermodern architecture and sculpture began in 1958 on what had been the site of the ultimately ill-fated Parisian defense (hence the name) against the invading Prussians. By the time the developers came to the area, La Défense was just a large traffic circle with a statue in the middle commemorating the battle—the statue still stands today, oddly isolated on an elevated island of grass. The developers sought to create an American-style business park, and they succeeded in building one of Europe's largest and most prestigious commercial neighborhoods with typical French flair.

La Défense is designed to continue the longest urban axis in the world, from the Louvre westward to the **Grande Arche de La Défense** (*see* Major Attractions, *above*), an enormous arch that hides an office building within its walls. The Grande Arche, along with La Défense's first building, the concrete, curvaceous **CNIT** (Centre National des Industries et des Techniques), draw thousands of tourists daily. The **esplanade,** the wide concrete promenade extending along the axis, is lined with big-name art, including a sculpture by Joan Miró that sparked furious controversy over its bizarre shape; Yaacov Agam's *Waterfall,* a fountain powered by 50 computer-controlled jets; and Takis's funky fountain filled with traffic signal–like lights. The Grande Arche de La Défense and the area surrounding it is especially worthwhile at night, when the bright lights and harsh geometrical shapes create a surreal atmosphere.

And the axis isn't stopping yet. Development contracts have been added past the original 1988 time line, and construction crews are extending Métro lines and unearthing bothersome cemeteries to the west of the Grande Arche. New proposals include the Tour Sans Fin (Endless Tower) designed by Jean Nouvel, which will be the tallest building in Europe and the fifth-tallest in the world. The Jardins de l'Arche, a huge park over an underground freeway, will probably be completed in 1997. Though it may not jive with your sense of aesthetics, La Défense is too enormous, popular, and spectacular to ignore. Visit the information center by the Grande Arche to pick up a map outlining all the sculptures and architectural details, including information about the history of La Défense. *Métro: Grande Arche de La Défense or Esplanade de La Défense.*

GARE DE L'EST AND GARE DU NORD

Tourists breeze through this quarter daily on their way from the center up to Montmartre; those who stop get a more satisfying taste of Paris than you could soak up from 38 portrait sittings on place du Tertre. This is a neighborhood filled with working-class people who shop at functional stores and eat at reasonably priced restaurants. Many of Paris's old *passages* (passageways) are here, but unlike the spruced-up ones in the center, these passages are old and crumbling, housing Indian restaurants or used-book vendors. If you're attracted to crumbly old-world charm, check out some passages (such as **passage Brady** and **passage Reilhac**) that branch off from the Boulevard de Strasbourg. The area right around the train stations can get a little sleazy, but if you head south toward **rue du Château-d'Eau** or east toward **quai de Valmy,** you'll be rewarded with a down-to-earth look at Paris. A few of the grand old cafés still call the area home, but their facades practically disappear amid the worn streets and stores around them.

Come to the 9th and 10th arrondissements to ramble, hit some of Paris's hottest clubs, and eat. A large Jewish population sustains kosher restaurants and bakeries, especially in the area above Métro Rue Montmartre, and Indian and Eastern European joints crowd the 10th. Head to **rue d'Enghien** for a great marketplace. Unfortunately, it isn't a good idea to come here alone at night, particularly if you're female or if you don't know exactly where you're going; it's one of Paris's worst areas for theft.

LES HALLES AND BEAUBOURG

Many Parisians believe that the day Les Halles marketplace left Beaubourg in 1969 was the day Paris irrevocably shuffled its priorities; tourism and consumerism were allowed to permanently supplant centuries of local tradition in a move that some call "McDonaldization." The Paris market had been here for nearly 800 years—ever since Philippe Auguste divided up the space, with central buildings for shops and surrounding open spaces for the fresh food market. The market became the central Paris meeting, drinking, and entertainment spot. In the mid-19th century, when Napoléon III complained that the market was disorganized, Victor Baltard created a covered market with glass-roofed pavilions supported by an iron frame, a design that became the model for markets all over Europe.

When the demolition of the market was settled upon in 1962, Parisians showed surprisingly little resistance; in 1969 the merchants were driven out of business or dispersed to the far corners of the city, and the 19th-century market hall was torn down and replaced with a gaping hole. As politicians haggled over the fate of the site, the wasteland came to be known as the "Largest Urban Hole in Europe." After 10 years of wrangling, developers had a brilliant idea: build a shopping mall. The multilevel, soulless structure you see today, the Forum des Halles, is the best they could come up with. Though the mall below ground is an indisputable mess, at least the streets of Les Halles have been spared from the property boom and hawkish developers. Sitting on top of the underground shopping monstrosity is a ghastly collection of fast-food stalls and tourist trinket shops, but many old-time bistrots have held on in the narrow surrounding streets. The area gets going at about 5 AM, when butchers and fish merchants arrive to set up shop, and the cafés are filled soon after with folks getting a coffee before the workday begins. Through the rest of the day, the streets fill up with students and street musicians, beer-drinking punk rockers and their dogs, wide-eyed tourists, and patrons of the porno video parlors. **Rue St-Denis** is both one of the sleaziest and one of the most inviting streets around; its bustling restaurants share centuries-old building space with equally busy sex shops.

Northern Les Halles has evolved into one of the hotter hot spots; a city project to redo the streets has proved to be successful, and hip cafés surround **rue Montorgueil,** lined with food markets and restaurants. The **Eglise St-Eustache,** at the northern edge of the **Jardin des Halles,** is an 18th-century Gothic wonder hiding a picturesque 1968 painting by Raymond Mason, *The Departure of the Fruits and Vegetables from the Heart of Paris.* In the other direction, to the south of the Forum, you have the **Fontaine des Innocents,** for ages the site of a common-trench cemetery, which was emptied into the Catacombes (*see* Dead Folk, *above*) after the overabundance of bodies pushed themselves above street level and the smell became unbearable. Now the public square here is filled day and night with Rasta bongo players, hair weavers, and a truckload of tourists gawking at the whole scene.

Farther south are small streets filled with jazz clubs and trendy shops until you hit **place du Châtelet** and its facing theaters. The square takes its name from a notoriously harsh prison that sat on the present site of Théâtre du Châtelet until its destruction in the 19th century. That random tower just off the place is the **Tour St-Jacques,** built as an addition to a church that was torn down during the Revolution. The tower has since served as Pasteur's lab for experiments on gravity, as a quarry, and currently as a meteorological observatory.

A couple blocks northeast from Châtelet is the best-known landmark of the neighborhood: the **Centre Georges Pompidou** (*see* Major Attractions, *above*). Tons of street musicians and performers gather on the sloping desert of a plaza in front of the Centre. Around the corner at place Igor-Stravinsky is Jean Tinguely's wild and fanciful fountain. A pair of big red lips, a rotund woman, a treble clef, and other wacked sculptures turn and gurgle in the spitting streams of water, a stark contrast to the sternly Gothic **Eglise St-Merri** nearby.

ILE DE LA CITE

The strategic location of this island in the Seine first drew a Gallic tribe, the Parisii, to the place they dubbed Lutetia in about 300 BC. Settling mainly on the island itself, they built wood bridges to the mainland. Caesar's rapid expansion plan hit Paris around 50 BC, and the Romans moved the hub to the Left Bank (though as late as the 4th century AD, Roman governors still slept in a palace on the island). Frankish kings took over that palace—now known as the **Conciergerie**—a couple centuries later, and it remained a royal residence until the 1300s; the Capetians alone lived here for 800 years.

Today, the tough Gauls have been replaced by tourists flocking to **Sainte Chapelle** and **Notre-Dame,** and milling around the expensive trinket shops that surround them. The desire to showcase Notre-Dame altered the soul of the island in the late 19th century: The tiny winding streets, churches, stalls, and houses crouching below it, along with an orphanage and invalids' hospital, were bulldozed to make way for the Haussmann aesthetic. The **Crypte Archéologique** (tel. 01–43–29–83–51), in the place du Parvis in front of the cathedral, became a museum after ruins were discovered in 1965 while building an underground parking structure here. Among the excavated details are parts of the 3rd-century wall of Lutetia; a Merovingian cathedral (Notre-Dame's predecessor) from AD 600; and bits of Roman and medieval houses. Plenty of diagrams, pictures, and photographs go along with the ruins, detailing the history of the isle. Admission to the crypt is 30F, 20F for students under 26. It's open daily 10–6 (shorter hours off-season).

For the most tranquil moment you are likely to have on the Ile de la Cité, head to the **square du Vert-Galant** (*see box* Pick a Park, *above*) at the island's western tip for a view out over the Seine, or picnic in the shady park of **place Dauphine.** The small garden behind Notre-Dame is another peaceful spot, where you can gaze at flying buttresses all day long. From the back of Notre-Dame head across the street and down the steep granite stairs to the **Mémorial de la Déportation,** a striking tribute to the 200,000 French sent to death camps by the Vichy government during World War II. Inside, 200,000 crystals memorialize the victims, and the walls are lined with moving quotations by famous French writers, poets, and philosophers, etched in angular, blood-red letters. It's worth bringing a dictionary to translate the passionate sentiments.

ILE ST-LOUIS

If it weren't sitting directly behind Notre-Dame, attached by a bridge, most tourists probably would never think of going to Ile St-Louis. But it is, and they do, and there is an entire street of restaurants and shops waiting to greet them. Actually, the narrow, **rue St-Louis-en-l'Ile** may be the most charming tourist street in Paris, and as a result plenty of locals join visitors here on warm days and clear evenings. You'll find most of them standing in line **Berthillon** (31 rue St-Louis-en-l'Ile, 4e, tel. 01–43–54–31–61), hands down Paris's best ice creamery. The relatively ignored Seine-side streets of the Ile St-Louis are some of the most enjoyable, with shady spots perfect to sit and savor your purchase.

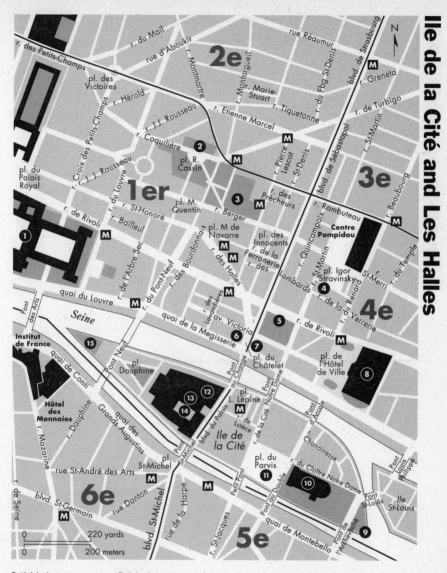

Cathédrale
Notre-Dame, **10**

Conciergerie, **12**

Crypte
Archéologique, **11**

Eglise
St-Eustache, **2**

Eglise St-Merri, **4**

Forum des Halles, **3**

Hôtel de Ville, **8**

Louvre, **1**

Mémorial de la
Déportation, **9**

Palais de
Justice, **13**

Sainte-Chapelle, **14**

Square du
Vert-Galant, **15**

Théâtre du
Chatelet, **6**

Théâtre de
la Ville, **7**

Tour St-Jacques, **5**

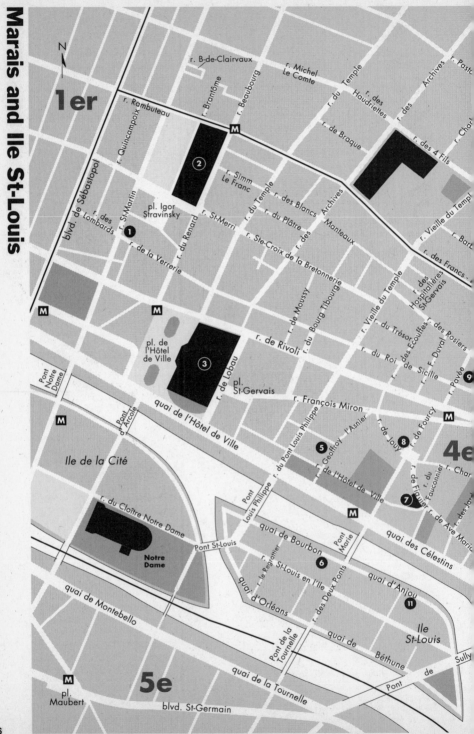

1er

N

r. B-de-Clairvaux

r. Michel
Le Comte

r. du Temple

r. des
Haudriettes

r. des

Archives

Past

r. Brantôme

r. Beaubourg

r. de Braque

r. des 4 Fils

r. Char

r. Rambuteau

r. Quincampoix

M

② 2

r. Simm
Le Franc

r. des Blancs

Archives

r. Vieille du Templ

r. Bart

blvd. de Sébastopol

r. St-Martin

r. des
Lombards

① 1

pl. Igor
Stravinsky

r. St-Merri

r. du Temple

r. du Plâtre

Manteaux

r. des Francs -

r. de la Verrerie

r. du Renard

r. Ste-Croix de la Bretonnerie

r. des

r. des Rosiers

M

M

pl. de
l'Hôtel
de Ville

③ 3

r. de Moussy

r. du Bourg Tibourg

r. de Rivoli

r. Vieille du Temple

r. des
Hospitalières-
St-Gervais

r. du Trésor

r. des Écouffes

r. du Roi de Sicile

r. Duval

r. Pavée

⑨ 9

r. de Lobau

pl.
St-Gervais

r. François Miron

M

Pont
Notre
Dame

Pont
d'Arcole

quai de l'Hôtel de Ville

Ile de la Cité

Geoffroy l'Asnier

⑤ 5

r. de Jouy

r. de Fourcy

⑧ 8

M

4e

r. Char

r. du Cloître Notre Dame

r. du Pont Louis Philippe

r. de l'Hôtel de Ville

r. de Figuier

r. du
Fauconnier

⑦ 7

r. de Ave Mari

Notre
Dame

Pont
Louis Philippe

Pont St-Louis

quai de Bourbon

Pont
Marie

quai des Célestins

r. du Regratier

r. St-Louis en l'Ile

⑥ 6

quai d'Anjou

⑪ 11

quai d'Orléans

r. des Deux Ponts

quai de Montebello

quai de
Béthune

Ile
St-Louis

de

Sully

Pont
de la
Tournelle

quai de la Tournelle

Pont

M

pl.
Maubert

5e

blvd. St-Germain

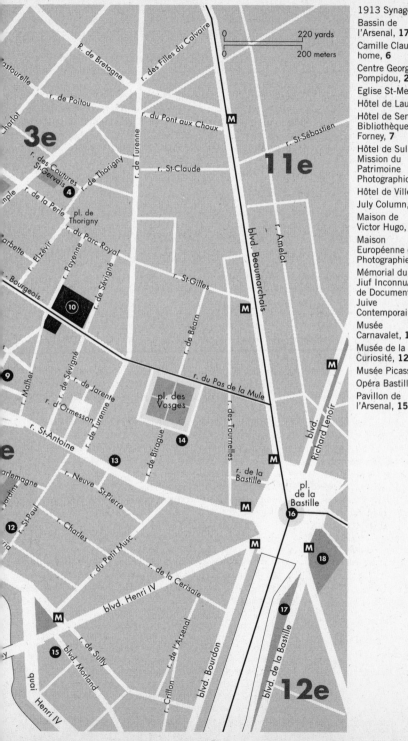

1913 Synagogue, **9**

Bassin de l'Arsenal, **17**

Camille Claudel's home, **6**

Centre Georges Pompidou, **2**

Eglise St-Merri, **1**

Hôtel de Lauzun, **11**

Hôtel de Sens/ Bibliothèque Forney, **7**

Hôtel de Sully/ Mission du Patrimoine Photographique, **13**

Hôtel de Ville, **3**

July Column, **16**

Maison de Victor Hugo, **14**

Maison Européenne de la Photographie, **8**

Mémorial du Martyr Jiuf Inconnu/Centre de Documentation Juive Contemporaine, **5**

Musée Carnavalet, **10**

Musée de la Curiosité, **12**

Musée Picasso, **4**

Opéra Bastille, **18**

Pavillon de l'Arsenal, **15**

For a while a canal divided the current Ile St-Louis in two; the halves were dubbed the Ile Notre-Dame and Ile aux Vaches, the latter given over to dairy cows and their attendants. And so it remained until the 17th century, when some land speculators joined the two islands, connecting them by bridges to the Ile de la Cité and the Left and Right Banks and selling plots to town house developers. After a while in the spotlight, the posh residences somehow lost their charm among the bourgeoisie, and artists, writers, and intellectuals like Cézanne and Baudelaire came to the island. The **Hôtel de Lauzun** at 17 quai d'Anjou was one of Baudelaire's haunts. As you wander around, keep an eye out for the building plaques describing who lived where when, and why it's important. The **quai d'Anjou** and **quai de Bourbon** boast some beautiful hôtels particuliers. A somber plaque adorns 19 quai de Bourbon: "Here lived Camille Claudel, sculptor, from 1899 to 1913. Then ended her brave career as an artist and began her long night of internment." Claudel's family committed her to an insane asylum where she was forbidden to practice her art until her death. Some of her works are displayed in the Musée Rodin (*see* Museums, *above*).

LOUVRE TO OPERA

Yeah, it's terribly expensive, snobbish, and packed with tourists. But any neighborhood that can boast the centers of the Western art, theater, and music worlds all within a 15-minute walk can't be all bad. The **Louvre** (*see* Major Sights, *above*) is the biggie here, displaying thousands of works in what was originally a royal palace. Just a block above it is the **Comédie Française** (*see* Theater, in Chapter 5), tacked onto another royal residence, the **Palais Royal** (*see* Parks and Gardens, *above*), and pointing the way up one of Haussmann's favorite boulevards, **avenue de l'Opéra**. On the avenue, notice the monotony of the structures and how closely the teeny balconies cling to the buildings; Haussmann wanted to ensure that you'd be struck by the grandeur of the street as a whole, with no one well-designed building stealing the show and no protruding terraces breaking the line straight down the street. At the end of this promenade is, of course, the **Opéra Garnier** (*see* Opera, Classical Music, and Dance, in Chapter 5).

If you didn't come to this district to follow the museum trail, pose with the pretentious, or shop in the nearby *grands magasins* (department stores), you'll probably come for practical reasons—it's home to all of the major airlines, travel agencies, and tourist bureaus. Off avenue de l'Opéra, however, you'll find the famous restaurants, age-old bistrots, and upscale shops that form the opulent heart of the quarter. Lately, a sizable Japanese population has moved in, bringing restaurants, bookstores, and specialty shops with them. North of the **Jardin du Palais Royal** is **rue des Petits-Champs,** whose bounty of iron-and-glass passages makes it one of the neighborhood's best spots for roaming. The street ends in the intimate **place des Victoires**; its matching facades were designed in 1685 by Versailles architect Hardouin-Mansart. Louis XIV was so pleased with the results that he had Hardouin-Mansart do another, the **place Vendôme,** on the other side of avenue de l'Opéra. Snobbish and self-important, place Vendôme is also gorgeous; property laws have kept away cafés and other such banal establishments, leaving the plaza stately and refined, the perfect home for the Ritz and Cartier (Chopin lived and died at No. 12). The column in the center of the place Vendôme has had numerous face-lifts, depicting everything from Louis XIV's curls blowing in the breeze to Napoléon's mug, depending on who needed a little self-glorification. The most noteworthy change was the toppling of Courbet's statue of Napoléon in 1871, when enraged Communards followed the lead of Courbet himself, heave-hoing and bringing the whole thing down into a pile of manure (which they'd heaped at the base). Courbet made a quick escape to Switzerland to avoid imprisonment and hefty fines, and eventually Napoléon was cleaned up and put back in the saddle, so to speak.

Next to the Eglise de la Madeleine you'll find the most beautiful pay toilets in all of Paris—a stunning display of art deco and porcelain. The cost for this luxury is a mere 2F.

West of the Louvre and Opéra is the decadent **Eglise de la Madeleine**; the surrounding area is where rich French do their shopping. **Place de la Madeleine** is home to a great flower market Tuesday–Sunday. To stroll among the well-heeled of Paris head to its version of Rodeo Drive, **rue du Faubourg-St-Honoré,** where ridiculously expensive clothes grace the windows of ridiculously expensive boutiques. While you're in the area, stop in and tell the president what you think of his country—the **Palais** de l'Elysée on place Beauvau (look for all the humorless cops hanging around) has been the official residence of the head of state since 1873.

LE MARAIS

Le marais translates as "the swamp." Although this title indicates the formerly overwhelming presence of the Seine in this area, the lively neighborhood of today is anything but a stick in the mud. The Marais covers the third and fourth arrondissements, and though its narrow streets become a bit too crowded in the summer, its eternally lively atmosphere makes it one of Paris's best areas for eating, drinking, singing, walking, and simply living.

Between its original existence as a swamp and its current one as a fashionable district inhabited by stylish Parisians and a thriving gay community, the Marais has seen royalty move in and out. When Henri IV installed his court here in the 17th century and built the place Royale (now the place des Vosges), the Marais was *the* place to live. Nobles flaunted money and prestige, building big, beautiful hôtels particuliers in the area. However, as soon as Versailles became the hot ticket, all those fickle French aristocrats followed Louis out there to kiss his feet, leaving the Marais virtually abandoned. Taking advantage of what had become basically worthless property, waves of Jewish immigrants put down stakes. The Revolution granted Jews religious freedom, and 100 years later Jews fleeing persecution in Poland and Russia came to Paris, living in squalid conditions in the Marais ghetto working mainly as peddlers and merchants. During World War II, the French police arrested thousands of Jews living in the Marais; the Vél d'Hiv roundup of July 16, 1942, when over 12,000 Jews were arrested in one day, marks the low point of the French collaboration. After the decimation of World War II, the Marais remained an old, decaying quarter until a 1962 law, the Loi Malraux, established a restoration program and saved the buildings from ruin. Developers started buying up property, fixing the facades of historic buildings, installing boutiques and galleries, and jacking up property values. The last 20 years have seen the transformation of the Marais into the trendy, artsy neighborhood that it is today, with a good mix of artists' studios and working-class folk. Jewish immigrants from North Africa have brought new life to the quarter, and you'll discover a hodgepodge of falafel stands, kosher butchers, and bookstores with tomes in Hebrew, Arabic, and French.

The **Jewish quarter,** centered on rue des Rosiers and rue des Ecouffes, adds to the Marais's bustling, sometimes bizarre, character: Hasidic Jews with beards and yarmulkes emerge from the kosher stores, passing young men in tight shirts heading to gay bars. Though interior visits are discouraged (most effectively by the locked gate), at least walk past the **1913 synagogue** (10 rue Pavée, 4e), designed by art nouveau whiz Hector Guimard. The **Mémorial du Martyr Juif Inconnu** (Memorial of the Unknown Jewish Martyr) and the **Centre de Documentation Juive Contemporaine** (17 rue Geoffroy-l'Asnier, 4e, tel. 01–42–77–44–72) share the same building. The memorial houses temporary art and history expositions, as well as the ashes of concentration camp victims; the center is a great resource for Jewish studies (*see* Resident Resources, in Chapter 1).

And at the end of rue des Francs-Bourgeois is the elegant **place des Vosges**: One look at the stylish red- and white-brick residences, flowing fountains, and manicured garden, and you'll understand why back in the old days this square was all the rage. In 1605, Henri IV initiated work to transform the square into the place Royale, though the poor guy died before he could move in. The king's and queen's residences, with the largest facades, face each other from across the plaza. Between them lay what belligerent Parisians used as jousting grounds, and so they remained until finally becoming an English-style park later in the century. The stately arcades under the mansions harbor the open gardens of the **Hôtel de Sully** and the **Maison de Victor Hugo** (*see* Museums, *above*). Try to come on a weekend afternoon, when sporadic free classical music concerts add to the already royal atmosphere.

Recipe for a postmodern Paris: one Middle Eastern falafel, a walk past the kosher stores on rue de Rosiers to the 17th-century place des Vosges, and a copy of Thomas Pynchon's Gravity's Rainbow.

Between the Seine and the rue de Rivoli lies the calmer part of the Marais, packed with beautiful old hôtels and green patches. Look for the tiny garden behind the **Hôtel de Sens**, a man-

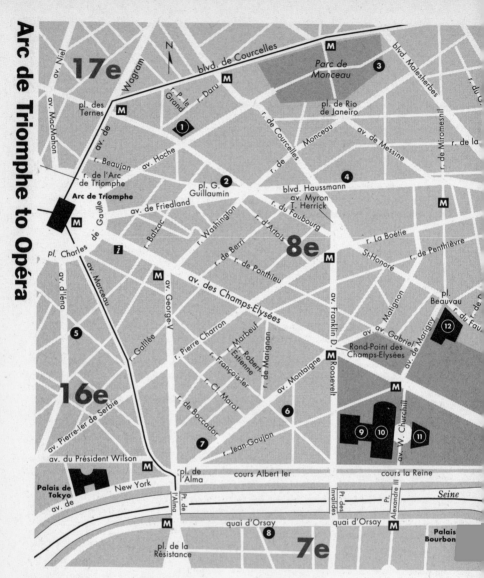

r. Chaptal ⑬

440 yards
400 meters

r. Pigalle
r. Clauzel
r. de la Rochefoucauld
r. d'Aumale ⑭
Notre-Dame-de-Lorette
r. des Martyrs
r. St-Lazare

r. d. Rome
r. des Londres
r. d'Amsterdam
r. de Clichy

du G. Foy
r. du Rocher

la Bienfaisance

Gare
St-Lazare

r. St-Lazare
r. de Châteaudun
9e
r. Taitbout
r. Laffitte
r. Geoffroy-Marie

pl.
St-Augustin
r. de la Pépinière

blvd. Haussmann
r. de Provence
r. de la Chaussée-d'Antin
r. La Fayette

blvd. Malesherbes
r. Pasquier
r. Tronchet
r. Auber
r. de Caumartin
r. Scribe
⑮
pl.
de l'Opéra
blvd. des Italiens
⑯ r. Favart
r. St-Marc

r. de Duras
f. d'Aguesseau
r. Boissy d'Anglas
Faubourg St-Honoré

㉒
pl. de la
Madeleine
blvd. de la
Madeleine
Capucines
r. des
blvd. des Capucines
r. de la Paix
Daunou
r. du Quatre-Septembre
r. St-Augustin
r. Ste-Anne
r. Chabanais
2e
r. Vivienne

r. Royale

pl.
Vendôme
av. de l'Opéra
r. des Petits-Champs
⑰

pl. de la
Concorde
r. de Castiglione
r. St-Honoré
r. St-Roch
r. de Richelieu
⑱
pl. des
Victoires

㉓
r. de Rivoli
r. des Pyramides
1er
⑳ ⑲

㉔
Jardin des
Tuileries
㉑
pl. du
Palais Royal
Louvre

Pt.
de la Concorde
quai des Tuileries
Jardin du
Carrousel

101

sion transformed into the Bibliothèque Forney, an art-history library (*see* Resident Resources, in Chapter 1). **Rues St-Paul** and **de l'Hôtel de Ville** overflow with dusty, insignificant-looking antiques shops that sometimes hide treasures. Of course, there are also plenty of cool-looking overpriced shops that offer everything but bargains.

Rues Ste-Croix-de-la-Bretonnerie and **Vieille-du-Temple** are the center of gay life in Paris, offering bars, bookstores, cultural info, and all the accessories needed for a night out at Le Queen (*see* Dance Clubs, in Chapter 5), like a feather boa and tight satin pants. This is one of the most stylish areas in town—you wonder how these guys can afford to buy Armani jackets when they're lounging around drinking cocktails at 3 PM. **Rue des Francs-Bourgeois** is another great street, full of sleek cafés and homey restaurants, and just north of it are a couple of the city's best museums: the **Musée Picasso** and **Musée Carnavalet** (*see* Museums, *above*).

MONTMARTRE

Rising above the city on the highest hill in Paris is Montmartre, site of the **Basilique du Sacré-Cœur** (*see* Major Attractions, *above*) and once home to a hefty artist community. Even now, after many of the artists have headed for cheaper quarters and tour buses deliver hordes to its minuscule streets, Montmartre remains first and foremost a village where a special breed of Parisian lives and drinks. A trip through the streets of this neighborhood will reward you with glimpses of gardens, small cafés filled with locals, and perhaps the sound of a practicing violinist. An essential part of the Montmartre experience is to sweat your way up the steep stairways that have graced many a Robert Doisneau photograph and afford incredible views of Paris. In the 19th century, vineyards and over 40 windmills covered Montmartre, then a country village. The only surviving windmill is the **moulin de la Galette,** on the corner of rue Lepic and rue Girardon. It is immortalized in Auguste Renoir's *Le Bal du Moulin de la Galette* (Ball at the Windmill of the Galette).

After Haussmann razed most of the working-class homes in the city center, this area saw a population boom. Among the newcomers were artists, drawn by cheap rents and the bohemian atmosphere. Picasso, Renoir, Dalí, Braque, and writer/poets like Apollinaire and Baudelaire all lived and worked here. The **Bateau-Lavoir** (13 pl. Emile-Goudeau; Métro: Abbesses) was an artists' colony where Picasso, Braque, Gris, and others had studios. Picasso painted the cubist classic *Les Demoiselles d'Avignon* here; supposedly a pack of prostitutes from Barcelona posed for the painting. Head south one block to the **place des Abbesses,** a tranquil old plaza with one of the two remaining art nouveau Métro entrances designed by Guimard. For more on the history and illustrious personalities of Montmartre, visit the **Musée de Montmartre** (*see* Museums, *above*), in the building where Renoir once had his studio.

Artist Address Book

Do the bogus artists at place du Tertre seem so tacky that you can't believe anyone cool ever lived around here? Well they did, and here's where you could have found them:

- *Cézanne: 15 rue Hégésippe-Moreau*

- *Manet: 77 rue d'Amsterdam and 39 rue de Léningrad*

- *Toulouse-Lautrec: 21 rue Caulaincourt, 19 rue Fontaine, and 30 rue Fontaine*

- *Van Gogh: 54 rue Lepic*

- *Renoir: 12 rue Cortot, 13 rue Ravignan, 8 allée des Brouillards, 22 rue Tourlaque, 73 rue Caulaincourt, 57 boulevard de Clichy, and 64 rue de La Rochefoucauld.*

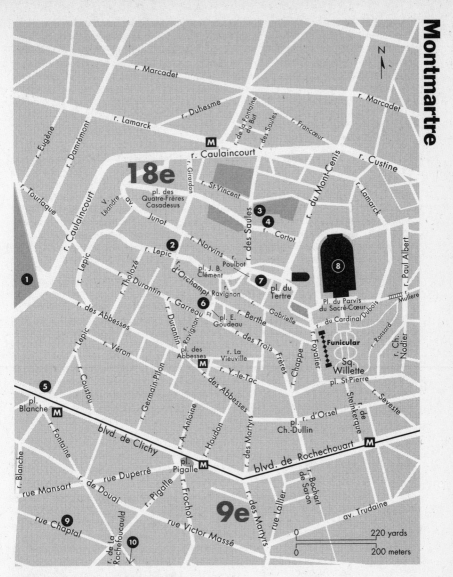

Basilique du
Sacré-Cœur, **8**

Bateau-Lavoir, **6**

Cimetière de
Montmartre, **1**

Espace Montmartre–
Dali, **7**

Moulin de la
Galette, **2**

Moulin Rouge, **5**

Musée de la Vie
Romantique, **9**

Musée de
Montmartre, **4**

Musée Gustave
Moreau, **10**

Vineyard, **3**

Where artists go, rich folk soon follow, and the area gradually filled with galleries, boutiques, and tourists like us. Today, the aggressive third-rate painters clustered around **place du Tertre,** one of the most tourist-attacked spots in the entire city, are the unfortunate reminders of Montmartre's artistic heritage. Real artists live behind the hill, often in million-dollar homes on **avenue Junot** or the picturesque **villa Léandre** just off it. To the east, on **rue des Saules,** is the last remaining **vineyard** in Paris, producing 125 gallons of wine per year. Nearby, off **place des Quatre-Frères-Casadesus,** is a small park where old men gather every day to play pétanque. The guy holding his head in his hands in the statue here is St-Denis, Paris's first bishop. Legend has it that the Romans beheaded him here in AD 250; he then picked up his head and carried it for 6 kilometers (4 miles) before calling it a day.

Montmartre became famous between 1880 and 1914, from the time when the first cabarets opened to the start of World War I. The cabarets, at the bottom of the hill near **place Pigalle** and **place de Clichy,** provided new excitement for the area's bohemians, as well as for students and bourgeois couples who came to the neighborhood for a show. The **Moulin Rouge** (*see* Cabaret, in Chapter 5), immortalized in Toulouse-Lautrec's posters and paintings, still cashes in on Paris's reputation as a city of sex and sin. The cabaret culture and the artistic community fed off each other: The artists provided the cabarets with patronage and publicity, and the cabarets provided the artists with the intrigue, alcohol, and occasional glimpse of dancers', uh, ankles they needed to stay "inspired."

In eastern Montmartre, demarcated by rue Doudeauville to the north and boulevard de la Chapelle to the south, is the **Goutte d'Or** (Drop of Gold), named after the white wine the vineyards here used to produce. A bastion of the Algerian independence party (the FLN) during the Algerian–French war, the area has absorbed constant waves of immigrants, most recently from the Antilles and Africa. Today, Muslim markets sit next to African textile manufacturers, wholesale grocers, and old horse butchers in this multiethnic working-class quarter. Huge crowds of people move through the streets while groups of men debate on corners; lone women may feel uncomfortable with the unwanted attention from men and the lack of other women. The neighborhood gets most festive on Sunday; streets are often blocked off for daylong street markets, and shops stay open later. Like Belleville, however, this center for immigrant communities is struggling against the modern "renovations" being inflicted upon many of Goutte d'Or's charming (albeit decrepit) buildings. Rents will soon shoot up, forcing many immigrants out of Paris and into cheaper housing in the suburbs.

MONTPARNASSE

The name Montparnasse is burdened with images of all kinds of brilliant expatriates doing silly drunken things in the years surrounding World War I. A quartet of cafés on the corner of **boulevards du Montparnasse** and **Raspail**—La Coupole, Le Dôme, Le Sélect, and La Rotonde—became the center for American writers who lived, lolled, loved, and left if the service displeased them. When the owner of Le Dôme fired his manager, threatened his waiters, and insulted his customers, they all regrouped a few weeks later at La Coupole, newly opened by the ex-manager. Americans liked to think that they held court on these corners, pointing to the presence of Ernest Hemingway, Gertrude Stein, Alice B. Toklas, Paul Bowles, Zelda and F. Scott Fitzgerald, Henry Miller, and Peggy Guggenheim. But they weren't the only people around—Pablo Picasso, Georges Braque, Juan Gris, Piet Mondrian, Leon Trotsky, Jean-Paul Sartre, Simone de Beauvoir, Albert Camus, Lawrence Durrell, Anaïs Nin, Jean Arp, Meret Oppenheim, Yves Tanguy, and Marcel Duchamp completed the picture, while an exiled Vladimir Lenin spent most of his time here shunning chitchat and honing his chess game.

The four cafés are still here, though only Le Sélect still has a stylish crowd. The rest of the neighborhood, on the surface anyway, looks like the same mixture of old buildings, manicured parks, and out-of-place new buildings that you see in the rest of Paris. The huge commercial center finished in 1973 detracts substantially from the neighborhood's charm, as does the **Tour Montparnasse,** the tallest office building (at 210 meters/690 feet) in the city. You can take an elevator up the sinister-looking tower to the rooftop bar where an overpriced drink will get you a spectacular view (but why subsidize an enterprise that ruins the skyline from every other vantage point?). Stretching out from the tower and the Gare Montparnasse train station are several remarkably uninspired commercial and residential developments. The **place du 18 juin 1940,** just north of the tower, commemorates the speech Charles de Gaulle gave in exile in London urging the French to resist the German invaders. The huge student population in Montparnasse, having fled the expensive fifth and sixth arrondissements, ushers in the latest (but not necessarily greatest) developments in nightlife along **boulevard du Montparnasse** and tucked into offshoots of **avenue du Maine.**

A few old sights are still worth visiting. The **Parc Montsouris** and **Cité Universitaire** area (*see* Parks and Gardens, *above)* is a great place to meet other foreigners in Paris. The **Cimetière du Montparnasse** has been packing them in for years, and the entrance to the network of **catacombs** is at place Denfert-Rochereau (*see* Dead Folk, *above*).

Montparnasse is probably best explored during the day, as you turn off the tree-lined boulevards onto scores of tiny streets and culs-de-sac lined with ivy-covered houses that look more like they belong in a country village than in Paris. **Villa Adrienne,** off avenue du Général-Leclerc, and **villa Hallé,** off avenue René-Coty, are both especially picturesque. Each house on villa Adrienne bears the name of a famous artist or philosopher instead of a numerical address. **Villa Seurat,** off rue de la Tombe-Issoire, saw the many comings and goings of Anaïs Nin, Henry Miller, and Lawrence Durrell. Several little streets leading away from Parc Montsouris off rue Nansouty, especially **square de Montsouris,** are likely to make you want to become a fabulously wealthy homeowner.

QUARTIER LATIN

The center of French intellectual life for over 700 years, the Quartier Latin has drawn the metaphysically restless, the politically discontent, the artistically inspired, and their hopeful wanna-

Rodin and Balzac

It made perfect sense that the greatest French writer of his time should be sculpted by the greatest French artist of his time, and so Société des Gens de Lettres president Emile Zola awarded to Auguste Rodin the commission to immortalize Honoré de Balzac. Despite the objections of society members, who saw the artist as out-of-touch and incompetent, Rodin accepted the proposal to erect a sculpture at the small place Guillaumin, near the intersection of avenue de Friedland and rue Balzac. Though his health was failing, Rodin traveled to the town where Balzac was born and sketched local peasants as models for the long-dead writer. Several nudes—many of which are at the Musée Rodin—were rejected by the society.

The final version of the sculpture, unveiled in 1898, was a towering image of the writer with a backward-arching body, shoulders draped by a formless dressing gown and hands clutched conspicuously at the waist. Rodin insisted that the work be mounted on a tall pedestal, forcing viewers to gaze up at the sculpture. The similarity between the work and a phallus is hardly accidental—both Rodin and Balzac were notorious for their high opinions of their own virility. The society refused the work and gave the commission to A. Jolguiere. This forgotten sculptor obediently produced a larger-than-life image of Balzac sitting fully clothed in an armchair, his feet surrounded by trite symbols of intelligence and artistry. This work was installed in the place in 1900 and has been largely neglected ever since. The original Rodin Balzac has since been placed on a traffic island on boulevard du Montparnasse at boulevard Raspail.

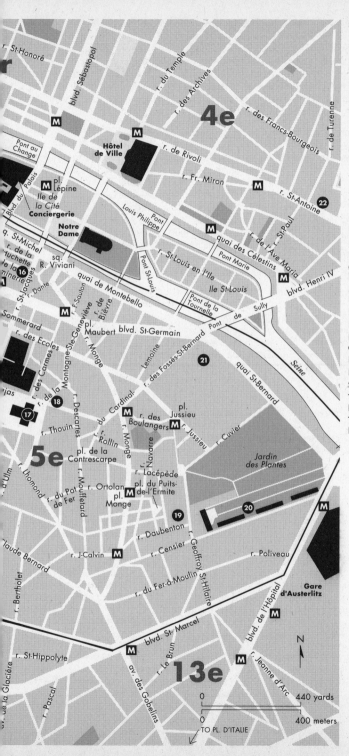

Montparnasse, Quartier Latin, and St-Germain

bes to the neighborhood's universities, cafés, garrets, and alleys. In 1099, Peter Abelard came to the area to study with a local monk. He became a master of dialectics (the discovery of truth through debate), and students from all over Europe came to study with him, including the young Héloïse, whose uncle had Abelard castrated when he learned of the couple's love. In 1215, the Parisian crown and the Roman papacy officially recognized the teachings going on in the area, though the growing school wasn't baptized until 1257, when it took on the name of Robert de Sorbon's (chaplain to Louis IX) neighboring boarding house. Latin became the fashionable language in and out of the classroom, hence the neighborhood's name.

The conservative **Sorbonne** had strong ties to the church; because of this, Rabelais was particularly fond of taking jabs at the university. In 1530 some disgruntled students and professors set up camp next door, establishing the Collège de France, where the classics were taught in—gasp!—Greek instead of Latin. Intellectual life plodded along for the next 250 years, until the Revolution turned all the abbeys and cloisters of the universities into quarries. The curriculum fell under the direction of the government until 1808, when the University of Paris took over the Sorbonne. It took the 1968 student uprisings against conservative faculty and obsolete teaching methods to bring the Sorbonne into the 20th century and to "encourage" the formation of the 13 specialized schools of the University of Paris.

The time-honored tradition of barricading streets in the Quartier Latin with pried-up cobblestones was brought to a close during the student rebellions of 1968: The government paved over every last tempting stone.

The presence of several institutions of higher learning, including the **Ecole Normale Superieure** on rue d'Ulm, keeps the neighborhood youthful, creative, and relatively liberal. Cafés, bookstores, bars, and cheap restaurants proliferate, and even the presence of millions of tourists doesn't break the mood (though it can seriously dampen it in summer). Down toward the Seine, the maze of streets surrounding **rue de la Huchette** are the ultimate experience in crowd tolerance, though you might find some good crêpes or street music there. Napoléon Bonaparte settled at 10 rue de la Huchette. Just to the west, **place St-Michel** and its fountain act as a meeting spot for tourists.

A good, safe, place to get lost is in the labyrinthine streets between place Maubert and the Seine; these streets manage to retain their medieval feel despite the presence of fast-food joints and expensive residences (Mitterrand's private home was at 22 rue de Bièvre). The **square René-Viviani,** just east of the Huchette madness, is a pleasant little park with the oldest tree in Paris, sprouted in 1601. **Shakespeare and Co.,** a handy refuge for Anglophones, is next door (*see* English-Language Bookstores, in Chapter 6). Don't forget to check out the bibliophilic *bouquinistes* (booksellers) along the Seine, where you can rummage through rare books, posters, and postcards.

The area around the Sorbonne and behind the **Panthéon** (*see* Dead Folk, *above*) merits serious exploration as well. Come evening, many students from the Ecole Normale Supérieure—"normaliens"—creep out for feeding and socializing on **rue Mouffetard,** and eventually congregate at the fountain at **place de la Contrescarpe.** After walking the length of rue Mouffetard, take a peek at the Eglise St-Médard (141 rue Mouffetard). Between 1728 and 1732, there was a series of miracles, séances, and visions in one of the chapels, causing the government great consternation; an anonymous pundit scrawled on a side door, "The King has decreed that God is prohibited from making miracles in this place." **Rue de la Montagne-Ste-Geneviève,** winding between the Panthéon and place Maubert, is one of the oldest streets in Paris, with a number of buildings dating from the Middle Ages.

Those in search of a less perfectly packaged part of the Quartier Latin should keep to the fringes and note the Eastern influence in the 13th arrondissement, where many Asian communities thrive. **Avenue des Gobelins** goes by the famous tapestry factory (a turn down the side street brings you to the leafy Square René le Gall) and directly to the **Place d'Italie.** Continue south on rue Bobillot to the charming **rue de la Butte aux Cailles,** a perfectly preserved example of old Paris. The little streets in this area offer inexpensive bars and restaurants, but the locals will not take kindly to a passel of loud Americans plunking down at a table—go exploring quietly by yourself or with one unobtrusive friend.

ST-GERMAIN-DES-PRES

This former haven for the intellectual, the beat, and the bohemian has relinquished its spirit to the hands of the mainstream, the upscale, and the comfortable. Where there used to be swinging jazz bars, bistrots, and bookstores, there are now clean, well-packaged, and rather sterile versions of the same; though plenty of students still roam the streets, they wear sport coats and Hermès scarves— few berets, very few berets. Still, on a sunny day, there are few places so golden as this sandstone quartier.

A short walking tour: Start at **Eglise St-Germain,** where monks once set up camp and blessed the area with an intellectual reputation, bringing international art and culture to the city. Rousseau and Voltaire, unable to get support elsewhere, were published in the St-Germain abbey. Literati continue to haunt the tables of **Les Deux Magots** and **Le Flore,** two overpriced cafés on boulevard St-Germain. Les Deux Magots was the favorite of Verlaine and Mallarmé, Le Flore of Jean-Paul and Simone, Camus, and Picasso, although only the Flore is still populated by French intellectuals. From the Eglise St-Germain, take **rue Bonaparte** toward the river and you'll soon reach the once-great **Ecole Nationale Supérieure des Beaux-Arts.** Take a detour to your right down **rue Visconti:** At No. 17 a young Balzac founded an unsuccessful press. On the other side of the Beaux-Arts school, Serge Gainsbourg had his Parisian digs at 5 bis rue Verneuil (today covered with spray paint) until his death in 1991. Similar in style and impact to American Bob Dylan in his song-writing and general presence, Gainsbourg became a folk hero and national idol for his poetic but risqué songs. Turn right at the river and walk past the **Palais de l'Institut de France** (at the corner of quai de Conti and Pont des Arts), the seat of the Académie Française, which Richelieu created in 1635 in an attempt to supervise the activities of Parisian intellectuals. The Académie is still around, defending the French language from foreign invaders—its latest stroke of brilliance was to *outlaw* the commercial use of non-French (read: English) words in France, though this was soon declared unconstitutional.

Set into the wall of the arcade-lined building across from the Senate (26–36 rue Vaugirard, 6e) is the last original marble "Mètre." In 1796, 16 of these plaques were strategically dotted around Paris by the National Convention in order to familiarize the public with the new "Enlightened" metric system. The fate of the Quarter-Pounder was thus sealed: Frenchies must settle for a "Royale with Cheese."

Walking along the Seine toward the Louvre, you pass **rue des Grands Augustins,** where at No. 5–7 Picasso enjoyed his last—and most luxurious—Parisian home from 1936 to 1955. Turn away from the river again on rue Dauphine, veering left at the fork a few blocks up, and you'll hit the **cour de Rohan,** where Dr. Joseph-Ignace Guillotin invented an execution device he described as a "puff of air on the neck" of the victim. Farther ahead, near Odéon, a statue of Danton marks where this great revolutionary once lived (Haussmann had his way with the actual building). Great streets branch south off place Henri-Mondor, including the tiny **rue de l'Ecole-de-Médecine,** where Sarah Bernhardt was born at No. 5. To the west lies **rue Monsieur-le-Prince;** No. 14 was home to American writer Richard Wright (from 1948 to 1959) and composer Camille Saint-Saëns (from 1877 to 1889). Head west a few blocks to **rue de Tournon,** whose 18th-century hôtels particuliers have housed too many celebrities to mention (read the plaques), among them Casanova (No. 27) and Balzac (No. 2). If you roam St-Germain with your eyes tilted upward, you'll find plenty of commemorative plaques to keep you busy.

Don't miss **rue St-André-des-Arts,** a pedestrian street roughly between place St-Michel and carrefour de Buci, lined with crêperies, postcard shops, and a good experimental cinema. The nearby **cour du Commerce St-André** (an alley between rue St-André-des-Arts and boulevard St-Germain) was opened in 1776 and saw all sorts of revolutionary activity, including the printing of Marat's *L'Ami du Peuple* at No. 8, the beheading of subversives at No. 9, and the daily life of Danton in his seven-room apartment at No. 20.

WHERE TO SLEEP

3

By Viviana Mahieux and Julia Švihra

Unless you have well-placed friends, Paris is not the cheapest place to spend a night. Single rooms in hotels start at about 100F for a dark, dingy room with a cigarette-burned bedspread, and a hall shower can cost you 10F–30F more. That said, checking into a 150F hotel usually means you're laying your body on something clean, dealing with someone nice, and leaving your bags somewhere safe. While the cheapest hotels in Paris are a bit farther from the center in **Belleville** (20e), **Montmartre** (18e), and **Montparnasse** (14e), monument-seekers willing to dish out the extra francs might be happiest in the more chic neighborhoods around the **Louvre** (1er) and **Opéra** (8e). **Les Halles** (1er), the **Marais** (4e), or the **Bastille** (11e) are great places to crash if nightlife is your raison d'être. At about 100F a night for a bed in a clean room with free showers and breakfast, youth hostels are still a bargain in Paris and are placed in some of the choicest locations. Despite the vicious early lockout hours, they're great places to meet foreign people, find travel companions, get tips, and hear about other travelers' adventures (or misadventures).

In summer, reserve at least a month in advance, particularly for hotels in the **Quartier Latin** (5e), **St-Germain-des-Prés** (6e), the **Marais** (4e), and near the **Louvre** (1er), by leaving a credit card number or a deposit for the first night. Make sure to confirm before you arrive. Because hostels book up quickly in summer, check in as early as 7 AM. AJF (*see* Visitor Information, in Chapter 1) specializes in student travel and can find you a cheap bed in a hostel for a 10F fee, but don't expect them to work miracles in high season. The tourist offices (*see* Visitor Information, in Chapter 1) can find you something at the last minute, but they don't exactly specialize in cheap rooms and they'll tack on an 8F–25F charge for their service. Innocent freeloaders who want to sleep under the stars should think again. Métro, bus, and train stations close between 1 AM and 5 AM, and most of Paris's parks are locked nightly or populated with people you wouldn't want to spend the night with. Find an all-night café or nightclub until morning, and crash on a nap-friendly bench or lawn during safer daytime hours.

Hotels

The French government uses a rating of one to four stars to indicate the percentage of rooms equipped with baths or other amenities. But this rating may not be a good indication of how nice the place is. Always ask to see a room before you take it. Room prices should be listed near the hotel's front door or on the wall behind the reception desk; the prices listed may or may not reflect room taxes, which run 1F–5F per person per night. Rooms marked *e.c.* or *c.t.* have a sink; rooms marked *douche* have a shower; and rooms marked *douche/WC* or *bain/WC* have a shower and a toilet, or a bath and toilet. If you're looking for the *prix plus bas* (lowest price), always ask for a room *simple* without toilet and shower, since French hotels almost invariably charge 30F–100F more for rooms with plumbing. On the other hand, hall showers (which cost zip–25F, depending on the owner's mood) are usually decent, as long as you're wearing thongs. *Petit déjeuner compris* means that breakfast is included in the price of the room; otherwise, the price for breakfast should be posted, and it's usually a bad deal. *The price categories in this book refer to the cost of a double room plus tax.* If a hotel has doubles for a wide range of prices, our price category will generally refer to the less expensive (usually showerless) doubles.

BASTILLE

Spreading over the 11th and 12th arrondissements on the Right Bank, the Bastille is all about cool cafés, cheap restaurants, and more bars than you could visit in a lifetime. Proximity to the Gare de Lyon is an added bonus, not to mention that most of the hotels listed below will have space long after cheap sleeps in the Quartier Latin and the Marais are gone. To find a place on your own, walk along **rue de la Roquette** or **rue de Charonne** and check out the side streets. If summer's in full swing and you don't have a reservation, try going north on **boulevard Voltaire,** which sees fewer tourists and has more welcoming (but still cheap) places to stay.

➢ **UNDER 175F** • Hôtel Nouvel France. This place is pretty squalid, but a nice indoor patio, garden, and its location redeem it a bit. Singles start at 120F, doubles at 150F; the few rooms with showers cost 180F. Monthly rentals (110F a night) are the specialty. These bargain rates can attract some sketchy dwellers, so don't leave without locking your door. *31 rue Keller, 11e, tel. 01–47–00–40–74. Métro: Bastille or Voltaire. From Bastille, walk down rue de la Roquette, turn right on rue Keller. 47 rooms, 5 with bath. Showers free.*

Modern's Hôtel. If you show the slightest knowledge of French, the eager owner will chat you up for hours. He offers clean, quiet quarters steps away from the Gare de Lyon and within walking distance from the Gare d'Austerlitz. The rooms are decent, although the carpeting makes you want to keep your shoes on. Singles are 140F, doubles 150F (210F with shower).

An American in Paris

Drawn to Paris by favorable exchange rates, the hypocrisy of Prohibition, and the disillusionment that followed World War I, many American writers, composers, and artists made the move to Paris in the 1920s and '30s (although Americans in the '90s have discovered that romance is cheaper by the koruna than the franc and have gone to Prague; see the Berkeley Guide to Eastern Europe). The romanticism of expatriate living—drinking red wine, shunning the French people, and not being able to sputter a single syllable of French—lingers on. Here's where some of these people lived or at least passed through:

AARON COPLAND: 30 rue de Vaugirard. COLE PORTER: 269 rue St-Jacques. JAMES BALDWIN: 170 boulevard St-Germain. JOHN DOS PASSOS: 45 quai de la Tournelle. ERNEST HEMINGWAY: 44 rue Jacob, 74 rue du Cardinal-Lemoine, 113 rue Notre-Dame-des-Champs, etc . . . WILLIAM FAULKNER: 26 rue Servandoni (entrance at 42 rue de Vaugirard). GERTRUDE STEIN and ALICE B. TOKLAS: 27 rue de Fleurus and 5 rue Christine. EZRA POUND: 70 bis rue Notre-Dame-des-Champs. ZELDA and F. SCOTT FITZGERALD: 14 rue de Tilsitt. HENRY MILLER: all over the place, but especially at 100 rue de la Tombe-Issoire.

11 rue d'Austerlitz, 12e, tel. 01–43–43–41–17. Métro: Gare de Lyon. Walk north on rue de Lyon, turn left on rue d'Austerlitz. 30 rooms, 14 with bath. Breakfast 20F, extra bed 40F, showers 15F.

Sainte Bastille Opéra. This hotel puts you 15 seconds from the Opéra Bastille and the lively rue de Lappe (not to mention the laundromat around the corner). Singles start at 120F, doubles at 160F. For friendly conversation or just some strong coffee, head to the bar next door, which is run by the same people. *6 rue de la Roquette, 11e, tel. 01–43–55–16–06. Métro: Bastille. 19 rooms, none with bath. Showers free.*

➢ **UNDER 200F** • **Hôtel de l'Europe.** This professional outfit offers big, clean, comfy rooms (often filled with busloads of German tourists). It's worth calling ahead. Singles and doubles are 185F, with shower 210F–230F. Ask for a room with a balcony. *74 rue Sedaine, 11e, tel. 01–47–00–54–38, fax 01–47–00–75–31. Métro: Voltaire. Walk NW on blvd. Voltaire, turn left on rue Sedaine. 26 rooms, 15 with bath. Breakfast 20F, extra bed 60F, showers 10F.*

Hôtel de Reims: A well-kept little hotel on a quiet street around the corner from the Gare de Lyon—so what if the woman who runs the place is curt? Rooms are in good condition but characterless. Singles and doubles are 175F without shower, 280F with shower and toilet. The wooded path a few steps from the hotel runs parallel to avenue Daumesnil and leads to the Bois de Vincennes. *26 rue Héctor-Ralot, 12e, tel 01–43–07–46–18. Métro: Gare de Lyon or Ledru-Rollin. From Gare de Lyon, cross rue de Chalon to rue Héctor-Ralot. 25 rooms, 10 with shower. Breakfast 30F, showers 15F.*

➢ **UNDER 225F** • **Grand Hôtel du Prince.** The entrance to this little hotel is downright grandiose, but relax—the newly renovated rooms are simple, cozy, and affordable. Singles and doubles with showers and TVs run 200F–230F. *106 blvd. Voltaire, 11e, tel. 01–47–00–95–09, fax 01–43–14–92–89. Métro: Voltaire. 25 rooms, 18 with bath. Breakfast 25F. AE, MC, V.*

Hôtel Baudin. Big, colorful, homey rooms and a location that's near the action AND safe and quiet make this a great place to stay. Singles cost 120F, 250F with shower; doubles start at 200F. Reserve at least a week in advance. *113 av. Ledru-Rollin, 11e, tel. 01–47–00–18–91. Métro: Ledru-Rollin. 19 rooms, 7 with shower. Breakfast 25F, showers 20F. AE, V.*

Nièvre-Hôtel. This hotel's cozy and unpretentious rooms make it more comfy than most budget deals . . . heck, even the folks could stay here. The Nièvre is clean, well maintained, and convenient—only two minutes from the Gare de Lyon and 10 minutes from the Bastille and its bars. Singles are 160F and doubles start at 200F. If you're lucky, you'll get to rub shoulders with the majestic cat that rules the place. *18 rue d'Austerlitz, 12e, tel. 01–43–43–81–51. Métro: Gare du Lyon. Walk north on rue de Lyon, turn left on rue d'Austerlitz. 25 rooms, 7 with bath. Breakfast 20F, showers 20F (towel 10F extra).*

Pax Hôtel. The Pax's fabulous location makes up for the chilly reception toward the backpacking set. Singles and doubles without shower are 220F–230F, or up to four people can live it up in one of the rooms with full bath, phone, and color TV for 300F–400F. It's no palace, but the rooms are meticulously maintained. *12 rue de Charonne, 11e, tel. 01–47–00–40–98, fax 01–43–38–57–81. Métro: Ledru-Rollin. Walk west on rue du Faubourg-St-Antoine toward the Bastille, turn right on rue de Charonne. 47 rooms, 40 with bath. Breakfast 30F. AE, MC, V.*

BELLEVILLE

As the Bastille becomes too trendy for its own good, young artists and musicians attracted by the cheaper prices have started to prowl around here in the immigrant-dominated Belleville. A stay here can be a relaxing respite from the swarm of August tourists—and it's a must for Jim Morrison devotees who plan on spending days elbowing crowds at nearby Père-Lachaise. Belleville, in the northern part of the 20th arrondissement, is not exactly a lodging mecca, though. Look around **place Gambetta** for hotels, but be careful wandering alone at night—women should be especially wary and prepared to dodge an occasional lewd comment.

➢ **UNDER 125F** • **Hôtel de Bordeaux.** This large hotel sits near the busy intersection of rue de Belleville and boulevard de Belleville, close to heaps of cheap restaurants. The dark

Auberge Internationale des Jeunes, **46**

Auberge de Jeunesse d'Artagnan, **28**

Auberge de Jeunesse Cité des Sciences, **8**

Auberge de Jeunesse Jules-Ferry, **25**

BVJ de Paris/Louvre, **20**

Grand Hôtel du Loiret, **33**

Grand Hôtel du Prince, **29**

Grand Hôtel Jeanne-d'Arc, **38**

Hôtel André Gill, **5**

Hôtel Andréa, **32**

Hôtel Baudin, **45**

Hôtel Bonne Nouvelle, **12**

Hôtel Caulaincourt, **1**

Hôtel de Bordeaux, **24**

Hôtel de la Herse d'Or, **41**

Hôtel de la Vallée, **22**

Hôtel de l'Europe, **30**

Hôtel de Lille, **18**

Hôtel de Reims, **50**

Hôtel du Brabant, **13**

Hôtel du Chemin de Fer, **26**

Hôtel du Commerce, **3**

Hôtel Haussman, **15**

Hôtel Henri IV, **31**

Hôtel La Fayette, **9**

Hôtel La Marmotte, **21**

Hôtel Métropole La Fayette, **10**

Hôtel Montpensier, **17**

Hôtel Nouvel France, **43**

Hôtel Paris-Opéra, **14**

Hôtel Pratic, **39**

Hôtel Richelieu Mazarin, **16**

Hôtel Rivoli, **34**

Hôtel Surcouf, **4**

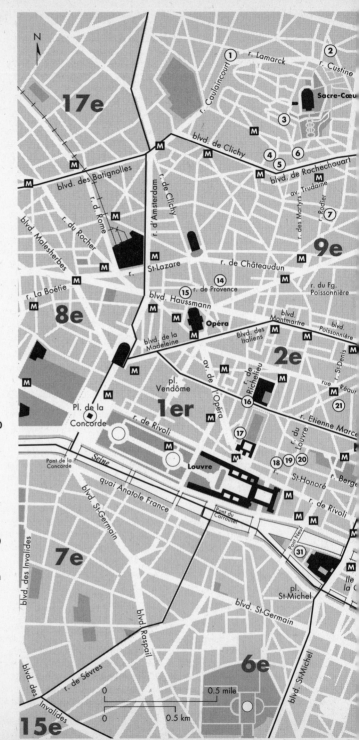

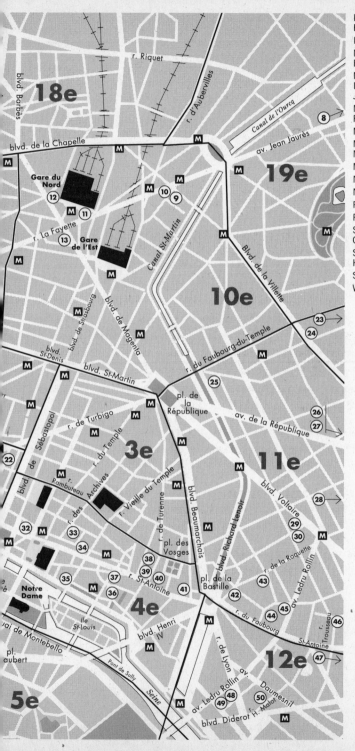

Hôtel Vieille France, **11**
Idéal Hotel, **6**
Maison des Etudiants, **19**
Maison Internationale des Jeunes, **47**
MIJE le Fauconnier, **36**
MIJE le Fourcy, **37**
MIJE Maubuisson, **35**
Modern's Hôtel, **49**
Nadaud Hôtel, **27**
Nièvre Hôtel, **48**
Pax Hôtel, **44**
Printana, **23**
Sainte Bastille Opéra, **42**
Société Modern Hôtel, **2**
Sully Hôtel, **40**
Woodstock, **7**

rooms are a little grim, but they're fairly clean, safe, and cheap. Singles are 100F–120F, doubles 120F–150F. A few larger doubles with bath and TV go for 200F. The happy man at the desk can almost always squeeze you in with a day's notice, but insist on getting the cheaper rooms, or else he'll happily squeeze you into the expensive ones. *3 rue Lémon, at blvd. de Belleville, 20e, tel. 01–40–33–98–15. Métro: Belleville. Walk south on blvd de Belleville, turn left on rue Lémon. 66 rooms, 34 with bath.*

➢ **UNDER 175F** • **Hôtel du Chemin de Fer.** Okay, so the rooms are a bit drab, and the reception none too friendly. At least you're steps away from Père Lachaise or the nearest Métro station, and the hotel's double-paned windows ensure peace and quiet. To soak up some French popular culture, ask for a room with a color TV (a 50F investment). Singles or doubles go for 170F–245F, or pick a tiny single room for 100F. *233 rue des Pyrénées, 20e, tel. 01–43–58–55–18. Métro: Gambetta. 33 rooms, 26 with shower. Showers 18F. AE, MC, V.*

➢ **UNDER 200F** • **Nadaud Hôtel.** The rooms, some with gorgeous views of Paris, are more than worth the price—doubles 195F and up (275F with shower). The friendly owners go out of

---

Have Wheelchair, Will Travel

Although Paris is slowly beginning to accommodate visitors in wheelchairs, low-end hotels aren't making much progress, with no elevators, too many stairs, and narrow hallways. Many of the hotels in prime locations (like the Louvre and Opéra area, or the Marais) are parts of historical neighborhoods, and are prohibited by law to make fundamental architectural changes. Unless you get a space in an accessible hostel or foyer, you're looking at around 450F a night, and it's usually not in a central neighborhood. Be sure to reserve ahead at these accessible, if not exactly budget, hotels—there are only a few adapted rooms, and these classy establishments fill up quickly. All accept major credit cards.

- *Grand Hôtel de France. Two double rooms are adapted (470F), though the entrance has one step. 102 blvd. de La-Tour-Maubourg, 7e, tel. 01–47–05–40–49. Métro: Ecole Militaire.*

- *Hôtel Campanile Italie Gobelins. Beyond the main entrance ramp there are two steps to the reception, but four rooms and their bathrooms are adapted and a deal at 420F. 15 bis av. d'Italie, 13e, tel. 01–45–84–95–95. Métro: Place d'Italie.*

- *Hôtel Urbis Jemmapes Louis Blanc. Two doubles with bath (440F) are adapted, and there are no steps. 12 rue Louis Blanc, 10e, tel. 01–42–01–21–21. Métro: Louis Blanc.*

- *Hôtel Urbis Lafayette. Everything is flat or reachable by elevator except for the back garden, which has one step. Three adapted rooms with bath go for 450F. 122 rue La Fayette, 10e, tel. 01–45–23–27–27. Métro: Gare du Nord (station is wheelchair accessible).*

- *Foyer International d'Accueil de Paris Jean Monnet. This huge foyer has several rooms and bathrooms adapted for disabled visitors. Singles are 260F. 30 rue Cabanis, 14e, tel. 01–45–89–89–15, fax 01–45–81–63–91. Métro: Glacière.*

their way to be helpful. Reservations are recommended at least a week in advance. *8 rue de la Bidassoa, near av. Gambetta, 20e, tel. 01–46–36–87–79, fax 01–46–36–05–41. Métro: Gambetta. 22 rooms, 13 with shower. Breakfast 27F, showers 20F. MC, V.*

➤ **UNDER 225F • Printana.** It's in the middle of great shops and restaurants, with stark but respectable rooms in a safe part of Belleville. Tiny, dormlike singles go for 140F, doubles for 200F (245F–295F with shower). Some rooms have balconies, but there are no hall showers. Ask for a room at the back, since the street tends to be noisy. *355 rue des Pyrénées, 20e, tel. 01–46–36–76–62. Métro: Jourdain. 41 rooms, 24 with shower. Breakfast 25F, elevator.*

GARE DE L'EST AND GARE DU NORD

The Gare de l'Est and Gare du Nord are close enough to merge; only a tiny block or two separates the rail lines stretching out behind each station. It's a great area to stay in if you arrive late, don't have a reservation, and are too tired to drag your belongings any farther. But stay away if you value peace and quiet (traffic roars all night long) or your wallet—foreign visitors have reported thefts here, some at gunpoint. If the hotels below are booked, walk straight from either station one block to **boulevard de Magenta** and its budget hotels.

➤ **UNDER 150F • Hôtel La Fayette.** If you speak French, this hotel's overworked Maghrebian receptionists are more than willing to share coffee and talk politics. The smallish rooms are clean, modest, and simple; the only frills are the hardwood floors and double-paned windows. Singles are 110F, doubles 135F–155F. The lone room with a private shower costs 226F. *198 rue La Fayette, 10e, tel. 01–40–35–76–07, fax 01–42–09–69–05. Métro: Louis Blanc. 21 rooms. Breakfast 20F, showers 20F. MC, V.*

Hôtel Métropole La Fayette. This place is literally in the middle of the street, on an island between three noisy avenues. Still, the La Fayette is a model of budget fare: clean enough, cheap, and convenient. Singles start at 110F (150F with shower), doubles from 130F (180F with shower). *204 rue La Fayette, 10e, tel. 01–46–07–72–69. Métro: Louis Blanc. 29 rooms, 22 with bath. Breakfast 15F, showers 20F. MC, V.*

➤ **UNDER 225F • Hôtel Bonne Nouvelle.** A two-minute walk from the Gare du Nord, this clean, comfortable establishment will welcome you (in English, no less) with not only a bed but your own telephone and shower. Request a room facing the courtyard, unless you'd prefer to hang out on an exhaust-filled balcony. The one single is 170F; doubles cost 220F. It's 20F extra for a TV. Reservations are recommended in summer. *125 blvd. de Magenta, 10e, tel. 01–48–74–99–90. Métro: Gare du Nord. 22 rooms, all with bath. Breakfast 20F, luggage storage.*

Hôtel du Brabant. This peaceful hotel on the tiny rue des Petits-Hôtels will welcome you Middle Eastern–style, with a blue mosaic reception area overflowing with plants. Come by in the morning—the friendly proprietor reserves a few rooms for stragglers even when it's really busy. The rooms, despite the no-smoking signs, are a bit musty but clean. Singles go for 140F–180F, doubles 200F (240F with shower) The nearby Marché St-Quentil is great for fresh produce. *18 rue des Petits-Hôtels, 10e, tel. 01–47–70–12–32, fax 01–47–70–20–32. Métro: Gare du Nord, Gare de l'Est, or Poissonnière. From Gare du Nord and Gare de l'Est, take blvd. de Magenta to rue des Petits-Hôtels. 35 rooms, 11 with bath. Breakfast 20F, showers 18F. MC, V.*

Hôtel Vieille France. Crawl into this comfy hotel a few steps from the station and let the pastel rooms, bouncy beds, and color TVs soothe you. Singles and doubles start at 195F without bath, then shoot up to 250F–320F with all the amenities. Triples are 330F–360F. *151 rue La Fayette, 10e, tel 01–45–26–42–37, fax 01–45–26–99–07. Métro: Gare du Nord. 40 rooms, some with bath. Breakfast 28F, elevator, showers 12F. Reservations advised. MC. V.*

LES HALLES AND BEAUBOURG

Central, lively, and cheap, Les Halles makes for a hip-happening place to crash . . . but not necessarily to get a lick of sleep. The quarter offers some great shopping and nightlife, and it's steps away from the Louvre and the Centre Pompidou. But be forewarned that above rue Réaumur, streets like rue St-Denis host some serious red-light activity, and sex shops galore attract a nice amount of sleaze. Keep an eye on your wallet and avoid wandering around at night with a big map and a puzzled look.

➤ **UNDER 225F** • **Hôtel Andréa.** Run around in the nearby Centre Pompidou, gorge yourself on a falafel in the Marais, and then plop down here for a siesta. Five modest doubles are 200F; spacious doubles away from the rue de Rivoli traffic with telephone and TV run 330F–350F. Call far ahead to reserve the cheaper rooms. *3 rue St-Bon, at rue de Rivoli, 4e, tel. 01–42–78–43–93. Métro: Hôtel de Ville or Châtelet–Les Halles. 26 rooms, 21 with bath. Breakfast 30F, luggage storage, showers 15F.*

Hôtel de la Vallée. Even though it's squeezed in between an erotic bookstore and a sex shop, this is actually quite a deal, due to the small but clean rooms and professional staff. Multitudes milling around the streets keep things relatively safe, although single women may have to endure a leer or two. Singles 155F, doubles 205F (285F with shower). *84 rue St-Denis, 1er, tel. 01–42–36–46–99. Métro: Etienne Marcel or Châtelet–Les Halles. From Etienne Marcel, walk south on rue Pierre-Lescot, turn left on rue Rambuteau to rue St-Denis. 32 rooms, some with bath. Breakfast 30F, showers 15F. Reservations advised. MC, V.*

Hôtel La Marmotte. The Opéra, the Louvre, and the Marais are all a 10-minute walk from this quiet corner of Les Halles, just up the street from the daily rue Montorgueil market. Your reward for conquering the vertiginous stairs: better-than-average rooms, all with TVs and telephones. Singles run 180F–270F, doubles 220F–230F. In the evening, locals fill the laid-back bar downstairs. *6 rue Léopold-Bellan, 2e, tel. 01–40–26–26–51. Métro: Sentier. Walk east on rue Réamur, turn right on rue des Petits Caneaux, which becomes rue Montorgueil, right on rue Léopold-Bellan. 16 rooms, most with bath. Breakfast 20F, showers 15F. AE, MC, V.*

LOUVRE TO OPERA

Anyone with a Napoleonic complex will want to stay here, smack in the historic heart of the city amid many of Paris's grandest monuments. The area isn't exactly infused with alternative youth culture (more like older ladies in fur coats), but it's definitely one of the most beautiful neighborhoods in Paris. Which means it's expensive: Unless you stay in a BVJ foyer (*see* Hostels and Foyers, *below*) or in one of the hotels below, you'll shell out at least 500F for a room.

➤ **UNDER 225F** • **Hôtel Haussmann.** In a nutshell, it's a clean, small, professional outfit that plops you right behind the Opéra and not far from the Gare St-Lazare. The English-speaking owner caters mostly to French couples; hence the slightly smoky rooms and mirrors everywhere (no, not over the beds). Reservations are a good idea. Singles run 200F–265F, doubles 200F–310F. *89 rue de Provence, 9e, tel. 01–48–74–24–57, fax 01–44–91–97–25. Métro: Havre-Caumartin. Walk north on rue de Caumartin, turn right on rue de Provence. 34 rooms, all with bath. Breakfast 25F, elevator. MC, V.*

Hôtel Henri IV. It's amazing that a budget hotel could exist in such a location—right on the Ile de la Cité, steps from Notre Dame but away from all grinding Parisian traffic. The atmosphere is rustic and charming, thanks largely to the humorous French proprietor who goes out of his way to make you chuckle. Shabby but comfy singles are 110F–270F, doubles 220F–270F, with breakfast included. Reserve far in advance. *25 pl. Dauphine, 1er, tel. 01–43–54–44–53. Métro: Pont Neuf. Cross Pont Neuf to Ile de la Cité, turn left on rue H. Robert. 22 rooms, none with bath. Reception open 8–7. Showers 15F.*

Hôtel de Lille. Reserve ahead for the best deal in the quarter, steps from the Louvre, the Palais Royal, and Les Halles. It's a family-run operation on a quiet street, with worn yet well-tended rooms. Singles 190F, doubles 220F–270F. *8 rue du Pélican, 1er, tel. 01–42–33–33–42. Métro: Palais Royal–Musée du Louvre. Walk east on rue St-Honoré, turn left on rue J.-J. Rousseau, left on rue du Pélican. 14 rooms, 6 with shower. Breakfast 14F, showers 30F.*

➤ **UNDER 250F** • **Hôtel Paris-Opéra.** If pink for girls and light blue for boys brings back unhappy childhood memories, please skip to the next review. Otherwise, the Paris-Opéra is a fine choice, with the Grands Magasins and the Opéra both around the corner. Ask for a room that's not facing the street and you'll get more sleep. Singles are 185F–210F, doubles

230F–330F, triples 350F. *76 rue de Provence, 9e, tel. 01–48–74–12–15, fax 01–40–16– 43–34. Métro: Chaussée d'Antin. Walk north on rue de la Chaussée-d'Antin to rue de Provence. 32 rooms, all with bath. Breakast 20F, elevator. AE, MC, V.*

Hôtel Richelieu Mazarin. This family-run hotel, five minutes from Garnier's Opéra and two from the Comédie Française, has rooms fit for a cardinal at refreshingly common prices: Singles are 190F–280F, doubles from 230F (300F with private shower). Reserve two weeks ahead for the two showerless rooms. There's a great boulangerie next door. *51 rue de Richelieu, 1er, tel. 01– 42–97–46–20, fax 01–47–03–94–13. Métro: Pyramides. Cross av. de l'Opéra, walk west on rue Thérèse to rue de Richelieu. 14 rooms, 12 with bath. Breakfast 25F, showers 10F.*

➢ **UNDER 275F** • **Hôtel Montpensier.** The Montpensier is high-class and run by a professional, welcoming, English-speaking staff—the lobby is so nice that backpackers may feel slightly out of place. The rooms aren't any great luxury . . . just clean and big. What you're really paying for is location: right below the Opéra, 60 seconds from the Louvre, and next door to the Comédie Française. Reserve ahead for one of the bathless, 250F singles or doubles (rooms with bath jump to 390F). *12 rue de Richelieu, 1er, tel. 01–42–96–28–50, fax 01– 42–86–02–70. Métro: Palais Royal–Musée du Louvre. Walk west on rue St-Honoré to rue de Richelieu. 45 rooms, 37 with bath. Breakfast 30F, showers 25F. AE, MC, V.*

LE MARAIS

The Marais is one of the best places to stay in Paris: You'll be sandwiched between Les Halles, the Bastille, and the Seine, and right around the corner from kosher delis, an active gay community, and loads of cool bars and cafés, which guarantee nonstop street life and a sumptuous night scene. Make your way into one of the quarter's famous *hôtels particuliers* (mansions) by staying at the fantastic foyers run by Maisons Internationales des Jeunes Etudiants (*see* Hostels and Foyers, *below*). Otherwise, scout out cheap sleeps in the streets just above **rue de Rivoli** near the Bastille.

➢ **UNDER 175F** • **Grand Hôtel du Loiret.** This recently renovated hotel has not lost any of its kitschy charm—it's still the sort of place where the wallpaper and bedspreads clash nicely. Even more appealing is its central Marais location and its able staff. Singles start at 140F, doubles at 160F (210F with shower). *8 rue des Mauvais-Garçons, 4e, tel. 01–48–87– 77–00. Métro: Hôtel de Ville. Walk east on rue de Rivoli, turn left on rue des Mauvais-Garçons. 30 rooms, 5 with bath. Breakfast 25F, elevator, showers 15F. MC, V.*

Hôtel de la Herse d'Or. The good news is that this place almost always has room and the accommodating manager is always cheerful and chatty. The bad news is that most of the rooms share an air vent that conducts the sound of your neighbors—snores, screams, and smoker's hack—better than fiber optics. Spacious singles and doubles start at 160F (280F with private bath). *20 rue St-Antoine, 4e, tel. 01–48–87–84–09, fax 01–42–78–12–68. Métro: Bastille or St-Paul. 39 rooms, 15 with shower. Breakfast 35F, luggage storage, showers 10F.*

Hôtel Rivoli. This hotel is not big on decorative frills, but it's friendly, clean, and popular with French folks (reservations are vital in summer). The rooms facing rue de Rivoli can be noisy, so try to get one overlooking the smaller rue des Mauvais-Garçons (translation: Bad Boys Street) instead. Singles are 140F–160F, doubles from 160F (220F with shower); triples are a deal at 240F. Check out the produce shop around the corner, or indulge in one of the many Chinese joints on rue de Venise. *44 rue de Rivoli, at rue des Mauvais-Garçons, 4e, tel. 01–42–72– 08–41. Métro: Hôtel de Ville. 20 rooms, 12 with bath. Breakfast 20F, showers 20F.*

➢ **UNDER 225F** • **Sully Hôtel.** The rooms, although dark, are clean and big, and the beds are firm enough to support even the weightiest of backpacks. You'll be around the corner from the beautiful place des Vosges and near the Sully hôtel particulier. There's no curfew, so take advantage of the Marais and Bastille nightlife at all hours. The lone single goes for 100F; otherwise doubles run 200F–280F, triples and quads 250F–280F. *48 rue St-Antoine, 4e, tel. 01–42–78–49–32. Métro: St-Paul. 22 rooms, 11 with bath. Breakfast 20F, showers 10F.*

➤ **UNDER 250F** • **Hôtel Pratic.** The Pratic is a charmer—all the rooms were redone in 1995, so they're in great condition, and it's in a fantastic location. Unless you mind the drifting sounds of an occasional impromptu jazz session in place du Marché-Ste-Catherine, ask for a room facing the scenic little square. A word to the grubby: If your room doesn't have a shower, you may have to descend as many as four flights to bathe. Singles are 150F, doubles with bath 230F (up to 340F for the deluxe with shower), triples 380F. Reserve a week in advance. *9 rue d'Ormesson, 4e, tel. 01–48–87–80–47, fax 01–48–87–40–04. Métro: St-Paul. Walk east on rue St-Antoine, turn left on rue de Sévigné, right on rue d'Ormesson. 22 rooms, 15 with shower. Breakfast 25F, luggage storage, showers 10F.*

➤ **UNDER 300F** • **Grand Hôtel Jeanne-d'Arc.** Come get your money's worth at this newly renovated splurge in the heart of the Marais. The large and modern rooms have a bathroom, telephone, television, and sometimes a couch. Singles and doubles are 295F–380F. The English-speaking, 100% female management is very sensitive to different travelers' needs: All rooms are safe for children, and come equipped with braille telephones. *3 rue de Jarente, 4e, tel. 01–48–87–62–11. Métro: St-Paul. Walk east on rue St-Antoine, turn left on rue de Sévigné, right on rue de Jarente. 63 rooms. Breakfast 35F. MC, V.*

MONTMARTRE

Even though it's on the northern edge of the city, Montmartre is a great place to experience Paris's diversity (sex shops, tourist traps, and old-style streets). Montmartre's distance from the center—most major attractions are 15 minutes by Métro—guarantees a few lodging bargains for starving artists (like those who once occupied the area). The nearer the sex shops of Pigalle, the cheaper and sleazier the rooms—be sure to specify one night, not one *hour*. The streets fanning out from **place des Abbesses** are full of cheap, sporadically respectable options.

➤ **UNDER 100F** • **Hôtel du Commerce.** The friendly proprietor's motto is it's better to have a full room than an empty one, so don't be afraid to negotiate. The rooms are less than inspiring, with peeling paint and uneven floors, but the mattresses are all in good shape. Many of the singles house waiters, waitresses, and artists who work in the hood. Reservations are not accepted, so arrive by 10 AM to secure a spot. This place is popular with the backpacking set due to the *hyper*-cheap prices. Singles and doubles are 85F–100F, with shower 110F–120F. *34 rue des Trois-Frères, 18e, tel. 01–42–64–81–69. Métro: Abbesses. Walk east on rue de La Vieuville to rue des Trois-Frères. 34 rooms, 7 with shower. Showers 15F.*

➤ **UNDER 125F** • **Hôtel Surcouf.** It's owned by the same guy who owns Hôtel du Commerce, and the same rules apply here for negotiating prices and making reservations. Ask for a street-facing room on the fifth floor for an incredible view of Paris. Singles and doubles 100F–120F (150F–160F with shower). *18 rue Houdon, 18e, tel. 01–46–06–41–30. Métro: Pigalle. Cross blvd. de Clichy to rue Houdon. 35 rooms, 11 with shower. Showers 15F.*

➤ **UNDER 150F** • **Société Modern Hôtel.** Stay here if you want to be near cafés, cheap restaurants, and working-class bars. The Sacré-Cœur is a 10-minute uphill walk to the south. Spartan rooms are brightened up a bit by fresh paint and wallpaper. Added frills are the friendly management and a laundromat around the corner. Singles and doubles go for 130F (170F–215F with shower). *62 rue Ramey, 18e, tel. 01–46–06–29–40, fax 01–46–06–48–74. Métro: Jules Joffrin. Walk south up the hill, turn left on rue Ramey. 64 rooms, 18 with shower. Breakfast 25F, extra bed 50F, showers 20F.*

The Métro station Abbesses, near the Sacré-Cœur, has one of the few remaining art nouveau Métropolitain archways, as well as a seven-flight, curving stairway whose walls are decorated with murals depicting Parisian life.

➤ **UNDER 175F** • **Hôtel Caulaincourt.** This hotel is in one of Paris's more tranquil neighborhoods, on a typically Montmartrois gravity-defying street of steps. Some of the smaller rooms, labeled "chambres d'artistes," have spectacular views over Paris and used to be rented out to artists. Singles are 125F–195F, doubles are 165F (195F–285F with shower); triples with shower are 230F–270F. Some rooms are rented out by the month, but they're pretty hard to snag. The Sacré-Cœur and place du Tertre are a 10-minute walk away. *2 sq. Caulaincourt, btw 63 and 65* rue Caulaincourt, 18e, tel. 01–46–06–42–99, fax 01–46–06–48–67. Métro: Lamarck-Caulaincourt. Climb the stairs, then turn right on rue Caulaincourt. 53 rooms, 35 with bath. Curfew 2 AM. Showers 20F. MC, V.

➤ **UNDER 200F • Idéal Hôtel.** Despite the curt, speed-talking Frenchwoman who runs the hotel, this is one of the best values in Montmartre. A respectable room for one starts at 125F, for two at 190F, for three at 250F. There's also a shower on every floor. Stay here and you're essentially at the foot of the stairs to the Sacré-Cœur and near loads of lively restaurants. Reserve at least 10 days in advance. 3 rue des Trois-Frères, 18e, tel. 01–46–06–63–63, fax 01–42–64–97–01. Métro: Abbesses. Walk east on rue Yvonne-Le-Tac to rue des Trois-Frères. 51 rooms, none with bath. Showers 20F.

➤ **UNDER 250F • Hôtel André Gill.** The rooms at this friendly hotel are some of the nicest around place des Abbesses—your tired feet will love the plush carpet, and some rooms even have stained-glass windows. The hotel is set in a peaceful courtyard off the street, so the sound of chirping birds makes the sex shops two blocks off seem miles away. Singles are 160F, doubles 240F (360F with shower). All prices except the 160F singles include breakfast. 4 rue André-Gill, at rue des Martyrs, 18e, tel. 01–42–62–48–48, fax 01–42–62–77–92. Métro: Pigalle or Abbesses. From Pigalle, walk east on blvd. de Clichy, turn left on rue des Martyrs. 33 rooms, 21 with bath. Showers 25F. AE, MC, V.

MONTPARNASSE

Montparnasse expands across the sprawling 14th arrondissement and nudges its way into neighboring Left Bank districts, including the Quartier Latin and St-Germain. You'll see students, professors, and businessmen guzzling coffee as they gab and read in Montparnasse's famous cafés, once the intellectual playground for Hemingway, Miller, and friends. The small hotels here tend to have more character than those in the Quartier Latin. Just be prepared to dodge shoppers and high-heeled speedwalkers along hotel-crammed streets like **rue d'Odessa, rue Delambre,** and **place Denfert-Rochereau.**

➤ **UNDER 200F • Hôtel de l'Espérance.** The "Hotel of Hope" is on a small street in the southern, less tourist-infested part of Montparnasse. Many of the comfortable TV-equipped rooms overlook cafés and restaurants, and the proprietess is energetic and eager to please. You're also right by a great market on rue Daguerre. Singles or doubles go for 190F (260F with bath), triples for 325F. Be sure to book well in advance. 1 rue de Grancey, 14e, tel. 01–43–21–41–04, fax 01–43–22–06–02. Métro: Denfert-Rochereau. Walk SW on av. du Général-Leclerc, turn right on rue Daguerre, right on rue de Grancey. 17 rooms, some with bath. Breakfast 25F, showers 20F.

➤ **UNDER 225F • Celtic Hôtel.** The Celtic has decent, quiet rooms with wooden armoires and ornamental fireplaces, if you can bear the pastel walls. Singles start at 190F, doubles at 220F, and all come with TV. No smoking is allowed, so your lungs can breathe easy here. Reserve at least a week ahead for the cheapest rooms. 15 rue d'Odessa, 14e, tel. 01–43–20–93–53, fax 01–43–20–66–07. Métro: Edgar Quinet. Walk west on blvd. Edgar-Quinet, turn right on rue d'Odessa. 36 rooms, some with bath. Breakfast 20F, showers 15F. MC, V.

➤ **UNDER 250F • Hôtel Baudelaire.** With his poetry inscribed on the walls, this hotel plays homage to the melancholy poet Charles Baudelaire (1821–67), conveniently buried in the nearby Cimetière du Montparnasse. The rooms themselves, however, are nothing to whine about—modern, spacious, and equipped with bathroom, TV, and phone. Singles 190F, doubles 240F, triples 340F. They also make reservations for the similarly priced **Hôtel Lionceau** around the corner at 22 rue Daguerre (tel. 01–43–22–53–53). 22 rue Boulard, 14e, tel. 01–44–10–72–44, fax 01–44–10–72–49. Métro: Denfert-Rochereau. Walk west on rue Froidevaux, turn left on rue Boulard. 26 rooms, all with bath. Reception open 7–7. Breakfast 25F. MC, V.

➤ **UNDER 275F • Hôtel des Académies.** It's on a quiet street full of art stores and students, and the rooms—simple, dark, and old—definitely appeal to starving-artist types. The frail proprietess keeps birds in the salon and an aquarium by the stairs. Singles are 190F–295F, doubles from 255F. 15 rue de la Grande-Chaumière, 6e, tel. 01–43–26–66–

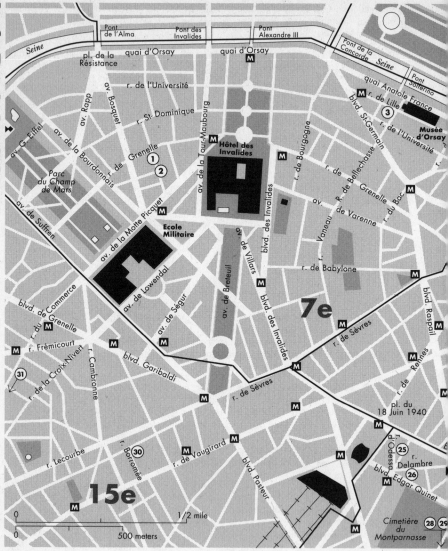

Left Bank Lodging

Seine

Pont de l'Alma

Pont des Invalides

Pont Alexandre III

Pont de la Concorde

Pont Solférino

pl. de la Résistance

quai d'Orsay

quai d'Orsay

Seine

quai Anatole France

r. de Lille

bvd. St-Germain

Musée d'Orsay

r. de l'Université

av. Rapp

av. Bosquet

r. St-Dominique

de Grenelle

av. de la Bourdonnais

av. de la Tour-Maubourg

r. de Bourgogne

r. de Bellechasse

r. de Grenelle

r. du Bac

av. G-Eiffel

Hôtel des Invalides

Vaneau

av. de Varenne

av. de Suffren

Parc du Champ de Mars

av. de la Motte Picquet

Ecole Militaire

bvd. des Invalides

av. de Villars

r. de Babylone

blvd. Raspail

av. de Lowendal

av. de Ségur

av. de Breteuil

blvd. des Invalides

7e

r. de Sèvres

blvd. de Commerce

r. du Grenelle

r. Frémicourt

r. de la Croix-Nivert

r. Cambronne

blvd. Garibaldi

r. de Sèvres

r. de Rennes

31

r. de Sèvres

pl. du 18 Juin 1940

r. Lecourbe

r. Borromée

r. de Vaugirard

blvd. Pasteur

30

25 r. Delambre

26 blvd. Edgar Quinet

15e

Cimetière du Montparnasse

28 **29**

0 — 1/2 mile

0 — 500 meters

Aloha Hostel, **30**
Les Argonautes, **9**
Association des Etudiants Protestants de Paris, **7**
BVJ de Paris/ Quartier Latin, **13**
Celtic-Hôtel, **25**
Grand Hôtel du Progrés, **18**
Grand Hôtel Lévêque, **2**
Hôtel Baudelaire, **29**

Hôtel de l'Espérance, **28**
Hôtel de Médicis, **16**
Hôtel de Nesle, **4**
Hôtel des Académies, **24**
Hôtel des Alliés, **21**
Hôtel des Bains, **26**
Hôtel du Brésil, **15**
Hôtel du Centre, **1**
Hôtel du Commerce, **12**
Hôtel du Globe, **6**

Hôtel du Petit Trianon, **5**
Hôtel Esmeralda, **10**
Hôtel Floridor, **27**
Hôtel Gay-Lussac, **19**
Hôtel Jean Bart, **22**
Hôtel le Central, **14**
Hôtel Marignan, **11**
Hôtel Résidence d'Orsay, **3**
Hôtel Stella, **8**

Three Ducks Hostel, **31**
Université de Paris Foyer International des Etudiantes, **17**
Villa "Les Camélias", **23**
Young and Happy Youth Hostel, **20**

3e

1er

Louvre

Pont Royal

Pont du Carrousel

Pont des Arts

r. de Rivoli

blvd. Sébastopol

r. Beaubourg

4e

r. de Rivoli

Pont Neuf

r. Jacob

r. des Sts-Pères

r. de Seine

r. Mazarine

r. Dauphine

Île de la Cité

Notre Dame

Pont d'Arcade

quai des Célestins

blvd. St-Germain

r. St-Andre des Arts

pl. St-Michel

Île St-Louis

Pont de la Tournelle

r. du Four

Monsieur le-Prince

r. de l'Odéon

quai de Montebello

Pont de Sully

quai St-Bernard

pl. Maubert

r. de Rennes

pl. St-Sulpice

r. St-Jacques

pl. de l'Odéon

r. des Ecoles

r. Monge

r. de Vaugirard

6e

Jardin du Luxembourg

r. Cujas

pl. du Panthéon

r. Descartes

5e

Jardin des Plantes

le Goff

Gay Lussac

r. Mouffetard

pl. de la Contrescarpe

pl. Monge

r. d'Assas

r. Guynemer

blvd. St-Michel

r. d'Ulm

r. Thomond

r. Monge

r. Censier

r. de la Grande Chaumière

blvd. du Montparnasse

r. Claude Bernard

20

blvd. Raspail

14e

r. Berthollet

blvd. St-Marcel

4 5 6 7 8 9 10 11 12 13 14 15 16 17 18 19 20 21 22 23 24 27 29

123

44. *Métro: Vavin. Walk east on blvd. du Montparnasse, turn left on rue de la Grande-Chaumière. 18 rooms, some with bath. Breakfast 27F, showers free.*

➤ **UNDER 300F** • **Hôtel Floridor.** This hotel in southern Montparnasse has become a kind of Bavaria West thanks to its connection with a German travel agency. All the rooms are well tended and have TVs; it's a little dark, but the beds aren't bad. The lone single (210F) isn't worth fighting for; you're much better off sharing a double for 240F–325F. Triples are 395F, and quads 480F. Give the hour of your arrival when you make your reservation and be prompt; they won't hold your reservation for very long. You can knock 25F off the price in low season by not taking the breakfast, but it's *obligatoire* in the summer (they'll serve it to your room upon request). *28 pl. Denfert-Rochereau, 14e, tel. 01–43–21–35–53, fax 01–43–27–65–81. Métro: Denfert-Rochereau. 60 rooms, some with bath. Elevator, extra bed 60F, showers 20F. MC, V.*

➤ **UNDER 325F** • **Villa "Les Camélias."** After walking along desolate streets covered with graffiti, you'll step into a wonderland of flowers and kitsch. The quiet, spacious rooms are lower octane than the lobby. Singles cost 295F, doubles 305F–355F, all with bath, TV, and phone. The hotel is east of the Gare Montparnasse and a short stroll from the Jardin du Luxembourg. *4 rue Jules-Chaplain, at rue Notre-Dame-des-Champs, 6e, tel. 01–43–26–94–92. Métro: Vavin. Walk north on blvd. Raspail, turn right on rue Bréa, right on rue Jules-Chaplain. 13 rooms. Breakfast 30F.*

➤ **UNDER 400F** • **Hôtel des Bains.** The downside: You're in the 400F price category, buddy. The upside: It's on a small street, managed by a multilingual staff, and newly renovated. It's almost too clean to have character, but it's situated around a quiet courtyard. One or two people pay 380F for a room with TV, phone—and a hair dryer. Suites for three to five people run 460F–630F. *33 rue Delambre, 14e, tel. 01–43–20–85–27, fax 01–42–79–82–78. Métro: Edgar Quinet. 41 rooms, all with bath. Breakfast 45F. Reservations advised.*

NEAR THE EIFFEL TOWER

This Left Bank quarter is Paris at its poshest—don't expect to find any cheap lodging here. Fancy apartments line the wide avenues, and hordes of tourists flock to the Eiffel Tower and Les Invalides before regrouping at an expensive restaurant or café. The bargains here are at small hotels, so book far in advance. If living it up in style is your Parisian fantasy, the seventh arrondissement might be just what you're looking for.

➤ **UNDER 225F** • **Grand Hôtel Lévêque.** This hotel—possibly the best deal in the seventh—is surrounded by fruit stands, pâtisseries, strung chickens, and all the trappings of a market street. The staff is friendly and occasionally English-speaking. Lug your baggage UP all those STAIRS and COLLAPSE in a clean, modern single or double (195F–290F, 315F–345F with full bath). Hall showers are free. *29 rue Cler, 7e, tel. 01–47–05–49–15, fax 01–45–50–49–36. Métro: Ecole Militaire. Walk NE on av. de La Motte-Picquet, turn left on rue Cler. 50 rooms, 48 with shower. Breakfast 25F. MC, V.*

Hôtel du Centre. It's on the same market-lined street as the Lévêque, with clean and modern rooms presided over by a stern, English-speaking proprietress. Singles and doubles start at 220F; rooms with full bath and TV peak at 360F. *24 bis rue Cler, 7e, tel. 01–47–05–52–33, fax 01–40–62–95–66. Métro: Ecole Militaire. Walk NE on av. de La Motte-Picquet, turn left on rue Cler. 30 rooms, all with bath. Breakfast 30F, elevator, showers 10F. AE, MC, V.*

➤ **UNDER 325F** • **Hôtel Résidence Orsay.** Fans of impressionism should book far ahead and hope for one of the four 320F singles or doubles that are a block away from the Musée d'Orsay. Miss them and you'll pay at least 420F to stay in super-clean rooms, with pastel decor and lots of natural light. The reception speaks English, but it's more fun to practice your French with the jovial porter. *93 rue de Lille, 7e, tel. 01–47–05–05–27, fax 01–47–05–29–48. Métro: Assemblée Nationale. 27 rooms, all with shower. Breakfast 35F, extra bed 90F. MC, V.*

QUARTIER LATIN

Home to the two snootiest schools in France and the tourists who buy their inauthentic T-shirts, the Quartier Latin remains one of the most heavily visited districts in all of Paris. This fact has unfortunately clobbered the housing situation, and unless leaky roofs or temperamental plumbing hold a rustic kind of charm for you, avoid the cheap hotels in this area. Those intent on sharing air with the stuffies and lolling about the famous Jardin de Luxembourg should reserve far in advance. Other places to try if the spots below are full are **rue Gay-Lussac** and its side streets heading away from the Jardin du Luxembourg, or the area between **rue des Ecoles** and **boulevard St-Germain** (near the Maubert-Mutualité Métro).

➤ **UNDER 150F • Hôtel du Commerce.** This ramshackle establishment offers no-frills lodging close to the action of the quarter. The spartan furnishings—a bed, Formica bedside table, and worn carpet—look like they came from a garage sale, but at these prices you could afford to redecorate your own room. Singles are 130F (160F with shower), doubles 140F (170F with shower), triples 210F, quads 260F. Unfortunately, the grinchlike owner doesn't take reservations, so show up early and give him your best smile. *14 rue de la Montagne-Ste-Geneviève, at rue des Ecoles, 5e, tel. 01–43–54–89–69. Métro: Maubert-Mutualité. Walk east on blvd. St-Germain, turn right on rue de la Montagne-Ste-Geneviève. 32 rooms, 5 with bath. Showers 15F.*

➤ **UNDER 175F • Hôtel de Médicis.** This hotel near the Panthéon and Sorbonne and, more importantly, a laundry has some of the best rooms in Paris if you're (1) not averse to the idea of a bedfellow, (2) olfactorily challenged, and (3) skimming the poverty line. Singles are impossible to get, thanks to a live-in population of artists and sedentary old men. Doubles with a desk, chair, sink, and bed are 160F–170F. *214 rue St-Jacques, 5e, tel. 01–43–29–53–64. RER: Luxembourg. Walk south on rue Gay-Lussac, turn left on rue St-Jacques. 27 rooms, none with bath. Showers 10F.*

➤ **UNDER 225F • Grand Hôtel du Progrès.** Now's your chance to set foot in a posh Haussmann creation, with spacious rooms reminiscent of another era. If you hang far enough over your balcony, you may glimpse the Panthéon or Jardin du Luxembourg—but be careful not to fall into the depths of car exhaust and poodle shit below. Simple singles are 120F–160F and doubles 220F (270F with private bath) with breakfast. Reservations may require a one-night deposit. *50 rue Gay-Lussac, 5e, tel. 01–43–54–53–18. RER: Luxembourg. 36 rooms, 6 with bath. Elevator, showers free.*

Hôtel des Alliés. The place fills up exceptionally fast in summer, even though it's in a working-class area on the far edge of the fifth arrondissement. Airy rooms are clean and basic, but the bath towels are more like washcloths. Singles from 145F, doubles 200F, 300F with bath. *20 rue Berthollet, 5e, tel. 01–43–31–47–52, fax 01–45–35–13–92. Métro: Censier-Daubenton. Walk west on rue de l'Arbalète to rue Berthollet. 43 rooms, 10 with shower. Breakfast 28F, luggage storage, showers 15F, towel 4F. MC, V.*

➤ **UNDER 250F • Hôtel le Central.** A friendly Portuguese family runs the small Central. Even though the halls are musty and the rooms dark and worn, an excellent location near rue Mouffetard and the Panthéon makes up for it. Singles are 150F, doubles 240F, triples 250F. If the wallpaper gets you down, go check out the nearby restaurants, crêperies, and bars. *6 rue Descartes, 5e, tel. 01–46–33–57–93. Métro: Maubert-Mutualité. Walk east on blvd. St-Germain, right on rue de la Montagne-Ste-Geneviève to rue Descartes. 16 rooms, all with bath.*

➤ **UNDER 275F • Les Argonautes.** Though the Greek restaurant downstairs hosts boisterous musicians almost every night, a peaceful night in this modern hotel a few steps from the Ile de la Cité is not out of the question. The rooms here are just the right size, with timbered ceilings and orange walls that only an optimist could love. Crowds (including lots of tourists) at surrounding bars and restaurants will keep you in safe company here, especially if you're traveling alone. Singles are 200F, and doubles start at 250F. *12 rue de la Huchette, 5e, tel. 01–43–54–09–82, fax 01–44–07–18–84. Métro: St-Michel. 25 rooms, all with bath. Breakfast 25F, extra bed 50F. AE, MC, V.*

Hôtel Gay-Lussac. Strung between the uptight vibes of the Grandes Écoles and the soothing tranquility of the Jardin du Luxembourg, this hotel sees plenty of academics and tourists alike. Clean and spacious doubles with the occasional faux-marble faux fireplace (got that?) cost 260F–400F; add 50F for an extra bed. Many rooms have been renovated. *29 rue Gay-Lussac, 5e, tel. 01–43–54–23–96. RER: Luxembourg. 44 rooms, 30 with bath. Breakfast 25F, elevator, showers 15F.*

➤ **UNDER 300F** • **Hôtel Marignan.** Finally! A hotel where zee people speak Eengleesh! You won't get any confused squints from the French-American couple that owns this hotel. Added bonus: Laundry is free. In summer, one person pays 190F, two pay 290F, three 390F, and four 480F (doubles and triples with private bath are 70F more); it's slightly cheaper the rest of the year because breakfast is not included nor required. Reserve in advance in the summer. *13 rue du Sommerard, 5e, tel. 01–43–54–63–81. Métro: Maubert-Mutualité or Cluny–La Sorbonne. From Maubert-Mutualité, walk south on rue des Carmes, turn right on rue du Sommerard. 30 rooms, some with bath. Breakfast 25F, showers free. Limited kitchen access.*

Hôtel Esmeralda. The chance to sleep in a loft bed may prompt you to reserve a frilly room in this 17th-century hôtel, five steps away from Notre-Dame—just be sure to reserve THREE months in advance in summer. In a gesture of wild generosity, the owner has reserved several singles without bath for a mere 160F per night. Doubles, all with shower, are 320F–490F. *4 rue St-Julien-le-Pauvre, 5e, tel. 01–43–54–19–20, fax 01–40–51–00–68. Métro: St-Michel. Walk east on quai St-Michel, turn right on rue St-Julien-le-Pauvre just before sq. René-Viviani. 19 rooms, 16 with bath. Breakfast 40F, showers 10F.*

➤ **UNDER 325F** • **Hôtel du Brésil.** This slightly upscale hotel near the Panthéon on the Jardin du Luxembourg has small, clean, pastel rooms with worn bedspreads but an energetic hostess. Breakfast is included in the price, and most rooms have TVs. Tiny singles start at 265F, doubles at 300F (340F with bath), and triples with bath at 535F. *10 rue Le Goff, 5e, tel. 01–43–54–76–11, fax 01–46–33–45–78. Métro: Luxembourg. Walk SE on rue Gay-Lussac, turn left on rue Le Goff. 30 rooms, some with bath. Elevator, showers free. MC, V.*

ST-GERMAIN-DES-PRES

St-Germain-des-Prés, on the Left Bank, cradles the oldest church in Paris (Eglise St-Germain) and borders the Seine. Although the area has been gentrified into a stupor, a few cheap hotels stubbornly remain, helping to retain a bit of the atmosphere that originally attracted poor bohemians. This is certainly one of Paris's safest neighborhoods, and provided you reserve far in advance, you can have a room near good shopping, a big park, young foreigners, and plenty of well-dressed French people.

➤ **UNDER 250F** • **Hôtel Jean Bart.** This hotel near the Jardin du Luxembourg has relatively clean, old-fashioned rooms, many with armoires and comfy beds. One person pays 190F–250F, two people pay 230F–300F. The prices are especially reasonable in August, when they drop 25F per person because breakfast is not required (nor offered). *9 rue Jean-Bart, 6e, tel. 01–45–48–29–13. Métro: St-Placide. Walk east on rue de Vaugirard, turn right on rue Jean-Bart. 36 rooms, 19 with shower. Curfew 1 AM. Showers 10F.*

You have a respectable chance of getting an Egyptian-themed room with access to a Turkish bath at the exotic Hôtel de Nesle, which does not accept reservations, even in summer.

Hôtel de Nesle. The Nesle—a bohemian backpacker haven with a Turkish bath and duck-filled garden—has more character than most other Parisian hotels combined. Each room has an enthusiastically executed historical theme, including an Egyptian room and a Molière room. The neighborhood is filled with oodles of art galleries, and there's a great daily market nearby. Singles without shower are 195F, and doubles run 220F–350F. They don't accept reservations, so arrive around 10 AM to see what's available. *7 rue de Nesle, 6e, tel. 01–43–54–62–41. Métro: Odéon. Cross blvd. St-Germain, walk north on rue de l'Ancienne-Comédie, turn right on rue Dauphine, left on rue de Nesle. 20 rooms, 10 with bath. Breakfast 25F, showers free.*

➤ **UNDER 275F** • **Hôtel Stella.** The Stella's location is ideal and the rooms clean, if spartan, with a bed, desk, and chair. It's a good deal for groups of all sizes: Singles cost 197F, doubles 256F–276F, and gargantuan rooms that can hold up to four cost 500F. To reserve a room you have to pay in cash by 11 AM the day of the night you plan to spend there. *41 rue Monsieur-le-Prince, 6e, tel. 01–43–26–43–49. Métro: Odéon. Walk west on blvd. St-Germain, turn left on rue de l'Odéon, left on rue Monsieur-le-Prince. 20 rooms, all with shower.*

➤ **UNDER 350F** • **Hôtel du Globe.** Authentically rustic rooms in the heart of the sixth arrondissement make this two-star hotel a fine splurge. You'll be surrounded by mirrors and dark florals grafted to the original stone walls and wood beams. The cheapest rooms are small but they all have good, firm beds. Singles start at 255F; doubles with bath run 330F–440F. Skip the 40F breakfast—one of the best bakeries in Paris, Gerard Mulot, is kitty-corner. Reserve at least two weeks ahead. *15 rue des Quatre-Vents, 6e, tel. 01–46–33–62–69. Métro: Mabillon. Walk east on blvd. St-Germain, turn right on rue de Seine, left on rue des Quatre-Vents. 15 rooms, all with bath. Closed Aug.*

Hôtel du Petit Trianon. This little hotel overlooks the markets on busy rue de Buci below. The rooms are bright and luxurious, but be forewarned that prices vacillate considerably depending on the season. In the winter, singles are 170F and doubles 260F, but come April singles go for 310F, doubles 320F–370F. *2 rue de l'Ancienne-Comédie, at rue St-André-des-Arts, 6e, tel. 01–43–54–94–64. Métro: Odéon. Cross blvd. St-Germain, walk north on rue de l'Ancienne-Comédie. 13 rooms, some with bath. Breakfast 20F, extra bed 80F, showers 30F.*

Hostels and Foyers

Paris's many hostels and foyers are clean, reliable, and safe, offering free showers and usually a coffee and baguette wake-up call. You can usually find a bed in a dorm-style room even at the height of tourist season. And for solo travelers—sick of being stiffed for a double in hotels—this is definitely the cheapest way to go.

Auberges de jeunesse (youth hostels) can be operated by Hostelling International (HI) or privately run. Although *foyers* tend to house young workers and students, they often have space for travelers in dormlike settings. The prices for either one run 100F–130F, although you might have to buy a membership card for HI hostels. To get a room in high season arrive between 8 AM and 10 AM or try reserving a room at the HI hostels. Hostels and foyers often have rules about curfews, late-night carousing, and alcohol intake, but that doesn't stop the occasional rowdy group from making your hostel experience a living hell.

HI HOSTELS Three hostels in Paris are run by the **Fédération Unie des Auberges de Jeunesse (FUAJ),** the French branch of Hostelling International. The price of a bed at 110F includes sheets, showers, and breakfast; best of all, there's no curfew, which is a rare thing among Paris's youth hostels. Most rooms are single-sex, unless it's really crowded; then they'll put you wherever they can. To reserve a space ahead of time at the Cité des Sciences or d'Artagnan hostels, mail them a check covering the first night or call the HI-AYH office in Washington, DC (tel. 202/783–6161) and give them your credit card number; they'll charge you for the price of a night's stay plus a $5 booking fee. If you want to stay at Jules Ferry, which accepts no reservations, show up well before 10 AM to secure a spot. All three HI hostels require a hostel card, which costs 100F at one of the FUAJ's four Paris offices. You can buy it on the spot when you arrive. Be sure to note the afternoon lockout hours (noon–2 PM). *FUAJ Centre National: 27 rue Pajol, 18e, tel. 01–44–89–87–27, Métro: La Chapelle. FUAJ Ile de France: 9 rue Notre-Dame-de-Lorette, 9e, tel. 01–42–85–55–40, Métro: Notre-Dame de Lorette. FUAJ Beaubourg: 9 rue Brantôme, 3e, tel. 01–48–04–70–40, Métro: Châtelet–Les Halles or Rambuteau. FUAJ République: 4 blvd. Jules-Ferry, 11e, tel. 01–43–57–02–60, fax 01–40–21–79–92. Métro: République.*

Auberge de Jeunesse d'Artagnan. This clean, enormous hostel is only steps away from Père-Lachaise, and it gets loud and packed in summer. A bed in a three- or four-bed dorm is 110F (including sheets and breakfast); beds in double rooms cost 121F (130F with private shower).

Three meals are served daily (menus for 28F–50F) at the very social bar and cafeteria. *80 rue Vitruve, 20e, tel. 01–43–61–08–75, fax 01–40–32–34–55. Métro: Porte de Bagnolet. Walk south on blvd. Davout, turn right on rue Vitruve. 411 beds. Reception open 8 AM–midnight. Lockout noon–3. Laundry, luggage storage 10F. Wheelchair access.*

Auberge de Jeunesse Cité des Sciences. Although technically in the Parisian *banlieue* (suburbs), this hostel is well served by the Métro, and within half an hour you can be smack-dab in the center of Paris. The mellow staff welcomes you to standard four- to six-bed dorm rooms. Though the rooms close every day noon–3PM, the small common area remains open and the reception is open 24 hours. Beds are 110F per night. *24 rue des Sept-Arpents, 93000 rue du Pré-St-Gervais, tel. 01–48–43–24–11, fax 01–48–43–26–82. Métro: Hoche. Walk south on rue du Pré-St-Gervais to rue des Sept-Arpents. 128 beds. Reception open 24 hrs. Laundry, luggage storage 10F. Wheelchair access.*

Auberge de Jeunesse Jules-Ferry. Come early and be ready to socialize, because this hostel is extremely popular and often full, with rowdy and friendly backpackers. It's also well located, overlooking a canal of the Seine and close to place de la République and the Bastille. Bed and breakfast in a dorm runs 110F (115F per person for the few doubles). Cheap food and groceries are close by, as are clubs and cafés. *8 blvd. Jules-Ferry, 11e, tel. 01–43–57–55–60, fax 01–40–21–79–92. Métro: République. Walk east on av. de la République, turn left on blvd. Jules-Ferry. 100 beds. Reception open 24 hrs. Lockout noon–2. Luggage storage 5F.*

PRIVATE HOSTELS **Aloha Hostel.** A secluded, tropical bungalow in Paris? No, but it's a welcoming place to stay all the same, with newly renovated rooms that sleep two to six. Supermarkets, laundromats, and some structure called La Tour Eiffel are all nearby—lone travelers will feel particularly safe in the midst of the hubbub. They usually let the maximum stay of one week (550F) slide during the school year. Come speak your native tongue with the friendly English-speaking staff. You pay 87F per person in a double, 97F for a dorm bed; summer rates go up 10F. *1 rue Borromée, 15e, tel. 01–42–73–03–03, fax 01–42–73–14–14. Métro: Volontaires. Walk west on rue de Vaugirard, turn right on rue Borromée. 130 beds. Curfew 2 AM, lockout 11–5. Reception open 8 AM–2PM. Limited kitchen access, luggage storage.*

Three Ducks Hostel. This American-infested hostel/bar is rambunctious and fun, what with all the cheap beers being consumed (9F). Some rooms have a shower; if not, you'll be queuing up in the communal courtyard for a shower booth. Beds are 77F–97F each (the higher price is in a double), 20F extra during the summer; sheet rental is 12F, and towels are 5F. Book ahead May–October by sending payment for the first night. Otherwise, call or arrive before 11 AM or after 5 PM to duke it out for the remaining beds. *6 pl. Etienne-Pernet, 15e, tel. 01–48–42–04–05, fax 01–48–42–04–05. Métro: Commerce. Walk south on rue du Commerce toward church; hostel is on your right. 95 beds. Curfew 2 AM, lockout 11–5. Kitchen, laundry next door, luggage storage, safe deposit box.*

Woodstock. This recently opened hostel was created in the same vein as the other hostels, with rooms sleeping three to six for 97F, showers, and a name sure to encourage some sort of rowdiness. Sheets are 15F, towels 5F. If this hostel is full, a seedier one, **Mike's Hostel,** is nearby on 122 boulevard de la Chapelle. *48 rue Rodier, 9e, tel. 01–48–78–87–76. Métro: Anvers. Walk south past pl. d'Anvers to rue Rodier. 75 beds. Curfew 2 AM, lockout 11–5. Kitchen facilities.*

Young and Happy Youth Hostel. Spectacularly located amid cafés, shops, and restaurants on rue Mouffetard in the Quartier Latin, the hostel is well known by American and Japanese travelers. The two- to six-bed rooms are standard but spotless and cost 97F per person, including breakfast. Sheets are 15F, towels 5F. Arrive before 11 AM or, to reserve, send a deposit for the first night. *80 rue Mouffetard, 5e, tel. 01–45–35–09–53. Métro: Monge. Walk east on rue Ortolan, turn left on rue Mouffetard. 75 beds. Curfew 2 AM, lockout 11–5.*

BVJ FOYERS These two foyers for travelers 16–35 balance smashing locations with immaculate rooms that hold up to ten people. Breakfast, sheets, shower, and a bed cost 120F per night, and both locations have kitchen facilities, 10F lockers, and a reception desk staffed 24 hours. Unfortunately you can't make reservations, so just show up at either foyer in the morning; you should get a space in any season, and if one place is full they'll call the other for you.

Singles cost 10F more at the Quartier Latin foyer. The Louvre location has a restaurant where guests at any of the four foyers can eat for 55F. They also have a shuttle service to either Orly (59F) or Charles de Gaulle (69F). Reserve beforehand at the desk. *BVJ de Paris/Louvre: 20 rue J.-J. Rousseau, 1er, tel. 01–42–36–88–18, fax 01–42–33–82–10. Métro: Palais Royal–Musée du Louvre. BVJ de Paris Quartier Latin: 44 rue des Bernardins, 5e, tel. 01–43–29–34–80, fax 01–42–33–40–53. Métro: Maubert-Mutualité.*

MIJE FOYERS Set up in medieval palaces and 18th-century hôtels particuliers in the Marais, **Maisons Internationales des Jeunes Etudiants (MIJE)** foyers are more comfortable than many hotels you're likely to stay in, except that they give you the boot after seven nights. The 125F rate includes sheets, breakfast, and showers. Doubles with private bath cost 150F. MIJE foyers don't accept reservations, so during high season show up at any location between 7 and 8:30 AM for a shot at one of the 450 beds. All three enforce a 1 AM curfew and offer free luggage storage. A restaurant in the Fourcy location offers meals to visitors (menus are 32F to 52F). To stay at a MIJE foyer you must be between the ages of 18 and 30. Beware of the lockout between noon and 4 PM. *Hôtel le Fauconnier: 11 rue de Fauconnier, 4e, tel 01–42–74–23–45, fax 01–42–74–08–93. Métro: St-Paul. Hôtel le Fourcy: 6 rue de Fourcy, 4e, tel 01–42–74–23–45, fax 01–42–74–08–93. Métro: St-Paul. Hôtel Maubuisson: 12 rue des Barres, 4e, tel. 01–42–72–72–09, fax 01–42–74–08–93. Métro: St-Paul or Hôtel de Ville.*

INDEPENDENT FOYERS **Association des Etudiants Protestants de Paris.** This large old foyer across the street from the Jardin du Luxembourg is one of the cheapest options in Paris (dorm beds 75F, singles 90F, breakfast included). Better yet, you can stay here for five whole weeks, even in summer, without a curfew or lockout. The fairly barren rooms are easier to swallow thanks to several big common rooms, a kitchen, and occasional parties with the full-time students who live upstairs. The residence claims to cater only to students aged 18–26, but they may be flexible. Show up early in the morning to get a bed for the night; the office opens at 8:45, and they don't take reservations. *46 rue de Vaugirard, 6e, tel. 01–46–33–23–30, fax 01–46–34–27–09. Métro: St-Sulpice. Walk east on rue du Vieux-Colombier, turn right at pl. St-Sulpice to rue de Vaugirard. Kitchen, luggage storage, membership fee 10F, sheets 20F.*

Auberge Internationale des Jeunes. Popular with European and American backpackers, this impeccable and modern hostel next to the place de la Bastille and 10 minutes from the Gare de Lyon is *the* place to meet up with other people raring to take advantage of the Bastille nightlife. The friendly (albeit hectic) management accepts reservations. Rooms for two to six people go for 90F a person with breakfast included. *10 rue Trousseau, 11e, tel. 01–47–00–62–00, fax 01–47–00–33–16. Métro: Bastille or Ledru Rollin. From Ledru Rollin, take rue du Faubourg St- Antoine to pl. de la Nation, turn left on rue Trousseau. 240 beds. Lockout 10–3. Reception 24 hours. Laundry, luggage storage. AE, MC. V.*

Maison des Etudiants. This fabulous house with flower-filled courtyard has doubles for 140F a person and singles for 160F (150F if you stay three weeks or more). Breakfast is included. There is a four-night minimum stay—perfect if you'll be spending days on end at the nearby Louvre. The maison is open year-round for students and for tourists in summer. *18 rue J.-J. Rousseau, 1er, tel. 01–45–08–02–10. Métro: Palais Royal–Musée du Louvre. Walk east on rue St-Honoré, turn left on rue J.-J. Rousseau. 52 beds.*

Maison Internationale des Jeunes. The managers of this somewhat sterile foyer—two Métro stops away from the Bastille—have no tolerance for "drinking, carousing, or late-night card playing." If you're under 30 you can stay in one of the two- to eight-bed rooms, though by some strange reasoning only mixed-sex couples can get a double. A night's stay plus breakfast costs 110F. There is a three-day maximum stay, which can be relaxed as long as you don't annoy the management and there's available space. Unlike most foyers, you can reserve space here up to 15 days in advance. *4 rue Titon, 11e, tel. 01–43–71–99–21, fax 01–43–71–78–58. Métro: Faidherbe-Chaligny. Walk east on rue de Montreuil, turn left on rue Titon. 175 beds. Curfew 2 AM. Sheets 15F.*

Université de Paris Foyer International des Etudiantes. During the school year this old wood-and-iron building houses only female students, while July–September anyone can stay (a majority of women still keeps beer-chugging contests to a minimum). Pluses include a rooftop terrace, theater, and cafeteria, not to mention its great location in the Quartier Latin. The rooms have wood floors and antique furnishings, but the bathrooms and kitchens have suffered from neglect. During the summer singles are 165F and doubles 115F per person, with a three-day minimum stay—be sure to reserve months in advance. Prices include breakfast and sheets. *93 blvd. St-Michel, 5e, tel. 01–43–54–49–63. RER: Luxembourg. 150 beds. Curfew 1:30 AM during school year. Reception open 9–noon and 6–1:30. Luggage storage.*

Longer Stays

So, the Paris bug has bitten. You've decided to make the BIG MOVE and boldly go where all expatriates have gone before. Be forewarned that even Parisians dream of finding a reasonable apartment in the city, so before your romantic hopes run amuck, prepare yourself for a long, tedious adventure. You'll probably end up paying at least 2,000F per month just to share a room in a one-bedroom apartment. It'll cost 2,500F or more for your own room in an apartment, or 3,000F–4,000F for a tiny studio. A *chambre de bonne* (maid's room) is a relatively cheap option at around 3,000F a month—usually in nicer and safer bourgeois neighborhoods, these little top-floor rooms often share a bathroom but don't have a kitchen.

STUDENT HOUSING Foyers and student dorms can be great housing options; a good place to start looking is the **Centre Régional des œuvres Universitaires et Scolaires (CROUS)** (39 av. Georges-Bernanos, 5e, tel. 01–40–51–37–17), which runs Paris's university residence halls and in July and August rents rooms for about 600F a month (if you're a student registered at a Paris school, and thus have access to social security). To snag one of these rooms, you'll have to go through a complicated bureaucratic process and document your financial situation. The Quartier Latin branch of the **BVJ** foyers (*see* Hostels and Foyers, *above*) also houses students and travelers, though if you're staying over two weeks, they slap a 250F membership fee on top of the 120F rate for a double room. Call or write ahead to get their application and see what's available. You can do the same for the female foyer **Union Chrétienne de Jeunes Filles** (22 rue Naples, 8e, tel. 01–45–22–23–49) or the all-male **Union Chrétienne de Jeunes Gens** (14 rue de Trévise, 9e, tel. 01–47–70–90–94) for summer lodging possibilities.

BULLETIN BOARDS Numerous bulletin boards post shared apartments, studios, and au pair jobs, and are ideal for anyone looking to stay at least a few months in Paris. Your first destination should be the **American Church** (65 quai d'Orsay, 7e, tel. 01–47–05–07–99), which has new listings every morning after 10 AM (after 2 PM on Sundays). **CROUS** (*see above*), the **American Library** (10 rue du Général-Camou, 7e, tel. 01–45–51–46–82), and **Shakespeare and Company** (37 rue de la Bûcherie, 5e, tel. 01–43–26–96–50) all have bulletin boards with apartment and room rentals. Students can also try the housing office of the **Union Parisienne des Etudiants Locataires** (120 rue Notre-Dame-des-Champs, 6e, tel. 01–46–33–30–78); it's open weekdays 2–6 (Wednesday 10–10).

NEWSPAPERS *France-USA Contacts* is a free paper with both housing and employment classifieds in English and French. It comes out every two weeks and is available at most English-language bookstores. The French newspaper *Le Figaro,* at all newsstands, also has good rental listings. Pick it up on a Monday and start calling immediately. *De Particulier à Particulier* comes out on Thursdays and is full of apartment rentals and shares; get it at any newsstand. Avoid rental agencies, which usually charge an entire month's rent for their service. If an ad says "p.à.p." or "part.," there's no agency involved.

FOOD

By Viviana Mahieux and Julia Švihra

Experiencing the French appreciation for fine food is much more than selecting a restaurant with "Chez" in the title, forking out a minimum of a three-digit sum in francs, and knowing the best vintages of *vin rouge* (red wine) and *vin blanc* (white wine). The best introduction to French food is the marketplace, where you'll see butchers nonchalantly toting whole pigs over their shoulders, crates of vegetables and fruits being transferred into neat pyramids of baskets, and exotic fish swirling in piles of ice at the *poissonerie* (fish market). Whether you buy the baguettes lined up soldier-fashion at the *boulangerie* (bread shop), pastries displaying themselves wantonly at the *pâtisserie* (pastry shop), or the strange cheeses emitting a thousand and one odors at the *fromagerie* (cheese shop), you'll soon discover that your francs will go much further at the markets than at those vulturous restaurants that advertise "cuisine traditionelle" and print their menus in English.

That said, it is imperative that you indulge in at least one drawn-out meal—or at least a coffee and a smoke—and treat the event as religiously as the French do. There are several places where you can accomplish this. One option is a **bistrot,** which is primarily a wine bar that offers plates of cheese and *charcuterie* (cold cuts) or even full meals as accompaniments. Bistrots that fit this description are listed near the end of this chapter (*see* Bistrots, *below*). A **brasserie** is a French pub that offers standard, single-course dishes traditionally (but not necessarily) served with a beer. Although not quite an eating institution, the most Parisian of all creatures is the **café** (*see* Cafés, *below*)—a mélange of sidewalk tables, surly waiters, and Parisians spewing forth fumes of espresso and Gaulois cigarettes.

In addition to the many crêperies and and sandwich joints springing up on Paris's side streets, you'll no doubt get the chance to sample the international culinary scene as you wander from one ethnic restaurant to another. While the **Marais** (3e, 4e) has some of the best falafel stands in Paris, **Belleville** (20e) is chock-full of Vietnamese, Chinese, and Thai restaurants. The large West African and Algerian immigrant population in **Montmartre** (18e) and near the **Bastille** (11e) has brought couscous to the forefront of Parisian food, although you might want to avoid the ghastly Tex-Mex eateries currently invading the more chic neighborhoods. And you can always trust the **Quartier Latin** (5e) to have anything from Greek to Lyonnais food at prices low enough to keep its student population sated.

The best deals for a full meal in restaurants are usually the *prix-fixe* (fixed price) menus, which can have an *entrée* (appetizer), a *plat* (main course), and *dessert,* for 60F and up. The lunch and dinner menus are usually the same, although lunch often costs a third less than dinner. It might sound elegant, but ordering *à la carte* (separately) is a sure-fire way to dine yourself into poverty. Some restaurants offer a filling *plat du jour* (daily special), which includes meat, veggies, and pasta or potatoes for as little as 50F. The commonly seen words *service compris* mean that tip is included in the prices. You can leave an extra 2F–5F *pourboire* (tip) for an extra-friendly server, but it's not an insult to leave nothing.

The French start their day with a *petit déjeuner* (breakfast), which usually consists of coffee and bread or croissants. Lunch, or *déjeuner* is normally served from noon until 2 or 2:30 and *dîner* (dinner) from 7 to 10 or 11. If we don't indicate hours for a restaurant listed below, you can assume it is open for lunch and dinner during these usual hours.

Restaurants

The following restaurants are arranged by neighborhood and price. If you're looking for a specific type of cuisine, flip to the Reference Listings at the end of this chapter. *The price categories listed generally refer to the price of a three-course dinner and a drink*—which means you can spend a bit less if you order carefully and forgo appetizers and wine.

BASTILLE

It's only fitting that a great nighttime area would have a great selection of restaurants. Take-out joints of all stripes serve cheap falafel and sandwiches along **rue de la Roquette**; on the rue's first block off place de la Bastille, homesick Americans take comfort from the thick pizza at **Slice.** Otherwise, you'll find plenty of cafés open late and many opportunities for quality meals, often served in converted art galleries. Keep in mind that the artsy crowd is often willing to pay a higher price. Edge northwestward out of the Bastille toward **place de la République** and along **boulevard Voltaire**; prices drop and ethnic eateries pop up more often.

➤ **UNDER 60F • Le Bistrot du Peintre.** This popular café and bar serves food until midnight and closes at 2 AM. The standard French cuisine includes a great *soupe à l'oignon* (onion soup; 30F) and the best *salade au chèvre chaud* (warm goat-cheese salad; 35F) in the city. The waiters are friendly and loyal regulars dominate the crowd, gobbling up hearty plats du jour like the *poulet moutarde* (mustard chicken; 62F). *116 av. Ledru-Rollin, at rue de Charonne, 11e, tel. 01–47–00–34–39. Métro: Ledru Rollin. Open Mon.–Sat. 7 AM–2 AM, Sun. 10 AM–9 PM. MC, V.*

Crêpes-Show. A cadaverous-looking mannequin beckons you into the Crêpes-Show, but luckily teen horror-flick gore is not what they serve here. Instead, you'll find fast, cheap, and filling fare dished out to everyone from students to heels and suits. The 39F lunch menu gets you a salad, a main course crêpe (like cheese and mushroom), and a dessert crêpe, while the 59F dinner menu includes all of the above with wine thrown in. *51 rue de Lappe, 11e, tel. 01–47–00–36–46. Métro: Bastille. Open daily 11:30–3 and 7–midnight.*

➤ **UNDER 80F • Café Moderne.** Despite its name, this restaurant seems more like an old Paris bistrot, with wooden tables, a mirrored bar, and *sympathique* atmosphere. Cherif, the congenial man behind the bar, won't take too many reservations (he likes to leave a bunch of tables free for friends and regulars). You may hear more Algerian than French, as locals congregate for the house specialty: mounds of couscous with raisins and pimento garnishing (50F–60F). The three-course lunch or dinner menu is 60F. *19 rue Keller, 11e, tel. 01–47–00–53–62. Métro: Bastille. Open Mon–Sat. 12–2:30 and 7–11. Closed Sun. MC, V.*

Restaurant Sarah. Ask locals where to get a great cheap meal, and they'll steer you toward the green doors of this Persian delight. The 30F plat du jour is always a good deal, or, for the total experience, get the 55F lunch menu with specialties like *tchelo kebab koubidee* (beef, onion, grilled tomatoes, and saffron rice). The four-course dinner menu is a deal at 65F. Add a quarter-bottle of wine (15F) and you'll be so happy you'll probably come back the next day. *10 rue Oberkampf, 11e, tel. 01–43–57–83–48. Métro: Oberkampf. Open daily noon–3 and 7:30–11.*

Le Temps des Cerises. This tiny lunch-only restaurant has been around since 1900; from the convivial atmosphere and the photos of old Paris, you might think you've jumped back in time. It's named after a revolutionary song, "The Time of Cherries"—if you didn't bring the sheet music, the words are written on the walls. Get here by noon to rub elbows with locals over a hearty 65F menu of traditional French home cookin' or one of the many meat and salad specials. Come later and you'll be in for a long, long wait. *31 rue de la Cerisaie, 4e, tel. 01–42–72–08–63. Métro: Sully-Morland or Bastille. Bar open until 8 PM. Closed weekends and Aug.*

Tokaj. Duck past hand-painted murals and seat yourself before heaps of steaming goulash (62F) to the sounds of soft Gypsy music. Originally from Budapest, the Brandt family relocated to Paris, where they are happily filling the stomachs of Parisians and tourists alike. The atmosphere is warm and the food fantastic. Treat yourself to the *hortubagy* (chicken-filled crêpe in paprika sauce; 58F) and a carafe of the house rosé (18F). *57 rue du Chemin-Vert, at blvd. Voltaire, 11e, tel. 01–47–00–64–56. Métro: Voltaire. Open Tues.–Sat. noon–2:30 and 7:30–10:30.*

Zagros. For those hankering after "Greco-Kurdish" cuisine, the cozy dining room of this restaurant feels like a real Greek home, and you might even get to tune in to the family argument drifting in from the kitchen. You can order excellent *moussaka* (56F) with rice and a mixed salad. The indecisive should opt for a generous *assiette zagros* (40F). Three-course lunch menus run 54F. *21 rue de la Folie-Méricourt, 11e, tel. 01–48–07–09–56. Métro: St-Ambroise. Open Mon.–Sat. noon–2 and 7–midnight. MC, V.*

All-Night Eateries

After-party hunger pangs at 3 AM just may make you slink into one of Paris's "24/24" (open 24 hours) restaurant chains. Batifol Opéra (36 blvd. des Italiens, 9e, tel. 01–45–23–09–34, Métro: Richelieu Drouot) serves hot and filling meals 24 hours daily. Pizza Pino (38 rue St-Séverin, 5e, tel. 01–43–54–70–53, Métro: St-Michel–Notre-Dame; 43 rue St-Denis, 7e, tel. 01–40–26–39–07, Métro: Châtelet–Les Halles) has a great variety of pizzas until 5 AM. Also try the Mustang Café (see Montparnasse, below), open until 5 AM, or the late-night bakery Le Terminus (10 rue St-Denis, 1er, tel. 01–45–08–87–97, Métro: Châtelet–Les Halles), which closes its doors at 3 AM.

- *Le Dépanneur. This diner/bar near Pigalle is styled in wood, with artsy chrome touches and comfy chairs. Big salads, hamburgers, and sandwiches run 40F–70F, a small carafe of wine 25F (15F during the day). It's open 24 hours. 27 rue Fontaine, 9e, tel. 01–40–16–40–20. Métro: Blanche.*

- *Le Grand Café. Finally—an all-night café. Too bad it's stuck in a neighborhood that goes to bed early. 40 blvd. des Capucines, 9e, tel. 01–47–42–19–00. Métro: Madeleine.*

- *Le Pigalle. While not necessarily in the greatest neighborhood, it's open Monday–Saturday until 5 AM. Chill out with some Vietnamese specialties after grooving all night at one of the nearby "boîtes" (dance clubs). 22 blvd. de Clichy, 18e, tel. 01–46–06–72–90. Métro: Pigalle.*

- *Pub St-Germain. Off boulevard St-Germain, this pub is always packed with foreigners and students. Over 450 international beers—26 on tap and more in bottles—accompany French pub food and occasional live jazz. Steak or lobster menus are 50F–78F. 17 rue de l'Ancienne-Comédie, 6e, tel. 01–43–29–38–70. Métro: Odéon. AE, MC, V.*

➤ **UNDER 100F** • **Naz Restaurant.** A laid-back crowd lingers over meals at this Indian-Pakistani place, which is best known for its curry and tandoori specials. *Poulet palak* (chicken curry with creamed spinach) runs 65F; a three-course menu is 59F–69F for lunch, dinner is 100F. Vegetarians should try the amazing *raita d'aubergine* appetizer (25F), made with grilled eggplant and spicy yogurt sauce. *19 rue de la Roquette, 11e, tel. 01–48–05–69–19. Métro: Bastille. Open daily noon–3 and 7–11. Closed Fri. lunch. AE, MC, V.*

➤ **SPLURGE** • **Chez Paul.** A modest sign welcomes you to the best splurge in the Bastille. The grilled salmon (80F), rabbit with goat-cheese sauce (75F), and escargots (40F) are delectable; spring for a bottle of wine (100F) and whip out that credit card. The place is crowded with locals and clued-in visitors, so make reservations. If you didn't plan ahead, get a drink at the bar or head over to Les Portes (*see* Bars, in Chapter 5) across the street and work up an appetite during your long, long wait. *13 rue de Charonne, at rue de Lappe, 11e, tel. 01–47–00–34–57. Métro: Bastille. Open daily noon–3 and 7:30–12:30. MC, V.*

BELLEVILLE

Belleville's African, Asian, and Eastern European restaurants are a refreshing alternative to standard Parisian cuisine—and they won't rip you off like some high-priced tourist traps. **Rue de Belleville, rue des Pyrénées,** and the streets stretching south from them offer some of the most varied and affordable dining in town, often in the front room of the owner's home. **Boulevard de Belleville** has cheap produce and scads of good Chinese and Laotian restaurants. Chinese residents prefer the well-stocked **Wing An** (7 rue de Belleville, 19e, tel. 01–42–38–05–24) for cooking ingredients, plus snacks to go. The Sephardic Jews in the area have opened up a kosher shop here and there; try the **Maison du Zabayon** (122 blvd. de Belleville, 20e, tel. 01–47–97–16–70), a kosher bakery with good pastries (8F–10F).

➤ **UNDER 40F** • **Restaurant Lao Siam.** Laotian and Thai specialties fill the vast menu of this humble Belleville institution, which focuses on basics like chicken with bamboo shoots (38F). The *omelette fou-yong* (23F) is a tasty option if you want to get filled up cheaply. *49 rue de Belleville, 19e, tel. 01–40–40–09–68. Métro: Belleville. Open daily 11 AM–11:30 PM.*

➤ **UNDER 60F** • **Da Lat.** This flashy restaurant is full of folks downing Da Lat's excellent Chinese/Thai cuisine. Almond chicken (40F), Thai chicken curry (31F), and crab salad (27F) are some of the favorites here. The 65F three-course menu is served piping hot all day. *19 rue Louis-Bonnet, 11e, tel. 01–43–38–22–72. Métro: Belleville. Open daily 11 AM–2 AM MC, V.*

Modas. This small, artsy crêperie high up on the rue de Ménilmontant has as much personality as Gabriel, its owner—which means it's colorful, chaotic, and extremely eccentric. Come and enjoy the rotating art exhibits along with Belleville regulars munching on a broad selection of crêpes (under 30F) and grilled meats (50F–60F). *110 rue de Ménilmontant, 20e, tel. 01–40–33–69–58. Open Tues.–Sun. noon–2:30 and 7–midnight.*

➤ **UNDER 80F** • **Restaurant Tai-Yien.** You know it's a good sign when 80% of a Chinese restaurant's clientele is Asian. The dining room may be a little dull, but customers stream in here for some of the best Chinese food in town. The simple stuff—like roast chicken with rice (42F)—is best. The adventurous should try the curried frog's legs (48F) or lamb with ginger and onions (60F). The three-course dinner menu is 63F. *5 rue de Belleville, 19e, tel. 01–42–41–44–16. Métro: Belleville. Open daily 10 AM–2 AM. MC, V.*

Le Vieux Byzantin. On a street jam-packed with sorry-looking stands of greasy Greek food, this cheery restaurant stands above the rest with its Greek and Turkish delicacies. Daily specials such as *chicken tagine* go for 35F. The 50F lunch menu is a deal. Fancier dinner menus run 70F to 95F. *128 rue Oberkampf, 11e, tel. 01–43–57–35–84. Métro: Ménilmontant. Open daily noon–3 and 7:30–midnight. Closed Sun. lunch.*

➤ **UNDER 100F** • **Chez Justine.** Chez Justine serves up heaps of traditional southern French cooking, complete with rustic log-cabin decor. The 70F lunch menu (52F without dessert and wine) and 85F dinner menu come with an all-you-can-eat appetizer buffet, a meat dish, such as *rôti de veau* (veal roast), dessert, and wine. *96 rue Oberkampf, 11e, tel. 01–43–57–44–03. Métro: St-Maur. Closed Sat. lunch, Sun., and Aug. AE, MC, V.*

➤ **SPLURGE** • **A la Courtille.** Relax on the terrace of this sleek bistrot with a breathtaking view over the city and the Parc de Belleville. Businesspeople fill it up at lunch and regulars come on evenings and weekends. Appetizers are 40F; courses like *steak tartare* are 75F–85F. Lunch is 70F–100F, dinner 150F–200F, but the wine will be worth it. *1 rue des Envierges, 20e, tel. 01–46–36–51–59. Métro: Pyrénées. Open daily noon–2 and 8–10:45. MC, V.*

CHAMPS-ELYSEES

Though it's one of Paris's best-known boulevards, with loads of theaters and clubs, the area around it is the worst neighborhood in which to seek out a decent meal for under 200F. Hunt around **rue La Boétie** and **rue de Ponthieu** for your most reasonable options. Restaurants here serve mostly traditional French fare for the ultrachic and ultrasleek. The rest of us just might have to grab a sandwich or duck into the closest *MacDo* (you can't get away from them).

➤ **UNDER 60F** • **Barry's.** This small, mirrored restaurant/deli is a popular lunch spot among the people who work in the area, which means it's chic but still affordable. Snag a seat indoors and try the 36F–49F roasted veal or curried chicken. Or get a 24F–29F *panini* (hot grilled sandwich) to go and picnic along the Champs-Elysées. *9 rue de Duras, 8e, tel 01–40–06–02–27. Métro: Champs-Elysées–Clemenceau. Open weekdays 8 AM–4 PM.*

Chicago Pizza Pie Factory. Happy-hour drinks (Monday–Saturday 6–8) are 50% off at this deep-dish pizza/sports bar institution. In addition to pizzas—84F for a two-person cheese pizza, 200F for the four-person everything-on-it—you can order all sorts of big salads (20F–55F), garlic bread (21F), and good ol' California wine. *5 rue de Berri, 8e, tel. 01–45–62–50–23. Métro: George V. Open daily 11:45 AM–1 AM. MC, V.*

GARE DE L'EST AND GARE DU NORD

A jazzy, post–World War II expatriate crowd ushered in new life to this inconspicuously cool neighborhood that spreads southwest of the Gares de l'Est and du Nord. Rather than the intellectual types who had schmoozed in the cafés of Montparnasse 10 years earlier, these expats were serious swingers. Happily, the spirit of the 1940s has been quietly maintained in a few restaurants near **place St-Georges,** as well as in the hidden jazz joints sprinkled around the area. With a large Jewish population, this area is also a good place for cheap kosher meals, as well as for falafel around **rue de Montyon.**

➤ **UNDER 60F** • **Restaurant Chartier.** Since the mid-1800s Chartier has served good, cheap meals to workers, bankers, students, and (now) tourists. The old revolving door whirls you into a big space with touches of brass and stained glass. Erratic, near-frantic service

---

I Ordered What?!

If you're an adventurous gourmet who has ordered one of the following dishes, here are some definitions to chew on:

• *Andouilletes: sausages stuffed with pork innards. They have a strong taste and are often eaten with mustard.* • *Boudin: a blood sausage made with onions and wheat grains.* • *Cervelle: pork or sheep brain cooked with butter and herbs.* • *Choucroute garnie: an Alsatian specialty consisting of a variety of sausages served on a bed of sauerkraut.* • *Foie gras: an expensive appetizer made of pure duck or goose liver. Pâté de foie gras is a less expensive version of it.*

demands that you assert yourself at times. The menu changes daily; main dishes include grilled steak with fries (46F) and grilled mackerel (36F). Desserts are 5F–20F, and half a carafe of passable red wine is 16F. The 80F menu, which includes dessert and wine, is the best way to sample everything. *7 rue du Faubourg-Montmartre, 9e, tel. 01–47–70–86–29. Métro: Rue Montmartre. Open daily 11–3 and 6–9:30. AE, MC, V.*

Van Gölu. Though the food is excellent, with a wide range of lamb dishes and tasty baklava, the entertainment is the main reason to come to this Kurdish institution. There's music every night, but try to make it for the weekend show when the belly dancer shimmies to the accompaniment of a *saz* (Turkish lute). You might even learn a few Turkish tunes from the crowd of regulars singing along. The 52F menu, complete with dessert and wine, is a small price to pay for the great floor show. *3 rue d'Enghien, 10e, tel. 01–47–70–41–01. Métro: Strasbourg–St-Denis. Open daily noon–2:30 and 8–2. Closed Sun. lunch.*

➤ **UNDER 80F** • **Bhai Bhai Sweets.** South of the Gare de l'Est on boulevard de Strasbourg is a crumbling old *passage* (an iron- and glass-covered passageway created during the 19th century). It houses about a dozen cramped Indian eateries, but Bhai Bhai is the best. The 70F lunch or dinner menu includes three courses, among them *bharta* (eggplant puree with onions, tomatoes, and spices) and *dal* (lentils). Vegetable beignets cost 16F, or try the tandoori chicken (18F). *77 passage Brady, 10e, tel. 01–42–46–77–29. Métro: Château d'Eau. Open daily noon–midnight. MC, V.*

Haynes. In 1947, Leroy "Roughhouse" Haynes decided that the French could use a little more soul in their diet. So he opened the first American restaurant in Paris, serving up a taste of his native Kentucky in the form of black-eyed peas, chicken gumbo, and whiskey sours. Haynes's kitchen not only gave Parisian cuisine a kick in the pants, it also became a favorite of expatri-

Vegetarian Grazing Grounds

The French's fondness for displaying pungent slabs of butchered meat swaying in the store windows has sent more than one vegan running for cover, but it's not impossible to find a good, meatless meal. Here's our pick of shops/restaurants that do their best to accommodate vegetarians:

- *Grand Appétit. 9 rue de la Ceuseiaie, 4e, Métro: Bastille, tel 01–40–27–04–95.*

- *Aquarius. 54 rue Ste-Croix-de-la-Bretonnerie, 4e, tel. 01–48–87–48–71. Métro: Hôtel de Ville.*

- *Country Life. 6 rue Daunou, 2e, tel. 01–42–97–48–51. Métro: Opéra.*

- *Entre Ciel et Terre. 5 rue Hérold, 1er, tel. 01–45–08–49–84. Métro: Les Halles or Louvre-Rivoli.*

- *Naturellement Vôtre. 12 rue Vitoure, 20e, tel. 01–43–70–07–24. Métro: Maraîchers.*

- *La Petite Légume. 36 rue des Boulangers, 5e, tel. 01–40–46–06–85. Métro: Cardinal Lemoine.*

- *Rayons de Santé. 8 pl. Charles-Dullin, 18e, tel. 01–42–59–64–81. Métro: Abbesses.*

- *Surma. 5 rue Daubenton, 5e, tel. 01–45–35–68–60. Métro: Censier-Daubenton.*

ate hepcats looking for a piece of home. You can still feast on fried chicken, T-bone steaks, and barbecued ribs (60F–90F) in this dimly lit, smoky club. When there isn't live piano music, Leroy gets out his great collection of jazz and blues. *3 rue Clauzel, 9e, tel. 01–48–78–40–63. Métro: St-Georges. Open Tues.–Sat. 7:30 PM–midnight. MC, V.*

Paparazzi. This boisterous Italian bistrot just north of the ninth arrondissement's best nightspots sees a young, good-natured crowd diving into varied plates of pasta (50F–60F) and megapizzas. At lunch people crowd in for the 60F menu and the *scampi fritti* (fried scampi; 55F). *7 bis rue Geoffroy-Marie, 9e, tel. 01–48–24–59–39. Métro: Rue Montmartre. Open Mon. noon–2:30, Tues.–Sat. noon–2:30 and 7:30–11:30. Closed 2 weeks in Aug. MC, V.*

➤ **UNDER 100F • A la Ville de Belgrade.** This dark place along a canal of the Seine serves up hearty, traditional, Eastern European food—we're talking serious stick-to-your-ribs stuff. A 58F lunch menu includes an appetizer, a main dish, and cheese or dessert. Order à la carte moussaka for 70F or *cassoulet* (white-bean-and-meat stew) for 65F, but save room for homemade baklava (27F). *153 quai de Valmy, 10e, tel. 01–46–07–60–93. Métro: Château Landon. Open Wed.–Mon. noon–2:30 and 7–10. Closed Tues. and Aug. AE, MC, V.*

Chalet Maya. Get this straight: This is not a chalet, and there's nothing Maya about it. Gay actor Jean Marais, heartthrob of teenage girls in the '40s, is the godfather of the restaurant's proprietor—check him out in the arty photos on the walls. But the real reason to come is the food, with entrées like penne with smoked salmon and main courses like duck baked with peaches, or curried lamb with plantains (60F). The place fills up after 10:30, when people file in for the 90F two-course menu. *5 rue des Petits-Hôtels, 10e, tel. 01–47–70–52–78. Métro: Gare de l'Est. Open Mon. 7:30 PM–11:30 PM, Tues.–Sat. noon–2 and 7:30–11:30. MC, V.*

➤ **SPLURGE • Julien.** This classy 1879 brasserie stands stylishly apart from its surroundings on a chaotic market street. High ceilings, mirrors, and tuxedoed waiters take you back to a golden era—on theater nights you'll still see decked-out dandies, playbills in hand, coming for the fantastic desserts (from 35F). The 51F *profiteroles* (ice cream inside a puff pastry smothered in chocolate) are Julien's specialty. Real food is good but expensive; try coming for lunch or after 10 PM, when the menu is 110F for two courses and a drink. *16 rue du Faubourg-St-Denis, 10e, tel. 01–47–70–12–06. Métro: Strasbourg–St-Denis. Open daily noon–3 and 7–1:30. AE, MC, V.*

LES HALLES AND BEAUBOURG

Les Halles has the unique distinction of having the worst crêpe stands in town, a trait indicative of the eating scene here as a whole. It's not that you *can't* eat well here—a few spots are actually quite good. However, plenty of places (particularly those south of the Forum des Halles) will happily take your francs for a plate of muck. The solution: On sunny days stroll down **rue Montorgueil**'s daily market and picnic in the park next to the Eglise St-Eustache. Or, grab a hot panini (18F–25F) from one of the stands lining **rue St-Denis** or **rue Rambuteau.** The best thing we can say about eating in Les Halles is that many restaurants stay open until the wee hours, including the **Pizza Pino** (open daily 11 AM–5 AM) on place des Innocents.

➤ **UNDER 60F • Dame Tartine.** Squeeze in with the yuppies at this restaurant-cum-art gallery next to the Centre Georges Pompidou on place Igor-Stravinsky. The specialty is the *tartines* (hot or cold open-faced sandwiches); try the *poulet aux amandes* (chicken with almonds; 30F). Add an inspiring glass of Bordeaux (15F), ponder the works by local artists, and watch the afternoon go by. They also have an offshoot called **Café Véry,** the first restaurant to open in the Jardin des Tuileries. *2 rue Brisemiche, 3e, tel. 01–42–77–32–22. Métro: Rambuteau or Châtelet–Les Halles. Open daily 11 AM–midnight.*

Jip's. This boisterous Afro-Cuban café/restaurant blares continuous reggae and salsa from a corner of Les Halles. The friendly (sometimes a bit too friendly), dreadlocked clientele comes for dishes such as *pescado en salsa* (fish with fresh salsa; 45F) or *manioc en frites* (fried manioc; 28F). Drop in anytime for some strong punch (36F) and a vibrant atmosphere. *41 rue St-Denis, 1er, tel. 01–42–33–00–11. Métro: Châtelet–Les Halles. Open daily noon–2 AM; noon–3:30 and 7–11 for meals.*

➤ **UNDER 80F** • **Au Petit Ramoneur.** This family-run place has been dishing out solid meals in Les Halles since way before the sex shops moved in. The 68F menu includes goodies like fried potatoes and sausage, tripe cooked in Calvados brandy, andouillettes, and salads, not to mention a half liter of wine or beer. At lunch the place is packed with working-class regulars who'll chat with anyone sitting nearby. *74 rue St-Denis, 1er, tel. 01–42–36–39–24. Métro: Les Halles or Etienne Marcel. Open weekdays 11:30–2:30 and 6–9:30. Closed end of Aug.*

Café de la Cité. Only a block from the Centre Georges Pompidou, this tiny brasserie is crowded with lunchtime regulars and offers good, hearty meals. At lunch all appetizers (including escargots or a meal-sized avocado salad) are 15F, main dishes 40F, and desserts only 15F. At dinner try the two-course menu (65F), with appetizers like tabouleh, and main dishes such as lasagne or grilled salmon. *22 rue Rambuteau, 3e, tel. 01–42–78–56–36. Métro: Rambuteau. Open daily noon–4 and 7–10:30.*

Japanese Barbecue. Some of the cheapest sushi in Paris passes over the counter of this friendly restaurant run by a Japanese family. While the dining room is simple, crowds fill the tables for the 45F lunch menu of soup, salad, and kebabs on rice. Sushi rolls start at 30F each; more elaborate fish specialties are 65F for three rolls. The cheapest dinner menu is 64F. The 80F sashimi menu is more than worth the splurge. If you eat at the counter, the guy at the grill might talk your ear off. *60 rue Montorgueil, 2e, tel. 01–42–33–49–61. Métro: Sentier or Les Halles. Closed Sun. MC, V.*

➤ **UNDER 100F** • **Entre Ciel et Terre.** This happy, crunchy place with wood-and-stone walls focuses on healthy gourmet meals of fruits and vegetables. They like to remind you of the great vegetarians of the world—Gandhi, Charles Darwin, Leonardo da Vinci, and Lenny Kravitz. The three-course vegetarian menu runs 90F, or try a tasty meal-size special like the *galette de céréales* (56F), a mix of different cereals and vegetables with a 15F glass of organic grape juice. Their apple crumble (29F) is delicious. *5 rue Hérold, 1er, tel. 01–45–08–49–84. Métro: Les Halles or Louvre-Rivoli. Open weekdays noon–3 and 7:30–10. MC, V.*

LOUVRE TO OPERA

Most of this neighborhood is going to be out of your range. On the upside, when you *do* sit yourself down for a bite here, it usually means you'll be served in true Parisian style. Workers from ritzy neighborhood shops find refuge on **rue du Faubourg-St-Honoré,** which has some good lunch deals. For Japanese restaurants and stores, check out **rue Ste-Anne** and, across avenue de l'Opéra, **rue St-Roch.** Some of the best sushi in town is served at **Foujita** (41 rue St-Roch, 1er, tel. 01–42–61–42–93), where a sushi sampler costs 100F.

A meal in Paris isn't complete without a glass of wine and a good toast. A few to try out on your French friends: "Tchin tchin!" (a formal version of cheers!), "A votre santé!" (To your health!), "A la tienne!" (Here's to you!), "On bascule!" (Bottoms up!).

➤ **UNDER 80F** • **Country Life.** For health nuts, this may be the best deal in town: 65F gets you unlimited access to the quality pickings of both a hot and a cold vegetarian buffet (dessert and drinks are extra). The hot dishes vary daily, from tofu curry to veggie lasagne. You can also ask for a take-out tray (29F for a small one, 49F for a large), and eat it in the great outdoors. The health-food store in front will tempt even the pickiest of herbivores with its wide selection of dried fruits, nuts, organic vegetables, and soy products. *6 rue Daunou, 2e, tel. 01–42–97–48–51. Métro: Opéra. Open weekdays 11:30–2:30 (Mon.–Thurs. also 6:30–10). Store open Mon.– Thurs. 10–10, Fri. 10–3. AE, MC, V.*

Le Gavroche. *"Tout le monde bascule!"* is shouted as everyone pounds a glass of the house Beaujolais at this lively neighborhood bistrot. A loyal group of middle-aged locals has been coming for years for the 70F menu of provincial specialties such as hearty *pot au feu* (beef and vegetable broth). Plan to stay awhile, as evenings here often end with rowdy sing-alongs. *19 rue St-Marc, 2e, tel. 01–42–96–89–70. Métro: Richelieu-Drouot. Open Mon.–Sat. noon–3:30 and 7–2. Closed Aug. MC, V.*

Higuma. Japanese and French businesspeople gather at lunch for Higuma's 63F menu (also offered at dinner), which includes a minisalad, soup, and *gyoza* (Japanese ravioli)—nothing fancy, but surprisingly hearty. *Oyakadon,* a bowl of rice covered with chicken, eggs, and onions, will fill up even the emptiest stomach. Grab a spot at the counter and watch the chefs' knives flailing around. *32 bis rue Ste-Anne, 1er, tel. 01–47–03–38–59. Métro: Pyramides. Open daily 11:30–3 and 5–10.*

L'Incroyable. The name refers to the self-proclaimed "Incredibles," a corrupt, egotistical group of nouveaux riches who sprang up after the Revolution—before Napoléon took over and put them in their place. Pick between the rustic, wood-paneled interior and the brightly colored tables in the front patio. The 75F (lunch 67F) traditional French menu includes *blanquette de veau* (veal cooked in butter and stock) and dessert: Do as an Incredible and indulge in the handmade pastries. *26 rue de Richelieu, 1er, tel. 01–42–96–24–64. Métro: Palais Royal–Musée du Louvre. Open Mon. noon–2:15, Tues.–Fri. noon–2:15 and 6:30–9, Sat. noon–2:15.*

Le Palet. Just above the Jardin du Palais Royal, Le Palet is so romantic and homey that you might find yourself falling for the suit-and-ties who come here for lunch. The filling 65F menu often includes tomato-and-mozzarella salad and steak; a slightly more elaborate 95F dinner menu has dishes like goat-cheese salad and *St-Pierre gratinée* (whitefish baked with cheese on top). *8 rue de Beaujolais, 1er, tel. 01–42–60–99–59. Métro: Palais Royal–Musée du Louvre. Closed Sat. lunch and Sun. MC, V.*

➢ **UNDER 100F** • **Yamamoto.** This crowded place serves excellent food to passing Japanese tourists—a sure sign that the food is good. Start off with a miso soup (20F), then try filling sushi rolls like *futo maki* (55F) or a sampler of six different kinds of sushi (95F). Wash it all down with a cold can of Sapporo (35F) or a warm sake (35F). *6 rue Chabanais, at rue des Petits-Champs, 2e, tel. 01–49–27–96–26. Métro: Quatre-Septembre or Pyramides. Closed Sun. MC, V (over 100F only).*

LE MARAIS

A variety of kosher restaurants, delis, and bakeries with Middle Eastern specialties indicate the strong presence of the Marais's Jewish community. Look no farther than the fantastic falafel stands on **rue des Rosiers** for the cheapest and tastiest meals in all of Paris. The Marais's other main contingent, its well-established gay crowd, means you'll also find more expensive, artsy, trendy joints; try instead the gay-owned restaurants, cafés, and bars on **rue Ste-Croix-de-la-Bretonnerie** and **rue Vieille-du-Temple.** The Marais café scene is swinging, so you won't have any trouble finding convivial spots to get your daily dose of espresso.

For cheap and delicious crêpes, head to the stand on the corner of rue de Rivoli and rue de Malher. Daniel, the ever-smiling cook, puts loads of Nutella in his 12F dessert crêpes—a sure sign of a good chef.

➢ **UNDER 40F** • **L'As du Fallafel.** The long line of hungry folks waiting for their falafel fix shows that the "masters of falafels" are doing something right. Lenny Kravitz paid homage to this standing room-only restaurant/grocery/deli in a *Rolling Stone* interview; now, it pays homage to him—the wall is adorned with pictures of Lenny and his girlfriend, the sexy French sugar-pop singer Vanessa Paradis. A falafel costs 20F, but shell out an extra 5F for the deluxe with grilled eggplant, cabbage, hummus, tahini, and hot sauce. Get a tiny 10F wine bottle to go with it, and you're set. *34 rue des Rosiers, 4e, tel. 01–48–87–63–60. Métro: St-Paul. Open Sun.–Fri. 10–10.*

Sacha et Florence Finkelsztajn. Walk through the brightly colored mosaic doorway and enter a world of Eastern European and Russian snacks and specialties. These stores/delis are Paris institutions; the rue des Rosiers location has been open since 1946. Small *pirojki* (pastries filled with fish, meat, or vegetables) cost 10F (20F for a large, almost meal-size version). Heftier sandwiches are 30F–40F. You can also get blinis, gefilte fish, and blueberry muffins. *Sacha: 27 rue des Rosiers, 4e, tel. 01–42–72–78–91. Métro: St-Paul. Open Wed.–Fri. 10–2 and 3–7, weekends 10–7:30. Closed July. Florence: 24 rue des Ecouffes, 4e, tel. 01–48–87–92–85. Métro: St-Paul. Open Thurs.–Mon. 10–1:30 and 3–7, Fri. and Sun. 9–7:30. Closed Aug.* **139**

➣ **UNDER 60F** • **Chez Rami & Hanna.** This place serves hearty, filling meals and a mean falafel almost rivaling that of L'As du Fallafel (*see above*) down the street. But here you can get your falafel to go (21F–24F), or sit down to dishes like the Israeli Platter (hummus, tahini, and falafel balls; 35F), spicy Moroccan salad (40F), or stuffed eggplant (60F) in the small, friendly dining room. *54 rue des Rosiers, 4e, tel. 01–42–78–23–09. Métro: Hôtel de Ville. Open daily 11–3 and 6–1:30.*

Le Petit Gavroche. You'll probably share a table and some smoke at this cramped bistrot, which intimates what the quarter was like before the chic set moved in. All kinds install themselves at the bar for a nightly glass of Bordeaux, while diners head upstairs for a filling 45F meal served until midnight. Don't expect fancy cuisine or reverent service, just good, substantial food and a casual atmosphere. *15 rue Ste-Croix-de-la-Bretonnerie, 4e, tel. 01–48–87–74–26. Métro: St-Paul. Open weekdays noon–3 and 7–midnight, Sat. 7–midnight. MC, V.*

La Theière dans les Nuages. The setting is small, cozy, and somewhat nondescript, but the great food and friendly service more than make up for the lack of atmosphere. This creole restaurant dishes out tasty specialities such as *poulet créole* (chicken with a sweet-and-sour sauce) and *marmite créole* (pork and bean stew). The speciality dishes change daily, and you can get a two-course 45F or 55F lunch menu (the 55F menu is also served at dinner). *14 rue Cloche-Perce, off rue de Rivoli, btw rue Vieille-du-Temple and rue des Ecouffes, 4e, tel. 01– 42–71–96–11. Métro: St-Paul. Open Mon.–Sat. noon–2:30 and 7–11.*

➣ **UNDER 80F** • **Chez Marianne.** You'll know you've found Marianne's place when you see the line of people reading the bits of wisdom and poetry painted across her windows. The restaurant/deli serves excellent Middle Eastern specialties like hummus and babaganoush; they serve couscous weekdays for 55F. The sampler platter lets you try four items for 55F, five for 65F, or six for 75F. If you don't want to wait, make reservations, grab something to go from the deli (featuring piles of dried fruits and nuts in bulk), or get a fabulous 25F Israeli-style falafel (with beets and cabbage) from the window outside. *2 rue des Hospitalières-St-Gervais, 4e, tel. 01–42–72–18–86. Métro: St-Paul. Open daily noon–3:30 and 7–midnight. MC, V.*

➣ **UNDER 100F** • **La Canaille.** The name means rascal or rabble-rouser—and that's exactly who came to this artsy joint to eat, drink, and sing protest songs in the early 1970s. Ever since, the place has stayed true to the ideals of fine food and drink, but the singing and rebellion, sadly, are on the wane. Both the 70F lunch menu and the three-course 90F dinner menu offer lots of choices, including grilled veal with macaroni. Meat portions are huge; for something light, try the 40F goat-cheese salad. *4 rue Crillon, 4e, tel. 01–42–78–09–71. Métro: Sully-Morland or Quai de la Rapée. Open weekdays noon–2:30 and 7:30–midnight, Sun. 7:30–midnight.*

The Studio. You could almost say you were at a Texas saloon except for two small details: no hard booze, and the romantic courtyard is filled with dozens of candlelit tables. Early evenings bring the sounds of the jazz and clomping feet of the dance school upstairs . . . another sure sign you're not in the Wild West. You'll find good ol' American spareribs (90F) here, as well as a hickory-smoked beef sandwich plate with coleslaw, green beans, and fries (70F). The week-end brunch of *huevos rancheros* (eggs with tortillas and salsa; 75F) brings a less smoochy crowd. *41 rue du Temple, 4e, tel. 01–42–74–10–38. Métro: Rambuteau. Open weekdays 7:30 PM–midnight, weekends 12:30–3 (Sun. until 3:30) and 7:30–12:30. AE, MC, V.*

➣ **SPLURGE** • **Le Gamin de Paris.** Candlelight gets you in the mood for fancy appetizers like escargots (40F) and salmon pasta (50F). Main dishes include beef fillets with shallots (90F) and roast duck with figs and raisins (90F). A weekday lunch special goes for 45F. Between meal-times, you can come for just a drink or a luscious homemade dessert, such as the *tarte-Tatin* (apple tart; around 30F). *49 rue Vieille-du-Temple, 4e, tel. 01–42–78–97–24. Métro: St-Paul. Open daily noon–3 and 7–midnight. Reservations required for dinner. MC, V.*

MONTMARTRE

The first rule of eating in Montmartre is: Don't buy anything near the tourist-infested Sacré-Cœur and place du Tertre, where you're sure to get screwed. If you insist on being in the shadow of the Sacré-Cœur, try going behind it to **rue Lamarck** and **rue Caulaincourt** for relatively cheap French fare. Better yet, head down the stairs toward **rue Muller,** where the food is cheaper and more ethnic. For the most authentic African cuisine, go east to the area between **rue de la Goutte-d'Or** and **rue Doudeauville.** Homey little restaurants and fresh produce shops abound on **rue des Abbesses,** but if you want something a bit different, try exploring along **rue des Trois-Frères.**

➤ **UNDER 40F** • **La Pignatta.** This Italian pizzeria and deli sells fresh pastas and panini with eggplant (16F–28F), some non-Italian items like hummus and tabbouleh (70F per kilo), and loaves of poppyseed bread (4F). You can also get a passable pizza for 30F. *2 rue des Abbesses, 18e, tel. 01–42–55–82–05. Métro: Abbesses. Open daily 9:30 AM–11 PM.*

➤ **UNDER 60F** • **Au Grain de Folie.** Although hardcore vegetarians may find some of the choices bland and somewhat pricey, this restaurant's redeeming dish is the *au grain de folie*, a refreshing and filling grain concoction accompanied by fresh veggies and topped with warm goat cheese. You can get soup and a tart for 60F; à la carte items run 45F–65F. Refuel with the 15F organic apple juice, because no matter where you're going in Montmartre, it's usually uphill. *24 rue de La Vieuville, 18e, tel. 01–42–58–15–57. Métro: Abbesses. Open weekdays noon–2:30 and 7–10:30, weekends noon–midnight.*

Le Fouta Toro. Get a whole day's worth of food for 50F. Some of the Senegalese dishes are terrific, like the *mafé au poulet* (chicken in peanut sauce) for 47F, but the seafood dishes could stand some improvement. Warm, cheery surroundings, jolly service, and huge portions make it a great dinner spot, packed with the working-class locals of northern Montmartre. *3 rue du Nord, 18e, tel. 01–42–55–42–73. Métro: Marcadet-Poissonniers. Open Wed.–Mon. 7:30–midnight (sometimes later).*

Rayons de Santé. The menu here is entirely vegetarian, featuring 20F–30F appetizers like vegetable pâté and artichoke mousse. Main courses (30F–35F) include spicy couscous with vegetables and soy sausage or vegetarian goulash. You can also choose between a 48F menu or a three-course (dessert included) 63F menu. Mornings, come for an omelette (30F) and then check out the mini health-food store in front. *8 pl. Charles-Dullin, 18e, tel. 01–42–59–64–81. Métro: Abbesses. Open Sun.–Thurs. 9–3 and 6:30–10, Fri. 9–3.*

➤ **UNDER 80F** • **Au Virage Lepic.** At a bend in one of Montmartre's steep and winding streets, Au Virage Lepic seems to belong to the last century—one can easily imagine Balzac's *ouvriers* (workers) huddling over some wine in the cozy dining room. The food is great, and the atmosphere casual and decidedly untouristed—the kind of place where today's Parisians come to argue art and politics over dinner and a cigarette. The *pavé au poivre*, a beefsteak with pepper, is 60F, or you can get a delicious *soupe à l'oignon* (onion soup) for 30F. *61 rue Lepic, 18e, tel. 01–42–52–46–79. Métro: Abbesses. Open daily 7 PM–2 AM.*

➤ **UNDER 100F** • **Au Refuge des Fondus.** Just when you think there's not enough oxygen in the room to support another body, the jovial proprietor asks you to scoot over so he can seat another dozen. You're sure to know your neighbors by the time you leave. The waiter simply asks "*viande ou fromage?*" (meat or cheese?) and "*rouge ou blanc?*" (red or white wine?), then sets you up with an aperitif, appetizers, fondue, dessert, and wine for 87F. You'll probably feel stupid drinking wine out of a baby bottle (no joke), but you'll also eat heaps of food and have a hell of a good time. *17 rue des Trois-Frères, 18e, tel. 01–42–55–22–65. Métro: Abbesses. Open daily 7 PM–2 AM. Reservations advised.*

La Bouche du Roi. The "Mouth of the King" is a self-proclaimed Franco-Benin enterprise that blends West African cuisine with traditional French cooking. Colorful tapestry seats and mellow African tunes will help you forget the mob scene at the Sacré-Cœur. Weekday nights often feature live music; Friday nights an African *conteuse* (storyteller) weaves her tales. But the real reason to come is the food: A 55F lunch menu (80F at dinner) offers specialties like *maffé* (beef in seasoned peanut sauce) and *tale tale* (fried bananas). Try the chicken cooked with plantains and coconut milk (60F) for a real treat. *4 rue Lamarck, 18e, tel. 01–42–62–55–41. Métro: Abbesses or Château-Rouge. Open Thurs.–Tues. 11:30–2 and 7:30–midnight. AE, MC, V.*

L'Eté en Pente Douce. This unassuming spot at the foot of stairs leading up to the Sacré-Cœur sees regulars filing in for fantastic dinners. The asymmetrical dining room feels like a country house, and outdoor tables are great for gazing at the beautiful nearby park. Large salads cost 45F–60F, meat dishes 60F–80F, and a delicious pear dessert with nuts is 30F. Reserve for dinner or come for lunch, when things are considerably calmer. *23 rue Muller, 18e, tel. 01–42–64–02–67. Métro: Château-Rouge. Open daily noon–3 and 7:30–11:15. MC, V.*

Le Kezako. This self-proclaimed hangout of Montmartre "professors, plumbers, and engineers" is among Paris's best tapas joints. Sophie and Miguel serve cheap Spanish food and a good sangria (65F per liter) in tiny, oddly mirrored rooms. A glass of sangria and a small tapa (22F) make a perfect snack, while a collection of four larger tapas (68F) makes a filling meal. The 85F menu includes paella, sangria, and coffee. *12 rue Véron, 18e, tel. 01–42–58–22–20. Métro: Abbesses. Open daily noon–2 and 7–11:30. MC, V.*

Le Pic à Vin. Alright, so it's touristy. But it's one of the cheapest snazzy meals around. And it's just far enough from the place du Tertre to keep the crowd pretty mellow . . . even if the menu *is* in four languages. Your 59F menu brings a two-course meal that could include a raw salmon fillet with lemon and herb-roasted chicken. A 97F super menu brings you more choices with dessert thrown in. *108 rue Lepic, 18e, tel. 01–46–06–19–29. Métro: Abbesses. Open Tues. and Thurs.–Sun. noon–3 and 6–11. AE, MC, V.*

MONTPARNASSE

Boulevard du Montparnasse marks the stark line between haughty St-Germain-des-Prés and the working-class district of Montparnasse. In recent years, however, obnoxious department stores like Galeries Lafayette have been built near the monolithic Tour Montparnasse; meals here can thus range from cheap and filling to expensive and insulting. If your budget is tight you can always get a good Breton crêpe around **rue d'Odessa** or **rue Daguerre**; the area was the original settling ground for Breton migrants looking for work in Paris at the turn of the century.

➤ **UNDER 60F** • **Chez Papa.** Rowdy waitresses serve southwestern French food at this crowded place across from the cemetery. Mongo salads packed with potatoes, ham, cheese, and tomato are known as *boyardes* and cost a piddling 35F. Escargots "Papa" (49F) come piping hot in a bright orange pot. The set menu goes for 50F day and night until 1 AM. At breakfast opt for an *omelette paysanne* (34F) filled with tomatoes, bacon, potatoes, and mushrooms. *6 rue Gassendi, 14e, tel. 01–43–22–41–19. Métro: Denfert-Rochereau. Open Mon.–Sat. 7 AM–2 AM, Sun. 10 AM–2 AM. AE, MC, V. Other location: 206 rue La Fayette, 10e, tel. 01–42–09–53–87; Métro: Louis Blanc.*

Mustang Café. This is the most popular of the many Tex-Mex café/bars in Montparnasse, drawing foreign students and Parisians. You won't be soaking up French culture, but you can have a respectable meal at almost any hour—they're open daily 9 AM–5 AM. Taco salads cost 49F, quesadillas 39F, enchiladas 59F, and Dos Equis 30F. Weekdays 4–7 margaritas and cocktails are half-price. Expect it dark, loud, and cramped. *84 blvd. du Montparnasse, 14e, tel. 01–43–35–36–12. Métro: Montparnasse. MC, V.*

➤ **UNDER 80F** • **Aux Artistes.** This restaurant is as artsy as its name suggests: worn, covered in paint and posters from top to bottom, and inhabited by cool people who were born halfway through a cigarette. The food is French, and the chicken dishes are especially good. For 75F you can choose among 29 appetizers, 35 main dishes, and several cheeses or simple desserts. Get a bottle of house wine (32F) to top it all off. *63 rue Falguière, 15e, tel. 01–43–22–05–39. Métro: Pasteur. Open weekdays noon–3 and 7–12:30, Sat. 7–12:30. MC, V.*

Pont Aven–Chez Melanie. Of the legions of crêperies below boulevard du Montparnasse, this one is among the best. Lively crowds of neighborhood students come for the *galette du jour* (buckwheat crêpe), plus salad and cider for 44F. A la carte galettes go for 15F–50F, dessert crêpes for 15F–40F. The lunch menu (64F) includes an appetizer, galette, and crêpe; the dinner menu (76F) has a salad, galette, and cider. *54 rue du Montparnasse, 14e, tel. 01–43–22–23–74. Métro: Vavin. Open daily noon–3 and 6–midnight. AE, MC, V.*

The restaurants in this area cater primarily to diplomats and politicians, stray groups of tourists, and a small handful of solemn locals. In other words, you won't be eating many meals here. **Rue de Babylone,** which attracts the shopping crowd, is a promising walk for a good lunch, and you might poke around the side streets near the **rue Cler** market. The cafés, haphazardly filled with students from nearby campuses, are also pleasant.

➤ **UNDER 100F** • **Au Babylone.** The proprietress hustles her family around the tables of this lunch-only restaurant, serving grilled specials to everyone from political bigwigs to students, all under the watchful gaze of ceramic Pope plates. The four-course 90F menu includes cheese and wine. Appetizers (try the 20F pâté Basque) are inexpensive, and main courses like a creamy veal stew or a plate of sausages are about 50F. The best deal is the wine: 12F for a half-bottle of house red. *13 rue de Babylone, 7e, tel. 01–45–48–72–13. Métro: Sèvres-Babylone. Closed Sun. and Aug.*

Bar de la Maison de l'Amérique Latine. Walk through the brightly lit gallery of Latin American art and past the expensive restaurant to this cultural center's cool and dark café-bar. A la carte dishes include Mexican quesadillas (64F) and Guatemalan stuffed peppers (60F), with appetizers like Argentinean empanadas (28F). Wash it all down with a 25F Corona. Although the bar fills up at mealtimes with handsome but snobby art enthusiasts and diplomatic attachés, it's a quiet place to study in the morning or late afternoon. *217 blvd. St-Germain, 7e, tel. 01–45–49–33–23. Métro: Rue du Bac. Café-bar open Oct.–Apr. 8:30–7:30; dinner served May–Sept. only. Closed weekends. AE, MC, V.*

Chez l'Ami Jean. If you're smitten with Basque food, the ebullient Jean and his family will dish you up some *pâté de campagne* (country-style pâté; 25F) and then treat you with specialties like trout meunière (55F) or Basque chicken (with tomatoes and red peppers, also 55F). Equally tempting desserts run 25F–40F. This is the meeting place for the North American Basque Organization, or the NABO. *27 rue Malar, 7e, tel. 01–47–05–86–89. Métro: Latour-Maubourg. Closed Sun. MC, V.*

➤ **SPLURGE** • **Au Petit Tonneau.** This gourmet, women-run restaurant bills its food *cuisine de femme.* Entrées at 40F precede main courses like *andouillettes de Troyes dijonnaise* (tripe sausages in mustard sauce; 65F) or duck breasts *au poivre vert* (with green pepper; 98F).

A Full Load of Courses

You'll hear mixed reviews of the university cafeteria-style restaurants, but dig this: You can get a three-course meal for about 15F. If you've been gnawing on bread and Brie for a week, this is nirvana. They're supposed to ask to see a student ID card (if you don't have one, the price gets jacked up 10F), but they often don't. Tickets come in sets of 10; if you only want one meal it'll cost 30F (just buy a ticket off a nice French student for the 15F deal). Lunch hours hover around 11:30–2; dinner is served 6:30–10. The "Resto-U" at 115 boulevard St-Michel (RER: Luxembourg) doles out all-you-can-eat couscous or lentils with meat, vegetables, salad, and bread.

For a complete list of university restaurants, stop by CROUS (39 av. Georges-Bernanos, 5e, tel. 01–40–51–37–17). Otherwise, try one of the following: 39 av. Georges-Bernanos, 5e, RER: Port-Royal; 10 rue Jean-Calvin, 5e, Métro: Censier-Daubenton; 3 rue Mabillon, 6e, Métro: Mabillon; 45 blvd. Diderot, 12e, Métro: Gare de Lyon; 156 rue de Vaugirard, 15e, Métro: Pasteur; Av. de Pologne, 16e, Métro: Porte Dauphine.

The dessert selection includes several liqueur-soaked sorbets (around 40F). *20 rue Surcouf, 7e, tel. 01–47–05–09–01. Métro: Invalides or Latour-Maubourg. AE, MC, V.*

QUARTIER LATIN

The Quartier Latin offers a slew of reasonable restaurants that keep its student population (and tourists) well fed. Competition is high among French, Greek, and Tunisian eateries on **rue de la Huchette.** For more upscale dining, try the area behind **square René-Viviani.** And, if you're really hard up, don't forget that you can always live off crêpes—whether they be smothered in Nutella or packed with *gruyère* (swiss cheese) and *jambon* (ham). Try **rue Mouffetard** for a mean 13F crêpe at one of the stands; you'll also find many French, Greek, and Mexican places offering a full meal for 50F-70F.

➤ **UNDER 40F** • **Al Dar.** The deli side of this otherwise expensive Lebanese restaurant offers delicious sandwiches (20F) and small plates (30F) of falafel and spicy chicken sausage. A variety of goodies costs 65F if you eat at the picnic tables outside, 60F if it's packed to go. The lack of a menu and hurried counterpeople can make it difficult to order, but pointing should do the trick. *8–10 rue Frédéric-Sauton, 5e, tel. 01–43–25–17–15. Métro: Maubert-Mutualité. Open daily 8 AM–midnight. AE, MC, V.*

➤ **UNDER 60F** • **Le Boute Grill.** Some Maghrebian expats feel this Tunisian restaurant serves the best couscous in Paris. The servings are enormous and come with a choice of—count 'em—14 combinations of meat, including one with tripe stuffed with herbs (52F). A three-course menu at 72F includes wine, but even the ravenous men hunched over their plates shudder at the thought of finishing it all. *12 rue Boutebrie, 5e, tel. 01–43–54–03–30. Métro: Cluny–La Sorbonne. Closed Sun.*

Cousin Cousine. This spacious, airy crêperie picks up on the French fetish for old flicks, with galettes named L'Ange Bleu (walnuts, blue cheese, crème fraîche; 35F) and Mad Max (ground beef, cheese, ratatouille; 41F). Simpler galettes start at 14F; the usual sundaes and flambéed crêpes are 30F-35F. A *bolée* (bowl) of cider starts at 14F. *36 rue Mouffetard, 5e, tel. 01–47–07–73–83. Métro: Monge. Open daily noon–11. MC, V (over 150F only).*

Le Jardin des Pâtes. The "Garden of Pasta" serves freshly made, organic-grain pastas (46F-73F) lavished with sauces like mixed vegetables with ginger and tofu; carnivores can sink their teeth into a smoked duck sauce with cream and nutmeg. Entrées, like the avocado paired with melon sorbet, are about 25F. The granola folk who own the restaurant have even found additive-free beers (24F). *4 rue Lacépède, 5e, tel. 01–43–31–50–71. Métro: Monge. Closed Mon. MC, V.*

La Petite Légume. This small restaurant near the Jardin des Plantes takes its vegetarianism seriously—most dishes use no dairy products, and several of the desserts are fat-free. Portions are generous, tasty, and relatively cheap: Grains with mixed vegetables cost 35F-40F, miso soup 30F, the vegetarian platter (tofu galette, vegetables, rice, and dried fruits) 60F. You can buy pastries (16F-32F) and whole-grain breads during the day. *36 rue des Boulangers, 5e, tel. 01–40–46–06–85. Métro: Cardinal Lemoine. Open Mon.–Sat. 9–2:30 and 7:30–10. AE, MC, V.*

Taco Mucho. While the name is absolutely unforgivable and the food only so-so, at least Taco Mucho (¡arriba!) is cheap. Or at least cheap for Paris, which means free chips and salsa, appetizers like gazpacho for 28F, main dishes for about 45F, and Dos Equis for 25F. Join local students and the odd professor for the two-course lunch menu (52F) or order *à emporter* and picnic at the nearby Jardin du Luxembourg. *206 rue St-Jacques, 5e, tel. 01–43–29–96–14. RER: Luxembourg. Open weekdays 11:30–3, Fri.–Sat. 7 PM–midnight. MC, V (over 100F only).*

➤ **UNDER 80F** • **L'Apostrophe.** Early diners get a deal at this romantic, country-style nook near the Panthéon. The 65F two-course menu (add 10F for dessert), served only until 8 PM, features appetizers like leek vinaigrette soup, main courses like pepper steak or shish kebabs, and banana flambée to finish it all off. Huge candles in bottles ensure a campy setting. *34 rue* *de la Montagne-Ste-Geneviève, 5e, tel. 01–43–54–10–93. Métro: Maubert-Mutualité. Open daily noon–2:30 and 6:30–midnight. MC, V.*

Bistrot de la Sorbonne. Swirl that glass of red wine (18F) and ponder the paintings of the Sorbonne in its halcyon days. The pleasant setting may urge you to bypass the basic 67F menu (salad, simple main course, and dessert) and get specialties like couscous or lamb tahini (75F). Half-liters of wine run 30F. *4 rue Toullier, 5e, tel. 01–43–54–41–49. RER: Luxembourg. Open Mon.–Sat. noon–3 and 7–11. MC, V.*

➤ **UNDER 100F • Surma.** Regulars fill the small dining room of this Indian restaurant across from the south wall of La Mosquée. The three-course menu is 98F (59F lunch with fewer choices), but you may do better ordering à la carte from among the 11 tandooris and 21 curries, priced 48F and up. Other highlights include *begun barta* (spicy roasted eggplant spread; 30F) and the fluffy cheese nan bread (19F). Top it off with a tiny pitcher of *citron lassi* (lemon yogurt drink; 20F). *5 rue Daubenton, 5e, tel. 01–43–36–31–75. Métro: Censier-Daubenton. Open daily 11:15–2:30 and 8–11. MC, V.*

ST-GERMAIN-DES-PRES

Beyond the chichi galleries and boutiques of St-Germain are plenty of substantial dining options. **Rue Monsieur-le-Prince** is one of the best restaurant streets in the city, featuring Asian spots with three-course menus for as little as 50F. **Rue des Canettes** and the surrounding small streets are best for crêpes and other fast eats; the classic French fare here often falls flat (let the crowds inside the restaurant be your guide). **Rue de Seine** and **rue de Buci** are packed with market stores, most of which have prepared foods to go and are open until 7 or 7:30.

➤ **UNDER 40F • Au Plaisir des Pains.** They pack pita pockets with fillings of your choice (grilled red peppers, tomato, mozzarella, and lettuce for 25F, other combinations 20F–30F), throw them on the grill, and then pack it up picnic-style for you (napkins and all). A good thing, considering the 10F charge to sit down and the Jardin de Luxembourg nearby. *62 rue Vaugirard, 6e, tel. 01–45–48–40–45. Métro: Rennes. Open Mon.–Sat. 10–8.*

Have you noticed those signs on brasserie windows boasting that they serve Poilâne bread? It all comes from a sublime St-Germain bakery at 8 rue du Cherche-Midi, where specials include a wheat loaf with nuts (25F) and apple tarts (12F).

➤ **UNDER 60F • Cosi.** The opera-loving New Zealander who owns this fancy sandwich shop can often be seen at the stone oven in back baking his trademark focaccia bread. You choose the ingredients—such as chèvre, spinach, smoked salmon, mozzarella, tomatoes, or curried turkey (30F–50F)—or you can just munch on the slightly salty bread *nature* for 9F. Add to this a glass of wine (14F), modern wood decor with photos of opera greats, a changing selection of opera music, and voilà: French deli. *54 rue de Seine, 6e, tel. 01–46–33–35–36. Métro: Odéon. Open daily noon–midnight.*

La Crêpe Canettes. This simple crêperie, decorated with posters from neighborhood art galleries, is a popular lunch spot. The 52F lunch or dinner menu includes a salad with walnuts, a galette, and Breton cider. The delicious fancier galettes come with smoked salmon or artichoke hearts (30F–49F) but be forewarned: The "vegetable" galettes are often NOT vegetarian, and vegans will have to resort to sucking down *pichets* (small pitchers) of cider (31F). Dessert crêpes are an extra 30F. *10 rue des Canettes, 6e, tel. 01–43–26–27–65. Métro: Mabillon. Open Mon.–Sat. noon–10; closed Mon. dinner. MC, V.*

Orestias. This restaurant is fine if you're in the mood for a boisterous meal; otherwise, the haphazard service may drive you nuts. It's owned by a Greek family that communicates by shouting: They shout at you to take a seat and then shout your order to the kitchen. Meals are typically a three-course affair (44F; two-course lunch menu, 37F) featuring a variety of grilled meats and desserts like baklava. Vegetarians may not enjoy the animal heads on the wall glowering down at patrons. *4 rue Grégoire-de-Tours, 6e, tel. 01–43–54–62–01. Métro: Odéon. Open Mon.–Sat. noon–2:30 and 5:30–midnight. MC, V.*

Besides bagels and sandwiches, the café across the street from Le Coffee Parisien has hard-to-come-by American products at jacked-up prices. Pop-Tart anyone?

➤ **UNDER 80F** • **Le Coffee Parisien.** This popular but tiny spot, frequented by St-Germain's young leisure class, serves brunch all day at the diner-style counter or at tables. We're talking *real* brunch, like eggs Benedict (70F), pancakes (50F), and eggs Florentine (70F). The 40F spinach salad is quite good. *5 rue Perronet, 7e, tel. 01–40–49–08–08. Métro: St-Germain-des-Prés. Open daily 10 AM–11:30 PM. MC, V.*

Restaurant des Beaux-Arts. Students and professors painted the frescoes on the walls and regularly fill up this lively, old-time establishment near the Ecole des Beaux-Arts. The three-course 75F menu with wine is extensive, including daily specials like fondue, rabbit, steak, or lamb. A budget tourist's favorite. *11 rue Bonaparte, 6e, tel. 01–43–26–92–64. Métro: St-Germain-des-Prés. Open daily noon–2:15 and 7–11.*

➤ **UNDER 100F** • **Chassagne Restaurant.** Locals linger in Chassagne's dark, rustic interior, and with a meaty three-course 85F menu (lunch 65F) with grilled specialties, this could be one of the best deals for a classic French meal. Servers may even attempt timid English translations if you look perplexed enough. *38 rue Monsieur-le-Prince, 6e, tel. 01–43–26–54–14. Métro: Odéon. RER: Luxembourg. Closed Sun. AE, MC, V.*

Les Jardins de St-Germain. This traditional restaurant near the Eglise St-Germain-des-Prés fills up at lunch with well-dressed professionals and students from the nearby business school. The 68F lunch menu (79F at dinner) includes a generously garnished main course, your choice of veggies, and dessert. The same owners run **La Ferme St-Germain** across the street; the two restaurants open alternately on Sundays. *14 rue du Dragon, 6e, tel. 01–45–44–72–82. Métro: St-Germain-des-Prés. Open Mon.–Sat. noon–2:30 and 7–11. MC, V.*

Le Petit Mabillon. In a section of St-Germain where restaurants are prohibitively expensive, this friendly Italian spot puts them all to shame with a delicious, filling three-course menu (77F). In good weather, sit outside and watch the crowds going to the market across the street. Pastas made fresh daily cost 55F à la carte. *6 rue Mabillon, 6e, tel. 01–43–54–08–41. Métro: Mabillon. Closed Mon. lunch and Sun. MC, V.*

Village Bulgare. Tucked into a quiet side street near the Pont Neuf, this restaurant was started by a Bulgarian dancer and his wife, who used to cook for homesick dance-troupe members. Sample Bulgarian specialties like *kebabtcheta* (a grilled meat roll; 52F) and *banitza* (a baked pastry filled with cheese; 35F); the three-course menu costs 85F. Their flyers deem it "Une cuisine qui chante" (cooking that sings). *8 rue de Nevers, 6e, tel. 01–43–25–08–75. Métro: Pont-Neuf. Open Tues.–Sat. noon–2 and 7:30–10, Sun. noon–2, and Mon. 7:30 PM–10 PM.*

➤ **SPLURGE** • **Le Bistrot d'Opio.** This restaurant opened last year to serve up delicious Provençal cuisine on a street packed with standard French restaurants. The 119F menu allows you to choose almost any entrée, main course, and dessert on the menu. Try the salmon baked on a bed of sea salt, or the duck prepared with honey and 19 spices, including anise and cloves. The chocolate fondant for dessert is a chocoholic's dream come true. *9 rue Guisarde, 6e, tel. 01–43–29–01–84. Métro: Mabillon. MC, V.*

Bistrots

There's a fine line between bistrots and their more expensive and largely British-run cousins, *bars à vin* (wine bars), but the perpetual feud between the French and Brits makes it a fairly serious faux pas to confuse the two. Bistrots, an obstinately Parisian institution, are all about wine—sold by the bottle or by the glass—and snacks like cheese and meat plates, although many of them are just as proud of their cuisine as they are of their wine. They often specialize in obscure regional vintages and sometimes buy grapes from the vineyards to blend themselves. And as long as you nod your head and smile knowingly as the *patron* (proprietor) explains his collection, everyone should get along smashingly.

Le Baron Rouge. Refreshingly mellow, the Red Baron has enough varieties of cheap wine—patrons draw straight from the barrel—to keep its poststudent crowd happy. Wine starts at 6F, meat plates at 35F, and smoked duck is 18F. The decor, like the crowd, is low-key and casual, with sawdust-covered floors, wooden tables, and friendly locals. About twice a week a live rock or blues band takes over, forcing some patrons out onto barrels set up on the sidewalk. *1 rue Théophile-Roussel, near pl. d'Aligre, 12e, tel. 01–43–43–14–32. Métro: Ledru-Rollin. Open Tues.–Sat. 10–10, Sun. 10–3.*

According to one theory, the word "bistrot" dates back to the early 19th century after the fall of Napoléon, when the Russian soldiers who occupied Paris supposedly banged on zinc-topped café bars yelling "buistra"—"hurry" in Russian.

Bistrot des Augustins. The Augustins, the best of several bistrots along the Seine in St-Germain, has a worn wood-and-brass bar, speckled mirrors, and shelves cluttered with dried flowers. When the weather is nice, the front doors open onto the street. Join the devoted clientele drinking quality wine by the glass (15F and up) and munching on goat cheese salads (40F) or liver terrine (32F). *39 quai des Grands-Augustins, 6e, tel. 01–43–54–41–65. Métro: St-Michel. Open daily 10:30–midnight. MC, V (over 100F only).*

Bistrot-Cave des Envierges. A cozy room and a few scattered sidewalk tables mark this old, casual bistrot just above the Parc de Belleville. Ten wines—five whites and five reds—are offered daily at 8F–12F a glass, and the list always features at least a couple of Loires. Snacks like gazpacho cost 30F, meat or cheese plates go for 45F. A cool, hang-loose crowd—not that there's ever much of one—makes this a great place to unwind. *11 rue des Envierges, 20e, tel. 01–46–36–47–84. Métro: Pyrénées. Open Wed.–Sun. 11:30–2:30 and 7–midnight.*

Le Bouchon du Marais. For a quieter meal at this bistrot, grab a table downstairs. For something more boisterous, reserve ahead for a table *à l'étage* (on the second floor). The patron specializes in Touraine wines and offers a wide selection by the glass (30F–40F). Otherwise, 70F gets you a glass of wine, a main dish, and dessert. They offer a *raclette* (fondue) menu (115F) in the winter, a perfect meal to have in the cozy, chalet-like upstairs. The walls are full of snapshots of the patron and his friends, all conspicuously drunk. *15 rue François-Miron, 4e, tel. 01–48–87–44–13. Métro: St-Paul. Open for lunch noon–2, dinner seatings past midnight. Closed Sun. AE, MC, V.*

Le Brin de Zinc. A relaxed crowd of locals gather on the sidewalk of the busy market street for an afternoon glass of wine (25F). Mingle with the suited regulars indoors, where you can order platters of cheese (50F) or meats (65F) with a bottle of wine (90F and up) from the well-stocked cellar. More substantial food, such as the *blanquette de veau* (veal cooked in butter and stock) is expensive (about 90F) but excellent, or stick to a cheap and delicious quiche Lorraine (25F). *50 rue Montorgueil, 2e, tel. 01–42–21–10–80. Métro: Etienne Marcel. Open Mon.–Sat. noon–3 and 7:30 PM–11:30 PM.*

Le Coude Fou. Yet another mellow Marais institution where you're bound to meet some cool people if you hang around long enough. Avoid the artsy, expensive food (70F–90F) and get a bottle of wine (90F and up) or a beer (20F); then join the regulars (including a fair number of anglophones) hunkered around tables made from wine crates. *12 rue du Bourg-Tibourg, 4e, tel. 01–42–77–15–16. Métro: Hôtel de Ville or St-Paul. Open daily noon–2 AM; food served daily noon–3 and 7:30–midnight. Closed lunch Sun. AE, MC, V.*

In mid-September, when the grapes on the vines outside Jacques Mélac's windows ripen, he closes off the street and holds his own private harvest festival. Everyone picks, the young'uns stomp, and the drinking goes on through the night.

Jacques Mélac. Since 1938 Jacques Mélac and son have been churning out some damn fine wine (with a few mediocre bottles thrown in occasionally to make sure you're awake). Look no further than the vines curling around this neighborhood bistrot to find the source of their labor. While Jacques offers a large selection of labels, definitely try his own award-winning 1981 wines (bottles start at 70F). The bar and dining room are packed with locals who aren't afraid to serve themselves when the waiters are a little slow. Omelettes (20F–50F) and plates of meats and cheese (20F–60F) may accompany the wine, but the waiters refuse to serve water with the food. *42 rue Léon-Frot, 11e, tel. 01–43–70–59–27. Métro: Charonne. Open Mon. 9–7, Tues–Fri 9 AM–midnight. Closed Aug. AE, MC, V.*

Le Relais du Vin. Eleven years ago, Mr. Beaugendre transformed his bar into a restaurant specializing in wines. The 18-wine-long list starts with a 65F bottle of Château Coquille 1992 rosé and winds up at a 1,400F Château Margaux 1976 Premier Grand Cru Classé; glasses of the less expensive stuff go for 12F–21F. For 40F you can compare small glasses of three different Burgundies. The menu runs 65F for two courses and a drink, 85F for three courses; lighter dishes such as spinach salad topped with raisins and cheese (40F) are served until past midnight. *85 rue St-Denis, at rue des Prêcheurs, 1er, tel. 01–45–08–41–08. Métro: Les Halles. Open Mon.–Sat. noon–2 AM. MC, V.*

Le Rouge Gorge. You won't find boisterous, glass-clinking guzzlers at this sophisticated southern Marais wine bar. The rustic and homey rooms give it the feel of an isolated country house, a good place to bring that edition of *War and Peace* and mull over life and a glass of white (from 15F) or red (from 12F) wine from Corsica. You can get decent plate of *figatelli* (spinach and polenta; 62F); desserts and cheeses cost around 30F. *8 rue St-Paul, 4e, tel. 01–48–04–75–89. Métro: Sully-Morland. Open Mon.–Sat. noon–3:30 and 5:30–11:30. Closed Aug. MC, V.*

Salons de Thé

While French cafés tend to appeal to chain-smoking, well-dressed crowds of chattering French people, salons de thé are wonderful, mellower institutions that no longer cater only to fussy matronly ladies. Regularly filled with students and artists seeking portions generous enough to share, the salons specialize in *tartes salées* (savory tarts with cheese and vegetables), *tartes sucrées* (dessert tarts), and, of course, tea. In the Marais they pop up on every corner, and gay proprietors can be less intimidating sources of information about gay life in the neighborhood than a bartender. That said, you'll see more women than men in salons de thé, and they're often alone, making these places a great refuge for single women travelers. They tend to be open in the afternoons, seeming to beckon just as your feet are rebelling against a day of marble-floored museums and cobblestone streets.

A Priori Thé. This small salon serves up large pots of tea (22F) in its comfortably worn room in the galerie Vivienne, an elegant renovated passage near the Bibiliothèque Nationale. Tables line the old glass-roofed galleria, making the place feel like a sidewalk café, only without the traffic and gloomy weather. Older women come here to sip on exotic teas (mango, mint, and almond are a few of the 25F options) and nibble on divine, although expensive, pastries (30F). It's the perfect place to catch up on your letter writing, and there's a funky postcard shop right next door. *35–37 galerie Vivienne, at 66 rue Vivienne, 2e, tel. 01–42–97–48–75. Métro: Bourse. Open Mon.–Sat. noon–6, Sun. 1–6.*

Caffé les Enfants Gâtés. A few blocks to the east you have the beautiful place des Vosges, in the other direction bars and restaurants—and in the middle of it all a café with low lights, tattered leather chairs, ceiling fans, and old movie posters. Coffee costs 15F and loose-leaf flavored teas 25F. Get a drink and stay as long as you like—the welcoming manager may even hand you a magazine from his huge stack. *43 rue des Francs-Bourgeois, 4e, tel. 01–42–77–07–63. Métro: St-Paul.*

La Charlotte de l'Isle. This minute salon de thé should really be called a *salon de chocolat;* birds and fish made of chocolate-dipped orange peels peer curiously out the front window, and they melt real chocolate bars for the sumptuous hot chocolates (20F). An ample selection of teas is available in bulk or by the cup (15F), and there's always an inventive selection of dessert tarts (15F–20F). Wednesday afternoons the friendly owner hosts reservation-only marionette shows. *24 rue St-Louis-en-l'Ile, 4e, tel. 01–43–54–25–83. Métro: Pont-Marie. Open Thurs.–Sun. 2–8. Closed July and Aug.*

Mariage Frères. This is the most reputable teahouse in Paris; the shop up front sells hundreds of varieties of loose leaves by the gram, as well as every device imaginable in which to brew them. A pot of tea in the chic salon at the back will run you 45F, desserts 45F–55F. Don't forget to visit their tea museum upstairs. Avoid the bland, overpriced brunch. *30 rue du Bourg-Tibourg, 4e, tel. 01–42–72–28–11. Métro: Hôtel de Ville or St-Paul. Closed Mon. Other location: 13 rue des Grands Augustins, 6e, tel. 01–40–51–82–50; Métro: Mabillon; closed Tues. AE, MC, V.*

La Mosquée. Inside Paris's main mosque, this salon de thé has an intricately tiled interior, Moroccan wood carvings, and tapestried benches. Let the Middle Eastern music lull you, and then visit the Turkish baths next door for pure decadence (*see box* Turkish Delights, in Chapter 2). Coffee or a teeny (but potent) glass of sweet mint tea is 10F; baklava and other pastries cost 11F–15F. *19–39 rue Geoffroy-St-Hilaire, 5e, tel. 01–43–31–18–14. Métro: Censier-Daubenton.*

Nezbullon. This salon de thé tends to attract a younger crowd and offers tea and cheap wine (9F–16F) by day. In the evenings people also come for the 39F three-course menu, which includes quiche and a salad. Pascal, the friendly, English-speaking owner, has a knack for card tricks and balloon art. *20 rue de La Vieuville, 18e, tel. 01–55–41–00-21. Métro: Abbesses.*

Cafés

Along with air, water, and the three-course meal, the café remains one of the basic necessities of life in Paris. You'll find a café on every corner and around every bend, and after a while you may notice that they all look the same. Only those who stick around long enough to make themselves regulars (or write entire books, as Simone de Beauvoir did) will discover their true intrigue. Those on the *grands boulevards* (such as boulevard St-Michel, boulevard St-Germain, and the Champs-Elysées) and in the big tourist spots (near the Louvre, the Opéra, and the Eiffel Tower, for example) will almost always be the most expensive and the least interesting. The more modest establishments (look for nonchalant locals) will give you a cheaper cup of coffee and a feeling of what real French café life is like.

If you can't stomach a deadly shot of espresso, swallow your pride and ask for a "café allongé." Waiters will smirk as they bring what's sometimes referred to as a "café américain": an espresso poured into a bigger cup and watered down.

Cafés are required to post a *tarif des consommations,* a list that includes prices for the basics: *café* (espresso), *café crème* (the same with hot milk), *chocolat chaud* (hot chocolate), *bière à la pression* (beer on tap), *vin rouge* (red wine), *kir* (white wine flavored with crème de cassis), and *citron* or *orange pressé* (fresh-squeezed lemonade or orange juice). They list two prices, *au comptoir* (at the counter) and *à terrasse* or *à salle* (seated at a table). Below we give the seated prices. If you just need a quick cup of coffee, take it at the counter and save yourself a lot of money. If you have a rendezvous, take it at a table, remember you're paying rent on that little piece of wood, and hang out as long as you like. Cafés are usually open until midnight or later and charge about 5F more per drink after 10 PM or so.

L'Allée Thorigny. A bright, simple café a few steps from the Musée Picasso provides everything you need: temporary shelter or a seat outside, a cup of coffee (9F), newspapers and magazines (from the newsstand on the corner), chessboards, and self-serve candy (14F for 100g). *2 pl. Thorigny, 3e, tel. 01–42–77–32–05. Métro: St-Paul or Chemin Vert. Open Wed.–Mon. 9:30–7.*

amnésia café. The music is just loud enough to keep conversations private at this dimly lit, predominantly gay café with big, comfy chairs. In fact, the atmosphere is so mellow, it might reconcile you with the preppy types that frequent it. Their scrumptious salad plates (45F–65F) offer more greenery than most cows could consume. A café costs 9F, café crème 14F, and a jumbo crème 18F; beers run 20F–30F. Nightfall ups both the prices and the crowd. *42 rue Vieille-du-Temple, 4e, tel. 01–42–72–16–94. Métro: St-Paul or Hôtel de Ville.*

Au Soleil de la Butte. Here you'll find the rare commodity of a good cup of coffee in an untouristy café near the Sacré-Cœur. A sparse local crowd hangs out on the covered terrace sipping café (10F) and beer (10F–15F). The menu is long and includes salads from 30F. This café has the dear idiosyncracy of also serving meals at off-times. Just be sure to walk down the stairs on the *east* side of the basilica, *away* from the tourist quagmire at place du Tertre. *32 rue Muller, 18e, tel. 46–06–18–24. Métro: Château Rouge.*

Brûlerie de l'Odéon. When you enter this old-fashioned coffee brewery specializing in teas, the friendly proprietress might engage you in conversation about the weather, even if you don't speak French. The decor (teak tables and coffee paraphernalia) is as low-key as the service. Café is 10F–11F, café crème 15F, and pastries 13F–20F. *6 rue Crébillon, 6e, tel. 01–43–26–39–32. Métro: Odéon. Open Mon.–Sat. 9:30–6:45.*

If you're wandering around and need to find a bathroom, one of the city's ubiquitous cafés may be your best bet. Not only are they on almost every street corner, but proprietors are required by law to let anyone use their bathrooms, whether they're patrons or not.

Le Café. The subdued name says it all. A young, goateed crowd and cool, low-key tunes keep the atmosphere about as mellow and unpretentious as it gets in Paris. Bring a book and munch on a zucchini and cheddar tart (45F) or a *croque monsieur* (grilled ham-and-cheese sandwich) with a side-salad (40F). Or bring a friend and sip kir (20F) while you play one of the backgammon, chess, or domino games they've got in back. *62 rue Tiquetonne, 2e, tel. 01–40–39–08–00. Métro: Etienne Marcel. Open Mon.–Sat. 10 AM–2 AM, Sun. 1 PM–2 AM.*

Café au Petit Suisse. It's at the edge of the Quartier Latin and across the street from the Jardin du Luxembourg, full of students, starving writers, and other locals. Sit in the cozy little room when the weather is rotten and, when it isn't, on the sunny terrace. With private booths and an indoor balcony, the Petit Suisse draws you in without being flashy or touristy. Café is 11F, café crème 18F, and cold drinks 18F–19F. *9 rue Corneille, at rue Vaugirard, 6e, no phone. Métro: Odéon. RER: Luxembourg. Closed weekends.*

Left Bank Literary Cafés

If you really want to sink a lot of money into a cup of café crème, stop by one of the cafés made famous by their artsy patrons of the 19th and early 20th centuries. On place St-Germain-des-Prés is Les Deux Magots, named after the grotesque Chinese figures inside. Still milking its reputation as one of the Left Bank's prime meeting places for the intelligentsia, Deux Magots charges hordes of tourists 21F for a stinking cup of coffee. Past patrons include Verlaine, Rimbaud, Mallarmé, André Gide, Picasso, Jacques Prévert, and André Breton. Jean-Paul Sartre and Simone de Beauvoir supposedly met here, but spent more time two doors down at the Café de Flore, hanging with his fellow angst-ridden friend Albert Camus.

Perhaps the most famous bastion of Left Bank café culture (and certainly one of the most expensive, having been turned into a pricey bar/restaurant), La Closerie des Lilas (171 blvd. du Montparnasse) marks its bar seats with plaques indicating who once sat there. For the price of an expensive drink, you can rest your buns where Baudelaire, Apollinaire, and Hemingway sat. Finally, Le Procope (13 rue de l'Ancienne Comédie), the self-proclaimed "first café in the world," was founded in 1689 and supplied coffee and booze to La Fontaine, Diderot, Rousseau, Balzac, Hugo, Voltaire, Napoléon, Robespierre, Ben Franklin, and Oscar Wilde. Now it's a stuffy restaurant.

Café Beaubourg. Style alert: The crowd here looks like it's been transplanted from some Saint-Tropez resort. Yet despite the intimidatingly slick exterior, the waiters are actually *friendly* and used to a fair amount of summer tourists. Best of all are the bookshelves filled with French titles that you can browse while you lounge in the shadow of the Centre Georges Pompidou. Tackle a large salad (45F–50F), but beware of the expensive coffee (14F, 17F after 7 PM). *100 rue St-Martin, 4e, tel. 01–48–87–63–96. Métro: Rambuteau. Open daily 8 AM–1 AM.*

Café de l'Industrie. This place is so cool that it doesn't even bother to open on Saturdays. Every twentysomething in town flocks to these large, smoky rooms where modern art hangs from the red walls. This is a great place for a light dinner and drink before hitting the Bastille scene. Sink into one of the corner cushy seats and hide out all day, or come later to schmooze with the French night owls at the bar. Beers are 16F. *16 rue St-Sabin, 11e, tel. 01–47–00–13–53. Métro: Bastille or Bréguet-Sabin. Open Sun.–Fri. 11 AM–2 AM. MC, V.*

Le Café du Trésor. Although it's tucked in a little side street off rue Vieille-du-Temple, this bright café is definitely an attention-grabber. The blue, yellow, red, and green tables are inscribed with bits of conversation (lest you run out of ideas), and the plush seats indoors accent the modern art on the walls. The handsome gay waiters will promptly equip you with beer (16F–28F) or *kir royal* (champagne with black currant liqueur; 40F). *5–7 rue du Trésor, 4e, tel. 01–44–78–06–60. Métro: St-Paul. Open daily 9 AM–2 AM.*

Café Marly. This flamboyant and unabashedly sophisticated café overlooks the Cour Marly in the Louvre's new Richelieu wing. The stunning view, name-dropping clientele, and reputation (the *International Herald-Tribune* did an article on the place) might justify paying 16F for a café or 35F for a chocolate tart, at least once. The extra-long hours are an added bonus. *Cour Napoléon, 1er, tel. 01–49–26–06–60. Métro: Palais Royal–Musée du Louvre. Open daily 8 AM–2 AM. MC, V.*

Café Wah-Wah. Here's a grungy Bastille café with decor that was lifted straight from San Francisco's Haight district or London's Camden Town. Don't be intimidated by the multiply pierced, tattooed regulars; the bar folk are real nice and the music's just loud enough to mask your bad French accent. Café is 6F, a pression 12F. Kirs are 15F. *11 rue Daval, 11e, tel. 01–47–00–08–48. Open daily 2 PM–2 AM. Métro: Bastille.*

Chez Camille. The outdoor terrace is only slightly larger than a balcony, and the cramped inside is painted a pale yellow. The patrons are young, hip and mostly male *Montmartrois,* who come regularly to enjoy the soft jazz and the cheap beer (10F–15F). *8 rue Ravignan, 18e, tel. 01–46–06–05–78. Métro: Abbesses. Open Tues.–Sun. 9 AM–2 AM.*

Les Colonies du Paradis. Okay, so the name (the Colonies of Paradise) is cheesy, and so is the Mariah Carey–style pop music they play. But this sunny, two-floor café is gorgeous and right off place de la Bastille. More importantly, their weekday happy hour (5 PM–8 PM) lets you sip tropical cocktails for only 20F. *3 rue du Faubourg St-Antoine, 11e, tel. 01–43–44–01–00. Métro: Bastille. Open daily noon–1 AM. MC, V.*

La Palette. This old, muted café amidst rue de Seine's galleries lets you sip a café crème (12F) or wine (20F) while contemplating the splotched palettes of local artists on the walls. The waiters are talkative and the clientele nocturnal—it's a good place for late-night socializing. Come on balmy evenings when everyone crowds the tables outside under the cherry trees. *43 rue de Seine, 6e, tel. 01–43–26–68–15. Métro: Mabillon. Open Mon.–Sat. 8 AM–2 AM.*

Pâtisserie Viennoise. A scaled-down version of its Austrian counterparts, this cramped local institution keeps aspiring doctors from the nearby Ecole de Médecine caffeinated. Pastries are created in the kitchen downstairs, including several variations on the chocolate torte (15F), each named for a famous composer; lesser pastries start at 5F. Café is 11F. *8 rue de l'Ecole-de-Médecine, 6e, tel. 01–43–26–60–48. Métro: Odéon. Closed weekends and Aug.*

La Pause. This smoky Bastille café (but what isn't smoky in Paris?) has an outdoor terrace overlooking the rue de Charonne, loaded with art galleries and music stores. Coffee is a reasonable 8F, crème 12F. If you're hungry, dig into the succulent salmon quiche (42F). A trendy, relaxed

French crowd, with a significant but not overwhelming contingent of motorcyclists, packs it all day. *41 rue de Charonne, 11e, tel. 01–48–06–80–33. Métro: Bastille or Ledru-Rollin.*

Sydney Coffee Shop. After you hike up a small 30° incline, a tiny little counter and two tables welcome you to this low-key, Australian Internet café. Foster's is 40F a pint, Melbourne bitter 30F. Check your e-mail for 1F a minute while you munch, since 35F specials make this a great lunch spot as well. Coffee is 12F. *27 rue Lacépède, 5e, tel. 01–43–36–70–46. Métro: Monge or Cardinal Lemoine. Open Tues.–Sat. 10–10.*

Markets and Specialty Shops

As well as a number of open-air markets, Paris hosts a whole medley of specialty shops and late-hour markets. **Monoprix** and **Prisunic** both house low-priced supermarkets, but you usually have to weave through clothing and perfume departments to reach the food. Monoprix is all over and usually open until 8 or 9; the Prisunic just off the Champs-Elysées (109 rue de La Boétie, 8e, tel. 01–42–25–10–27) is open Monday–Saturday until midnight. On most side streets, especially in budget lodging areas, look for *alimentations générales*—small grocery stores that offer standard snack items at steep prices. They're generally open until 9 or 10 PM.

To see French connoisseurship at its most prestigious and pretentious, check out the world-famous Fauchon (26 pl. de la Madeleine, 8e, tel. 01–47–42–60–11) and Hédiard (21 pl. de la Madeleine, 8e, tel. 01–42–66–44–36). You won't be able to afford to fill your stomach, but we can guarantee a Pantagruelian feast for the eyes, the exotic produce, chocolates, and rows of glass jars glistening in elaborate displays.

A lifesaver for anyone on a budget, **Ed l'Epicier** is the cheapest supermarket in Paris. Although the selection varies, you can always find the basics (pasta, rice, beans, meat, cheese, wine, chocolate) for way less than anywhere else. Bring your own grocery sacks. *84 rue Notre-Dame-des-Champs, 6e. Métro: Notre-Dame des Champs. Other locations: 80 rue de Rivoli, 4e; Métro: Hôtel de Ville. 123 rue de Charonne, 11e; Métro: Bastille.*

OPEN-AIR MARKETS

There is no better way to experience the "real" Paris than by joining the haggling, pushing, pointing, and shouting that takes place at Paris's 84 open-air markets. Don't be intimidated, because not much French is needed—shopping in markets merely requires a little body language. The best time to go is in the morning, when you'll get the best selection and the merchants will be more patient with your halting French. Unless you see a sign saying "Libre Service" (self-service), the grocer chooses your items for you. You can, however, object to anything she chooses or tell her which ones you prefer. Pointing should do the trick if you don't speak any French.

The list "Les Marchés de Paris" at the tourist office will give you a detailed plan of all the markets; otherwise pick and choose from the following. The cheapest market is on **place d'Aligre** (12e; open Mon.–Sat. 8–1 and 3–7, Sun. 8–1). Here you'll find fresh fruit, veggies, cheese, pastries, kosher butchers, coffee, clothing, flowers, and cooking utensils. The market at **place Monge** (5e; open Wed., Thurs., and Sun. 7 AM–1:30 PM) is another well-known cheapie. Paris's biggest outdoor market is held on **boulevard de Reuilly** between rue de Charenton and place Félix-Eboué (12e; open Tues. and Fri. 7 AM–1:30 PM). More permanent covered markets take place on **rue Mabillon** (6e), **rue de Bretagne** (3e), and **rue l'Olive** (18e). Hours for these markets are Monday–Saturday 8–1 and 3–7, Sunday 8–1. For organic food head to the **Marché Biologique** (6e; open Sun. 7 AM–1:30 PM), on boulevard Raspail between rue du Cherche-Midi and rue de Rennes.

One of the most enjoyable market streets is **rue Montorgueil.** For Chinese, Vietnamese, and Thai food, check out the excellent daily **Chinese market** near Paris's Chinese district in the 13th arrondissement; take the Métro to Porte de Choisy and you can't miss it. If you're still not satisfied, try the south end of **rue Mouffetard** (5e), **rue de Buci** (6e) near St-Germain, **rue Daguerre** (14e) in Montparnasse, and **rue Lepic** (18e) in Montmartre, all with astounding arrays of produce, cheeses, meats, breads, candies, and flowers.

NON-FRENCH FOODS

At larger supermarkets it's easy to become frustrated by the limited range of non-French foods they tend to offer. Luckily, most French people fulfill these needs in specialty stores. American and British goods are most common in neighborhoods like St-Germain and the Marais, kosher food is common in the Marais (4e), and Asian and Middle Eastern supplies are plentiful around Belleville (19e), Chinatown (13e), and the 10th arrondissement.

Hate to burst your bubble, but most of the boulangeries in Paris aren't allowed to make their own bread because you need a special permit to own an oven. To have a real loaf of bread baked by real Parisian boulangers, look for a blue and yellow sign in front of the boulangerie saying ARTISAN BOULANGER.

La Grande Epicerie. Perhaps the best part of the department store Au Bon Marché (*see* Grands Magasins, in Chapter 6) is the gourmet grocery attached. Other than the finest brands and the highest prices on all your usual French supplies, this place has sections devoted to American, British, Italian, Indian, and kosher goods. The excellent produce section here, though pricey, has a much wider selection than the typical market. *38 rue de Sèvres, 7e, tel. 01–44–39–81–00. Métro: Sèvres-Babylone. MC, V.*

Izraël. This small, packed shop in the Marais specializes in hard-to-find goods from all over the world, including huge bins of rices, grains, and olives, some prepared dishes, and shelves of prepackaged goods. Pick up anything from Indonesian soya sauce (15F) to barbecue sauce (50F) to Kraft marshmallow spread (30F). Be careful reaching for things—one false move can bring the whole store crashing down on you.(spoken from experience). *30 rue François-Miron, 4e, tel. 01–42–72–66–23. Métro: St-Paul. Open Tues.–Sat. 9:30–1 and 2:30–7. MC, V.*

Mexi & Co. If you're tired of faux Mexican food, this specialty store sells your basic Mexican and Latin American goods at high prices: A can of refried beans costs 16F, a kilo of flour tortillas 36F. At several sidewalk tables or the inside bar you can sip on a Tecate (18F) while munching on the chicken burrito plate (29F) or free chips and salsa. *10 rue Dante, 5e, tel. 01–46–34–14–12. Métro: Maubert-Mutualité or Cluny–La Sorbonne. Open weekdays 10:30–8 (Fri. until midnight).*

Ste-Kioko. Come here for fresh and packaged Japanese foods. *46 rue des Petits-Champs, 2e, tel. 01–42–61–33–66. Métro: Pyramides. Open Mon.–Sat. 10–7.*

Supermarché Asia-France International. Everything Belleville's Asian population could possibly desire—dozens of different types of noodles, spicy sauces, and cheap produce—constitute the bulk of this supermarket's stock. *48 blvd. de Belleville, 20e, tel. 01–40–33–43–33. Métro: Couronnes. Open Tues.–Sun. 9–8.*

Tang Frères. This chain of Chinese supermarkets (with a largely Vietnamese clientele) sells Asian produce and packaged items—anything from tea to preserved squid intestines. The atmosphere is strictly Hong Kong, with groping hands and lashing elbows everywhere. *168 av. de Choisy, 13e, tel. 01–44–24–06–72. Métro: Place d'Italie or Tolbiac. Open Tues.–Sun. 10–7.*

Thanksgiving. Don't do major shopping here; it would be cheaper to have mom Federal Express a care package from home. But when you *gotta* have Oreos, you can get 'em here for 50F. Other finds include Jell-O (12F), peanut butter (32F), Pop Tarts (35F), and a good selection of California wines. The restaurant upstairs sells "New York" bagels and cream cheese with lox (65F), or baked potatoes with cheddar or spinach (25F). *20 rue St-Paul, 4e, tel. 01–42–77–68–29. Métro: St-Paul. Open daily 11–8 (Sun. until 6). AE, MC, V.*

SWEETS

If you've reached the bottom of your Nutella jar and your sweet tooth still wants more, hightail it over to one of Paris's fabulous *boulangeries* (bakeries), *pâtisseries* (pastry shops), or *confiseries* (candy shops). Luscious French desserts are everywhere, so it's important that you pick up some of the vocabulary: *chausson aux pommes* (an apple turnover that puts Ronald McDonald to shame); *religieuse* (a puff pastry filled with chocolate- or coffee-flavored whipped cream and drizzled with chocolate); *madeleines* (sponge-cake dipping cookies that are not quite as orgasmic as Proust implies); the *opéra* (a triple-decker chocolate and cream indulgence); *tartelettes* (minitarts); and *choux à la crème* (round, cream-filled pastries).

The French term for window-shopping, "lécher les vitrines," literally means "to lick the windows," which is what you'll be tempted to do outside Paris's pastry shops.

Parisians have to admit that Belgian chocolates are better than French ones. Accept this fact and be glad that Belgium isn't far away, ensuring easy access to their celebrated *pralines* (filled chocolates). If you're hunting for gourmet chocolate, seek out **Léonidas** (7 rue des Innocents, 1er, tel. 01–42–36–11–92; Métro: Châtelet–Les Halles), or the oldest sweet shop (AD 1761) in Paris, **A la Mère de Famille** (35 rue du Faubourg-Montmartre, 9e, tel. 01–47–70–83–69; Métro: Rue Montmartre). Proving that the French can do chocolate cheaply is **Le Chocolatier de Paris** (71 rue de Tolbiac, 13e, tel. 01–45–86–38–39; Métro: Nationale), where a kilo (2.2 lbs) costs just 100F. Also worth a visit is **La Charlotte de l'Isle** (24 rue St-Louis-en-l'Ile, 4e, tel. 01–43–54–25–83), which only opens Thursday to Sunday 2 PM–8 PM, but has sumptuous dark chocolate and a cute little tea room where you can enjoy it. Across the street is **Berthillon** (31 rue St-Louis-en-l'Ile, 4e; Métro: Pont Maire, tel. 01–43–54–31–61), whose ice creams and sorbets are ambrosia for the mortals. Try the apricot sorbet, which tastes like real apricot. They're open Wednesday to Sunday 10–8.

Reference Listings

BY TYPE OF CUISINE

AMERICAN

UNDER 60F

Chicago Pizza Pie Factory
(Champs-Elysées)
La Theière dans les Nuages
(Marais)

UNDER 80F

Le Coffee Parisien (St-
Germain-des-Prés)
Haynes (Gare de l'Est and
Gare du Nord)

UNDER 100F

The Studio (Le Marais)

CHINESE/ SOUTHEAST ASIAN

UNDER 40F

Restaurant Lao Siam
(Belleville)

UNDER 60F

Da Lat (Belleville)

UNDER 80F

Restaurant Tai-Yien
(Belleville)

CREPERIES

UNDER 60F

Cousin Cousine (Quartier
Latin)
La Crêpe Canettes
(St-Germain-des-Prés)
Crêpes-Show (Bastille)
Modas (Belleville)

UNDER 80F

Pont Aven–Chez Melanie
(Montparnasse)

DELIS

UNDER 40F

Al Dar (Quartier Latin)
L'As du Fallafel (Le Marais)
Au Plaisir des Pains (St-
Germain-des-Prés)
La Pignatta (Montmartre)
Sacha et Florence
Finkelsztajn (Le Marais)

UNDER 60F

Barry's (Champs-Elysées)
Cosi (St-Germain-des-Prés)

UNDER 80F

Chez Marianne (Le Marais)

EASTERN EUROPEAN

UNDER 40F

Sacha et Florence
Finkelsztajn (Le Marais)

UNDER 80F

Tokaj (Bastille)

UNDER 100F

A la Ville de Belgrade (Gare
de l'Est and Gare du Nord)
Village Bulgare
(St-Germain-des-Prés)

FRENCH

UNDER 60F

Le Bistrot du Peintre (Bastille)
Chez Papa
(Montparnasse/Gare de
l'Est and Gare du Nord)
Cousin Cousine (Quartier
Latin)
La Crêpe Canettes
(St-Germain-des-Prés)
Crêpes-Show (Bastille)
Dame Tartine (Les Halles
and Beaubourg)
Modas (Belleville)
Le Petit Gavroche (Le Marais)
Restaurant Chartier (Gare de
l'Est and Gare du Nord)

UNDER 80F

L'Apostrophe (Quartier Latin)
Au Petit Ramoneur (Les
Halles and Beaubourg)
Au Virage Lepic (Montmartre)
Aux Artistes (Montparnasse)
Bistrot de la Sorbonne
(Quartier Latin)
Café de la Cité (Les Halles
and Beaubourg)
Le Gavroche (Louvre
to Opéra)
L'Incroyable (Louvre
to Opéra)
Le Palet (Louvre to Opéra)
Pont Aven–Chez Melanie
(Montparnasse)
Restaurant des Beaux-Arts
(St-Germain-des-Prés)
Le Temps des Cerises
(Bastille)

UNDER 100F

Au Babylone (Near the
Eiffel Tower)
Au Refuge des Fondus
(Montmartre)

La Canaille (Le Marais)
Chalet Maya (Gare de l'Est
and Gare du Nord)
Chassagne Restaurant
(St-Germain-des-Prés)
Chez Justine (Belleville)
Chez l'Ami Jean (Near the
Eiffel Tower)
L'Eté en Pente Douce
(Montmartre)
Les Jardins de St-Germain
(St-Germain-des-Prés)
Le Pic à Vin (Montmartre)

SPLURGE

A la Courtille (Belleville)
Au Petit Tonneau (Near the
Eiffel Tower)
Le Bistrot d'Opio
(St-Germain-des-Prés)
Chez Paul (Bastille)
Le Gamin de Paris (Le Marais)
Julien (Gare de l'Est and Gare
du Nord)

GREEK

UNDER 60F

Orestias (St-Germain-
des-Prés)

UNDER 80F

Le Vieux Byzantin
(Belleville)
Zagros (Bastille)

INDIAN

UNDER 80F

Bhai Bhai Sweets (Gare de
l'Est and Gare du Nord)

UNDER 100F

Naz Restaurant (Bastille)
Surma (Quartier Latin)

ITALIAN

UNDER 40F

La Pignatta (Montmartre)

UNDER 60F

Le Jardin des Pâtes
(Quartier Latin)

UNDER 80F

Paparazzi (Gare de l'Est and
Gare du Nord)

UNDER 100F

Le Petit Mabillon
(St-Germain-des-Prés)

JAPANESE

UNDER 80F

Higuma (Louvre to Opéra)
Japanese Barbecue (Les
Halles and Beaubourg)

UNDER 100F

Yamamoto (Louvre to Opéra)

LATIN AMERICAN/TEX MEX

UNDER 60F

Jip's (Les Halles and
Beaubourg)
Mustang Café (Montparnasse)
Taco Mucho (Quartier Latin)

UNDER 100F

Bar de la Maison de
l'Amérique Latine (Near
the Eiffel Tower)

SPANISH

UNDER 100F

Le Kezako (Montmartre)

TURKISH/MIDDLE
EASTERN/NORTH AFRICAN

UNDER 40F

Al Dar (Quartier Latin)
L'As du Fallafel (Le Marais)

UNDER 60F

Le Boute Grill (Quartier Latin)

Chez Rami & Hanna
(Le Marais)
Van Gölu (Gare de l'Est and
Gare du Nord)

UNDER 80F

Café Moderne (Bastille)
Chez Marianne (Le Marais)
Restaurant Sarah (Bastille)
Le Vieux Byzantin (Belleville)
Zagros (Bastille)

VEGETARIAN

UNDER 60F

Au Grain de Folie
(Montmartre)
La Petite Légume (Quartier
Latin)
Rayons de Santé (Montmartre)

UNDER 80F

Country Life (Louvre to Opéra)

UNDER 100F

Entre Ciel et Terre (Les Halles
and Beaubourg)

WEST AFRICAN

UNDER 60F

Le Fouta Toro (Montmartre)

UNDER 100F

La Bouche du Roi
(Montmartre)

SPECIAL FEATURES

DINNER AND
ENTERTAINMENT

UNDER 60F

Van Gölu (Gare de l'Est and
Gare du Nord)

UNDER 80F

Haynes (Gare de l'Est and
Gare du Nord)

UNDER 100F

La Bouche du Roi
(Montmartre)

OUTDOOR DINING

UNDER 40F

Al Dar (Quartier Latin)

UNDER 60F

Dame Tartine (Les Halles and
Beaubourg)

UNDER 80F

Au Petit Ramoneur (Les
Halles and Beaubourg)
L'Incroyable (Louvre to Opéra)

UNDER 100F

L'Eté en Pente Douce
(Montmartre)
Le Petit Mabillon
(St-Germain-des-Prés)
The Studio (Le Marais)

SPLURGE

A la Courtille (Belleville)

TAKE-OUT

Al Dar (Quartier Latin)
L'As du Fallafel (Le Marais)
Au Plaisir des Pains
(St-Germain-des-Prés)
Barry's (Champs-Elysées)
Chez Marianne (Le Marais)
Chez Rami & Hanna
(Le Marais)
Country Life (Louvre to Opéra)
La Pignatta (Montmartre)
Sacha et Florence
Finkelsztajn (Le Marais)
Taco Mucho (Quartier Latin)

AFTER DARK

5

By Viviana Mahieux and Julia Švihra

Whether you're a jazz fiend or a clubhead, a patron of the arts or a lounge lizard seeking refuge in a dark smoky bar, Paris's labyrinthine streets provide ample destinations for nocturnal creatures. From opulent opera houses to low-key bars, dance floors in 17th-century caves, or just a stroll along the light-splintered Seine—if you don't seek out the nightlife, it will find you.

There are a million tempting ways to blow money if you happen to have it: theaters, discos, concert halls, films, legendary cabarets, or one of the 40F *bateaux-mouche* (fly boats) that cruise along the river (*see* Getting Around Paris, in Chapter 1). Jazz and an up-and-coming world music scene add even more sparks to the city's nightlife. For events info, consult the ubiquitous advertisement boards or check in *Pariscope* (3F, available Wednesdays at any kiosk), a weekly entertainment bible with an English-language section that lists nighttime activities all over the city. *Lylo,* short for *les yeux les oreilles* (eyes and ears), is a free monthly detailing the goings-on around town, and its listings include info about cover charges, types of music, and wheelchair accessibility. Pick it up at a bar or concert hall.

But a night out doesn't have to be expensive to be fun. Grab a bottle of wine and hang out with the French youth smoking and pretending to ignore each other on the steps of the Opéra Bastille. Better yet, take that bottle to the Pont des Arts and sit down among slobbering couples, drummers, and Rollerbladers to watch the sunset and listen to amateur musicians. Another great place is on the banks of the Seine on the Ile St-Louis; before national holidays this little island is thronging with musicians, students, and anyone else who doesn't have to get up in the morning. In the summer, place des Vosges, place St-Catherine, and the front of the Centre Pompidou are all home to impromptu guitar, jazz, and accordion music as well. Come nightfall, La Défense becomes an enormous illuminated skateboarder haven. The esplanade looks much more eerie and futuristic when the sleek high-rises are bathed in orange city lights. For info on the many free classical concerts performed in the city's churches, concert halls, and museums, *see* Opera, Classical Music, and Dance, *below.*

Gay life in Paris has its geographic base in the Marais, though it's not the raging scene that American city kids might be used to. During the afternoons and early evenings, Marais cafés cater to mixed crowds and the gay atmosphere is subtle. Lesbian life is still less visible. Try contacting the **Maison des Femmes** (8 cité Prost, 11e, tel. 01–43–48–24–91), a feminist/lesbian resource center and cafeteria, or the **Centre Gai et Lesbien** (3 rue Keller, 11e, tel. 01–43–57–21–47) for info on events. The free monthly *Illico,* found in gay bars and cafés, has a calendar of gay events, including tea dances, lectures, and concerts, as well as topical essays and a number of risqué pretty-boy pictures. *Double-Face,* a monthly aimed pri-

157

marily at men, lists gay and gay-friendly bars, clubs, and pick-up spots. It's free at Les Mots à la Bouche (*see* Bookstores, in Chapter 6) and some bars. Otherwise, it costs 8F at a kiosk.

Bars

Most Parisian bars (at least the ones that aren't open as cafés earlier in the day) open around 6 PM and close at 2 AM, even on weekends. Cafés, bars, and *boîtes* (dance clubs) in Paris tend to mutate over the course of an evening—something that was a restaurant at lunch could become a bar at 8 PM and then a dance club until sunrise. This means that a place we call a café (*see* Cafés, in Chapter 4) could wind up being a great place to have a drink after dinner or to listen to live music on certain nights. If you want a relatively quiet place, try hitting bars during the *apéritif* (around 6 PM). That's when Parisians congregate to decide where they want to meet up later, and it's a good time to meet people before everyone is too drunk.

Law requires that prices be posted, but if they're not, expect to pay 20F–35F for a draft beer, referred to as *une pression, une demi-pression,* or simply *une demi* (all mean a half-pint on tap). Wine costs about the same as beer, and cocktails are generally too expensive to bother with. The cheapest beer tends to be in more out-of-the-way, working-class neighborhoods such as **Belleville** and **Montparnasse**, where locals relax with friends. The **Marais** and the **Bastille** get a lot pricier, with a stylish crowd and a great gay scene along **rue Ste-Croix-de-la-Bretonnerie**. **Les Halles** is where you're going to end up shelling out 50F for a beer so you can hear the accompanying jazz.

BASTILLE

The Bastille is still the hottest nightlife area in town, welcoming hordes of Parisians, knowing visitors, and new arrivals who have discovered that the Left Bank is no longer where it's at. However, "where it's at" does not translate to "cheaper beer"—you have to pay for the atmo-

Fruity Brewski

Beer isn't always made exclusively from barley and hops. If the usual stuff triggers your gag reflex, try some of these flavored varieties:

- **Kriek, black cherry–flavored beer.**
- **Panaché, a mixture of half-beer and half-lemonade.**
- **Becasse, a Belgian strawberry-flavored beer.**
- **Pêcheresse, peach-flavored beer.**
- **Pelforth Framboise, dark beer with raspberry flavoring.**
- **Monaco, a light beer with grenadine syrup.**

Other fruity drink options include:

- **Kir, white wine flavored with cassis.**
- **Diabolo, tonic water flavored with grenadine.**
- **Cidre, cider, choose between doux (sweet) and sec (dry).**
- **Calvados, an apple brandy.**

sphere and attitude that come with your drinks. The block-long **rue de Lappe** has more bars per meter than any other street in Paris, while **rue de la Roquette** starts off crowded at place de la Bastille and grows desolate to the north. Side streets like **rue de Charonne** and **rue Keller** harbor low-key joints and a generally local scene. You might want to drop by **Dame Pipi** (9 rue de Charonne, 11e, tel. 01–48–05–05–83) and lounge on their wacky fuschia seats. **La Galoche d'Aurillac** (41 rue de Lappe, 11e, tel. 01–47–00–77–15) is much more homey; go there to mingle with the grandmothers at the bar and check out the clogs hanging from the ceiling.

Bar des Ferrailleurs. This bar can immediately be identified by the weird, rusty iron things hanging from its windows and the friendly, unpretentious crowd inside. Sink into the incredibly comfortable velvet seats in the back (you might have trouble standing up again), or stand in the more lively area around the bar. Sip 22F beers or a 40F Long Island iced tea to a steady stream of jazz. *18 rue de Lappe, 11e, tel. 01–48–07–89–12. Métro: Bastille.*

La Bastide. This cramped bar in the heart of the Bastille serves some of the cheapest beer (14F–20F) in the neighborhood, making it a haven for young scruffy types and serving as a reminder of the Bastille's working-class roots. The steady flow of jazz, blues, and beer encourages all kinds of sing-alongs. *18 rue de Lappe, 11e, tel. 01–47–00–26–72. Métro: Bastille.*

Café de la Plage. Soul, funk, blues, and jazz tracks accompany drinks (beers 25F–35F, aperitifs 30F) and idle chat at this Franco-British bar. Drinks cost more in the *cave* (cellar) during the weekend DJ shows, when the place becomes one of the coolest dance scenes in town (cover 50F). The crowd is young and congenial and wants to be in a band. *59 rue de Charonne, 11e, tel. 01–47–00–91–60. Métro: Charonne. Bar opens at 10 PM, disco at 11 PM.*

Le Lèche Vin. Jesus and Mary smile benevolently as you down draughts in this kitch bar lined with Christmas-tree lights and religious paraphernalia. The scene is weird and fun, reminiscent of a grungy Seattle bar, with a much less image-conscious crowd than in most of the Bastille. A demi-pression goes for 10F. *13 rue Daval, 11e, tel. 01–48–05–16–75. Métro: Bastille.*

Les Portes. If the madness of rue de Lappe and rue de la Roquette gets to be too much, take a break at this laid-back bar with occasional jazz in the cellar (except in summer). Prices hover at about 22F for a kir and 25F for draft beer; the best deal is the giant 30F kriek. Incredibly, prices *don't* go up during performances. Take a table outside and watch the drunken revelers stumble home from rue de Lappe. Performance schedules vary, so be sure to call ahead. *15 rue de Charonne, 11e, tel. 01–40–21–70–61. Métro: Bastille.*

Sans Sanz. This huge, two-story bar/restaurant is a favorite among those who are cool—and know it. After 10 PM, that means a *lot* of people. Choose between the throbbing techno scene downstairs and the more sophisticated second floor, where you can eat fancy food and spy on the downstairs crowd via video screen. Beers run about 25F. *49 rue du Faubourg-St-Antoine, tel. 01–44–75–78–78. Métro: Bastille. Open weekdays 9 AM–2 AM, weekends noon–2 AM.*

Tapas Nocturne. This festive hole in the wall is *the* place to come and fuel up before, during, and after bar hopping. Dip into the sangria (20F) and soak up the alcohol with a few *tapas* (spanish appetizers; 30F–50F) such as the *tortilla española*. Weekend nights offer live Spanish music and a long wait after 10 PM. *17 rue de Lappe, 11e, tel. 01–43–57–91–12. Métro: Bastille. Open Mon.–Sat. 7:30 PM–2 AM.*

BELLEVILLE

The truly hip are truly fickle, so they are constantly on the hunt for new haunts to colonize. In recent years, the Bastille was transformed from a working class *quartier* (neighborhood) to a mecca for the funky. Now that the metamorphosis is complete, cool Parisian youth have moved on to greener pastures: multicultural, immigrant-rich Belleville. Artsy cafés with cheap beer and grungy patrons have recently been popping up around **avenue de Belleville** and **rue de Ménilmontant**.

Café Charbon. In this beautifully restored 19th-century café, a trend-setting clientele schmoozes to the jazz playing in the background. The atmosphere gets even livelier at night when a DJ takes over. *109 rue Oberkampf, 11e, tel. 01–43–57–55–13. Métro: Ménilmontant.*

Lou Pascalou. This low-key neighborhood joint features pool tables indoors and melancholy youth on the terrace. Cheap (12F) beers and the requisite jazz background music make this a good place to catch a glimpse of old Belleville life. *14 rue des Panoyaux, 20e, tel. 01–46–36–78–10. Métro: Ménilmontant.*

Le Soleil. Come here on sunny afternoons to enjoy a cold beer (20F) on the crowded terrace. Regulars come on a daily basis and stay for hours at a time: You'll soon notice that everybody seems to know each other. It's a good place to hang out if you made the trip to Paris to meet the city's unique breed of musicians and artists. *136 blvd. de Ménilmontant, 20e, tel. 01–46–36–47–44. Métro: Ménilmontant.*

CHAMPS-ELYSEES

The Champs-Elysées (Les Champs to the initiated) and the streets branching off from it are *not* the budget traveler's domain. Bars and clubs are filled with models, wealthy foreigners, diplomats, and those who hope to meet them; this is the playground of the rich and beautiful with bucks to blow. Be prepared to be turned away at the door if you don't fit the clientele mold. Mixed-sex groups and couples are usually okay, but big groups of men or women often get the brush-off. To blend in, you need high fashion and even higher heels. It's a lot of hassle for the privilege of spending 50F on a beer, but if you seek the sleek, head to **Doobies** (2 rue Robert Estienne, 8e, tel. 01–53–76–10–76), tennis star Yannick Noah's contribution to Parisian snobbery, where you can mix and mingle with all sorts of important types. The **Chicago Pizza Pie Factory** (*see* Restaurants, in Chapter 4) is a good place to socialize with Americans (and the French people who want to meet them) while sipping a 35F beer and watching sports on TV. At **Planet Hollywood** (78 av. des Champs Elysées, 8e, tel. 01–53–83–78–27), you could stare at Schwarzenegger's *Terminator* costume while sipping a 60F Terminator cocktail, though we're not sure why you would. Some of the best entertainment is just to grab your own brew at **Prisunic** (109 rue de la Boétie, 8e, tel. 01–42–25–10–27) and then watch the hopefuls clamor over each other to get into clubs like the **Queen** (*see* Dance Clubs, *below*), where the stylish party crowd flutters, or **Les Planches** (40 rue Colisée, 8e, tel. 01–42–25–11–68), where rich suburban kids flaunt their required jackets and ties.

LES HALLES

Though Les Halles is most frequented for its live-jazz bars, a number of watering holes cater to those who'd prefer to pay a reasonable price for a beer and listen to a record instead. At night the area is almost as touristy as during the day, but it catches some gay nightlife from the nearby Marais and still lures a fair number of Parisians with relatively cheap drinks and plenty of late-night eateries. Unaccompanied women should be careful at night, especially around the deserted sex shops of northern Les Halles.

Banana Café. Gay waiters with big muscles serve 30F beers at this snazzy Les Halles bar. The interior is sleek and dim, while the terrace right near Fontaine des Innocents is prime people-watching territory. Most nights, the downstairs area becomes a small, sweaty boîte. *13 rue de la Ferronnerie, 1er, tel. 01–42–33–35–31. Métro: Châtelet. Open nightly 4 PM–dawn.*

Le Baragouin. This friendly northern Les Halles joint features bizarre decor (such as the aluminum foil backdrop behind the bar) and reasonable drinks. Come before 9 PM and squeeze in for happy hour, when a beer at the bar costs just 8F. The crowd is young, blonde, and looks as Californian as Parisians possibly can. The pool tables in the back room often host rowdy games. *17 rue Tiquetonne, 2e, tel. 01–42–36–18–93. Métro: Etienne Marcel.*

La Baraka. All bars should be like La Baraka: It's laid-back, friendly, and serves lots of cheap, cheap beer (9F–13F before 10 PM, 13F–16F after). A small room dotted with jazz memorabilia, La Baraka is the spot of choice for artsy types, thanks to the theater school next door. The charming couple who've been running the place for years give everyone a warm reception while pumping a steady stream of jazz, blues, and rock into the room. They also serve great tapas (12F a plate). *6 rue Marie Stuart, 2e, tel. 01–42–36–10–56. Métro: Etienne Marcel. Open daily 5 PM–2 AM.*

Comptoir. Facing the leafy Jardin des Halles, this sleek art deco bar with neon lights lining the ceiling will provide you with a kir (25F) or a frothy beer (23F–28F). Come early for a quiet drink, or around midnight if you prefer to see the place packed and happening. *37 rue Berger, tel. 01–40–26–26–66. Métro: Les Halles. Open weekdays noon–2 AM, weekends until 4 AM.*

Flann O'Brien. Live, potentially obnoxious rock or blues music (you are strongly encouraged to sing along) accompanies pints of frothy Guinness (17F–32F) four or five nights a week. Don't miss the happy (three) hours 6–9. *6 rue Bailleul, 1er, tel. 01–42–60–13–58. Métro: Louvre-Rivoli. Open daily 4 PM–2 AM.*

LE MARAIS

An artsy, gay neighborhood, the Marais is filled with all kinds of people and all kinds of nocturnal options. In the evenings, the bars and cafés overflow with a mixed crowd, but as the night settles in, most places turn almost exclusively gay. **Rue Vieille-du-Temple** is the main drag; in addition to the bars listed below, check out the sprawling, cushy couches at the **Majestic Café** (34 rue Vieille-du-Temple, 4e, tel. 01–42–74–61–61), where a beer goes for 20F underneath a red light and tacky statues. At **Le Pick-clops** (cnr rues Vieille-du-Temple and du Roi-de-Sicile, 4e, tel. 01–40–29–02–18) Rolling Stones posters surround a semi-pretentious but fun crowd downing 20F beers. After your revelries, head over to **Chez Rami & Hanna** (*see* Restaurants, in Chapter 4), which serves great falafel until 1:30 AM.

After midnight Thursday–Saturday, come to the tiny, nondescript Café au Vieux Paris (72 rue de la Verrerie, 4e), when song lyrics are handed out as the resident accordion player gets going. Audience participation is not optional. Drinks are 20F.

L'Apparament Café. Dim lights, soft music, comfortable seats, and a strong coffee (12F) or mixed drink (50F)—this place has all you need after trekking around the Marais all day. Flip through a magazine or play a board game to collect your energy before you hit the bars. *18 rue des Coutures-St-Gervais, 3e, tel. 01–48–87–12–22. Métro: Filles du Calvaire. Open weekdays noon–2 AM, Sat. 4 PM–2 AM, Sun. noon–midnight.*

Au Petit Fer à Cheval. A mixed bunch of locals fills this tiny bar all day and into the night. It's got an impressive range of seating options for such a small place; the best spot is right up against the horseshoe-shaped bar where the drinks are cheaper (café crème 15F, beer 25F). *32 rue Vieille-du-Temple, 4e, tel. 01–42–72–47–47. Métro: Hôtel-de-Ville. Open 9 AM–2 AM.*

Bar d'Arts/Le Duplex. Art exhibits and loud alternative music characterize the dim, cool atmosphere of this gay men's bar full of sexy, young, tortured-artist types. Women are welcome but are usually few and far between. A pression costs 25F. *25 rue Michel le Comte, 3e, tel. 01–42–72–80–86. Métro: Rambuteau.*

The Lizard Lounge. In the afternoon, students from the school of industrial design across the street mingle under the high ceilings and brick walls of this airy lounge. At night, a more diverse crowd crams into the red booths to drink 20F–35F beers and munch on chips and salsa. The bar downstairs has blaring techno, a pool table, and a little more elbow room. *18 rue Bourg-Tibourg, 4e, tel. 01–42–72–81–34. Métro: Hôtel de Ville. Open 11 AM–2 AM.*

Both Le Central (33 rue Vieille-du-Temple, 4e, tel. 01–48–87–99–33) and Le Quetzal (10 rue de la Verrerie, 4e, no phone) are prime places to scope the gay scene. Le Quetzal will even provide you with a visiting card so you can jot down your name and number and hand it to the guy of your choice.

MONTMARTRE AND PIGALLE

While Montmartre nightlife consists of neighborhood bars and pubs filled with locals (and tourists eager to join the scene), Pigalle, famed for its abundance of sex shops, strip shows, and prostitution has a little more, uh, action. To avoid the worst, steer clear of **rue Pigalle** and stay north of **boulevard de Clichy.** For the more wholesome Montmartre scene, head up streets like **rue Lepic** and **rue Caulaincourt.** Insomniacs and those who have missed the last Métro should be sure to hit **Le Dépanneur** (27 rue Fontaine, 9e, 01–40–16–40–20) for a '50s-style diner meal anytime, day or night.

Le Gerpil. Though only a few steps north of Pigalle, this simplest of bars is wholly Montmartre. The proprietor alternates sips of gin with *bises* (kisses) for all his regulars and vows that he has "only good music" for his powerful cassette player. Request a little old-time French accordion or some flamenco guitar. Pressions run 15F–20F. *14 rue Germain-Pilon, 18e, tel. 01–42–64–16–78. Métro: Pigalle. Closed Sun.*

Lily la Tigresse. For a mild taste of Pigalle's traditional charms, come to this large, red velvet–lined space with bar-top dancers. The crowd is surprisingly wholesome, and there's plenty of plush seating. The scowling, brawny doorman doesn't like single-sex crowds, so be sure to come with a mixed bunch. Expect to pay 80F for a drink. *98 rue Blanche, 9e, tel. 01–48–74–08–25. Métro: Pigalle. Open 10 PM–dawn.*

Ministry. This place features cobweb-covered skeletons and (astonishingly, considering the neighborhood) no prostitutes. The atmosphere is surprisingly relaxed, and the leather-clad crowd is friendly. Beers are 21F–25F, Martinis 25F. Don't miss the *voyante* (psychic) sessions that take place every full moon. *1 rue Mansart, 9e, tel. 01–42–82–08–88. Métro: Blanche. Open weekdays 6 PM–2 AM, weekends also 4 AM–8 AM.*

Le Moloko. Cool people and those merely aspiring to be so fill this *branché* (hip) bar/boîte until 6 AM. The three rooms include a dance floor, a smoky, plush sitting room, and a lounging "salon." Admission is free, so splurge on a Molokococktail (55F–65F), or sip a 35F beer. *26 rue Fontaine, 9e, tel. 01–48–74–50–26. Métro: Pigalle. Open 9 PM–5 AM.*

Le Sancerre. A nightly gathering of jovial Montmartrois fills up this established neighborhood bar; during the day, young artist types sun themselves outside and roll their eyes at the passing tourists. The 12F pression doubles in price after 10 PM. *35 rue des Abbesses, 18e, tel. 01–42–58–08–20. Métro: Abbesses. Open 9 AM–2 AM.*

QUARTIER LATIN

Though most spots near the river are intolerably touristy and expensive, there are some mellow bars up the hill from **boulevard St-Germain,** near **place Maubert,** and on **rue Mouffetard,** where crowds of students can actually afford the beer. English-speaking folks tend to hang out around here, so it's a good place to meet Brits, Aussies, Canadians, or—if you've had any trouble finding them—Americans.

Café Oz. A bunch of Aussies runs this small, convivial bar where Foster's on tap is 35F a pint. The sign outside claims ON PARLE FRANÇAIS (We speak French), but they must not get much practice: American college students have taken over, along with foreign students from other countries who adopt the place from semester to semester. *184 rue St-Jacques, 5e, tel. 01–43–54–30–48. Métro: Cluny–La Sorbonne. RER: Luxembourg. Other location: 18 rue St-Denis, 2e, tel. 01–40–39–00–18. Métro: Les Halles.*

Le Manhattan. Only men are admitted to this cool weekend bar/dance club. The boys arrive after 1 AM, then hang around and boogie until dawn drinking 37F beers. The club's business card doubles as a date card—on the back you can write your name and number and hand it to that hot man you've been watching all night. *8 rue des Anglais, 5e, tel. 01–43–54–98–86. Métro: Maubert-Mutualité. Closed Mon.–Thurs.*

Le Piano Vache. University students come here in groups to rest heavy elbows on the tables, chain-smoke, and solve the world's problems. The bar is sufficiently dark and the music sufficiently angst-inspiring to keep you from getting too optimistic. Beer is 30F, 40F after 10. On Wednesdays pastis is a mere 10F, making this a great introduction to the anise-flavored drink, and most afternoons there's a drink *du jour* for 15F. *8 rue Laplace, 5e, tel. 01–46–33–75–03. Métro: Cardinal Lemoine.*

Polly Maggoo. This little bar using old newspapers for wallpaper uses backgammon boards and an odd mix of jazz and Neil Diamond music to lure its clientele—a mix of old-time regulars, nocturnal alcoholics, and unsuspecting passersby caught by its red glow after the other bars have closed. You can drink and dawdle over a 30F glass of mediocre wine or a 15F *pression. 11 rue St-Jacques, 5e, tel. 01–46–33–33–64. Métro: St-Michel.*

ST-GERMAIN-DES-PRES

For what used to be the swingingest quartier around, St-Germain's nightlife has fallen pretty flat. Most of the jazz bars have tried unsuccessfully to go upscale, and the bars are overrun by foreigners about 20 years behind the times. The spots that have managed to keep a low profile have done the best, holding on to a loyal clientele and almost justifying the 30F and up that you'll pay for your beer. Most of the good bets are between **boulevard St-Germain** and the **Jardin du Luxembourg.**

Le Birdland. A soothing, well-lit bar with a big jazz collection, the Birdland caters to a crowd of varying ages with cocktails (70F) named after your favorite jazz musicians. They play Monk, Bird, and other jazz greats until 6:30 AM nightly except Sunday, when they quit early. Beer is 35F. *20 rue Princesse, 6e, tel. 01–43–26–97–59. Métro: Mabillon.*

Chez Georges. As the nostalgic decor suggests, this upstairs bar has been serving glasses of red wine, pastis, and beer (20F–30F) to older men in work clothes for the past 60-odd years. Down in the basement, local students crowd around tiny tables. Don't be intimidated if the place looks packed—there's always room to squeeze in somewhere, and the regulars are more than willing to make new friends. *11 rue des Canettes, 6e, tel. 01–43–26–79–15. Métro: Mabillon. Closed Sun.–Mon. and mid-July–mid-Aug.*

La Paillotte. Nurse a cocktail (51F) until dawn in this dark, smoky joint, which is decorated like a beach hut with fake grass roofing. The owner stations himself at the bar to greet you and keeps a close eye on the turntable—he has one of the best classic jazz collections in Paris. Beers are 25F at the bar, 40F seated. *45 rue Monsieur-le-Prince, 6e, tel. 01–43–26–45–69. Métro: Odéon. Closed Sun.*

Cabaret

The Paris cabaret, which hit its peak early this century, is seeing something of a revival these days. Cabarets most often involve a series of solo musicians, singing quartets, and other groups. If you find yourself in the Marais, check out **Le Piano Zinc** (49 rue des Blancs Manteaux, 4e, tel. 01–42–74–32–42) for gay shows. Call ahead to see what's happening. Otherwise, the greatest concentration of cabarets is still up on Montmartre hill—just be sure you choose the right kind of club.

Some of the tackiest, most famous cabaret venues in town—**Le Moulin Rouge** (pl. Blanche, 9e, tel. 01–46–06–00–19), **Les Folies-Bergère** (32 rue Richer, 9e, tel. 01–44–79–98–98), and the **Crazy Horse** (12 av. George V, 8e, tel. 01–47–23–32–32)—manage to draw a crowd despite the 500F admission. The Folies reopened a few years ago under a new director who is trying to give cabaret a more contemporary, intellectual flair.

Au Lapin Agile. This venue on Montmartre's back side has been around since 1860, including a stint under the ownership of Aristide Bruant, the famous Parisian cabaret balladeer. Today it's still serving up classic French oldies—largely to French tourists—in a dark, close room. Any evening sees solo pianists, singers, and other musicians, who rotate from 9 PM to 2 AM. Entrance with one drink is 110F, 80F for students; second drinks go down to 30F. *22 rue des Saules, 18e, tel. 01–46–06–85–87. Métro: Lamarck-Caulaincourt. Closed Mon.*

Au Pied de la Butte. It's got everything you ever hoped for from a Paris cabaret, including glittery, flashy numbers interspersed with Edith Piaf favorites. Though the focus is on singers, you'll also see comedians, magicians, balloon artists, and more. Grab a spot at one of the small tables, pay 80F for a drink, and stay as long as you like—things usually wind down around 3 AM, later on weekends. *62 blvd. Rochechouart, 18e, tel. 01–46–06–02–86. Métro: Anvers.*

Dance Clubs

Hefty covers, discriminatory door policies, and a scrambling crowd of rich, spoiled teens—how you perceive Paris's *boîte de nuit* (nightclub) scene depends on how keen you are to mix with territorial regulars. At its best, Paris's *boîtes de nuit* offer incredible people-watching opportunities and a good lesson in how to dish out French attitude.

If your face doesn't grace the cover of *Vogue,* it's hard to get around the usual 60F–150F cover charge. Your best bet is to hook up with someone who has a pass; fickle staff members hand out passes inside the boîtes to those deemed cool enough to be invited back. Youth hostels and student housing facilities are good places to ask around about passes. Once you plunge into this scene, make sure you have a lot of stamina, since the music usually goes until at least 4 AM—though by no means do you have to head home right after. Chances are, you'll have no trouble finding something to do until the Métro starts running again at 5:30 AM. Many clubs also host weekly afternoon "tea dances," gatherings where couples often dance the swing and more traditional steps. Tea dances are often men- or women-only; check *Pariscope* for listings.

In gaining admission, women have an advantage over men; at heterosexual places, guys are better off finding one or two women to accompany them. Following these guidelines will also up your chances: (1) Dress well. This means sleek and sophisticated for Champs-Elysées clubs, outrageous and scantily clad for Pigalle haunts, and funky and retro for the Bastille. (2) Arrive early (between the 11 PM opening time and midnight). Until you become known at a particular disco door, this little trick greatly improves your shot at getting in—and at getting in free. (3) Avoid going in big same-sex groups (except, of course, to gay clubs). Most places prefer mixed groups and couples. Two big-name clubs to avoid are **La Locomotive** (90 blvd. de Clichy, 18e, tel. 01–42–57–37–37; Métro: Blanche) and **La Scala** (188 bis rue de Rivoli, 1er, tel. 01–42–60–45–64; Métro: Palais Royal–Musée du Louvre), which play mostly mainstream house music for young and pouty crowds bathed in cheesy laser-light effects.

Les Bains. This former Turkish bath is now an exclusive disco with the highest ratio of models to real people found anywhere outside the pages of *Elle.* If the extremely choosy doorwoman decides you look okay, and if you don't mind forking over 100F–140F you'll find rooms full of self-absorbed people and a DJ who couldn't mix his way out of a paper bag. *7 rue du Bourg-l'Abbé, 3e, tel. 01–48–87–01–80. Métro: Etienne Marcel. Open Tues.–Sun. midnight–5 AM.*

The Little Sparrow

Born in Belleville in 1915 (and abandoned on someone's doorstep shortly thereafter), Edith Piaf began singing in cafés and on the streets of Paris by age 15. Often called "the Little Sparrow," Piaf soon became famous for her expressive, tremulous voice, performing in many cabarets and even a few plays and films. However, one look at a photo of this waifish, saucer-eyed singer, and you'll know that life was not all song and dance for this troubled woman; Piaf's career was filled with tragic relationships and drug addiction. After a serious illness, she made a comeback in 1961, but died two years later. Parisians have passion for Piaf, and the songs she made famous—including "La vie en rose," "Je ne regrette rien," "Milord," and "Mon Dieu"—are likely to pop up in any cabaret show.

Chez Moune. This old, dark cabaret in Pigalle is a women's disco during the week and a cabaret by women for women on Fridays and Saturdays. The 130F cover includes one drink; after that you're on your own. The club also has a 75F, women-only tea dance on Sunday afternoon at 4:30. *54 rue Pigalle, 9e, tel. 01–45–26–64–64. Métro: Pigalle. Open daily midnight–dawn.*

L'Escale. This South American- and Cuban-influenced club has been playing cha-cha music for musicians, intellectuals, and supposedly even Sartre and Simone de Beauvoir since the 1950s, but you wouldn't know it just passing by—the dance floor is in the cave downstairs. The crowd runs from age 20 to 70, and most of the patrons have outgrown the groping stage—no matter what the music suggests. Cuban and South American bands play nightly. On weekends the first drink is 100F, 60F thereafter. *15 rue Monsieur-le-Prince, 6e, tel. 01–43–54–63–47. Métro: Odéon. Closed Mon.*

Les Folies Pigalle. Decorated like a 1930s bordello, this small, red-hot gay club plays techno and hip-hop for a crowd crammed onto the two-level dance floor. Frequent drag shows might spotlight a faux Cher, Barbra Streisand, or Boy George, and weekends feature giddy theme nights. Lately they've been trying to bring in more women with male strip shows (for women only) on Wednesday nights when they take it all off. Admission depends on the show; the raunchier it is, the steeper the price—anywhere from 45F to 150F. Check the schedule posted outside. Weekend mornings the party goes on until noon. Drinks are 50F. *11 pl. Pigalle, 9e, t▮▮ 48–78–25–56. Métro: Pigalle. Open daily midnight–dawn.*

▮▮ge. Descend the glittered corridor to this hopping disco that lays down house and ▮ a stylish lesbian crowd. Weekends are the most fun—and the toughest nights for men to get in. Weeknights, however, see a mixed crowd lounging on the low, red velvet couches downstairs. The cover is 100F with one drink included, except for women-only Saturdays when cover is 60F; after that, drinks cost 70F. Saturday and Sunday mornings, this becomes the after-hours spot of choice for not-so-straight hedonists with dance fever. *3 cité Bergère, 9e, tel. 01–42–46–50–98. Métro: Rue Montmartre. Open daily midnight–6 AM.*

Keur Samba. The richer, more stylish, and more African you look, the better your chances of gaining entry into this super-sleek club near the Champs-Elysées. The music ranges from reggae to African soukous, American hip-hop, and house. Dress up and bring generous funds for the 120F entrance and first drink; don't even think about buying another (100F) unless you can convince one of the rich-kid regulars to spring for it. *79 rue la Boétie, 8e, tel. 01–43–59–03–10. Métro: St-Philippe du Roule. Open daily.*

Le Monocle. A fun lesbian crowd converges nightly at this boîte that features sporadic sexy "spectacles." It's open early for intimate drinks and later becomes one of the best places to dance among women. Men are sparse here. The cover charge is 150F including one drink; additional drinks start at 100F. *60 blvd. Edgar-Quinet, 14e, tel. 01–43–20–81–21. Métro: Edgar Quinet. Closed Sun.*

Le Palace. This super '80s extravaganza remains popular despite flights of fashion and the fickleness of disco patrons. It's not quite the "in" spot that it once was, but it still manages to pack in about 2,000 hot, sweaty dancers a night. The cover varies between 50F and 100F, and all styles are welcome—just be sure you have one. DJs from London play everything from disco to house to Motown. The Sunday afternoon tea dance (5–10 PM; cover 60F) has become an institution in the gay community. Drinks go for 50F. *8 rue du Faubourg Montmartre, 9e, tel. 01–42–46–10–87. Métro: Rue Montmartre. Closed Mon.*

Le Queen. This high-profile, super-cool gay nightclub on the Champs might admit a woman if she's accompanied by a man; on Thursday nights all genders are more than welcome. Everyone gyrates to house music on the vast dance floor (Monday is '70s night), and the whole scene is outrageous, right down to New Age cocktails like the Love Bomb (created with plant extracts) and the occasional hilarious appearances of "Big Dick Man." The cover is free during the week

If you actually go to clubs to hear the music and dance, try to find a club featuring a guest (and preferably foreign) DJ. Otherwise, you might be subjected to badly remixed techno all night.

(except on Mondays, when it's 50F) and 80F on the weekend. Dress hot, bright, tight, and gay. *102 av. des Champs-Elysées, 8e, tel. 01–42–89–31–32. Métro: George V.*

Rex Club. With its huge red billboard screaming at you from three blocks away, the Rex is no hidden secret. Inside, the decor is high '70s, with a roller-rink dance floor and mirrored backdrop. Different nights feature different types of music, including soul, thrash funk/rock, and "exotic." The cover varies from free to 100F depending on the night's theme. Beer is always 30F. Couples of all ages come to the afternoon tea dances (30F) to twist and tango. *5 blvd. Poissonnière, 2e, tel. 01–42–36–83–98. Métro: Bonne-Nouvelle. Closed Sun.–Tues.*

Film

On any given night, the range of films screening in Paris is phenomenal. That obscure documentary that only lasted a week at your local art-cinema back home might play here on a regular basis, even if the attendance rarely hits double digits. You'll also find low-budget films in a dozen or so languages. The small, funky cinemas where you'll find such films are mostly clustered in and around the Quartier Latin. Often they have a limited but obscure collection and show the same 40 or 50 films over and over—which means that if you missed the last screening of *Prospero's Books*, it'll probably be back in a week or two.

Paris also has big, flashy cinemas that offer blockbuster films, plush seats, and good sound. Two of the biggest and flashiest are **Gaumont Grand Ecran** (30 pl. d'Italie, 13e, tel. 01–45–80–77–00) and **Max Linder Panorama** (24 blvd. Poissonnière, 9e, tel. 01–48–24–88–88), both of which have immense screens and seat hundreds of people; Max Linder is also wheelcha̶͟ ̶el. 01–̶ sible and tends to carry cult and classic films. The Champs-Elysées is another good sp̶ for new (and expensive) screenings. France is very proud of its technological mo̶ which include the **Dôme Imax** (La Défense, tel. 01–36–67–06–06), showing 3-D natu̶

̶at Privilè
̶unk for

What's in a Rave?

Describing the extremely popular rave scene in Paris, one local put it: "Good thing there's a lot of drugs, because it's the only way you can stand the music." However, if the never-ending monotonous beats and the packed dance floor of the average rave party do appeal to you, check out techno stores like BPM and Rough Trade (see Specialty Shops, Records, CDs, and Cassettes, in Chapter 6), where flyers listing addresses and phone numbers are constantly replenished. This is also a fine place to get advice on which dances are cool and which are no better than high school canteens.

There are basically two kinds of raves: Those that take place at clubs hosting theme nights, and private ones held in venues that change week by week. Entry prices run 50F–150F, with 20F beers. Although some get pretty outrageous in decor, Dr. Seuss hats are few and far between—jeans and T-shirts are the regular uniform. Flyers usually say (in English) "no drugs," yet practically everyone manages to swallow, inject, or smoke something before entry. (Of course, we strongly discourage drug purchases at raves; besides the possible medical and legal consequences, LSD and MDMA cost considerably more in France than in the United States, with prices starting at 100F a hit.) And be careful before boarding a "navette gratuite" (free shuttle) that whisks you out of Paris— you may get trapped in Techno Hell with no way to get home until 6 AM.

and **La Geode** (26 av. Corentin-Cariou, tel. 01–36–68–29–30), which has the largest movie screen anywhere, ever (*see* Museums, Cité des Sciences et de l'Industrie, in Chapter 2.).

Almost all foreign films are played in the *version originale* (original language) with French subtitles, marked "v.o." in listings; the abbreviation "v.f." (*version française*) means a foreign film is dubbed in French. Occasionally, French films show with English subtitles; look for the words "sous-titres anglais" in the listing. Both of Paris's entertainment weeklies, *L'Officiel des spectacles* and *Pariscope,* have comprehensive film listings—prices normally run 35F–55F with some discounts for students. Some theaters will only accept ISIC cards as proof of student status. Nearly all theaters offer the reduced rate to everyone on Mondays. On one day in June, during the **Festival du Cinéma,** theaters across Paris let you see all the movies you want for the price of one.

Cinéma Gaumont la Pagode. Although the selection of first-run French and international films is pretty standard here, you've never seen another theater like this in your life. In 1896, the wife of the owner of Au Bon Marché (*see* Grands Magasins, in Chapter 6) built what was to become the most fashionable salon in Paris; it became a theater in 1931, and filmmaker Louis Malle rescued it from wreckers 40 years later. The silk-and-gilt Salle Japonaise is the best place to watch a film. A tiny café takes over the garden in summer. Tickets are 43F–46F, 36F–37F for students and on Wednesdays. *57 bis rue de Babylone, 7e, tel. 01–36–68–75–07. Métro: St-François Xavier.*

Cinémathèque Française. Founded in 1936 by Henri Langlois, this is a world-famous cinephile heaven, where different classic French and international films play every day. Film schedules often pay homage to a certain filmmaker, with a few unrelated pieces thrown in for variety. Tickets are 28F, 17F for students, 30F for afternoon films at the Faubourg-du-Temple address. The Chaillot location has a tiny film museum. *Palais de Chaillot at Trocadéro, 16e, tel. 01–47–04–24–24. Métro: Trocadéro. Other location: 18 rue du Faubourg-du-Temple, 11e, tel. 01–47-04-24-24; Métro: République.*

L'Entrepôt. This all-in-one cinema, café, bar, restaurant, and bookstore is a must for film lovers. The three cinemas host a variety of festivals and show some great art and international films. Hang around the bar with other types who are suffering for their art and maybe an independent filmmaker will discover you. Film tickets are 39F, 29F for students. *7 rue Francis-de-Pressensé, 14e, tel. 01–45–43–41–63. Métro: Pernety.*

Le Grand Rex. The grandest of Paris's cinemas, this movie palace should not be confused with the other smaller Rexes that don't have the painted ceiling, the cloud machine, or the same capacity (2,750 seats). The memorable and much-photographed facade was designed in 1932; unfortunately, much of the interior has been chopped up into smaller screens, each showing mainstream films. Seats are 46F, 36F students and senior citizens. Matinees at 11 AM go for 25F. *1 blvd. Poissonnière, 2e, tel. 01–36–65–70–23. Métro: Bonne-Nouvelle.*

Le Lucernaire. This multimedia supercenter has two stages, three cinemas, occasional concerts, art expositions, a restaurant, and a café. The film selection is eclectic, specializing in the foreign and the rare; seats cost 41F, 30F for students. On one of the stages, *Le Petit Prince* has been running for nine years; shows cost 118F–140F, 71F–84F for students, and still less if you spring for a 100F membership card. *53 rue Notre-Dame-des-Champs, 6e, tel. 01–45–44–57–34. Métro: Notre-Dame des Champs.*

Passage du Nord-Ouest. This café/cinema screens artsy flicks to accompany your café crème. The schedule is very erratic: One week may see only one or two showings, the next a miniature film festival. Entry costs around 30F. Most films play in the afternoon to make way for the jazz and world music concerts at night. *13 rue du Faubourg Montmartre, 9e, tel. 01–47–70–81–47. Métro: Rue Montmartre.*

The Lumière brothers, inventors of the "Cinématographe" (a precursor to the movie projector), showed their first film—the first public showing of any projected film ever—in 1895 in a café at 14 boulevard des Capucines.

Studio 28. This famed Montmartre venue gained notoriety for being brave enough to show avant-garde pieces such as Buñuel and Dali's *Un chien andalou* and François Truffaut's early films. The "studio" even boasts decor painted by Jean Cocteau. Recently renovated with plush seats and Dolby sound, this theater remains faithful to art movies while throwing in the occasional box-office hit. Films screen weeknights at 7 and 9; Saturdays at 3, 6, and 9; and Sundays at 3, 5, and 7. Tickets are 35F, 28F for students. *10 rue Tholozé, 18e, tel. 01–46–06–36–07. Métro: Blanche.*

Vidéothèque. While hard-core moviegoers may scoff at the idea of videotapes, the Vidéothèque is one of Paris's most important resources for moving images. A full day of audiovisual stimulation costs just 30F; the daily program can vary from a score of avant-garde shorts to a handful of feature-length films from the 1930s, all screened either in an immaculate projection room or on private consoles. The auditorium is also a forum for symposia and lectures, drawing a host of international critics and filmmakers eager to argue about the meaning of the tracking shot. *2 Grande Galerie des Halles, 1er, tel. 01–40–26–34–30. Métro: Les Halles. Open Tues.–Sun. 12:30–8:30 PM.*

Live Music

This town has loved jazz for as long as jazz has been around. American artists flocked here during the post–World War II boom and fostered an appreciative and innovative atmosphere for their music making. There's still some fine music being played in Paris, but while young French groups try earnestly to catch the beat, these days it's hard to find truly jazzy dives. For some time now African, Caribbean, and South American music has been moving in, spicing up the club circuit; many "jazz" joints have a weekly *zouk* (Caribbean dance music) or salsa night.

Most jazz clubs are in Les Halles, St-Germain, or the Quartier Latin. You can usually stay all night for the price of a drink—a 50F–100F drink, that is. For cheaper shows, keep an eye on some of the museums and cultural centers around town (the Musée Guimet and Institut du Monde Arabe, for example); they occasionally host free or almost-free concerts. One particularly good venue for world music and jazz is the café/cinema **Passage du Nord-Ouest** (*see* Film, *above*). Latin rhythm has been taking Paris by storm. For one of the best dance floors, check out **L'Escale** (*see* Dance Clubs, *above*), which has Cuban and South American bands nightly and one of Paris's best salsa dance floors. The free monthly *Paris Boum-Boum* (available at cafés) has a section on world-music happenings around town.

If jazz sounds about as exciting to you as staring at a brick wall, there are plenty of places where you can mosh to your heart's content with a bunch of hot and sweaty punkers. Rock and punk are alive and well in Paris—and usually cheaper to hear than jazz. For most thrash and punk shows, look to the Pigalle area. The **Elysée Montmartre** (72 blvd. de Rochechouart, 18e, tel. 01–42–52–25–15) is one of the better venues for alternative bands, but they also show reggae and heavy metal bands. **Le Bataclan** (50 blvd. Voltaire, 11e, tel. 01–47–00–30–12) is good for international pop. **Le Divan du Monde** (75 rue des Martyrs, 18e, tel. 01–44–92–77–66) presents great if not hyper-famous bands in a smaller setting. Cover usually varies between 60F and 80F. **Hot Brass** (211 av. Jean-Jaurès, 19e, tel. 01–42–00–14–14) hosts some of the best Latin jazz and funk bands of Paris. For bigger shows you can reserve tickets (50F–120F) in advance at **Virgin Megastore, Rough Trade,** or **FNAC** (*see* Specialty Shops, Records, CDs, and Cassettes, in Chapter 6).

Au Duc des Lombards. Quality European blues and jazz acts regularly fill up this Les Halles club for 10:30 PM shows. The secret to this place, though, is attending the jam sessions played by local groups most nights between 8 and 9:30, when beers only cost 30F (they cost 50F when the headliner's playing). Get here even earlier for 8F beers and hang out with the bar crew. A potentially hefty cover charge might apply if the band is especially good and/or famous. The restaurant upstairs serves passable meals for around 100F until 4 AM every night but Sunday. *42 rue des Lombards, 1er, tel. 01–42–33–22–88. Métro: Châtelet.*

Le Baiser Salé. This bar's small, potentially hot upstairs room is the perfect venue for small, potentially hot ensembles. Sit back on your velvety turquoise seat and listen to music ranging from blues to fusion to Afro-jazz. They have nightly concerts at 8 PM and 10:30 PM, and cover varies between 30F and 90F. Beers cost about 25F. *58 rue des Lombards, 1er, tel. 01–42–33–37–71. Métro: Châtelet.*

Le Bistrot d'Eustache. This small, classic café/bar across from its eponymous cathedral is well loved by young Parisians without a lot of money. Lounge singers perform weekend nights 10:30 PM–4 AM. A frustrating column in the middle of the room means that only three tables and the bar have an unobstructed view of the musicians. Beers cost 15F at the bar, around 40F seated; snacks run 30F and up. *37 rue Berger, 1er, tel. 01–40–26–23–20. Métro: Les Halles.*

Le Caveau de la Huchette. This classic *caveau* (underground club) has been serving up swing and Dixieland to hepcats since the 1950s. The young, wholesome crowd of tourists and students still swing dance here like it's going out of style. Cover is 65F, 75F on weekends; students pay 5F less. *5 rue de la Huchette, 5e, tel. 01–43–26–65–05. Métro: St-Michel.*

La Chapelle des Lombards. This chapel (complete with fake stained glass and pews) religiously serves up high-quality live Latin, zouk, and African music. It calls itself a tropical disco, and the crowd is as "world" as the music; everyone really gets into the shows, making a dance floor out of everything. Cover for concerts costs 100F, 120F weekends, one drink included. *19 rue de Lappe, 11e, tel. 01–43–57–24–24. Métro: Bastille.*

La Cigale. This old-style theater-turned-concert hall is just the right size for a good mosh pit. Big names (as well as small ones) make frequent appearances, churning out loud, fast rock and indie music for a chain-smoking audience. A small bar in the basement keeps you fueled with 25F beers. The cover charge runs 80F–150F; for the really popular groups, buy your tickets in advance at FNAC or Virgin Megastore. *120 blvd. Rochechouart, 18e, tel. 01–49–25–81–75. Métro: Pigalle.*

Every June 21, France comes alive with free music in celebration of the summer solstice. During this Fête de la Musique, Paris's churches, clubs, parks, and squares fill with musicians and onlookers. You owe it to yourself to stay out all night.

Gibus. Finally, a Parisian dive where nobody gives a damn what you wear and the doorman is capable of smiling. For a sense of its history, check out the photos by the bar: the Police, the Clash, the Pretenders, the Stray Cats, and Deep Purple are among the bands who have appeared here. The Gibus remains faithful to loud rock, metal, and punk, and all shows range 50F–60F with one drink included; a second beer is 25F. *18 rue Faubourg-du-Temple, 11e, tel. 01–47–00–78–88. Métro: République. Open Tues.–Sat. 11 PM–5 AM.*

La Java. Parisians hooked on Latin rhythm give La Java the thumbs up, and with good reason. The city's best salsa and samba bands frequently animate the place, and the enthusiastic crowd has as many experts as clumsies. Most importantly, male patrons are there to dance, not grope their partners. Cover is 50F–100F with one drink. Salsa plays on Fridays, samba on Sundays. *105 rue Faubourg-du-Temple, 10e, tel. 01–42–02–20–52. Métro: Belleville. Open Wed.–Sun. 11 PM–5 AM.*

New Moon. Formerly a women-only cabaret, New Moon is now one of the better places in Paris to *pogo* (slam) to the latest in punk, funk, rock, and thrash. Cover is usually is 50F–60F with a drink included; big-name bands can drive the price up to 150F. Check *Pariscope* for a schedule. *66 rue Pigalle, 9e, tel. 01–45–95–92–33. Métro: Pigalle. Open Mon.–Sat. 11 PM–dawn.*

New Morning. This is Paris's big-time jazz club. All the greats have sweated on its stage at one time or another: Archie Shepp, Dizzy Gillespie, Miles Davis, and Celia Cruz, among them. The quality and reputation remain exceptional, and the repertoire now includes reggae, salsa, and Latin jazz. Cover for the dark, 600-seat club is 130F–150F. Drinks are 30F. Concerts start at about 9 PM; check *Pariscope* to see who's playing. *7–9 rue des Petites-Ecuries, 10e, tel. 01–45–23–51–41. Métro: Château d'Eau.*

L'Opus Café. Opened in March of 1995 and run by a bunch of young French hipsters, L'Opus Café is fast becoming the cool hangout for twentysomethings who look like they were born smoking in the back of a blues bar. Tables are scattered downstairs and in an upstairs loft, with no seat more than 20 feet from the stage. The music swings back and forth between French and English rock, blues, soul, and swing orchestras. The cover charge swings between zero and 100F. *167 Quai de Valmy, 10e, tel. 01–40–34–70–00. Métro: Louis Blanc.*

Slow Club. This classic swing/jazz dance hall has been around for decades, seducing jazz greats such as Miles Davis into a show or two. Every night, bands play Dixieland, bebop, blues, oldies, rock, and jazz to an older crowd of swing dancers. Cover charge is 60F during the week (55F for students under 25) and 75F weekends, and drinks are 25F and up. *130 rue de Rivoli, 1er, tel. 01–42–33–84–30. Métro: Châtelet.*

Opera, Classical Music, and Dance

The performing arts scene in Paris is overwhelming, with two of the world's greatest opera houses, more than 150 theaters, and a daily dose of at least a dozen classical concerts. There are opportunities for everyone, whether in the form of costly tickets to snooty musical societies, free concerts in churches and cathedrals, or flute sonatas on the banks of the Seine. Scan the first 70 pages of *Pariscope* each week for listings, and look for the words *entrée gratuite* or *entrée libre* ("freebie," in other words). The posters and notices pasted on the walls of Métro stations are also good ways to keep up with the calendar.

There is plenty of free music in Paris. **Eglise St-Merri** (78 rue St-Martin, 4e, tel. 01–42–71–93–93) has free classical concerts Saturdays at 9 PM and Sundays at 6 PM; **L'Eglise Américaine** (65 Quai d'Orsay, 7e, tel. 01–47–05–07–99) has choral and organ music Sundays at 6 PM; and the **Conservatoire National Supérieur de Musique** (209 rue Jean Jaurès, 19e, tel. 01–40–40–45–45) frequently has afternoon student concerts. Other venues worth checking for free concerts include the **Musée d'Art Moderne** (11 av. du Président Wilson, 16e, tel. 01–53–67–40–00), the **Maison de Radio France** (116 av. du Président Kennedy, 16e, tel. 01–42–30–15–16) and the **Cité de la Musique** (221 av. Jean-Juarés, 19e, tel. 01–44–84–44–84). **Conservatoire Paul Dukas** (45 rue de Picpus, 12e, tel. 01–43–47–17–66) has free concerts on Tuesdays at 7 PM. **Eglise de la Madeleine** (pl. de la Madeleine) has free concerts on Sundays at 4 PM; call 01–42–30–10–45 for info.

Tickets to major performances are not impossible to get if you use a little foresight. At most venues, the box office starts selling tickets two weeks before a performance, though a limited number are available one month in advance if you charge by phone. Day-of-performance tickets are often available for students ages 25 and under; depending on the show, you should arrive 15–90 minutes early to try for any leftover tickets—sometimes excellent seats can be had for as little as 10% of the original price. Of course, you can always get tickets by phone from **FNAC** (tel. 01–40–41–40–00) or **Virgin Megastore** (tel. 01–49–53–50–50), though you'll pay a service charge and availability may be limited.

In 1994, French designer Christian de Portzamparc was awarded the Pritzker Prize, the world's most prestigious honor for an architect. Evaluate his sinuous forms yourself by checking out the Conservatoire National at the Cité de la Musique or the Café Beaubourg across from the Centre Pompidou.

Centre Georges Pompidou—IRCAM. One of the four divisions within the Centre Georges Pompidou (*see* Major Attractions, in Chapter 2), the IRCAM (Institut de Recherche et Coordination de l'Acoustique et de la Musique) takes care of the "gestural" arts. Performances at the institute's multipurpose hall, under the place Igor-Stravinsky, include contemporary music, computer-generated videos, dance, drama, lectures, philosophy seminars, and debates. The center's mediathèque is open to the public and specializes in the latest technological innovations. *31 rue St-Merri, on pl. Igor-Stravinsky, 4e, tel. 01–42–17–12–33. Métro: Rambuteau. Tickets sold at the counter on the ground floor. Open weekdays 9:30–1 and 2–6 (Fri. until 5). Wheelchair access.*

Conservatoire National Supérieur de Musique et de Danse. Since its founding in 1784, the Conservatoire has featured concerts by its budding students. Most are free and impromptu—stop by and check the info desk for flyers and schedules. In early 1995, the Conservatoire's performance space in the

Parc de la Villette's Cité de la Musique more than doubled; it now includes more performance rooms and a small museum for kids. Designed by Christian de Portzamparc, the complex has been one of the quieter successes of Mitterrand's Grands Travaux—not likely to make the tourist circuit, but the international music community has taken notice. *209 av. Jean Jaurès, 19e, tel. 01–40–40–46–46. Métro: Porte de Pantin. Wheelchair access.*

Eglise de la Madeleine. Though it's one of the gloomier churches in Paris (*see* Houses of Worship, in Chapter 2), the Madeleine is a spectacular concert hall; to be an organist here is one of the most coveted musical appointments in Paris. The expansive nave hosts several classical concerts every week, and admission usually runs around 140F, 100F for students. There are free Sunday concerts at 4 PM. *Pl. de la Madeleine, 8e, tel. 01–42–65–52–17. Métro: Madeleine.*

Maison de Radio France. The government's broadcasting center until the privatization of the airwaves, this vast complex is now home to countless radio and TV stations. In addition to studios, meeting halls, and a small museum devoted to the entire establishment (tours in French are 14F, 7F students), the complex includes the smallish, modern Salle Olivier Messiaen, home to the **Orchestre National de France,** which also performs regularly at larger venues. You might enjoy stopping by to catch a rehearsal—you're not really supposed to be here, but act like you are, and the guards may not notice. Seats are available one month before a show, or turn your radio dial to 91.7 or 92.1 (France Musique) to hear the concert for free. You will also find legitimately free orchestra soloist concerts and 30F jazz concerts. Call 01–42–30–10–45 for performance dates. Historic note: The streets behind the Maison de Radio France serve as a kind of showcase for France's best art nouveau architect, Hector Guimard. Most of his interesting stuff is on rue La Fontaine, including No. 14, the beautifully detailed Castel Béranger (1894)—his best-known work. *116 av. du Président Kennedy, 16e, tel. 01–42–30–15–16. Métro: Renelagh or Bir-Hakeim. RER: Maison de Radio France. Box office open Mon.–Sat. 11–6.*

Opéra Bastille. In his quest to join the likes of Louis XIV and Napoléon III as one of the grand builders of Paris, President Mitterrand had the Opéra Bastille built on place de la Bastille to

Quel Guignol!

In French slang, to be a "guignol" means to be a clown, and to "faire le guignol" (act like a guignol) means to act silly. This is a pretty good indication of what to expect from a guignol show. These traditional puppet farces have entertained French children for centuries, and they continue to do so to this day (along with their parents, who might not want to admit they enjoy the skits as much as their kids). Here are a few good places to catch a show:

* *Guignol de Paris. Set outdoors in the Parc des Buttes Chaumont, these puppets attract kiddies daily at 3 PM. Parc des Buttes Chaumont, btw av. Bolivar and rue Botzaris, 19e, tel. 01–43–64–24–29. Métro: Buttes Chaumont.*

* *Marionnettes des Champs Elysées. This theater specializes in guignol classics. Shows happen daily at 3 PM, 4 PM, and 5 PM. Rond Point des Champs Elysées, btw av. Matignon and av. Gabriel, 8e, tel. 01–40–35–47–20. Métro: Champs-Elysées–Clémenceau.*

* *Marionnettes du Champ de Mars. You can catch a show daily at 3:15 PM and 4:15 PM. Champ de Mars, 7e, tel. 01–48–56–01–44. Métro: Ecole Militaire.*

replace the renowned Opéra Garnier (*see below*). Mitterrand's three-billion-franc project was the city's second redefinition of the opera house and an ambitious attempt to become (once again) the center of European opera. Designed by Uruguayan-born Canadian architect Carlos Ott and inaugurated on July 13, 1989, the Bastille received resoundingly negative criticism and was unflatteringly compared to a sports arena. Nonetheless, those who have condemned the building's appearance enthusiastically file in to experience the "perfect" acoustics and clear sight lines available to all 2,700 of the democratically designed seats. Downstairs from the Grande Salle, the Studio Bastille challenges strict traditionalists by offering "Parallèles," an experimental, inexpensive program of recitals and films related to the operas; tickets cost around 25F. Taking part in all the excitement and controversy requires minimal planning: Tickets go on sale at the box offices two weeks before any given show or a month ahead by phone. Schedules and tickets are available at either Bastille or Garnier. Seats range from 60F to 600F for most shows. Concerts go for 45F–225F. Student and youth (under 25) rush tickets cost 100F just before a performance, and anyone else can also try to buy any remaining seats. Bring a book and get in line a couple hours in advance if you want a chance at a seat. *120 rue de Lyon, 12e, tel. 01–44–73–13–99 (info) or 01–44–73–13–00 (reservations). Métro: Bastille. Box office open Mon.–Sat. 11–6:30. Wheelchair access.*

Opéra Comique. The seasons are shorter, the director is less flamboyant, and the late 19th-century building is less grandiose than the Opéra Bastille or Opéra Garnier; the Opéra Comique stages a dozen operas and concerts each season in a more intimate setting than the other major theaters can offer. Concerts by the Orchestre Symphonique Français cost only 50F for any seat in the house; other performances cost 40F–500F, with 50F rush tickets available 15 minutes before curtain time to students and those under 26. *5 rue Favart, 2e, tel. 01–42–29–12–20. Métro: Richelieu-Drouot. Box office open Fri.–Wed. 11–7, Thurs. 1 hr before curtain.*

Opéra Garnier. The most pompous of all Parisian buildings, the Opéra was built by Charles Garnier after he won an architectural competition in 1861. Unable to settle upon any one style, Garnier chose them all: a Renaissance-inspired detail here, a rococo frill there, Greek shields put up at random. The regal lobby, with grand stairways and a mirrored ballroom, is as big as the auditorium; together they cover more than 3 acres. The hall itself is rich, velvety, and gaudy, with an extraordinary number of gilt statuettes and a ceiling repainted by Marc Chagall in 1964; if you're one of those who spent 30F for the sans-visibilité (without visibility) seats, at least you'll have images from Chagall's favorite operas and ballets to stare at. Those who spring for the 30F visitors' fee (18F students) are allowed to climb the ornate stairway and check out the plush auditorium. A small museum features Degas's simple portrait of Wagner. Performance tickets (30F–590F) go on sale a month in advance over the phone or two weeks in advance in person. Call or stop by to reserve seats, but you must go in person for the 30F–60F cheapie seats. You can also try to get rush tickets sold 45 minutes before a performance. *8 rue Scribe, 9e, tel. 01–47–42–57–50. Métro: Opéra. Open daily 11–4:30.*

Sainte-Chapelle. The intimate size and utter exquisiteness of this building make seeing a concert at Sainte-Chapelle (*see* Major Attractions, in Chapter 2) worth the cost and hassle of getting a ticket. Most seats start at 120F, and the concerts, mainly small classical ensembles, often sell out early. For tickets, come as soon as they're put on sale and expect to wait in line. *4 blvd. du Palais, 1er, tel. 01–42–05–25–23. Métro: Cité.*

Salle Pleyel. Another grand old hall, this one has the unique distinction of having hosted Chopin's last public performance. These days it's the main stomping ground of the Orchestre de Paris. The hall also sees some dance and jazz, including regular stops by the Golden Gate Quartet. Tickets are sold on a looser schedule than at other theaters; call about specific shows. *252 rue du Faubourg-St-Honoré, 8e, tel. 01–45–63–07–40. Métro: Ternes. Box office open Mon.–Sat. 11–6.*

Théâtre de la Ville. The fraternal twin of the Beaux-Arts Châtelet across the way, the Théâtre de la Ville stages contemporary dance and music in its starkly renovated theater. In 1899, Sarah Bernhardt bought the theater, named it after herself, and began performing regularly. When the city took over, it naturally renamed the hall after itself, and now only the café next door and the fine print over the theater's entrance display Sarah's name. Tickets for most shows cost 90F–140F and have to be purchased two weeks in advance. *2 pl. du Châtelet, 4e, tel. 01–*

42–74–22–77. Métro: Châtelet. Box office open Mon.–Sat. 9–8 (Mon. until 6). Wheelchair access on the Seine side of the building.

Théâtre des Champs-Elysées. This large, fancy musical theater stages a bit of everything—operatic soloists, ballets, orchestras, marionette shows, and jazz acts. Tickets generally run 40F–700F. For students, all seats are half-price (or even less) 30 minutes before the show. *15 av. Montaigne, 8e, tel. 01–49–52–50–50. Métro: Franklin D. Roosevelt. Box office open Mon.–Sat. 11–7.*

Théâtre Musical de Paris. Ideally located on the place du Châtelet by the Seine, the Théâtre Musical is less self-important than its famous cousins, the Opéras Bastille and Garnier. The excellence of the theater's productions tends to draw a devoted crowd—nobody claps between arias by mistake. The hall is discreet by Parisian standards, though no late 19th-century theater could forgo frilly detailing and plush red velvet. Tickets cost 70F and up; 50F rush tickets are available 15 minutes before curtain time to students with ID or those under 20. The theater is also continuing its "Midis Musicaux" (Musical Noons) series, with concerts in the foyer on Monday, Wednesday, and Friday starting at 12:45; seats cost 50F. The "Dimanches Musicaux" (Musical Sundays) start at 11:30 and cost 80F. *1 pl. du Châtelet, 1er, tel. 01–40–28–28–40. Métro: Châtelet. Box office open daily 11–7. Wheelchair entrance at 17 bis av. Victoria.*

Theater

The Parisian theatrical scene goes back to 17th-century French playwrights like Corneille, Racine, and Molière. If this nearly 400-year-old tradition intimidates you a bit, note that Paris has also been a center for great 20th-century experimental theater; Antonin Artaud, Samuel Beckett, Jean Genet, and Jean-Paul Sartre all staged works here in the 1930s, '40s, and '50s. The legacy of the absurdists lives on, for example, at the stubborn Théâtre de la Huchette, which has been playing Ionesco's *La Leçon* and *La Cantatrice chauve* for years.

If you're in search of discount tickets and have the patience to wait in line, check out the discount kiosks at the **gare Montparnasse** (pl. Raoul Dautry, 15e; Métro: Montparnasse-Bienvenue) and at the **Madeleine** (15 pl. de la Madeleine, 8e; Métro: Madeleine). They're open Tuesday–Saturday 12:30–8, Sun. 12:30–4. They sell tickets for same-day performances at up to half the original price. For students and those under 26, the **Kioske Paris-Jeunes** (25 blvd. Bourdon, 4e; Métro: Bastille) specializes in youth discount tickets.

While not uniformly responsive, many Parisian theaters have been making a concerted effort to accommodate patrons in wheelchairs; call one month in advance for tickets and access information for all theaters. Most antiquated houses have clumsy ramps and elevators, while new or renovated theaters have tried to achieve barrier-free access. Some theaters also have begun to provide services for the hearing- and sight-impaired.

Les Bouffes du Nord. Founded by British theater man Peter Brook, whose influence ensures a repertoire of out-of-the-ordinary productions and eccentric comedies, this performances in this beautifully decrepit theater feel otherworldly. Tickets are cheap: 60F–130F. *37 bis blvd. de la Chapelle, 10e, tel. 01–46–07–34–50. Métro: La Chapelle.*

Chaillot. Founded by Jean Vilar in post–World War II Paris as part of the movement to revive live theater, France's first *théâtre national* stages highly regarded theatrical and musical productions in its two halls under the terrace of the Trocadéro. Tickets run 80F–150F, depending on the show and your status; discounted student rush tickets are available on the day of the performance. *1 pl. du Trocadéro, 16e, tel. 01–47–27–81–15. Métro: Trocadéro. Box office open Mon.–Sat. 11–7, Sun. 11–5.*

Comédie-Française–Salle Richelieu. The Comédie–Française traces its origins to 1680, when Louis XIV merged Molière's acting company with other troupes, establishing the first completely French theater. The group lost its lease in 1770, but Louis XV saved the Comédie-

Française by ordering the construction of the Odéon; four years later the troupe was brought under even tighter royal control with the construction of the Théâtre Français (now called the Salle Richelieu) in the Palais Royal. Since then, this stage has been the permanent playground for the ghosts of Great French Theater. The Comédie-Française has a reputation as a bastion of traditionalism; the fact that the lobby holds the chair in which Molière collapsed and died after a performance in 1673 only reinforces this myth. The company, however, doesn't always produce Racine and Molière; sometimes they branch out to Camus. Tickets run 45F–165F, with 60F rush tickets available 45 minutes before curtain time to students and those under 25. *2 rue de Richelieu, 1er, tel. 01–40–15–00–15. Métro: Palais Royal–Musée du Louvre. Box office open daily 11–6.*

Comédie-Française/Théâtre du Vieux-Colombier. Founded in 1913 by Jacques Copeau, the Théâtre du Vieux-Colombier has traditionally staged the works of controversial playwrights, including Sartre, Federico García Lorca, and Arthur Miller. The company folded 60 years after its opening, but the state acquired the theater in 1986, putting it under the control of a Comédie-Française eager to have a venue for non-Molière productions. The theater was beautifully renovated in 1993 and now stages plays by Calaferte and Duras, among others. Saturday readings offer a more alternative spectacle (60F, 50F rush). All seats are 150F; 60F rush tickets are available 45 minutes before curtain time to students and those under 25. *21 rue du Vieux-Colombier, 6e, tel. 01–44–39–87–00. Métro: St-Sulpice. Box office open Tues.–Sat. 11–7, Sun. 1–6. Wheelchair access.*

Odéon Théâtre de l'Europe. Under the direction of Lluís Pasqual, the Odéon has made pan-European theater its primary focus. Unless it's Shakespeare, plays that have been translated into French have supertitles in the original language. Tickets run 50F–170F, with half-price rush tickets available 50 minutes before curtain time. Student tickets are always 20F less, but if you're a regular theatergoer you might as well buy the Carte Complice Jeune for 100F and get all tickets for a mere 30F each (if you're over 26, or not a student, you still get 25% off with the Carte). The basement holds the experimental Petit Odéon, where all seats cost 70F. *1 pl. Paul Claudel, 6e, tel. 01–44–41–36–36. Métro: Odéon. Box office open Mon.–Sat. 11–6:30.*

Théâtre de la Bastille. Experimental theater and dance productions go on in this black-toned, minimalist hall. Tickets are almost always 100F, 70F–80F for students. *76 rue de la Roquette, 11e, tel. 01–43–57–42–14. Métro: Bastille.*

Théâtre de la Huchette. It was at La Huchette that Eugène Ionesco—whose death in 1994 saddened the literary and dramatic worlds—founded and developed a theatrical and philosophical style that came to be known as Theater of the Absurd. Parisians, while somewhat confused by Ionesco's surreal story lines, were so smitten by his words that *La Cantatrice chauve* (The Bald Soprano) has been performed every night here since its premiere in 1950. Both it and Ionesco's 1951 play *La Leçon* (The Lesson) have played at La Huchette for years, although plays by Tennessee Williams have been creeping in. Tickets are generally 100F (80F for students 25 and under except for Saturday performances). *23 rue de la Huchette, 5e, tel. 01–43–26–38–99. Métro: St-Michel. Box office open Mon.–Sat. 5–9:30. Wheelchair access.*

Théâtre National de la Colline. This glass-and-concrete mass of urban sophistication behind place Gambetta is a major part of the emerging *nouvelle culture* (new culture) of Belleville and produces large-scale, mildly controversial plays (a lot of Beckett and Lamas). All seats run 160F, 120F for students and those under 25. Classical concerts produced by Radio France (seats 100F) are given from time to time. There are no rush tickets, but students 25 and under can get 80F seats for Saturday afternoon performances in the Grande Salle and for Wednesday shows in the Petite Salle. *15 rue Malte-Brun, 20e, tel. 01–44–62–52–52. Métro: Gambetta. Box office open Tues.–Sat. 11–8, Sun. and Mon. 11–6. Wheelchair access.*

CAFE THEATER This subgenre of Paris theater is devoted to low-budget and potentially subversive productions. Unless your French is pretty good, you'll have a hard time understanding, but it's still worth it—these little shows often present funny views and critiques of French society and culture. Despite the name, most café-théâtres do not sell refreshments. Some well-known and popular venues include **Au Bec Fin** (6 rue Thérèse, 1er, tel. 01–42–

96–29–35), with fairly large-scale productions, and **Le Point Virgule** (7 rue Ste-Croix-de-la-Bretonnerie, 4e, tel. 01–42–78–67–03), which specializes in comedy.

Café d'Edgar. Tongue-in-cheek skits are the specialty at this small, red-benched café-théâtre in Montparnasse. Three shows are performed nightly except Sunday, and the price is 80F a show, 65F for students during the week. *58 blvd. Edgar-Quinet, 14e, tel. 01–42–79–97–97. Métro: Edgar Quinet.*

Café de la Gare. A happy crowd piles onto wooden benches to catch the comedies at this popular theater where the young Gérard Depardieu and Miou-Miou have played. On stage are two quality 90-minute shows per night with tickets between 80F and 100F each. *41 rue du Temple, 4e, tel. 01–42–78–52–51. Métro: Hôtel-de-Ville. Closed Sun.–Mon.*

ENGLISH-LANGUAGE THEATER Theater enthusiasts who aren't quite ready to brave the French language should keep an eye out for Paris-based English-language troupes such as **Dear Conjunction,** the **Gare St-Lazare Players,** and the **On Stage Theater Company.** Larger troupes like the **Royal Shakespeare Company** also occasionally pass through town.

Théâtre de la Main d'Or. The student-oriented company **American Conservatory Theater (ACT)** (tel. 01–40–33–64–02) is based here and performs both in this former garage and at schools throughout Paris. Tickets are 180F–100F, 80F for students. *15 passage de la Main d'Or, 11e, tel. 01–48–05–67–89. Métro: Ledru-Rollin. Wheelchair access.*

Théâtre de Nesle. Although not exclusively English-language, this theater frequently hosts the On Stage Theater Company with modern plays by the likes of Harold Pinter and Bertolt Brecht. Tickets run 80F, 60F for students. *8 rue de Nesle, 6e, tel. 01–46–34–61–04. Métro: Odéon. Box office open Tues.–Sat. 10–7.*

SHOPPING  6

By Viviana Mahieux and Julia Švihra

Paris is a paradise for fashion victims, but it can terrorize those of us who fear well-coiffed ladies brandishing tiny, manicured dogs. It's not uncommon to see speedwalking Parisians slow to a crawl as their eyes lock on to an attractive *vitrine* (shop window)—even if the price tag glares with a red 1,800F. Truth is, shopping here can be contagious, and if you don't buy something—a book, shoes, lingerie (this *is* Paris)—you're missing out on a truly Parisian experience.

To really absorb Parisian *mode* (fashion), browse through the monolithic *grands magasins,* department stores with a minimum of three levels and maximum breathing space of two square feet. When shopping for clothes, keep in mind that the consumer in France is less privileged than in the United States. Often you're not allowed to try on heavily discounted items before buying, and returns are virtually unheard of (though exchanges are usually okay). Most stores in Paris stay open until 6 or 7 PM and close on Sundays, and many take a lunch break sometime between noon and 2 PM. Consequently, Saturday is shopping hell.

Some shopping lingo: soldes (sale); braderie (clearance); promo (sale); d'occasion or brocante (secondhand); nouveautés (new arrivals); dépôts-ventes (last season's unsold clothes); fripes (used clothing).

If you want to avoid getting smooshed to death *and* going broke, follow the majority of Parisians to flea markets (*see below*), used bookstores, vintage clothing shops, and tiny, nondescript boutiques. If you wander about Paris's two main flea markets, **St-Ouen** and **Montreuil,** you'll encounter a sizeable immigrant population where African, Arab, and Asian influences mingle to create a vibrant and dynamic atmosphere.

Shopping by Neighborhood

BASTILLE Now that the press has announced that the Bastille is Paris's newest ultracool neighborhood, true hipsters are hightailing it out of here (you can't be hip if everybody knows about you). During the day, Bastille is like a sleepy colony of vampires—there are a few people milling around, but most are saving up their energy for the bars and clubs. There are still a few good places to shop, though. The area around **rue Daval, rue de la Roquette,** and **rue des Taillandiers** has small, self-consciously cool boutiques that sell platform shoes, vintage dresses, and handcrafted jewelry. Rue des Taillandiers is also home to **Godjo Bastille** (26 rue des Taillandiers, 11e, tel. 01–48–06–64–75), an African gallery with artwork, jewelry, drums, and bags. This is also the area for all things techno: Rave info, clothing, CDs, and vinyl are all clustered around **rue Keller** and **rue de Charonne.** If you want to get a dose of transcendental ecstasy before heading off to your rave, visit **Dojo Zen** (17 rue Keller, 11e, tel. 01–48–05–47–43) for meditation partners and paraphernalia.

CHAMPS-ELYSEES This part of the eighth arrondissement is the shopping ground of the rich and beautiful Parisian elite. It's doubtful you'll find anything here you can afford, and even if you do, you won't have anywhere to wear it. There is the Champs-Elysées, of course, with its car dealerships, designer boutiques, and fast-food chains, but much more impressive are the streets and squares off it. **Rue du Faubourg-St-Honoré** is notorious for its posh boutiques; if you're determined to buy something along this strip, 30F will get you a small bag of Godiva chocolates at the corner of rue Castiglione. Equally hopeless is **avenue Montaigne,** housing the workshops of designers like Chanel, Christian Dior, and Valentino. **Place de la Madeleine** and the surrounding streets also cater to the upper crust. While walking through the eighth, chant "thousands of francs, thousands of francs," so you don't accidentally fall in love with anything.

LES HALLES AND BEAUBOURG Expect lots of D'OCCASION (used) signs: Here you'll find secondhand CDs, secondhand hats, secondhand shirts, secondhand shoes, and firsthand Parisians. For fun and trashy used clothes, try **rue St-Martin** and **rue St-Merri. Rue de la Grande-Truanderie** is home to the best collection of 50F Hawaiian shirts in all of Paris. The lower part of **rue St-Denis** has a slew of stores selling used leather jackets, but avoid **place des Innocents,** which is littered with the same chains you see everywhere—Kookai, ProMod, Burger King, and Pizza Pino. One of the most successful shopping malls in all of France, **Forum des Halles** is amazingly ugly but it does have a few decent boutiques.

Just a few blocks from Les Halles, the staid, elegant **Louvre** sprawls out in regal contrast. However, below lurketh **Le Carrousel du Louvre** (99 rue de Rivoli), open 10 AM–8 PM every day except Tuesday. This big, fancy mall jammed under the Louvre contains over 30 big-name stores (among them Virgin Megastore and Esprit) as well as a restaurant court. This is all worth a look if only to see the inverted glass pyramid that plunges into its center; the design is by the inimitable I. M. Pei, the architect responsible for the pyramid at the Louvre's entrance.

LE MARAIS Like the Bastille, the Marais houses many a trendy, artsy clothing boutique. On the downside, the Marais tends to be a bit more elegant and expensive than the Bastille. Good streets to browse (but not necessarily buy) are on the northern side of the Marais; they spike off the **rue des Francs-Bourgeois** on the way to the utterly posh place des Vosges. The streets around **rue Ste-Croix-de-la-Bretonnerie** and **rue Vieille-du-Temple** are good for feather boas and tight, satin hotpants—everything you need for a night in drag. **Son et Image** (8 rue Ste-Croix-de-la-Bretonnerie, 4e) specializes in vintage clothes for gay men and has a great collection of 30F shirts and 80F sweaters. If you're Jewish and/or heavy into matzo balls, **rue des Rosiers** and **rue Pavée** have a couple kosher delis and bookstores with Jewish cultural info.

Looking for that special something for your special someone (a whip, perhaps . . .), Rue St-Denis, around rue Etienne-Marcel, and place Pigalle are brimming with sex shops dying to cater to your every fetish.

MONTMARTRE Somehow, Montmartre manages to combine a small town's intimate atmosphere with a big city's cosmopolitan panache. **Rue des Abbesses** is a perfect place to stroll among fruit stands, wine shops, and fishmongers. **Rue Houdon** and **rue des Martyrs** are sprinkled with boutiques selling vintage clothing, ethnic jewelry, and used books, valiantly resisting the tourists trekking up to the Sacré-Cœur. Stay away from the sleazy area near place Pigalle unless, of course, you like that sort of thing.

QUARTIER LATIN The shops in the Quartier Latin cater to the local student population, so this is where you'll find the coolest and wackiest stores, not to mention some of the nation's strongest coffee. Although **boulevard St-Michel** is schlocky and crowded, the smaller streets around **place Maubert** in the fifth arrondissement offer fantastic specialty bookstores (*see* Specialty Shops, Bookstores, *below*). The ubiquitous tiny music stores have excellent collections of rare and/or used vinyl, while more domestic shoppers might prefer the no-nonsense housewares and furniture that fill vast stores in the outer fifth. The shopping strip of **rue Mouffetard** tries to be more offbeat than it actually is; its saving grace is an open-air produce market that lures locals out into the swarms of tourists browsing through all the jewelry and clothing stores.

ST·GERMAIN-DES-PRES Boutiques are the name of the game here. The less expensive (but more interesting) stores spiral off the small streets around the **rue de Buci** market below **boulevard St-Germain,** but the serious shopping happens above the strip. **Rue de Rennes** is a major shopping hub, and the narrow streets all along it offer clothing, antiques, gifts, and art stores. Good shopping streets include **rue St-Placide,** which is home to the five-shop markdown bliss of **Le mouton à cinq pattes** (*see* Specialty Shops, Clothing, *below).* Rue de Rennes itself has some vintage clothing stores, and **rue de Sèvres** boasts affordable chains and small names alongside the priceless untouchables.

Want a souvenir that you don't have to lug around? Tattoos start at 500F (we didn't say it would be cheap). Try Absolute Tattoo (3 rue André-Mazet, 6e, tel. 01–43–25–40–94), or check the side streets around Montparnasse. For piercings, try 3D (7 rue Tiquetonne, 2e, tel. 01–40–26–42–50).

Grands Magasins

They're big, they're intimidating, they're *really* expensive, but they're worth a visit. You can gawk at the ornate architecture, scoff at prices, and marvel at the historical value of it all; some of these stores have been around since 1869. Just take a deep breath, practice your *pardon-nez-moi,* and ogle away.

Au Bon Marché. The world's oldest grand magasin has a central structure designed by Mr. Eiffel himself, but architectural historians weep and moan about subsequent alterations. While you're here, don't miss the gourmet grocery-store annex **La Grande Epicerie** (*see* Markets and Specialty Shops, in Chapter 4). *Rues de Sèvres and de Babylone, 7e, tel. 01–44–39–80–80. Métro: Sèvres-Babylone. Open Mon.–Sat. 9:30–5. AE, MC, V.*

Au Printemps. Au Printemps bills itself as "the most Parisian store," but it's basically the same as any other large department store. Unless you climb all the way to the colorful, domed top-floor café, the building itself is not very appealing, as modernization has marred most of the original 19th-century decor. You are also invited to Au Printemps's free fashion show every Tuesday at 10 AM (also Fridays at 10 AM March–October). Arrive early to pick up an invitation at the info desk on the ground floor. *64 blvd. Haussmann, 9e, tel. 01–42–82–50–00. Métro: Havre-Caumartin. Open Mon.–Sat. 9:30–7, Thurs. 9:30–10. AE, MC, V.*

BHV. The unglamorous Bazar de l'Hôtel de Ville is slightly cheaper than the others, specializes in housewares, and has a huge hardware department in the basement. While the clothing selection is minimal, BHV does have an entire floor dedicated to books. *52 rue de Rivoli, 4e, tel. 01–42–74–90–00. Métro: Hôtel de Ville. Open Mon.–Sat. 9:30–7 (Wed. until 10). AE, MC, V.*

Galeries Lafayette. The highlight here is a central gallery featuring counters of designer beauty products under a stained-glass dome. After wading through the trendy boutiques and stylish shoppers, climb up to one of the six interior wrought iron balconies for a little perspective on the frenzy below. To witness French haute couture's last gasps, wander through the empty boutiques on the sixth floor. *40 blvd. Haussmann, 9e, tel. 01–42–82–36–40. Métro: Chaussée d'Antin. Open Mon.–Sat. 9:30–7 (Thurs. until 9). AE, MC, V.*

La Samaritaine. This sprawling magasin dominates a whole section of rue de Rivoli east of the Louvre. La Samaritaine has what locals generally consider the best view of Paris—check out the tiled panorama upstairs that indicates the city's major monuments. Even more exciting is the big, curvy slide (used for transporting merchandise) that snakes through the middle of the store, tempting brave souls to hop on for a free ride. *19 rue de la Monnaie, 1er, tel. 01–40–41–20–20. Métro: Pont Neuf. Open Mon.–Sat. 9:30–7 (Thurs. until 10). AE, MC, V.*

Flea Markets

If you are excited by the prospect of shopping in Paris, imagine finding 20 acres of stuff you can actually afford. Parisian *marchés aux puces* (flea markets) sell old treasures, vintage clothing, handmade fashions, shoes, appliances, and (you will soon discover) a lot of junk. Don't ever pay the asking price and keep haggling, or you'll wonder why you paid 600F for a pair of pink plastic shoes. Keep a close eye (and firm hand) on your wallet; pickpockets thrive in the crowded conditions.

Paris also has several specialized outdoor markets, including a **stamp market** at the corner of avenues de Marigny and Gabriel (8e) on Thursdays, Saturdays, and Sundays. Three **flower markets** brighten the city streets Tuesday–Sunday from 8 AM until about 7; the main one, at **place Louis-Lépine** (4e) on the Ile de la Cité, turns into a bird and pet market on Sundays, while the markets at **place de la Madeleine** (8e) and **place des Ternes** (8e) stick to flowers and such.

MARCHE AUX PUCES ST-OUEN First you have to decide which of the seven markets composing this sprawling giant sounds most tempting. A few of the markets, such as **Marché Jules Vallès** (on rue Jules Vallès, at rue du Plaisir) have a bit of everything—from African masks to dusty 19th-century watches. **Marché Bison** (85 rue des Rosiers) and **Marché Cambo** (next door) specialize in fancy antiques, which means they're good when it's raining 'cause they're covered. **Marché Ralik** (rue Jean-Henri-Fabre) makes up for in prices what it lacks in originality. It specializes in used Levi's; you have to look a little to find the other secondhand clothes. The little shops that mushroom around the various markets are especially worthwhile: Most offer quality vintage leather, African crafts, and records. *Métro: Porte de Clignancourt, 18e. Open Sat.–Mon. 7:30–7.*

MARCHE AUX PUCES MONTREUIL This market is smaller and funkier than **St-Ouen,** so it's a good place to come if you don't have a whole day to spare. Asian and African trinkets abound, and you can even find used cars. But above all, this market is the best place to get used and vintage clothing. Come on Monday mornings, when it's less crowded. *Métro: Porte de Montreuil, 20e. Open Sat.–Sun. 7:30–7, Mon. 7:30–1.*

Specialty Shops

ART SUPPLIES

Art supplies in Paris can be pretty reasonable if you nose around enough. Prices may seem high, but don't forget—this is where the masters at the Ecole des Beaux-Arts in Saint Germain seek out their burnt sienna. Also try gallery districts like the Bastille, where shops have exotic materials such as handmade Japanese paper and fewer of the traditional, classroom-oriented materials you'll see elsewhere.

L'Artiste Peintre. The friendly, sympathetic staff give a 10% discount off their already low prices if you can pass yourself off as a Beaux Arts student. Their stock is either expensive, high-quality stuff or cheap-o schlock. *54 blvd. Edgar-Quinet, 14e, tel. 01–43–22–31–71. Métro: Edgar Quinet. Open Mon.–Sat. 9:30–7. MC, V.*

C.T.S. Individual- and industrial-size containers of paints, plasters, and other materials brewed from C.T.S.'s own recipes sit alongside more mainstream brands. A 20-ml tube of house extrafine oil paint starts at 20F. *26 passage Thiéré, 11e, tel. 01–43–55–60–44. Métro: Bastille. Open weekdays 9–1 and 2–6:30, Sat. 9–1.*

Graphigro. Parisian art students frequent this chain, which sells all types of paints, papers, tools, and other materials. The two-story branch on rue de Rennes will satisfy the needs of a serious artist, while celebrants can decorate one of several masks for under 30F. Rembrandt oil paints in 17-ml tubes are 14F–68F. *133 rue de Rennes, 6e, tel. 01–42–22–51–80. Métro: Rennes. Open Mon.–Sat. 10–7. MC, V (over 50F only).*

PAPER Stock up on paper at any store labeled PAPETERIE. There are plenty on the Left Bank—two good places to try are the downstairs papeterie of **Eyrolles** (57–61 blvd. St-Germain, 5e, tel. 01–44–41–11–73) and **Gibert Joseph** papeterie (30 blvd. St-Michel, 5e, tel. 01–44–41–88–66), with its own discount line of notebooks and stationery. If you want to splurge, **rue du pont Louis-Philippe** near rue Rivoli in the Marais has a few good stores that sell everything from recycled to handmade paper; try **Papier Plus** (tel. 01–42–77–70–49), **Calligrane** (tel. 01–48–04–09–00) or **Mélodie Graphique** (tel. 01–42–74–57–68).

PHOTOGRAPHY EQUIPMENT **FNAC Service** has over 40 locations in France, with the mother store at 136 rue de Rennes in Montparnasse (*see* Bookstores, *below*). For photography and other electronic equipment, **InterDiscount** will be happy to let you use your credit card for good deals on cameras (a basic 35mm camera can be had for 99F), Walkmans (as low as 29F), and film (24-exposure Kodak 200 for 30F); locations in Paris include 97 rue Monge (5e, tel. 01–45–35–00–13), 45 avenue du Général-Leclerc (14e, tel. 01–43–27–79–11), and 9 blvd Poissonnière (2e, tel. 01–42–36–02–72).

BOOKSTORES

While bookstores of all shapes and subjects are spread throughout Paris, bookstores specializing in art, literature, economics, politics, language, gastronomy, and ethnic studies are most abundant on the Left Bank. The best place to look for lit crit and philosophy texts is in the areas that spawn them, specifically **boulevard St-Michel** near the Ecole Normale Supérieure, **place de la Sorbonne,** and all of those pesky little streets tucked in between. Gibert Joseph, Presses Universitaires, and the FNAC in Les Halles are also good places to try. Finally, be sure to check out the *bouquinistes* (booksellers) along the Seine, particularly between **boulevard du Palais** and the **Pont au Double** (*see box, below*).

A tire-d'ailes. This little bookshop on pleasant Ile St-Louis offers an international selection of poetry and might sell you just the thing to woo that scornful *Parisienne.* Or join the ranks of poets railing against romance—the nearby Pont St-Louis is a great place for declamations of all sorts. *81 rue St-Louis-en-l'Ile, 4e, tel. 01–40–46–89–37. Métro: Pont Marie. Open Tues.–Sat. 11–7, Sun. noon–8. MC, V.*

Boulinier. This totally wacky four-story jumble sells new and used music, comic books, videotapes, and even scholastic books—all it takes is some scrounging around to find a good deal. *20 blvd. St-Michel, 5e, tel. 01–43–26–90–57. Métro: St-Michel. Open Mon.–Sat. 10 AM–midnight, Sun. 2 PM–midnight. V.*

FNAC. This multistory chain with four major locations in the city actually sells a great deal more than mere books—like music, computer software, photo equipment, videos, and concert tickets, all for reasonable prices. Books are all new here and cover a wide variety of subjects. *1 rue Pierre-Lescot, 1er, tel. 01–40–41–40–00. Métro: Châtelet–Les Halles. Other locations: 136 rue de Rennes, 6e, tel. 01–49–54–30–00; Métro: St-Placide. 26–30 av. des Ternes, 8e, tel. 01–44–09–18–00; Métro: Ternes. 4 pl. de la Bastille, 12e, tel. 01–43–42–04–04; Métro: Bastille. All open Mon.–Sat. 10–7:30. MC, V.*

Gibert Jeune. More student-oriented than its counterpart Gibert Joseph, Gibert Jeune sells heaps of new and used books—not only scholarly ones, but also colorful, hardback art books (175F–240F new) that look most at home on coffee tables. Some of the stores have specialties like science, religion, or fiction, so consult the yellow awnings in front of the several branches clustered on place St-Michel. You can sell books (including quality English fiction) at the 5 place St-Michel location. The selection of English literature at the 10 place St-Michel site is terribly conservative and boring, but if you're determined to work your way through Dickens, titles go for 10F–15F less here than at other English-language bookstores. *2–10 pl. St-Michel and 27 quai St-Michel, 6e, tel. 01–43–25–70–07. Métro: St-Michel. Open Mon.–Sat. 9:30–7:30. MC, V (over 100F only).*

Gibert Joseph. No one can get through the Quartier Latin without encountering this chaotic store or its alter ego, Gibert Jeune. Books here are moderately priced and run from the general (tourism, language aids) to the very specific (particularly in economics, politics, literature, and anthropology). *26 blvd. St-Michel, 6e, tel. 01–44–41–88–88. Métro: Cluny–La Sorbonne. Open Mon.–Sat. 9:30–7:30. MC, V (over 100F only).*

La Hune. This sleek bookstore is a landmark for the *intellos* at Café de Flore and Les Deux Magots. Belles-lettres are downstairs, but the main attraction is the international, comprehensive collection of books on art and architecture upstairs. Stay here until midnight with all the other people pretending to be genius-insomniacs. *170 blvd. St-Germain, 6e, tel. 01–45–48–35–85. Métro: St-Germain des Prés. Open Mon.–Sat. 10 AM–midnight. MC, V.*

Librairie Gallimard. This bookstore buys and sells new (and some used) literature and literary criticism. If you heard about it or read it in a French class, it's probably here. *15 blvd. Raspail, 7e, tel. 01–45–48–24–84. Métro: Rue du Bac. Open Mon.–Sat. 10–7. AE, MC, V.*

ENGLISH-LANGUAGE BOOKSTORES Paris has several English-language bookstores, among them **Brentano's** (37 av. de l'Opéra, 2e, tel. 01–42–61–52–50), **Galignani** (224 rue de Rivoli, 1er, tel. 01–42–60–76–07), and **W. H. Smith** (248 rue de Rivoli, 1er, tel. 01–44–77–88–99). They all stock big, shiny, expensive books in English—a single paperback volume can cost 75F or more. All three accept credit cards and are closed Sundays. If you need to stock up on novels in English, head to **Albion** (13 rue Charles V, 4e, tel. 01–42–72–50–71).

The Abbey. This Franco-Canadian enterprise specializes in literature from Québec, with new and used titles in French and English. They wait to get contemporary American works until the books are published in the United Kingdom. *29 rue de la Parcheminerie, 5e, tel. 01–46–33–16–24. Métro: St-Michel. Open Mon.–Sat. 10–7.*

Shakespeare and Company. The daring founder of the original institution, Sylvia Beach, published Joyce's *Ulysses* in 1922 after it was deemed obscene and turned down by other publishers. The current owner, George Whitman, claims Walt as an ancestor and will say anything to capitalize on the reputation of Beach's salon; he adopted the name years after the first Shakespeare and Company closed. Nowadays you can find new and used books for as little as 10F. The selection is haphazard and poorly organized, but you'll be subsidizing the friendly staff who will let you hole up in the back and read an entire novel if it's raining outside. The store periodically hosts poetry readings and literary discussions in English. Check out the bulletin board for apartment rentals, goods for sale, and French–English conversation exchanges. *37 rue de la Bûcherie, near quai Montebello, 5e, tel. 01–43–26–96–50. Métro: St-Michel. Open daily noon–midnight.*

Tea and Tattered Pages. This tiny, cluttered, and eminently comfortable little bookshop and tearoom near Tour Montparnasse is a better place to huddle over a pot of tea (20F, 25F for two) and a plate of brownies (20F) than actually buy used English-language books—too many pulp thrillers (Tom Clancy for 40F). The sweet-tempered staff is as American as the menu (cheesecake! bagels with cream cheese! lox!), and the only French you'll hear will be a commercial on the classical radio station. There's a basket of free books in front for the especially hard-up. *24 rue Mayet, 6e, tel. 01–40–65–94–35. Métro: Duroc. Open daily 11–7.*

Village Voice Bookshop. Easily the best English-language bookstore in Paris, the Village Voice is beloved by expatriate reading groups who order their titles here; as a result the literature section is comprehensive and often experimental, while the nonfiction section is filled with titles

Les Bouquinistes

They crowd around the river like green flies, hawking plastic Eiffel Towers and other offensive tourist paraphernalia, or so it seems at first glance. Truth is, many bouquinistes are bona fide bibliophiles—careful collectors who have spent a lifetime dealing in classics, as well as posters (30F–100F), comic books (35F), magazines, postcards, poetry and literature (10F–30F), pocket books (15F), and sometimes even sheet music. They open shop Monday through Saturday at 10 AM (more or less) and pack up around 6, but much depends upon their mood, the weather, and the crowds.

published by university presses. East Coast thirtyish women with doctorates form the bulk of their clientele. *6 rue Princesse, 6e, tel. 01–46–33–36–47. Métro: Mabillon. Open Mon. 2–8, Tues.–Sat. 10–8. AE, MC, V.*

FEMINIST BOOKSTORES **La Fourmi Ailée.** This bookstore has a large selection of literary works by or about women. The refined tearoom in back often hosts the lesbians-who-lunch set who murmur romantically to one another over plates of scones (34F), but you'll be just as comfortable reading alone with a pot of tea (26F). On the weekend they do a full brunch. *8 rue du Fouarre, 5e, tel. 01–43–29–40–99. Métro: St-Michel. Open Wed.–Mon. noon–7.*

La Librairie des Femmes. This feminist bookstore is strong on theoretical feminist texts, many of which it publishes, and weaker on activist/radical/lesbian books. There's a nice section of feminist texts throughout history (all translated into French), and quite a bit about women's health issues. The English section includes translations of French women authors like Colette and Anaïs Nin. *74 rue de Seine, 6e, tel. 01–43–29–50–75. Métro: Mabillon. Open Mon.–Sat. 10–7. V.*

GAY AND LESBIAN LITERATURE **Les Mots à la Bouche.** Paris's only overtly gay bookstore features magazines, art, photography, novels, and poetry in French and English. Come here to pick up gay and lesbian guidebooks to France, and to find out what's going on around town. They also sell videos. *6 rue Ste-Croix-de-la-Bretonnerie, 4e, tel. 01–42–78–88–30, fax 01–42–78–36–41. Métro: Hôtel de Ville. Open Mon.–Sat. 11–11, Sun. 2–7. MC, V.*

SPECIALTY BOOKSTORES **Arcane 22.** This low-key bookstore near the Centre Beaubourg features literature on white magic, yoga, and spiritualism. Non-French readers can come for the incense, crystals, candles, tarot cards. You can also pick up a copy of *Le Nouvel Age* (10F), which lists upcoming lectures and cultural events. *12 rue des Lombards, 4e, tel. 01–42–72–62–31. Métro: Châtelet. Open Mon. 1:30–7, Tues.–Sat. 10–noon and 1:30–7. MC, V.*

Attica. Attica has all you need to learn a language, including children's grammar books and corny language tapes. *64 rue de la Folie-Méricourt, 11e, tel. 01–48–06–17–00. Métro: Oberkampf. Open Tues.–Sat. 10–7, Mon. 2–7. AE, MC, V.*

Aux Films du Temps. Film buff heaven, with technical books on filmmaking and film history as well as big, glossy posters and movie stills. *8 rue St-Martin, 4e, tel. 01–42–71–93–48. Métro: Châtelet. Open Tues.–Sat. 11:30–7:30, Mon. 2–7:30. V.*

Cosmos 2000. The mellow, chain-smoking woman who runs Cosmos doesn't care if you settle into a chair and read *bandes-dessinées* (comic books) for hours. She also carries a small number of used fantasy/science-fiction books in English (20F–30F). Be warned: Some of these comics aren't for kids, given their sexual and violent tone. *17 rue de l'Arc-de-Triomphe, 17e, tel. 01–43–80–30–74. Métro: Charles de Gaulle–Etoile. Open Tues.–Fri. 2–7:30, Sat. 11–6:30.*

L'Harmattan. "Au carrefour des cultures" (at the crossroads of cultures) is how this impressive bookstore/publisher likes to describe itself: They specialize in African, Arabic, Spanish, Portuguese, Latin American, and Asian literature. *16–21 rue des Ecoles, 5e, tel. 01–46–34–13–71. Métro: Maubert-Mutualité. Open Mon.–Sat. 10–7. MC, V.*

L'Introuvable. The place for para-literature: spy novels, science fiction, mysteries, and westerns. The English-speaking shop owner carries nothing but first-run editions, mostly in French. *25 rue Juliette-Dodu, 10e, tel. 01–42–00–61–43. Métro: Colonel Fabien. Open Tues.–Fri. 3–7, Sat. 4–7. MC, V.*

La Librairie du Monde Libertaire. Paris's main anarchist bookstore is pretty low-key. The shop's monthly newsletter, "Le Monde Libertaire," lists in-store lectures and seminars. *145 rue Amelot, 11e, tel. 01–48–05–34–08. Métro: Filles du Calvaire. Open weekdays 2–7, Sat. 10–7. MC, V.*

La Librairie Gourmande. The certified antiquarian owner hoards her collection of precious antique cookbooks behind a glass counter. Other books of equal gastronomic caliber, however, are offered for less, and she has a delicious collection of reproductions of old food advertisements. *4 rue Dante, 5e, tel. 01–43–54–37–27. Métro: St-Michel. Open daily 10–7. MC, V.*

La Librairie Musicale de Paris. This place stocks all things musical: metronomes, musical anthologies, and sheet music on everything from French oldies to grunge. *68 bis rue Réaumur, 2e, tel. 01–42–72–30–72. Métro: Réaumur-Sébastopol. Open weekdays 10–12:45 and 2–7, Sat. 10–7. AE, MC, V.*

CLOTHING

If the stuffy salespeople in gallery-style boutiques don't have what it takes to woo you away from your money, there are plenty of other places with good deals on clothing, especially if you work for it. With four Paris locations, **Tati** (4 blvd. de Rochechouart, 18e, tel. 01–42–55–13–09; 13 pl. de la République, 3e, tel. 01–48–87–72–81; 140 rue de Rennes, 6e, tel. 01–45–48–68–31; 106 rue du Faubourg-du-Temple, 11e, tel. 01–43–57–92–80) is a menagerie of cheap polyester clothing and bargain-basement housewares piled higgledy-piggledy in bins. Couture it isn't, but everyone needs underwear. Go to the main store on boulevard de Rochechouart for the most intense Tati experience. You can also try the **Salvation Army** (12 rue Cantagrel, 13e, tel. 01–43–83–54–40); it's not necessarily the height of fashion, but it's cheap as hell and you never know what you'll find. It's also good for furniture.

If you want to drop a bundle on your feet, **André** and **Eram** are two shoestores that you'll see all over Paris. A cheaper option is to browse along the stores on boulevard St-Michel (5e), avenue du Général-Leclerc (14e), and rue Grégoire de Tours (6e). For some less mainstream styles, don't overlook the flea markets, or the tiny shops along the Halles. If you (stupidly) packed shoes that are killing your feet, **Anatomica** (14 rue de Bourg-Tibourg, 4e) has Birkenstocks for 450F and up.

Eurofripe Mod. This vintage shop feels like a boutique with its impeccably organized racks, but the '70s-style shoes, jeans, and leather are well worth the trip. Also, check out the clothing creations handmade on the premises. *15 rue Daval, 11e, tel. 01–48–06–24–29. Métro: Bastille. Open Mon. noon–8, Tues.–Sat. 11–8. Sun. 2–7. AE, MC, V.*

Guerrisold. Used leather jackets in bomber and '70s styles for 50F, long wool coats 50F–100F, trench coats 50F–100F, shoes for 30F, sweaters for 10F. Period. Most clothes are of mediocre quality, but you can't beat the prices. Guerrisold stores have sprouted all over Paris, but the one on boulevard Rochechouart has the broadest selection. *17 bis blvd. Rochechouart, 9e, tel. 01–42–80–66–18. Métro: Barbès-Rochechouart. Other location: 21 blvd. Barbès, 18e, tel. 01–42–52–39–24; Métro: Château Rouge. Both open Mon.–Sat. 9:30–7.*

Kiliwatch. What to wear to the rave? Two floors of '70s vintage, fuchsia platform sneakers, and ultratight neon Lycra creations come to the rescue. They even have an Internet café on the ground floor where you can sip an espresso and sort out all the rave flyers spread out on the counter. *3–5 rue d'Argout, 2e, tel. 01–40–26–21–45. Métro: Sentier. Other location: 64 rue Tiquetonne, 2e, tel. 01–42–21–17–37; Métro: Etienne Marcel. Both open Mon. and Wed. 1–7, Tues., Thurs., Fri. 10:30–7, Sat. 10–7:30. AE, MC, V.*

Orlando Curioso. Silver and gold lamé shrouds the tiny confines of this tightly packed store, which concentrates on the romantic and masculine aspects of women's clothing. Wool suit jackets are 100F, dresses and poet blouses 50F–100F. The hat selection is inspiring but surprisingly expensive. *78 rue de Rennes, 6e, tel. 01–42–22–28–66. Métro: St-Placide. Open weekdays 11–6:30.*

Terrain Vogue. On a street filled with cool art galleries, bars, and music stores, Terrain Vogue remains hip without charging ridiculous prices. The selection is limited but good, with a nice collection of funky jewelry. Dresses run around 100F, while '60s-style polyester shirts go for 60F. *13 rue Keller, 11e, tel. 01–43–14–03–23. Métro: Ledru Rollin or Bastille. Open Mon.–Sat. 11–8.*

Tosca. Everything here dates from the '30s, '40s, and '50s and has been amassed personally by the one-time actress who owns the place. Most of the clothing is costly, excluding the decent selection of dresses for about 150F. She's also got some incredible hats. *1 rue des Taillandiers, 11e, tel. 01–48–06–71–24. Métro: Ledru Rollin or Bastille. Open daily afternoons or by appointment.*

DEGRIFFES If you can't leave this city without buying *something* with a designer label, the *magasins de dégriffés* are your best bet. "Dégriffés" (meaning de-clawed—go figure) stock surplus merchandise and slightly damaged goods. These stores are packed with good stuff and charge up to 70% less than normal retail stores. Unfortunately, this doesn't mean they're a steal—most manage to charge 100F for a T-shirt anyway. **Basic Dressing** (13–15 rue du Pont au Choux, 3e, tel. 01–42–77–26–29) is an outlet store with plenty of semifancy stuff your parents would approve of, while **La Citadelle** (1 rue des Trois-Frères, 18e, tel. 01–42–52–21–56) has a little bit of everything—from wacky creations to corporate duds.

Le mouton à cinq pattes. Real and aspiring designers come to this treasure trove to drop off their damaged and outdated extras. The direct translation, "five-legged sheep," is slang for "the unattainable." The store has eight locations in Paris. *8–18 rue St-Placide, 6e, tel. 01–45–48–86–26. Métro: Sèvres-Babylone. Other locations: 15 rue Vieille-du-Temple, 4e, tel. 01–42–71–86–30; Métro: Hôtel de Ville. 19 rue Grégoire-de-Tours, 6e, tel. 01–43–29–73–56; Métro: Mabillon or Odéon.*

FRILLS **Herbier de Provence.** The French response to the Body Shop specializes in aromatherapy oils and sells all types of magic potions, such as cellulite cream (162F). They also have bath products made with natural ingredients (soaps with your choice of scent go for 9F). *Carrousel du Louvre, 99 rue de Rivoli, 1e, tel. 01–40–20–00–64. Métro: Palais Royal. Open Wed.–Mon. 10–8. MC, V.*

L'Occitane. This airy little store on the Ile St-Louis has more ways to scent your body than you may have thought possible, although they sternly warn you they will not package the soaps (14F for 100g, 22F for 250g) as gifts. Almost all their products are made in the south of France. *55 rue St-Louis-en-l'Ile, 4e, tel. 01–40–46–81–71. Métro: Pont Marie. Open Tues.–Sat. 10:30–7:30, Sun. 10:30–7, Mon. 2:30–7. MC, V.*

Parfums de Femme. This chain of perfumeries guarantees the lowest prices on perfumes and potions, with brands like Dior, Givenchy, Lancôme, and Biotherm. *189 rue St-Jacques, 5e, tel. 01–43–25–44–22. RER: Luxembourg. Open Mon.–Sat. 10–7. MC, V.*

Virginie Boutique. Finally a boutique where they don't make you feel like an intruder for walking in. The friendly owner, Virginie, has been here for 30-odd years and all her jewelry—most of it big, chunky, and colorful—is handcrafted in France by artist friends of hers. *13 rue de l'Odéon, 6e, tel. 01–43–26–55–29. Métro: Odéon. Open Tues.–Sat. 10–1 and 2–7.*

HOUSEWARES AND FURNISHINGS

Prices on just about everything drop as you stray from Paris's heavily trod districts. Still, there are a few cheapo places poking out of well-known streets if you look hard for them. If you have the patience to wade through all the junk at **Tati** (*see* Clothing, *above*), you can find cheap cooking utensils and bowls (5F). Also try **boulevard Barbès** and **boulevard de Rochechouart,** where you'll find inexpensive, low-quality dishes, utensils, and other household items. The Brit-owned **Conran Shop** (117 rue du Bac, 7e, tel. 01–42–84–10–01) carries slightly more expensive items—you'll recognize their stock from your Crate and Barrel catalogue.

A. Simon. While there are a few cooking utensils and pots tucked in the corners, A. Simon specializes in the tools of bistrots—carafes, café bowls, escargot baking dishes—that are hard to find outside France. The showroom is crammed with china and flatware. *36 rue Etienne-Marcel, 2e, tel. 01–42–33–71–65. Métro: Etienne Marcel. Open Mon.–Sat. 8:30–6:30. AE, MC, V.*

Hall Bazaar. For those days when you really need a juicer that looks like a cactus, or a candle holder made out of Nestlé cans. *89 rue St-Denis, 1er, tel. 01–45–08–14–39. Métro: Les Halles. Open Tues.–Sat. 10–7, Mon. 1–7. MC, V (over 100F only).*

La Vaissellerie. If you can't afford the discount ceramics inside and have no particular use for an ornate tea set, try the more practical items outside: bowls (12F–15F), tea baskets, silverware, and the like. *85 rue de Rennes, 6e, tel. 01–42–22–61–49. Métro: St-Sulpice. Open Mon.–Sat. 9:30–7. MC, V.*

APPLIANCES AND ELECTRONICS **La Cape.** The Cape (Centrale d'Achat pour Etudiants) is a discount store available expressly for anyone with a student ID, and they're not very picky about what kind. Come for electronics and appliances like stereos, Walkmans, headphones, film, TVs . . . everything at prices slashed for a student budget. *28 rue du Chemin-Vert, 11e, tel. 01–43–57–68–56. Métro: Chemin Vert. Open Tues.–Sat. 10:30–7. MC, V.*

FURNITURE For cheap furniture, you might try the Salvation Army (*see* Clothing, *above*), and the flea markets (*see above*). Next, head for **Bricodidi** (16 rue Monge, 5e, tel. 01–43–54–32–43), which sells cheap, simple wood furniture like chairs (95F), tables (180F), and shelves (260F), as well as hardware and kitchen items. Handy types can try **Castorama** (1 rue Coulaincourt, 18e, tel. 01–45–22–17–11), an enormous store filled with cheap assemble-it-yourself furniture.

OUTDOOR EQUIPMENT

If someone swiped your backpack, you can get another at **Passe Montagne** (39 rue du Chemin-Vert, 11e, tel. 01–43–57–08–47). Although they have several stores in Paris, this is the only one that rents equipment (tents, sleeping bags, camping stoves). The knowledgeable staff caters mostly to rock climbers and can outfit you with all you need to scale the Eiffel Tower. If you've decided to brave the traffic and cycle your way through Paris, **Point Vélos** (83 blvd. St-Michel, 5e, tel. 01–43–54–85–36) sells used bikes (starting at 700F), and promises to repair your cycle within 24 hours.

Au Vieux Campeur. There are 17, count 'em, 17 branches compressed within a few blocks in the Quartier Latin. The main shoe stores are at 50 rue des Ecoles and 38 rue St-Jacques; camping gear is at 6 rue Thénard; backpacks are at 80 boulevard St-Germain; and everything you need for water sports is at 5 place Paul-Painlevé. The main store has a climbing wall so that passsersby can watch your moves. *Main branch: 48 rue des Ecoles, 5e, tel. 01–46–34–02–04. Métro: Maubert-Mutualité. Open Mon.–Sat. 10:30–7 (longer hrs in summer). MC, V.*

RECORDS, CDS, AND CASSETTES

Record shops may abound in Paris, but music sure doesn't come cheap: Expect a new CD to run you 100F minimum. If you can afford it, some branches of **FNAC** (*see* Bookstores, *above*) sell "new" music plus concert tickets. Also try **FNAC Musique Bastille** (4 pl. de la Bastille, 12e, tel. 01–43–42–04–04) or **FNAC Forum** (1–7 rue Pierre-Lescot, in Forum des Halles, 1er, tel. 01–40–41–40–00). The latter has a good world-music department but rarely ventures far from the mainstream. The **Virgin Megastore** (52 av. des Champs-Elysées, 8e, tel. 01–40–74–06–48) is just that—a megalith with a megaselection, a million listening stations, and some great prices on new albums. If you're looking for alternative music and lesser-known bands that FNAC ignores, dive into the Megastore's second location in the Carrousel du Louvre at 99 rue de Rivoli. On the Left Bank, **Paris Musique** (10 blvd. St-Michel, 5e, tel. 01–43–26–96–41) gives a 20% discount on new releases.

Gilda. This place has been around since the '60s and now sells used CDs for 60F and under. Many collectors do a lot of selling and buying here, so the selection is always changing; you might have to come more than once to get what you want. CDs run 25F–60F, and tapes are 25F. They've also got some used books in English in the back for about 15F. *36 rue des Bourdonnais, 1er, tel. 01–42–33–60–00. Métro: Châtelet–Les Halles. Open Mon.–Sat. 10–7.*

O'C.D. This music store with listening tables and a coffee machine buys, sells, and exchanges new and used CDs with prices from 55F to 85F. They carry a lot of new French music, as well as rock, jazz, acid jazz, techno, New Age, and opera. *26 rue des Ecoles, 5e, tel. 01–43–25–23–27. Métro: Maubert-Mutualité. Open Tues.–Sat. 11–9, Sun. and Mon. 2–7.*

Rough Trade. The granddaddy of all the music stores clustered around rue de Charonne and rue Keller, Rough Trade primarily sells imports. This is definitely the first place to look for info on bands passing through Paris. Downstairs is devoted to vinyl techno and house music with current rave info. Upstairs features indie, ambient, and some spoken word, along with a desk that sells concert tickets. You can listen before you buy, and the staff is very helpful (and usually speaks English). *30 rue de Charonne, 11e, tel. 01–40–21–61–62. Métro: Ledru Rollin or Bastille. Open Mon.–Sat. noon–7. AE, MC, V.*

DANCE AND TECHNO **BPM records.** Look no further for your techno needs; you can hear the pulsating beat of this all-vinyl record store from a block away. This is also a hot spot for rave and jungle party info, so check out the flyers. *1 rue Keller, 11e, tel. 01–40–21–62–88. Métro: Bastille. Open Mon.–Sat. noon–8. MC, V.*

JAZZ AND WORLD MUSIC **Paris Jazz Corner** (5 rue de Navarre, 5e, tel. 01–43–36–78–92) is staffed by people who know all about the jazz, blues, and world music they have on vinyl and CD, both new (80F–100F) and used (25F–50F). For African music and salsa, try the specialty record stores **Afric' Music** (3 rue des Plantes, 14e, tel. 01–45–42–43–52) or **Anvers Musique** (35 blvd. de Rochechouart, 9e, tel. 01–42–80–18–56). For Arabic music, try **Le Disque Arabe** (116 blvd. de la Chapelle, 18e, tel. 01–42–54–95–71).

Crocodisc. This two-room store has both new and used jazz and rock in one room (records as low as 10F, tapes 25F, CDs 70F–120F) and reggae, salsa, Brazilian, African, and Middle Eastern music in the other. *40–42 rue des Ecoles, 5e, tel. 01–43–54–33–22. Métro: Maubert-Mutualité. Open Tues.–Sat. 11–7. MC, V.*

CrocoJazz. Crocodisc's offspring has not only jazz and blues but Cajun and gospel music as well. Used cassettes start at 40F (100F for three). New discs cost 90F, imports 100F–120F. **La Dame Blanche** is just across the street if you want to compare prices. *64 rue de la Montagne-Ste-Geneviève, 5e, tel. 01–46–34–78–38. Métro: Maubert-Mutualité. Open Tues.–Sat. 11–1 and 2–7. MC, V.*

PUNK AND ALTERNATIVE **Parallèles.** A hip crowd moves in and out among the eclectic mix of rock fanzines and underground newspapers devoted to ecology and socialism. There's a good selection of used indie CDs (25F and up). New CDs start at 60F. They've also got vinyl and a big collection of rock anthologies (many in English). *47 rue St-Honoré, 1er, tel. 01–42–33–62–70. Métro: Châtelet–Les Halles. Open Mon.–Sat. 10–7. MC, V (over 120F only).*

Le Silence de la Rue. This tiny shop's flaming red exterior attracts pierced patrons looking for the latest deals in indie, garage, punk, noise, and all things alternative. CDs run 85F–120F. There's a big vinyl collection, and you can ask to hear something before you buy it, provided it's not on sale. *8 rue de la Fontaine-du-But, 18e, tel. 01–42–55–61–34. Métro: Lamarck-Caulaincourt. Open Mon.–Sat. noon–7:30. MC, V.*

WINE

To come to France and not purchase a bottle of wine is a punishable offense. Good (if not famous) wines can be found for under 30F a bottle, some for as little as 8F. The chain **Nicolas** has locations all over Paris, especially around marketplaces. Worth trying are their brightly labeled "Les Petites Récoltes Nicolas" for 11F–19F.

Caves des Abbesses. The owner really knows his grape juice. He follows independent growers for years before buying their wine, often bottling it himself and then reselling it cheaply. Bottles start at 8F, though most run 10F–20F. *43 rue des Abbesses, 18e, tel. 01–42–52–81–54. Métro: Abbesses. Open Tues.–Sat. 9–1 and 2–8, Sun. 2–8. MC, V.*

Grains Nobles. At this boutique at the foot of the Panthéon, you can sign up for one or a series of wine-tasting classes, which take place at 7:30 PM several times a month. Those between the ages of 18 and 25 can try to get into the five-wine "initiation pour jeunes oenophiles" for 90F (those older than 25 will have to fork over 390F, but the wines will be better). Otherwise, just buy a couple of bottles at discount prices. *5 rue Laplace, 5e, tel. 01–43–54–93–54. Métro: Maubert-Mutualité. Open weekdays 10:30–6.*

Juveniles. At this Brit-owned cellar, 12 wines (12F–40F) and several sherries (30F–45F) are offered by the glass, so you can try before you buy. You can hardly resist a *tartelette de légumes* *au pistou* (pesto vegetable tarte; 36F) or 35F rabbit brochettes with chutney while you're sampling the main attraction. The owner sells over 60 of his favorite wines from around the world for 40F–175F a bottle. Food is served Tuesday–Friday noon–11, Monday and Saturday noon–3 and 7–11. *47 rue de Richelieu, 1er, tel. 01–42–97–46–49. Métro: Palais Royal–Musée du Louvre. Open for drinks Mon.–Sat. 11 AM–midnight. MC, V.*

Nectar France. This small shop sells a wide range of regional and imported beers, liquors, and a good selection of wine. Prices are what you'd find in a grocery store, only you'd have to visit about 43 grocery stores to compile this collection, and the staff gives good advice. Wine-sized bottles of corked *kriek* (cherry-flavored beer) go for 27F. *25 rue des Ecoles, 5e, tel. 01–43–26–99–43. Métro: Maubert-Mutualité. Open Mon.–Sat. 10–8. MC, V.*

ILE-DE-FRANCE

7

By Viviana Mahieux and Julia Švihṛa

Unless you were born in a café, there comes a point when you need a short escape from the city. With its rural pace, peaceful villages, and impressive châteaux, the Ile-de-France is an ideal getaway (and you can easily zip back to Paris if you need an urban fix). The Ile-de-France completely surrounds Paris, so it's fairly easy to spend a morning in a Paris museum and an afternoon in the Forest of Fontainebleau, or gawking at the cathedral at Chartres, or biking in Compiègne. At the other end of the spectrum are the region's hardcore tourist sites: The palace at Versailles, the controversial Disneyland Paris, and Parc Astérix, all of which have their share of outrageous prices, heavy crowds, bad food, and bratty kids.

While not exactly an *île* (island), the Ile-de-France is cordoned off from the rest of the country by three rivers: the Seine, Marne, and Oise. These and the region's many brooks and streams have long stood to defend the area and keep it lush, two factors that once attracted royalty with a get-away-from-the-masses mindset. Forests stocked with easily catchable animals were also a big draw, enticing rich hunters who, presumably, needed all the help they could get. Today, the region's châteaux stand as monuments to the wealth, power, and aim of the French monarchy.

On summer weekends, Parisians flock to the forests and small towns of the Ile-de-France, while tourists make their way to its châteaux and palaces, driving prices for food and lodging turret-high. The only way to eat without plunking down serious cash is to picnic; luckily, this is one of the best ways to enjoy the countryside, and markets are plentiful. Budget lodging is even easier, thanks to youth hostels that have snuck in among the châteaux and cathedrals in towns like Chartres, Vernon (near Giverny), and Compiègne. As a general rule, well-touristed towns make their *fermeture hebdomadaire* (weekly closing) on Tuesday, so museums and markets may be closed—call ahead if in doubt.

Versailles

Louis XIII originally built the château in Versailles as a rustic hunting lodge in 1631, but when Louis "Sun King" XIV converted it from a weekend retreat to the headquarters of his government, he didn't cut any corners. Architect Louis Le Vau restored and added to the original lodge, while Charles Le Brun handled the interior decoration. Jules Hardouin-Mansart later remodeled the whole thing, expanding on Le Vau's improvements. They began in 1661 and spent the next 50 years designing everything his royal acquisitiveness could want, including a throne room dedicated to Apollo, the king's mythological hero. Jacques-Ange Gabriel later added an opera house so Louis XV could be entertained at home without troubling himself to mingle with the common folk. Reconstruction efforts aimed at bringing the entire estate back

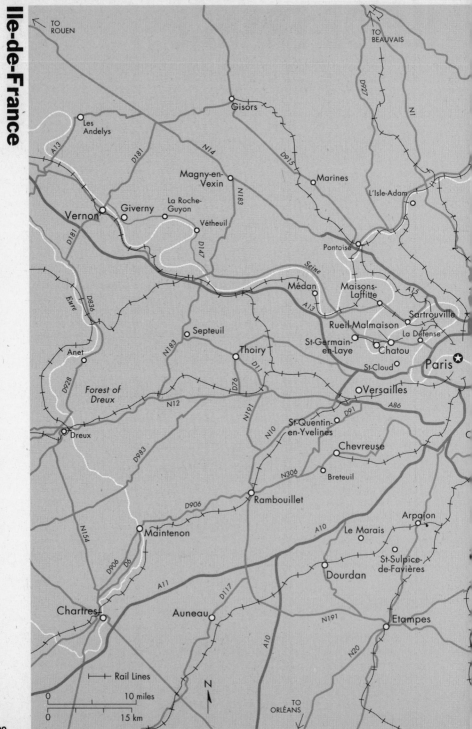

Ile-de-France

TO ROUEN

TO BEAUVAIS

D927

N1

Gisors

Les Andelys

D181

N14

D915

Marines

L'Isle-Adam

Magny-en-Vexin

N183

La Roche-Guyon

Giverny

Vernon

D181

Vétheuil

D147

Pontoise

Seine

Emre

D836

Médan

Maisons-Laffitte

A15

A13

Sartrouville

Septeuil

N183

Rueil-Malmaison

La Défense

St-Germain-en-Laye

Chatou

Paris ★

Anet

D928

Thoiry

D76

D11

St-Cloud

Forest of Dreux

N12

D91

○Versailles

A86

N191

N10

St-Quentin-en-Yvelines

Dreux

D983

Chevreuse

N306

Breteuil

D906

Rambouillet

Arpajon

Maintenon

A10

Le Marais

St-Sulpice-de-Favières

N154

D906

D6

Dourdan

Chartres

A11

Auneau

D117

N191

Etampes

A10

N20

TO ORLÉANS

├──┼── Rail Lines

N

0 ——— 10 miles
0 ——— 15 km

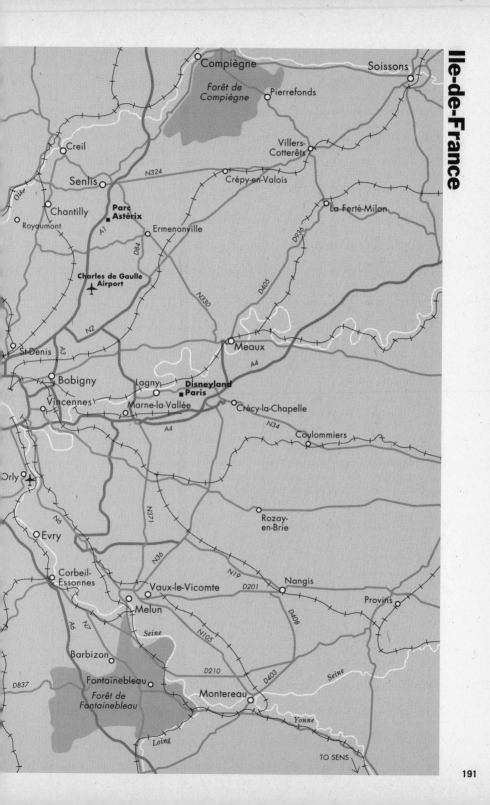

Île-de-France

Compiègne
Soissons
Forêt de Compiègne
Pierrefonds
Creil
Villers-Cotterêts
Senlis   N324   Crépy-en-Valois
Oise
Chantilly   Parc Astérix   La Ferté-Milon
Royaumont   Ermenonville
A1   D84   D936
Charles de Gaulle Airport   N330   D405
N2
St-Denis   A3   Meaux
Bobigny   Lagny   A4
Vincennes   Disneyland Paris
Marne-la-Vallée   Crécy-la-Chapelle
A4   N34   Coulommiers
Orly
N6   N371   Rozay-en-Brie
Evry
N36
Corbeil-Essonnes   N19   Nangis
Vaux-le-Vicomte   D201   Provins
A6   N7   Melun   D408
Seine
Barbizon   N105
D837   D210   D403   Seine
Fontainebleau   Montereau
Forêt de Fontainebleau   Yonne
Loing   TO SENS

191

to how it looked when the Sun King lived here will continue for the next couple of decades; billboards provide updates on what's currently being worked on.

Your best strategy at Versailles is to look beyond the overflowing trash bins and cigarette-butt-littered cobblestones and imagine what life was like here during the two centuries that it served as the home of French royalty. Picture France's overdressed nobility promenading through the gardens plotting dangerous liaisons, perhaps fawning over the king and queen in the dazzling **Galerie des Glaces** (Hall of Mirrors). Imagine Louis XVI and Marie Antoinette entertaining in the **Grands Appartements,** decorated with sumptuous marble, gilded bronzes, and ceiling paintings of mythological figures. Now imagine the day in 1789 when a revolutionary mob marched the 15 miles from Paris to Versailles to protest the bread shortage, only to find Louis lounging in this pleasure palace. It's no wonder they forced the king to leave Versailles and set up camp at the Tuileries Palace in Paris, where they could keep an eye on him.

BASICS There are three **Offices de Tourisme** locations in Versailles. The branch (tel. 01–39–53–31–63) opposite the Gare Rive Gauche train station in Les Manèges, a shopping mall, is closed on Mondays. Another office (tel. 01–39–50–36–22), just north of the château next to the auto entrance at 7 rue des Réservoirs, is closed on Sundays. May through September a third, constantly crowded office sets up Tuesday–Sunday at the château's main gate. All three locations have loads of brochures and helpful English-speaking employees, and all are open until around 6 PM.

COMING AND GOING The cheapest way to reach Versailles from Paris is via the **yellow RER Line C** to Versailles–Rive Gauche (40 min, 16F). Otherwise, trains from Paris's Gare Montparnasse stop at Gare des Chantiers (rue des Etats Généraux) south of the château, while trains from Paris's Gare St-Lazare arrive at the Gare Rive Droite behind place du Marché de Notre-Dame, just northeast of the palace. All three stations are within walking distance of the château.

FOOD Picnicking is the cheapest and easiest way to eat here. If you don't bring your own food, be prepared to work up an appetite walking to the nearest sandwich shop **Classe Croûte,** in the Les Manèges shopping mall just across from the Gare Rive Gauche. Decent sandwiches here cost 17F–30F. Otherwise there's a **Monoprix** market on avenue Général de Gaulle, five minutes to your right as you exit the Gare Rive Gauche. If you're not hot on the picnic idea, try one of the small restaurants behind place du Marché de Notre-Dame (about three blocks northeast of the château entrance), or one of the brasseries on avenue de Paris, the main street that runs smack dab into the château's gates. The farther you get from the château, the better luck you'll have finding something that isn't priced for tourists with a capital T. If you have the time, walk five blocks southeast of the château to **Traiteur Philippe Joly Charcutière** (62 rue d'Anjou, tel. 01–39–50–28–46), and stand in line with the locals for a freshly made sandwich (10F–20F).

WORTH SEEING It's hard to tell which is larger at Versailles—the tremendous château that housed Louis XIV and 20,000 of his courtiers, or the 20,000 visitors standing in front of it. You may be able to avoid the hour-and-a-half wait for a tour if you arrive here at 9 AM sharp, when the château opens. The hard part is figuring out where you're supposed to go once you arrive: There are different lines depending on tour, physical ability, and group status. Frequent guided tours in English visit the private royal apartments. More detailed hour-long tours explore the opera house or Marie Antoinette's private parlors. The opera house is especially interesting because the architect, wanting the acoustics of a violin, built the hall entirely of wood, and then had it all painted to resemble marble. You can go through a few rooms, including the Hall of Mirrors, without a tour—by means of yet another line, of course. To figure out the system, pick up a brochure at the information tent at the gates of the château, or consult the info desk at the ticket center. *Tel. 01–30–84–76–18. Admission: 45F, 35F under 26 and Sun., under 18 free. Tours: 25F–50F. Open Tues.–Sun. 9–6:30 (Oct.–Apr. until 5:30).*

If you don't feel like hassling with crowds and lines, or if you don't have any money left but still want to say that you've been to Versailles, check out the free **gardens** in back. This is where you'll find Versailles's hundreds of famous fountains. By the way, if you're wondering why the fountains don't work, they do—but you'll have to come on a Sunday and shell out 18F to see them in action. However, ongoing reconstruction means they may not oblige even then. For a real spectacle, come on one of several Saturdays during summer for the **Fêtes de Nuit,** when the fountains come to life with music and lights. Ask at a tourist office for dates and ticket prices, which range from 70F to 185F. Otherwise, lose the tourists huddled around the fountains and discover 250 acres of gardens a little further away from the château. Tourist brochures request you not picnic on the lawns, but they don't say anything about the grottoes, groves, and grassy areas scattered throughout the woods. Chances are good that you won't run into a gendarme if you stay away from the main attractions. *Gardens open daily 7–sunset, weather permitting.*

A guide written by Louis XIV himself, *Manière de montrer les jardins de Versailles* (The Manner of Showing the Versailles Gardens), is being consulted as the gardens are returned to their Sun King days. Le Nôtre's gardens are brimming with walkways, pools, viewpoints, woods, velvet lawns, a **Colonnade** of 24 marble columns, an **Orangery** and tons (literally) of statuary. Perhaps most impressive are sculpture groupings emerging from two pools: the **Neptune Basin's** sea god with dragons and cherubs and the **Apollo Basin's** sun god with dragons and cherubs and the **Apollo Basin's** sun god in his chariot emerging amid sea monsters to bring light to the world. Beyond the Apollo Basin is the **Grand Canal,** which Louis XIV equipped with brightly colored gondolas. Today you can pay about 25F for a boat ride down the canal, though tours may be interrupted by the area's renovations.

Rent bikes in Petite Venise, at the head of the Grand Canal, directly behind the château. Bikes cost 30F an hour, and you must leave an ID as a deposit. The dirt trails lead you into the forest or to the farthest end of the canal.

In the northwest corner of the gardens are the smaller châteaux, the **Grand Trianon** and the **Petit Trianon,** used as guest houses for everyone from Napoléon I to Richard Nixon. Although you can go inside, there's not much here, and the visit is particularly anticlimactic if you've just toured the big château. Behind the Petit Trianon is the **Hameau de la Reine** (Hamlet of the Queen), a collection of cottages where Marie Antoinette came to play peasant among the real-life versions who were recruited to fill her wonderland. You can reach this corner of the gardens on a tram (29F) that leaves every 35 minutes from the north side of the château, but walking is cheaper. *Admission: Grand Trianon 25F, 15F under 26 and Sun., under 18 free; Petit Trianon 15F, 10F under 26 and Sun., under 18 free. Combined ticket 30F, 20F under 26. Both open May–Sept., daily 10–6:30; Oct.–Apr., Tues.–Fri. 9–12:30 and 2–5:30, weekends 10–5:30.*

Chartres

Travelers who make their way to Chartres to see the **Notre-Dame de Chartres** cathedral are following in the footsteps of religious pilgrims who began coming to the city over 1,000 years ago: In the late 9th century, King Charles the Bald presented Chartres with the *sacra camisia* (sacred tunic) of the Virgin Mary, turning the city into a hot spot for the Christian faithful. The magnificent Gothic cathedral here was built in the 12th and 13th centuries, in appreciation of the miraculously unsinged state of Mary's tunic after the original church burned to the ground in 1194.

Like the cathedral, the old part of town has been preserved in its cloak of mellowing old stone. The signposted **route touristique** behind the cathedral takes you along cobblestone streets past riverbanks dotted with old wash houses, stone buildings, and a bridge all but demolished by World War II bombing. But stray from the path and you'll be slapped by modern apartment buildings and whizzing traffic. (Sometimes old pieces of buildings have been reworked into new ones—all it takes is a watchful eye to see through the modern exterior and into the past.) Slackers who prefer a ride on a choo-choo to walking can take the **Promotrain** (30F) instead, which passes by all of Chartres's major sights and leaves from place de la Cathédrale mid-March–October between 10 and 7. However, the grandeur of the cathedral is best appreciated after an hour of winding around narrow passages and suddenly seeing it loom above.

BASICS The **Office de Tourisme** is well stocked with info about the cathedral, town, and special events in the region. Hotel reservations cost 10F. *Pl. de la Cathédrale, tel. 02–37–21–50–00. Open weekdays 9:30–6:30, Sat. 9:30–6, Sun. 10:30–12:30 and 2:30–5:30.*

COMING AND GOING Hourly trains make the 50-minute, 138F round-trip from Paris's Gare Montparnasse to Chartres's **train station** (pl. Pierre Sémard, tel. 02–37–28–50–50), which puts you within walking distance of the cathedral; a map in the station shows you exactly where to go. You can check your bags from 8 AM to 7:30 PM for an extortionate 20F, or put them in equally expensive lockers.

WHERE TO SLEEP The **Auberge de Jeunesse** is the only affordable place to crash in Chartres. Its ugly exterior doesn't reflect the clean, comfortable, quiet interior. Each room has two to eight beds, a sink, and plenty of storage space. The hostel is toward the bottom of the old town, across the river from the cathedral—a well-marked 20-minute walk from the train station or a five-minute trip on Bus 3. Beds are 70F, including breakfast. *23 av. Neigre, tel. 02–37–34–27–64, fax 02–37–35–75–85. 16 rooms. Curfew 11:30 PM. Reception open noon–10. Laundry 20F, sheets 16F. Closed last 3 weeks in Dec.*

FOOD Chartres has not made much (okay, any) name for itself in the culinary world, but you'll do fine if you avoid the area surrounding Notre-Dame and stick to the old town south of the cathedral—rue Noël Ballay, rue du Cygne, and rue du Bois-Merrain Marceau are good bets for grocery stores and inexpensive restaurants. **Feu Follet** (21 pl. du Cygne, tel. 02–37–21–24–06) is the place for cheap hamburgers (11F) and crêpes. For more substantial meals, the restaurants on rue de Porte Morard are frequented by students, and there are several pizza and pasta places where a hot meal can be had for under 50F.

WORTH SEEING The **Notre-Dame de Chartres** cathedral has survived seven centuries of wars. If that doesn't impress you, consider the fact that it features over 2,000 square meters (21,500 square feet) of glass, including 12-meter- (38-foot-) high stained-glass windows, some of which date back to 1210. The oldest window is *Notre Dame de la Belle Verrière* (Our Lady of the Beautiful Window), in the south choir. Note the smaller windows depicting the guilds that sponsored the artwork—a good indication of commercial enterprise in the so-called Dark Ages. Also noteworthy are the mismatched towers, the result of lightning striking the north tower in the 16th century, decapitating its spire. Don't spend all your time looking up, though; the black and white pattern on the floor of the nave is the only one of its kind to have survived from the Middle Ages. The faithful were expected to travel along its entire length (about 300 meters, or 984 feet) on their knees. Malcolm Miller, who looks like he stepped right out of an *Addams Family* episode, gives fabulous tours in English daily at noon and 2:45 PM, providing info on the narrative stained glass and his own travels for 25F. Otherwise, you can head out the cathedral's south door to La Crypte across the street and rent a Walkman and a (vastly inferior) tape-recorded tour in English (30F). For an additional 20F that might be better spent elsewhere, you can climb the north tower for a view of the city. Organ recitals are given July–October on Sunday at 4:45 PM free of charge, though definitely not free of tourists. Show up early to stake out a seat. *Open daily 7:30–7:30.*

The **Musée des Beaux-Arts,** behind the cathedral, sits in the former bishop's palace. The collection of drawings, tapestries, and archaeological finds will be interesting only to those who have a real fascination with Chartres's history. If anything interesting is unearthed during the excavation of the medieval convent in front of the cathedral, the museum may get a needed infusion of artifacts. Check the sign in front of the museum to see if the changing contemporary exhibit is truly worth 20F (10F students). *29 cloître Notre-Dame, tel. 02–37–36–41–39. Open Apr.–Oct., Wed.–Mon. 10–1 and 2–6; Nov.–Mar., Wed.–Mon. 10–noon and 2–5, Sun. 2–5.*

The **Centre International du Vitrail** displays temporary exhibits of stained-glass works from the Middle Ages to the present. The exhibition shop in the same complex has beautiful pictures and gift items of old and new glass works. Admission to the exhibition shop is free, but that doesn't mean you'll escape with your wallet unscathed. *5 rue du Cardinal-Pie, tel. 02–37–21–65–72. Open daily 9:30–12:30 and 1:30–6 (weekends from 10). Admission: 20F, 12F students.*

Giverny

From 1883 until his death in 1926, Claude Monet painted some of his most famous works in (and of) the gardens at Giverny, 80 kilometers (37 miles) outside Paris. The gardens themselves are a work of art that Monet spent several years perfecting before he began re-creating them on canvas. He planted colorful checkerboard gardens, installed a water lily pond, put up a Japanese bridge, and finally decorated the interior of his house to match it all. Ultimately, he would paint the same scene in different seasons, weather conditions, and times of day, thus developing innovative techniques for capturing light, water, and reflections on canvas.

The 142F round-trip train-and-bus ride may sound extravagant for a day trip, but it's worth it if you're a fan of impressionism. For the full effect, come midweek in the morning to avoid the crush. The colors radiate best on sunny days, especially in late spring. Don't limit yourself to the gardens, though; Monet's large collection of Japanese prints, a great source of inspiration to French impressionists, cover the walls of his house and are worth seeing if the crowds have not reached asphyxiating numbers. Otherwise, the few rooms are sparely furnished and decorated only with Monet reproductions and his family's (limited) artistic efforts.

If you want to see "real" paintings, walk down the street to the **Musée Américain** (35F, 20F students, same hours as the Monet museum), with its excellent collection of American impressionist works influenced by Monet. Founded in 1992, the museum handsomely houses Sargents and Cassatts as well as lesser-known painters, along with an expensive restaurant and a beautiful garden "quoting" some of Monet's plant combinations. It makes an elegant respite from the hordes up the street. *Tel. 02–32–51–28–21. Admission: gardens 25F; gardens and house 35F, 25F students. Open Apr.-Oct., Tues.-Sun. 10–6.*

BASICS The **Office de Tourisme** in the nearby town of Vernon has brochures on Monet's time at Giverny. There's enough information at the train station if you're just planning a short trip, but be sure to stop in here for trail maps if you want to hike or bike in the surrounding forest. *36 rue Carnot, tel. 02–32–51–39–60. Open Tues.-Sat. 9:30–noon and 2:30–6:30, Sun. and Mon. 10–noon.*

COMING AND GOING Trains leave every couple of hours from Paris's Gare St-Lazare for the 50-minute, 65F ride to Vernon; buses meet the trains and whisk you away to Giverny for 11F more. The last bus back to Vernon from Giverny leaves around 5 PM, so check with the driver before you settle down for a late afternoon *pastis* (anise liqueur). If you have the time and energy, the 6-kilometer (3½-mile) stretch from Vernon to Giverny is nice and flat with a slight incline at the end: If you want a bike for the ride to Giverny and around town, rent one at the train station in Vernon for 55F a day (plus a 1,000F or credit-card deposit); bikes must be back by 8:30 PM. From the train station, walk (or bike) through town along rue d'Albuféra to the river, cross the bridge, and hang a right on the road to Giverny, the footpath is off to the left of the main road. Food is ridiculously expensive in Giverny itself, so bring a picnic from Paris or stock up at the numerous grocers and pâtisseries lining rue d'Albuféra.

WHERE TO SLEEP **Auberge de Jeunesse.** If you decide that Giverny deserves more than a day trip, the youth hostel in nearby Vernon is clean, spacious, and only 45F a night. The sprightly man who runs the place advises you on how best to spend your time in Giverny. The big garden doesn't quite rival Monet's, but it connects the hostel to a great 20-site campground with kitchen and laundry facilities and hot showers, all for 25F a night. *28 av. de l'Ile-de-France, tel. 02–32–51–66–48. From Vernon train station, walk 2 km (1¼ mi) on road marked PARIS. 16 beds. Breakfast 18F, sheets 17F. Reception open 8–10 and 6:30–8:30. Reservations advised.*

OUTDOOR ACTIVITIES The rolling hills and tree-lined river meandering between Vernon and Giverny are loaded with trails ideal for hiking and biking. About 20 trails climb up hills or run alongside the shady river; to find the best of them, pick up the hiking guide from the tourist office. You can also get information about gîtes d'étape (rural dorms) and chambres d'hôte (bed & breakfasts) in the area that will put up one or two car-less people for around 50F. If you plan to bike the rougher trails, you'll need a VTT (mountain bike); **Martin Cycles** in Vernon (84 rue Carnôt, tel. 02–32–21–24–08) rents them for 100F a day, 150F for Saturday through Monday (4,000F or credit-card deposit required, reservation recommended).

Chantilly

An impressive Renaissance castle, immense stables, and a famous horse-racing track all work together to recommend this quaint, tranquil little town 45 kilometers (30 miles) north of Paris. Hop off the train, ponder the sights, refuel at a café, and you'll be rested and ready to leave by early evening. Which is a good thing, since there are no cheap places to sleep ("budget" rooms start at a hefty 220F).

If you've come to Chantilly for the horse races, save yourself the racetrack admission by sitting on the grass next to the bleachers.

If spending the day at the track is your cup of tea, note that Chantilly's only official horse races are held in June, with the major international events on the first and second Sundays and smaller races on various weekdays. However, it's not uncommon to see low-key races throughout the year, so don't be deterred from coming in spring or fall. You can enter the stands on the far side of the racing oval for 40F (20F students) and bet the rest of your cash on a sure thing. Call the **S.E.C.F.** (tel. 03–49–10–20–39), which organizes the international events, for race info and schedules.

BASICS The **Office de Tourisme** is run by a bunch of locals who know the area like the back of their hand. They hand out brochures on horse races and the different combinations of tickets you can buy for the museums, château, and park. It also has the most confusing hours in all of France. *23 av. Maréchal Joffre, tel. 03–44–57–08–58. Open May–Sept., Mon. and Wed.–Sat. 9–12:30 and 2:15–6:15, Sun. 9–12:30; Oct.–Apr., Mon. and Wed.–Sat. 9–12:30 and 2:15–6:15 (Nov.–Feb., Sat. until 5:15).*

The Château of Chantilly had an excellent reputation for fine cuisine in the 17th century and today remains the eponym for fresh whipped cream. Anything you order "à la chantilly" will come with a dollop of the stuff, which is worlds better than the plasticky, super-sweet Cool Whip popular in the United States.

COMING AND GOING You can reach Chantilly from Paris's Gare du Nord on **RER Line D** or on the regular train (both 40 min, 39F). From Chantilly's train station, head straight down rue des Otages, hang a shallow left when it ends, and head back through the wooded trails; a beautiful 15-minute walk across a field brings you to the stables. If there are races going on, you'll have to scoot around the outskirts of the field. Otherwise you can just walk straight across (provided no one too official is watching). If you want to bus it, hop on any city bus passing in front of the station.

FOOD The grocery store **Kandi** (55 rue du Connetable, tel. 03–44–57–01–47) has all you need for snacks on the lawns. **A la Renommée** (9 rue de Paris, tel. 03–44–57–01–13), a charcuterie near the tourist office, will custom-make sandwiches for 18F and stocks 6F sodas. Surprisingly, the snack carts at the entrance of the château won't completely rip you off. Restaurants around town tend to be pricey and not terribly exciting (serving your basic 90F menu or 40F salad). One exception is **La Calèche** (3 av. du Maréchal Joffre, tel. 03–44–57–02–55), near many of the fancier restaurants but with a tasty plat du jour for 49F. Most town eateries also offer a ton of expensive desserts topped with mounds of *chantilly* (whipped cream).

WORTH SEEING Chantilly's château came first and the stables and racetrack later, but older isn't always better—even in France. The spectacular stables, the **Grandes Ecuries,** which hold the **Musée Vivant du Cheval** (Living Museum of the Horse), house an elite cadre of race-horses in luxury (note the arched, molded ceilings). Surprisingly, the stables aren't just for show; the horses in them are actual racehorses. In the rooms around the training courtyard is a huge, well-done collection of jockey uniforms, harnesses, bits, biological diagrams—everything imaginable to do with horses. The museum visit includes a casual show-off session for the horses. On Sunday afternoons at 3:15 and 4:45 the show goes upscale with costumes, music, and special tricks; admission, however, doubles. *Tel. 03–44–57–13–13. Admission:*

50F, 45F students. Open Apr. and Sept.–Oct., Wed.–Mon. 10:30–5:30; May–June, daily 10:30–5:30; July–Aug., Wed.–Mon. 10:30–5:30, Tues. 2–5:30; Nov.–Mar., Wed.–Mon. 2–4:30, weekends and holidays until 5:30; closed Dec. 1–15.

A visit to the **Château de Chantilly** is just icing on the cake. It makes the stables more elegant, and the stables make the château more realistic. Both conjure up images of leisurely picnics with men toting pocket-watches and women in large, flowery hats. Located behind the stables and totally surrounded by water, the château houses a so-so collection of furniture, paintings, and clothes, including Napoléon's hat. The **Musée Condé,** displaying mostly mediocre paintings and sculpture, claims to be one of the "most beautiful museums in France." We wouldn't go that far, but, since admission is included with château entrance, you can judge for yourself. *Tel. 03–44–54–04–02. Admission: 39F, 34F students. Open Mar.–Oct., Wed.–Mon. 10–6; Nov.–Feb., Wed.–Mon. 10:30–12:45 and 2–5.*

Versailles landscape architect André Le Nôtre also created Chantilly's château **gardens.** Beyond the grandiose fountains by the castle, they stretch to either side encompassing bridge-linked canals, lily ponds, and clearings in manicured woods. Each section of the garden represents a period of history from the 17th to 19th century: **Le Jardin Français** (the French Garden), laid out in the 1600s, is the most formal and full of flowers; **Le Petit Parc** (the Little Park) and **Le Hameau** (the Hamlet), which inspired similar gardens at Versailles, are from the 18th century; and **Le Jardin Anglais** (the English Garden) is from the 19th century. As usual, you're not supposed to hang out on the grass of the formal gardens, but you're welcome to picnic on the lawns in front of the château. *Admission: 17F, free with château visit. Open 10 AM–dusk when the château is open.*

CHEAP THRILLS **L'Aérophile** is the world's largest helium balloon, and it hovers 150 meters (450 feet) in the air, giving fantastic views of Chantilly's château, stables, and gardens, not to mention neighboring towns and, on clear days, the Eiffel Tower. The balloon is attached to a cable right next to Le Hameau in the gardens, so you don't exactly feel as free as a bird, but a good breeze can make it pretty exciting. Real hot-air balloon rides cost over 1,200F, so enjoy the cable. *Admission: 45F (after you've paid the 17F park fee). Open Apr.–Nov., weekdays 2–7, weekends 10–7.*

NEAR CHANTILLY

SENLIS Just a short bus ride from Chantilly, the tiny medieval, cobblestone passageways of well-preserved Senlis are worth a visit. Based on the Roman town of Augustomagus founded in AD 8, the village found God in the 4th century and was home to some of the first kings in France. Access to the park, where you can wander through the mossy ruins of the old château, is a mere 5F (3F students). Don't confuse this with the slightly bloodthirsty **Musée de la Venerie** (25F, 13F students), located inside the park; hourly tours take you through three floors of hunting trophies, hunting scenes, and hunting costumes, all to the blare of hunting horns. The **Rendez-vous de Septembre,** held in odd-numbered years, turns the old town totally pedestrian and totally touristed (call ahead to avoid the exact weekend).

➤ **BASICS** • **Buses** meet almost all trains to Chantilly for the 20-minute ride to Senlis's defunct brickwork train station (14F). The **Office de Tourisme** (pl. du Parvis Notre-Dame, tel. 03–44–53–06–40) has plenty of information about Senlis and the surrounding area. It's open Wednesday to Monday 10–noon and 2:15–6:15, and closed December 15 to January 31.

➤ **WHERE TO SLEEP AND EAT** • Senlis caters to well-heeled French tourists, so the cheapest hotel is the **Hotel du Nord** (110 rue de la République, tel. 03–44–53–01–16), which gets you pretty and clean Munchkin-size rooms for 220F. A fun place for dinner is **Le Gril des Barbares** (19 rue de Châtel, tel. 03–44–53–12–00), with three-course meals in a 12th-century cave for 120F; most other restaurants are filled with middle-aged tourists. You can pick up groceries at the **Prisunic** on rue de la République, while place de la Halle, just southeast of the ramparts, is filled with "sandwicheries."

Compiègne

It's possible to do Compiègne itself in an afternoon, but you'll have to move fast to see the château, the forest, and nearby Pierrefonds all in one swoop. You may be tempted to stay a little longer than you expect—biking the Oise Valley is a welcome change from fighting Métro crowds, and tossing back cold beers with the students of the Université de Technologie de Compiègne (UTC) is a lot cheaper here than in Paris.

The real draw in Compiègne, however, is the natural element: Locals and tourists focus as much attention on Compiègne's surrounding forest as on the town itself, and rightly so. It's nice for hiking, and the tourist office can give you information about free guided walking tours run by Compiègne AVF Accueil on the weekends. If you don't have a lot of time, the real way to go is to rent a bike (see Outdoor Activities, below), which will get you to the **Clarière de l'Armistice** and to **Pierrefonds** (see Near Compiègne, below) without dealing with infrequent buses. It's a straight shot to Pierrefonds, but once you enter the maze of trails, you'll get lost if you don't have a map—pick up a free one when you rent a bike, or buy the 15F *Circuits Pédestres* (Walking Tours) booklet at the tourist office. Pennypinching souls with a poor sense of direction should note that all trail markers have a red dash in the direction of Compiègne. Once you enter the forest you're truly spoiled—it's flat, easy riding with gorgeous, varying scenery.

BASICS The bustling **Office de Tourisme** next to the Gothic Hôtel de Ville is jam-packed with leaflets and brochures on Compiègne, the forest, and the castle at Pierrefonds. *Pl. de l'Hôtel de Ville, tel. 03–44–40–01–00. Open Mon.–Sat. 9:30–12:15 and 1:45–6:15, Sun. 9:30– 12:30 and 2:30–5; Nov.–Easter, closed Sun.*

COMING AND GOING Trains leave at least three times a day from Paris's Gare du Nord for the 69F, one-hour trip to Compiègne. The train and bus station is across the river from the center of town—a five-minute walk, max. Just cross the bridge to the right of the station and continue straight on rue Solferino through to place de l'Hôtel de Ville. On the other side of the place, rue Solferino turns into rue Magenta. Head off to your left for the château and to your right for the cobblestone pedestrian zone. City Buses 1, 2, and 5 are free and run from the station into the center of town (except on Sundays).

WHERE TO SLEEP Cheap options are few and far between, and all are a good deal less charming than the hostel at Pierrefonds (see Near Compiègne, below). Two of the best choices are the **Hôtel du Lion d'Or** (4 rue Général Leclerc, tel. 03–44–23–32–17, fax 03–44–86– 06–23), with cute, small singles for 120F and doubles for 150F; and the **Hôtel St-Antoine** (17 rue de Paris, tel. 03–44–86–17–18), with doubles for 95F–140F.

Auberge de Jeunesse. The only real budget accommodation in town, this conveniently located hostel offers bunk-filled rooms for only 30F a night, plus 13F for sheets. The showers are hot and the rooms are clean, but the hostel has one big drawback: The woman who runs it would rather let you sleep in the streets than break her precious 10 PM curfew. *6 rue Pasteur, tel. 03– 44–40–72–64. Reception open 7–10 AM and 5–10 PM. HI card required. Closed mid-Sept.–Mar.*

FOOD Brasseries abound around place Hôtel de Ville and in the pedestrian area, but they're not cheap. Try **Le Songeons** (40 rue Solférino, tel. 03–44–40–23–98), one block down toward the river from the center, for a decent 50F plat du jour. **Stromboli's Pizzeria** (2 rue des Lombards, in passage la Potene, tel. 03–44–40–06–21), closed Sundays, is a local favorite, a fact which comes in handy when you're trying to find the passage. You may have to wait a while to be seated, but the crispy-crust pizzas and pungent pastas (37F–50F) are worth it. Pass the time with a glass of wine in the friendly, close quarters. For picnic packers, the open-air **Marché Place du Change** behind the pedestrian zone, open until 12:30 PM on Wednesdays and Saturdays, will ready you for the road. Otherwise, **Djerba Market** (cours Guynemer, tel. 03– 44–40–01–36), open daily 8–8, is an absolute treasure, with everything from trail mix to fresh Sicilian olives, homemade couscous, fruit, and vegetables. **Monoprix** on rue Solferino has the cheapest bulk grocery supplies.

WORTH SEEING Compiègne is a mix of shaggy half-timbered houses and modern stucco buildings that went up after World War I flattened parts of the town. In fact, the armistice ending the war was signed in a railway car just 6 kilometers (3½ miles) away from the then wiped-out town. If you rent a bike (see Outdoor Activities, below), you can visit the railcar in a memorial park called the **Clarière de l'Armistice** (tel. 03–44–85–14–18) and pay 10F to look through the windows at memorabilia of the event. (No buses come here, and it's closed Tuesdays.)

The last weekend in May, Compiègne hosts the Foire aux Fromages et aux Vins, a big wine-and-cheese fair complete with wandering minstrels and Frenchies hell-bent on beating last year's record consumption of 58,000 bottles of wine and 17,000 pieces of cheese.

Louis XV built **Château de Compiègne** in the 18th century, and it's a grand estate like Fontainebleau, not a Sleeping Beauty–type structure. It saw some war action of its own, losing all of its furniture during the Revolution. Never one for futons and milk crates, Napoléon redid the whole thing in marble, gold, and silk, though all that's left is some old furniture and flaking gold paint. You can see everything during a drab one-hour guided visit. But you won't get much out of it if you don't speak French, and from the looks of the park and gardens behind the château, Compiègne's royalty must have spent most of their time in the backyard. The colorful English **garden** and wide expanse of grass and trees make one of the nicest hang-out spots in France, and it's free—the gate is right off place du Château. Admission to the château also gets you into two museums. At the **Musée de la Voiture** (Car Museum) in the north wing, follow the animated tour guide to get the lowdown on the cars. One used for picnics looks like an early rendition of the Batmobile, but the others just look like ornate chariots. Old-fashioned bicycles sneak their way in, too. The ho-hum **Museum du Second Empire** is a mishmash of furniture, clothes, and art set up in stark rooms. *Tel. 03–44–38–47–00. Admission: 32F, 20F ages 18–25 and Sun. Open Wed.–Mon. 9:15–5:30 (Oct.–Mar. until 3:45).*

Though it doesn't sound particularly exciting, the **Musée de la Figurine Historique** in the passage next to the tourist office has a collection of superbly detailed dolls, fully decked out in costumes. *Tel. 03–44–40–72–55. Admission: 12F, 6F students. Open Tues.–Sat. 9–noon and 2–6, Sun. 2–6 (Nov.–Feb. until 5).*

AFTER DARK **Au Bureau** (17 pl. de l'Hôtel de Ville, tel. 03–44–40–10–11) makes a good starting point for an evening out. In booths surrounded by English pub paraphernalia, you can enjoy a 45F pizza as you down your first cold one. Once you're ready, ease over to the bar to choose from over 100 beers from 20-odd countries or order a "meter" of beer. For a cozier, more student-oriented scene, try the **Sweet Home Pub** (cnr rues St-Corneille and d'Austerlitz), where things get wild later in the evening as more and more 25F brews are consumed. For dancing, try **Le City Hall** (27 pl. Hôtel de Ville, tel. 03–44–40–80–40), where the young and studious get hot and sweaty.

OUTDOOR ACTIVITIES Endless trails—paved, unpaved, and downright sloshy—wind through shady groves of birch, oak, and French broom in the **Forêt de Compiègne.** There are only a couple of steep trails, but you'll have plenty of opportunities for exploration and discovery. The man at **Picardie Forêts Vertes** (4 rue de la Gare, tel. 03–44–90–05–05) is terrific, but you need to call the day before you want a bike; he'll have it waiting for you at the station. Tell him what you want to explore and how steep a ride you want, and he'll give you a map with your own personalized route. His office is just to your right as you exit the train station, but he is seldom there; you'll have better luck on weekends and holidays, when you can find him at the Carrefour Royal by the campground. All of this pampering has a price, of course—120F per day.

NEAR COMPIEGNE

PIERREFONDS Tucked away in the Forêt de Compiègne, the 12th-century **Château de Pierrefonds** has round towers with pointy tops, cannon notches in the walls, a moat—everything a proper château should have. Between the château and a lake, half-timbered houses and teardrop spires rise out of Pierrefond's tiny village; the interior of the château is decorated with

Between April and September, get wet and wacky on the lake at Pierrefonds with a pedal boat (48F for two people) or rowboat (25F per person), each rented by the half hour.

medieval memorabilia. *Tel. 03–44–42–80–77. Admission: 28F, 18F students. Open May–Aug., daily 10–6; Sept.–Apr., daily 10–12:30 and 2–5.*

➤ **COMING AND GOING** • Getting here from Compiègne is a beautiful and easy bike ride—a flat 14 kilometers (8½ miles) through lush green forest—and the initial view of the château as you round the final curve is worth the effort. Buses from Compiègne only run three times daily (fewer on Sunday, none on holidays) from the station and charge 13F; if you get stranded in Pierrefonds the taxi will cost a whopping 180F.

➤ **WHERE TO SLEEP AND EAT** • The **Château de Jonval** (2 rue Séverine, tel. 03–44–42–80–97) has been converted into a hostel with rooms for two to eight people. Ever wondered what it would be like to open the window of your own castle bedroom and gaze across a tiny valley at a majestic medieval château glistening in the morning light? Here's your chance to find out. For 70F (plus a 30F membership fee per room), you get a simple bed and breakfast, but the superb setting makes it worthwhile. Cheap picnics are difficult to come by, so stock up in Compiègne. Crêpe fans should check out **Ty Breiz** (8 rue du Beaudon, tel. 03–44–42–86–62), where the oversized, delicious galettes (25F–40F) put anything you get in Paris to shame.

Fontainebleau

If you love the sight of a richly decorated château but can't handle Versailles's waves of slobbering tourists, head for Fontainebleau, a quick 65 kilometers (40 miles) south of Paris. Elaborate, garish, and even occasionally beautiful, Fontainebleau's castle technically dates back further than Louis XIV's palace at Versailles. And if the château's regimented gardens seem too uptight, forage in the thick forest nearby (*see* Outdoor Activities, *below*).

BASICS Those interested only in Fontainebleau's château can pick up everything they need at the main entrance. If the forest is calling, however, the **Office de Tourisme** has some crucial items, including a very detailed forest map (35F) and the schedules of irregular local buses. The hard part is finding the office. Hint: Look behind the carousel on the place du Napoléon Bonaparte. *31 pl. du Napoléon Bonaparte, tel. 01–64–22–25–68. Open weekdays 9:30–12:30 and 2–6:30, Sat. 9:30–6:30, Sun. 10–12:30 and 3–5:30; Oct.–Apr., closed Sun.*

COMING AND GOING Trains leave every hour from Paris's Gare de Lyon and cost 39F for the 40-minute trip. The 3-kilometer (2-mile) walk from the train station in Avon to the château takes about 30 uninteresting minutes along avenue Franklin Roosevelt, unless you stop to rent a bike (*see* Biking, *below*). Or take **Bus A/B** (every 15 min) from the station until you see the château. During high season, when the bus is crowded, most visitors slip on without a ticket; honest types buy the 9F ticket on board.

During the fall, many go mushroom hunting in the Fontainebleau forest and feast on fungi, all for free. But don't even THINK about doing this yourself without taking your finds to a pharmacist to verify they're NOT poisonous, as dangerous lookalikes abound.

FOOD At **Au Délice Impérial** (1 rue Grande, tel. 01–64–22–20–70), near the tourist office, large salads set you back only 38F. A few doors over, **La Taverne Alsacienne** (23 rue Grande, tel. 01–64–22–20–85) serves a 58F three-course menu with French specialties. Otherwise, there are a few mediocre crêperies on rue Montebello, where crêpes go for 15F–35F, and several great specialty shops in the pedestrian zone around rue des Sablons. For general groceries there's a **Prisunic** a few blocks from the center toward Avon on rue Grande.

WORTH SEEING The **gardens** of Fontainebleau, like the château, reflect a mix of styles. Designed in part by Versailles's landscape architect extraordinaire, André Le Nôtre, they don't quite achieve the same magnificence. Yet the nice thing about these gardens (and

Fontainebleau in general) is that they are relatively untainted by tourists. Locals fish for salmon and carp in the Grand Canal and walk their dogs along Le Prairie, the grassy expanse on the edge of the sculptured gardens. If you have a burning desire to know more about Napoléon or French military history, there's always the **Musée Napoléonien d'Art et d'Histoire Militaire** (88 rue St-Honoré, north of rue de France; open Tues.–Sat. 2–5), which claims to be the third-biggest military museum in France. Whoopee.

➤ **CHATEAU DE FONTAINEBLEAU** • In 1528, King François I had license to kill just about anything he wanted, so no one complained when he commissioned this upscale hunting lodge—and we're talking *way* upscale. The château has been used as both a hunting lodge and an official residence for nearly eight centuries by more than 30 sovereigns. Each king who lived here left his mark—a tower here, a staircase there—with additions that reflect the style of his period. Because of these hundreds of years of architectural influences, Napoléon I called Fontainebleau "La Maison des Siècles" (The House of Centuries).

One 35F ticket (22F students) lets you into the **Grands Appartements** and the **Salles Renaissances,** the fully furnished living quarters of François I, Napoléon III, and all the royalty in between. The same ticket admits you to the **Musée Napoléon I** (15 rooms filled with arms, guns, hats, uniforms, and other relics of Napoléon's life) and the **Musée Chinois,** which holds the Empress Eugénie's private collection of Chinese goodies. An extra 15F (10F students) allows you into the kings' private rooms, the **Petits Appartements.** If you really have your heart set on seeing these smaller rooms, call ahead (tel. 01–60–71–50–70) to find out if tours are running that day. In addition, there are regular free concerts on the castle's organ in the **Chapelle de la Trinité**; call 01–64–22–68–43 for information. *Open June–Oct., Wed.–Mon. 9:30–5; Nov.–May, Wed.–Mon. 9:30–12:30 and 2–5.*

OUTDOOR ACTIVITIES The château's gardens back right onto 17,000 hectares (42,000 acres) of the **Forêt de Fontainebleau,** one of the biggest national forests in France. If you want to play in the woods, don't come on a Monday, however, when most of the rental-equipment facilities are closed. The tourist office sells a 35F topo guide called *Guide des Sentiers de Promenades dans le Massif Forestier de Fontainebleau,* which covers paths throughout the forest. For a good view of the whole beech-, birch-, and pine-covered expanse, head up to the **Tour Denecourt,** about 5 kilometers (3 miles) northeast of the château.

➤ **BIKING** • The trails here are a dream—endless and totally unrestricted. The tourist office has trail maps and guides, but you can easily explore the former hunting grounds on your own. **A la Petite Reine** (32 rue des Sablons, tel. 01–60–74–57–57) rents mountain bikes for 80F per weekday, 100F per weekend day with a 2,000F or credit-card deposit. **Mountain Bike Folies** (246 Grande rue, tel. 01–64–23–43–07) is another rental option with similar prices. Both offer half-day rentals for 50F–80F. Most of the steeper trails are west of town, but ask the bike store people to point out the best places to ride on your map.

➤ **CLIMBING** • Rock clusters and small gorges abound, but getting the gear and then both the gear and yourself to them is tricky. **Top Loisirs** (16 rue de Ferrare, tel. 01–60–74–08–50) rents gear in town but doesn't open until 10 AM, and if you're relying on buses to get here, the day will be over before you touch rock. Your best bet is to rent in Paris, then arrive in town early enough to stop at the tourist office to book one of the many guides. Once you've done that, you can check the bus schedules or walk the 5–8 kilometers (3–5 miles) to your climbing spot.

Disneyland Paris

It's controversial, it's expensive, and it's a hell of a lot of fun. Though the park's chances of survival were shaky for a while—it lost almost $1 billion in 1993—attendance and, more importantly, length of stay, have been on the upswing. It's the money you spend on hotels, food, and felt hats with plastic ears that really brings in the bucks—and the longer you stay, the more felt hats with plastic ears you're likely to buy. Frequent cold, damp weather hasn't helped attendance either, but you'd think they'd have thought of that before they started construction. But no matter how you feel about the Disneyfication of Europe, it can be tempting to blow a month's pay on the spotless grounds, good rides, and long lines that characterize this meticulously conceived fantasy world. Basically, Walt has taken the best attractions of the American Disney parks and rolled them into one condensed version. **Star Tours, Captain Eo, Big Thunder Railroad, It's a Small World, Peter Pan** . . . they're all here, and more state-of-the-art than ever. New stuff includes **Indiana Jones and the Temple of Peril,** with Disney's first-ever roller coaster loop, and the $120 million **Space Mountain,** the scariest Disney ride ever. It's also a trip watching otherwise elegant Parisians try to figure out what a drinking fountain is. Although Adventureland's **Middle Eastern Grand Bazaar** and Fantasyland's **Alsatian Village** give the park a bit of *faux* international flair, it's definitely more "Disneyland" than "Paris." The American Old West theme seems to find its way into everything, and the Roaring Twenties are bigger here than they ever were in the States.

While Disneyland Paris will never be a travel bargain, you can save money by timing your visit carefully. Rates do not simply rise with the temperature; they fluctuate with school and national holidays, weekends, and season. During most of June, for example, entrance costs 175F, while during February and March (ski season) it jumps back up to 250F. Call ahead to verify prices for specific dates—going a day later could make a big difference. Lines within the park are usually ridiculous on weekends, but apparently everyone rushes to get here first thing in the morning, then poops out by early afternoon. As always, Disney is careful about wheelchair accessibility, though for most of the good rides you must have an attendant to help you leave the chair. Pick up the pamphlet "Guest Special Services Guide" for specific accessibility info. *Tel. 01–60–30–60–30. Take RER Line A to Marne-la-Vallée/Chessy (35F). Admission: 175F–250F. Open daily 9–7 (until 11 in summer).*

WHERE TO SLEEP It's so expensive to stay here that it's no wonder no one spends the night. The least expensive hotels within the resort, the **Hotel Santa Fe** and **Hotel Cheyenne,** offer rooms for up to four people at 300F–650F, and April through September the **Davy Crockett Ranch** offers cabins for up to six people from 475F. Hotel/park admission packages can make a night here slightly more attractive. For reservations call 01–49–41–49–10 (from the United States call 407/W–DISNEY; from the United Kingdom call 0171/753–2900).

FOOD Though most budget visitors just smuggle food into the park, a few restaurants inside actually have menus that won't break your bank, including the **Café Hyperion** (inside Videopolis in Discoveryland), with a menu from 40F; the **Pizzerria Bella Notte** (Fantasyland), with a menu from 50F; and the **Cowboy Cookout Barbeque** (Frontierland), also with a menu from 40F. The restaurants serve mostly American-style food.

Putting the Paris in Disneyland Paris

The following are quirks unique to Mickey's European pied-à-terre:

- *Wine is served in the park (they changed their no-alcohol policy in 1993).*

- *Tombstone inscriptions at Phantom Manor: "Jasper Jones, loyal manservant, kept the master happy. Anna Jones, faithful chambermaid, kept the master happier."*

- *No Mickey walking around—he was too mobbed by kiddies, so he stays in one spot, and you have to line up to see him.*

- *Cast members look like they need a cigarette.*

- *If you so much as think about sitting on the lawn, "happy" Disney characters lose the grin and use the whistle.*

Elsewhere near Paris

PARC ASTERIX All French kids know comic book hero Astérix and his loyal, larger sidekick, Obélix. In the year 50 BC, these stubby Gauls beat up invading (and usually pretty idiotic) Romans trying to attack their village in Brittany. A swig of magic potion makes Astérix invincible in battle, and menhir-toting Obélix fell into a vat of the stuff as a child and was permenantly fortified. Read one of the comic books before you go to get the most out of this cartoon world.

If you think you know amusement parks, this French-style one could be a real eye-opener. You learn about French history on your way from one attraction to the next (only in Paris would they lump an amusement park with an historical lesson), from a Gaul village with print makers and potters, to a little Roman village, to a miniaturized version of Paris complete with a Dixieland band. Most of the attractions are glorified versions of carnival rides, spinning and twirling you around until your lunch makes an encore appearance. There are some fun ones, though, like the ultra-loopy **Goudurix** roller coaster and **Grand Splatch**, which will get you soaked. Be warned that some attractions close on weekdays—call ahead if you have your heart set on any ride in particular. *Tel. 01–44–62–34–04. Admission: 160F, 110F under 12. Open mid-Apr.–mid-Oct., weekends 10–6 (until 7 PM on peak days); also open weekdays July–Aug.; for other weekdays, call ahead.*

If you decide to make the Parc Astérix investment, come on a weekend when it's nice and crowded. When it's empty, it's really empty, and there's nothing more depressing than a lonely amusement park.

➤ **COMING AND GOING** • From Paris, take **RER Line B3** to the Charles de Gaulle/Roissy terminus (34F), where you can catch a special 15F shuttle (20 min) that runs to the park (9:30–1:30) and back (4:30–park closing) every half hour. Food, of course, is expensive . . . no ancient France prices here. If you don't want to sneak in a picnic, you might decide to skip lunch.

PROVINS If you've never seen a fortified medieval town, visiting Provins is a must. Built mostly in the 12th and 13th centuries, the *ville haute* (upper village) is entirely surrounded by stone ramparts and has all kinds of medieval stuff to explore. See the tower where they used to keep criminals; an enormous church with imposing wooden doors and a big, black dome; an executioner's house; subterranean passages running under the whole town; tiny, flowered, cobblestone streets; and, of more recent origin, a beer garden where locals come to hear live music. From the train station, walk across the bridge, through the commercial center, and up the hill, following the signs that say ITINÉRAIRE PIÉTON (pedestrian route).

If you hit Provins in late May or early June, you'll find the Fête Médiévale, when the whole town dresses up, acts like barbarians from the Middle Ages, and eats a lot of junk food. Entrance is 30F, free if you have a medieval costume lying around.

The ramparts and medieval building are courtesy of the Count of Champagne, who brought money, people, and ideas to Provins in the early 13th century, turning it into a major commercial center. People came to buy, sell, and trade their goods, paying taxes to the count, who, in turn, offered them protection. Apparently the system worked; the count made enough money to build the town and the convent in the neighboring forest. Everything was running smoothly until river transportation became all the rage in Europe, and Provins found itself high and dry. Eight centuries later, without its superpower status, it's merely a great day trip from Paris.

➤ **BASICS** • The hour-long train ride will set you back 70F. Take one of the three morning trains from Paris's Gare de l'Est; the only afternoon train is at 4 PM and won't leave you enough time to return to the city. If you miss the last train to Paris, the nightlife isn't exactly kicking in Provins, but you can find cheap hostel-like housing (50F–80F) at **Le Chalet** (3 pl. Honoré de Balzac, tel. 01–64–00–02–27). For a bit more luxury check out the beautifully converted farmhouse at **La Ferme du Châtel** (5 rue de la Chapelle St-Jean, tel. 01–64–00–10–73), where fancy doubles are 260F. As for food, it's all cutesy, overpriced meals in the walled village, but there's a **Monoprix** market on your walk from the train station where you can stock up on cheap grub.

ST·GERMAIN·EN·LAYE Scale down Versailles, take away 95% of its tourists, plop it down on a terrace overlooking the Seine, and you have the château of St-Germain-en-Laye. The original château here, the first palace built by French royalty outside Paris, was started by Louis VI, known as Le Gros (the Fat), in the early 12th century as a defensive stronghold. François I and his successors transformed St-Germain from a fortress to a royal residence. Louis XIV then called in Hardouin-Mansart and Le Nôtre to make additions and improvements. Never satisfied, he finally abandoned the château entirely and built Versailles.

Thanks to Napoléon III, the château now houses the **Musée des Antiquités Nationales** (admission 22F, 15F students; open Wed.–Mon. 9–5:15), an archaeological collection from paleolithic times to the Middle Ages. If that's not your thing, you can enjoy an unobstructed view of the Seine and the distant Paris skyline from the **Petite Terrasse** in front of the château. Protected from the forest by the château walls, the **Grande Terrasse** offers a 4-kilometer (2½-mile) loop for joggers and serious promenaders. The gardens are free, open until 9:30 PM, and stretch into the endless Forêt de St-Germain, which is dotted with picnic tables. The tourist office can give you maps for trails as long as 18 kilometers (11 miles) in this dense but relatively flat forest. All this serenity is just a 20-minute RER ride from Paris. Take the **Red Line A1** from La Défense for 10F50, or buy a Métro ticket good from the center of Paris for 16F.

➤ **BASICS** • The **tourist office** is set up in Claude Debussy's house and can give you minimal info on the few museums in the area, as well as surrounding places of interest. *38 rue au Pain, tel. 01–34–51–05–12. From the Métro, head right toward town center; rue au Pain is on left. Open Tues.–Fri. 9:15–12:30 and 2–6:30, Sat. 9:15–6:30; also Mar.–Oct., Sun. 10–1.*

French Glossary

The French are not known for being tolerant of foreigners who butcher their language. But, even if you haven't spent a few years mastering the language's uvular r's and labial u's, a good phrase book, a small dose of humility, and a great deal of *politesse* should help. Remember to use "Madame" and "Monsieur" when addressing people you don't know. Living Language™ cassettes, CDs, phrase books, and dictionaries make it easy to learn the essentials. If you can't find them at your local bookstore, call 800/733–3000.

PRONUNCIATION

French is not an easy language for English speakers to pronounce. The vowel and nasal sounds are difficult; consonants at the end of words are usually not pronounced; and, when a word ending in a consonant is followed by a word beginning with a vowel, the two words are often run together (this is called *liaison*). At least you can almost always count on the stress being on the last syllable. Here's a little guide to get you started:

a like the **a** in saw
e like the **ea** in earth
é and *è* like the **ay** in hay
eu and *œ* like the **oo** in hoof
i like the **i** in magazine
o like the **o** in no
ou like the **oo** in zoo
u like **oo** with your lips pursed
ui a short "wee" sound
oi a short "wah" sound

NASAL SOUNDS Nasal sounds in French are much less pronounced than they are in English. They aren't easy to develop an ear for, but there are really only three of them: the nasal in *faim* (hungry) or *vin* (wine), the nasal in *bon* (good), and the nasal in *an* (year).

CONSONANTS Consonants resemble English a lot more closely than the vowels, with a few exceptions: s is often pronounced **z** as in "rose"; **ch** is always **sh** like "shoe"; **j** has a soft **zhuh** sound; **ll** is often like the **y** in yam; and **th** is always **t**.

French	Pronunciation	English
Basics		
Bonjour	Bohn-zhoor	Hello
Bonsoir	Bohn-swahr	Good evening
Bonne nuit	Bun-wee	Good night (before going to bed)
Comment allez-vous?	Cummunt-allay-voo	How are you?
Je vais bien	Zhuh-vay-bee-en	I'm fine
Ça va?	Sah-vah?	How's it going?
Ça va	Sah-vah	It's going fine
D'accord	Dah-core	Okay
Au revoir	Oh-vwahr	Goodbye
Excusez-moi	Ex-cuze-ay-mwah	Excuse me

Parlez-vous anglais?	Par-lay-voo-zang-lay	Do you speak English?
Je ne parle pas français	Zhun-parl-pah-frawn-say	I don't speak French
Je suis américain(e)	Zhuh-sweez-ahm-air-ee-can(nuh)	I'm American
Je suis australien(ne)	Zhuh-sweez-oh-stray-lee-en(nuh)	I'm Australian
Je suis canadien(ne)	Zhuh-swee-cah-nah-dee-en(nuh)	I'm Canadian
Je suis anglais(e)	Zhuh-sweez-ahn-glay(glezz)	I'm English
Je suis écossais(e)	Zhuh-sweez-ay-coss-ay(ezz)	I'm Scottish
Je suis irlandais(e)	Zhuh-sweez-eer-lahn-day(dezz)	I'm Irish
Etudiant(e)	Ay-too-dyahn(tuh)	Student
Je ne comprends pas	Zhuh-nuh-cum-prond-pah	I don't understand
Pardon	Pahr-dohn	Sorry/excuse me
Je ne sais pas	Zhun-say-pah	I don't know
S'il vous plaît	See-voo-play	Please
Merci	Mehr-see	Thank you
De rien	Duh-ree-en	You're welcome
Non	Noh	No
Oui	Wee	Yes
Où est/sont . . .	Oo-ay/sohn	Where is/are . . .
Les toilettes	Lay-twah-lett	Bathroom
La poste	Lah-pust	Post office
La laverie	Lah-lahv-ree	Laundromat
La banque	Lah-bonk	Bank
Ça coûte combien?	Sah-coot-cohm-bee-en	How much does this cost?
Avez-vous...	Ah-vay-voo	Do you have...
Fermeture annuelle	Fair-muh-toohr-ahn-yoo-ell	Annual closure
En vacances	On-va-cons	On vacation
Jour ferié	Zhoor-fehr-ee-ay	Holiday
Ouvert(e)	Oo-vehr	Open
Fermé(e)	Fair-may	Closed
Que sont vos horaires?	Keuh-sohn-vohs-orr-air	What are your hours?
A quelle heure...?	ah-kell-uhr	At what time..?.
Entrée	Ohn-tray	Entrance
Sortie	Sore-tee	Exit
Hôtel de ville	Oh-tell-duh-veel	City hall
Rez-de-chaussée	Ray-duh-shoh-say	Ground floor
Sous-sol	Soo-sull	Basement
Zone piétonne	Zunn-pee-ay-tunn	Pedestrian zone
Quartier	Car-tee-ay	District

Emergencies and Medical Aid

La police	La-poh-lees	Police
Arrêtez!	Ah-reh-tay	Stop!
Aidez-moi!	Ay-day-mwah	Help me!
Au secours!	Oh-suh-coor	Help!
En cas d'urgence	Ohn-cah-doohr-zhonce	In case of emergency
Fichez-moi la paix!	Fee-shay-mwah-lah-pay	Leave me alone!
Je suis malade	Zhuh-swee-mah-lahd	I'm sick
Appelez un médecin	Ah-pul-lay-uh-medd-sahn	Call a doctor
J'ai mal à la tête	Zhay-mall-ah-lah-tett	I have a headache
J'ai mal à l'estomac	Zhay-mall-ah-less-tum-ock	I have a stomach ache
L'hôpital	Loh-pee-tall	Hospital
La pharmacie	Lah-farm-ah-see	Drugstore
Ordonnance	Orr-dunn-ons	Prescription

Un médicament	Uh-may-dee-cah-mon	Medicine
Une aspirine	Oon-ass-pee-reen	Aspirin
Un préservatif	Uh-pray-zurve-ah-teef	Condom

Coming and Going

Aller-simple	Ah-lay-sam-pluh	One-way
Aller-retour	Ah-lay-ruh-toor	Round-trip
A pied	Ah-pee-ay	On foot
Assurance	Ah-soor-ohns	Insurance
Auto-stop	Oh-toe-stop	Hitchhiking
La banlieue	Lah-bahn-lee-yeuh	Suburbs
Consigne	Kohn-seen-yuh	Luggage storage
Correspondance	Kor-eh-spohn-dawnse	Connection
La fin de la ligne	Lah-fahn-duh-lah-leen-yuh	The end of the line
Vente de billets	Vahnt-duh-bee-yay	Ticket office
Un billet pour . . .	Uh-bee-yay-poor	A ticket for . . .
Composter votre billet	Com-poh-stay-votra-bee-yay	Validate your ticket
Circule tous les jours	Seer-cool-too-lay-zhoor	Runs every day
Sauf dimanche	Soaf-dee-mansh	Except Sundays
Combien de kilomètres?	Com-bee-en-duh-kee-loh-met	How many kilometers?
Je vais à . . .	Zhuh-vay-ah	I'm going to . . .
Je voudrais descendre à . . .	Zhuh-voo-dray-day-son-drah-ah	I want to get off at . . .
Le train part à quelle heure?	Luh-trahn-pahr-ah-kel-euhr	What time does the train leave?
Un plan de la ville	Uh-plohn-duh-lah-veel	City plan/map
Une carte routière	Oon-cart-roo-tee-air	Road map
L'aéroport	Lay-roh-por	Airport
La gare	Lah-gar	Train station
Chemins de fer	Shuh-man-duh-fair	Train tracks
Quai	Kay	Platform
Couchette	Coo-shett	Sleeping compartment
La gare routière	Lah-gar-roo-tee-air	Bus station
Car	Cahr	Tourist bus
Arrêt	Ah-ray	Bus stop
Location de voitures	Loh-cah-see-ohn-duh-vwah-toor	Car rental agency
Essence	Ess-onse	Gas
Un pneu	Uh-puh-nuh	Tire
Feu rouge/vert	Fuh-roozh/vayr	Red/green stoplight
Une motocycle	Oon-moe-toe-see-cluh	Motorcycle
Autoroute	Oh-toe-root	Highway
La route pour . . .	Lah-root-poor	The road to . . .
Pont	Pohn	Bridge
Station de métro	Stah-see-ohn-duh-may-tro	Subway station
Tarif	Tah-reef	Fare
Ticket journalier	Tee-kett-zhoor-nall-ee-ay	One-day pass
Traverser	Tra-vayr-say	To cross
Un vélo	Uh-vay-loh	Bicycle

Where to Sleep

Une auberge de jeunesse	Oon-oh-bayrge-duh-zhoo-ness	Youth hostel
Une gîte d'étape	Oon-zheet-day-top	Rural hostel
Un refuge	Uh-ruh-fyooge	Mountain shelter
Un camping	Uh-camm-ping	Campground
Un emplacement	Un-omm-plass-mont	Campsite

Une chambre	Oon-shahm-bruh	Room
Une chambre pour deux	Oon-shahm-bruh-poor-duh-pair-sunn	Double roompersonnes
Je peux la voir?	Zhuh-puh-lah-vwarr	Can I see it?
On reste pour . . . jours	Ohn-rest-poor . . . zhoor	We're staying for . . . days
Avec	Ah-veck	With
Sans	Sahn	Without
Une douche	Oon-doosh	Shower
Un lavabo	Uh-lah-vah-boe	Sink
Draps	Drah	Sheets
Calme	Call-muh	Quiet
Le petit déjeuner	Luh-puh-tee-day-zhuh-nay	Breakfast
Compris	Cum-pree	Included

Food

Alimentation	Ah-lee-moan-tah-see-ohn	Food
Boulangerie	Boo-lahn-zhuh-ree	Bakery
Supermarché	Soo-pehr-mar-shay	Supermarket
J'ai faim	Zhay-fah	I'm hungry
Je voudrais . . .	Zhuh-voo-dray	I'd like . . .
Est-ce que service est compris?	Ess-kuh-sayr-veese-ay-com-pree	Is the tip included?
Je ne peux pas manger de . . .	Zhuh-nuh-puh-pah-mon-zhay	I cannot eat . . .
Je suis végétarien(ne)	Zhuh-swee-vay-zhay-tay-ree-en	I'm a vegetarian
Le plat du jour	Luh-plah-doo-zhoor	Dish of the day
Une bouteille de . . .	Oon-boo-tay-duh	A bottle of . . .
Un verre de . . .	Uh-vayr-duh	A glass of . . .
L'addition	Lah-dee-see-ohn	Bill/check
Pain	Pah	Bread
Agneau	Awn-yoe	Lamb
Beurre	Buhr	Butter
Bifteck	Beef-tek	Beef steak
Champignons	Shahm-peen-yohn	Mushrooms
Chocolat	Sho-coh-lah	Chocolate
Confiture	Coh-fee-toohr	Jam
Eau gazeuse	Oh-gahz-uzz	Sparkling water
Fromage	Fro-mawzh	Cheese
Fruits de mer	Fweed-mehr	Shellfish
Jambon	Zham-bohn	Ham
Jus	Zhoo	Juice
Lait	Lay	Milk
Lapin	Lah-pah	Rabbit
Marrons	Mah-rohn	Chestnuts
Miel	Mee-ell	Honey
Moutarde	Moo-tard	Mustard
Oeuf	Uff	Egg
Poivre	Pwah-vruh	Pepper
Poisson	Pwah-sohn	Fish
Pomme	Pohm	Apple
Pommes de terre	Pohm-deuh-tehr	Potatoes
Porc	Pohr	Pork
Poulet	Poo-lay	Chicken
Rôti	Roh-tee	Roast
Sel	Sell	Salt
Sucre	Soo-cruh	Sugar

Viande	Vee-ahnd	Meat
Vin (rouge/blanc)	Vahn-(roo-zhuh/blahn)	Red/white wine
Vinaigre	Veen-ay-gruh	Vinegar
Yaourt	Yah-oort	Yogurt
Une assiette	Oon-ah-syet	Plate
Une fourchette	Oon-for-shet	Fork
Une cuillère	Oon-kwee-yay	Spoon
Un couteau	Uh-coo-toe	Knife
Une serviette	Oon-sehr-vee-et	Napkin
A point	Ah-pwah	Medium rare
Bien cuit	Bee-en-coo-ee	Well-done
Saignant	Senn-yahn	Rare (literally, bleeding)
A Emporter	Ah-ohm-poor-tay	Take-out

Numbers

Un/une	Uh/Oon	One
Deux	Duh	Two
Trois	Twah	Three
Quatre	Cat-ruh	Four
Cinq	Sank	Five
Six	Sees	Six
Sept	Sett	Seven
Huit	Weet	Eight
Neuf	Nuff	Nine
Dix	Deece	Ten
Onze	Ohn-zuh	Eleven
Douze	Dooz	Twelve
Treize	Trehz	Thirteen
Quatorze	Ka-torz	Fourteen
Quinze	Kanz	Fifteen
Seize	Sez	Sixteen
Dix-sept	Deece-set	Seventeen
Dix-huit	Dee-zweet	Eighteen
Dix-neuf	Deece-nuff	Nineteen
Vingt	Vahnt	Twenty
Trente	Tront	Thirty
Quarante	Cahr-ont	Forty
Cinquante	Sank-ont	Fifty
Soixante	Swah-sont	Sixty
Soixante-dix	Swah-sont-deece	Seventy
Quatre-vingts	Cat-ruh-vahnt	Eighty
Quatre-vingt-dix	Cat-ruh-vahnt-deece	Ninety
Cent	Sohnt	One hundred
Mille	Meal	One thousand

Days and Months

Dimanche	Dee-monsh	Sunday
Lundi	Lun-dee	Monday
Mardi	Mar-dee	Tuesday
Mercredi	Mehr-cruh-dee	Wednesday
Jeudi	Zheuh-dee	Thursday
Vendredi	Vohn-druh-dee	Friday
Samedi	Sam-dee	Saturday
Janvier	Zhahn-vee-ay	January
Fevrier	Feh-vree-ay	February
Mars	Mahss	March
Avril	Ah-vreel	April

Mai	May	May
Juin	Zhoo-wahn	June
Juillet	Zhwee-ay	July
Août	Oot	August
Septembre	Sep-tohm-bruh	September
Octobre	Ok-toh-bruh	October
Novembre	No-vohm-bruh	November
Decembre	Deh-sohm-bruh	December

Index

Notes

Notes

Notes

Notes

Notes

Notes

TELL US WHAT YOU THINK

We're always trying to improve our books and would really appreciate any feedback on how to make them more useful. Thanks for taking a few minutes to fill out this survey. We'd also like to know about your latest find, a new scam, a budget deal, whatever . . . Please print your name and address clearly and send the completed survey to: The Berkeley Guides, 515 Eshelman Hall, U.C. Berkeley, CA 94720.

1. Your name _____

2. Your address _____

_____ Zip _____

3. You are: Female   Male

4. Your age: under 17   17–22   23–30   31–40   41–55   over 55

5. If you're a student: Name of school _____ City & state _____

6. If you're employed: Occupation _____

7. Your yearly income: under $20,000 $21,000–$30,000 $31,000–$45,000
$46,000–$60,000 $61,000–$100,000   over $100,000

8. Which of the following do you own? (Circle all that apply.)

   Computer   CD-ROM Drive   Modem

9. What speed (bps) is your modem?

   2400   4800   9600   14.4   19.2   28.8

10. Which on-line service(s) do you subscribe to apart from commercial services like AOL?

_____

11. Do you have access to the World Wide Web? If so, is it through a university or a private service provider? _____

12. If you have a CD-ROM drive or plan to have one, would you purchase a Berkeley Guide CD-ROM? _____

13. Which Berkeley Guide(s) did you buy? _____

14. Where did you buy the book and when?   City _____ Month/Year _____

15. Why did you choose The Berkeley Guides? (Circle all that apply.)

Budget focus	Design
Outdoor emphasis	Attitude
Off-the-beaten-track emphasis	Writing style
Resources for gays and lesbians	Organization
Resources for people with disabilities	More maps
	Accuracy
Resources for women	Price

Other _____

16. How did you hear about The Berkeley Guides? (Circle all that apply.)

Recommended by friend/acquaintance   Bookstore display   TV

Article in magazine/newspaper (which one?) _____

Ad in magazine/newspaper (which one?) _____

Radio program (which one?) _____

Other _____

17. Which other guides, if any, have you used before? (Circle all that apply.)

Fodor's	Let's Go	Rough Guides
Frommer's	Birnbaum	Lonely Planet

Other _____

18. When did you travel with this book?   Month/Year _____

19. Where did you travel? _____

20. What was the purpose of your trip?

Vacation	Business	Volunteer
Study abroad	Work	

21. About how much did you spend per day during your trip?

$0–$20	$31–$45	$61–$75	over $100
$21–$30	$46–$60	$76–$100	

22. After you arrived, how did you get around? (Circle all that apply.)

Rental car	Personal car	Plane	Bus
Train	Hiking	Bike	Hitching

23. Which features/sections did you use most? (Circle all that apply.)

Book Basics	City/region Basics	Coming and Going
Hitching	Getting Around	Where to Sleep
Camping	Roughing It	Food
Worth Seeing	Cheap Thrills	Festivals
Shopping	After Dark	Outdoor Activities

24. The information was (circle one):   V = very accurate   U = usually accurate

                                              S = sometimes accurate   R = rarely accurate

Introductions	V U S R	Worth Seeing	V U S R
Basics	V U S R	After Dark	V U S R
Coming and Going	V U S R	Outdoor Activities	V U S R
Where to Sleep	V U S R	Maps	V U S R
Food	V U S R		

25. I would _____ would not _____ buy another Berkeley Guide.

26. Which of the following destinations are you planning to visit in the next five years?

The Americas
Chicago
Washington, D.C.
New Orleans
Los Angeles
Boston
Austin
The Midwest
The South
The Southwest
New England
The Pacific Northwest
Hawaii
Canada
South America

Middle East/Africa
Turkey
Israel
Egypt
Africa

Europe
Spain
Portugal
Greece
Russia
Scandinavia
Berlin
Prague
Rome

Australia/Asia
Australia
New Zealand
Vietnam
Philippines
Indonesia
Thailand
Singapore
Malaysia
Cambodia
India/Nepal